THE LOUISIANA PURCHASE AND ITS PEOPLES

PERSPECTIVES FROM THE NEW ORLEANS CONFERENCE

THE LOUISIANA PURCHASE AND ITS PEOPLES

PERSPECTIVES FROM THE NEW ORLEANS CONFERENCE

Edited by
Paul E. Hoffman

Louisiana Historical Association and
Center for Louisiana Studies
University of Louisiana at Lafayette
Lafayette, Louisiana

Cover image is adapted from Frank Bond, *Louisiana and the Louisiana Purchase* (Washington, D. C., 1912), map 4.

Library of Congress Catalog Number: 2003114056
ISBN Number: 1-887366-51-2

Publication of this book has been made possible in part through a grant from the Louisiana Endowment for the Humanities, a state affiliate of the National Endowment for the Humanities. The opinions expressed in this book do not necessarily represent the views of the Louisiana Endowment for the Humanities or the National Endowment for the Humanities.

Published by the Louisiana Historical Association and the Center for Louisiana Studies, University of Louisiana at Lafayette.

Contents

Illustrations

Preface

These essays were first presented at the Louisiana Purchase Bicentennial Conference, a project of The Historic New Orleans Collection and the Louisiana Historical Association (LHA). The Conference was held at New Orleans, January 22-25, 2003. Dr. Stephen A. Webre, then president of the LHA, initiated planning for such a conference in 1997. The planning group early determined that the full historical ramifications of the Purchase could not be explored in even a three-day conference; indeed they are still being revealed. What could be done, and what had special attraction because the conference was to be held in New Orleans, was to explore the colonial and early national periods, to about 1860. The Civil War is generally recognized as among *the* major historical consequences of the Purchase because the latter led to increased sectional tensions over the spread of slavery and the balance of political power in the U.S. Congress. To that basic historical period we added what is sometimes called the pre-history of the region because we understood that any understanding of the colonial and early national periods necessarily had to begin with the history of Native Peoples before 1699 as well as afterward.

Between the concept and the reality, many scholars across the United States generously gave their advice as to appropriate speakers if they were themselves unable to participate. Dr. James Horn, Saunders Director, the International Center for Jefferson Studies, provided the planning team with a number of important suggestions for the organization of the Conference. This help, and that of many colleagues in Louisiana, is gratefully acknowledged.

A conference of this scale required considerable financial support. Thanks to the generous support of the following organizations and individuals the Conference brought together the twenty-two scholars whose work you are about to read and over five hundred persons who devoted two and a half days to attending these remarkable presentations. Support for the Conference and events associated with it was provided by Department of Culture, Recreation and Tourism, State of Louisiana, Bicentennial Commission; Bank One; the Louisiana Endowment for the Humanities; K-Paul's Louisiana Enterprise, Inc.; Louisiana State University System; Citigroup Asset Management; Associated Office Systems; René Bistro; St. Denis J. Villere & Company; Dorian M. Bennett Realtors, Inc.; El Corte Inglés; French Heritage Society; the Program for Cultural Cooperation between Spain's Ministry of Education, Culture and Sports and United States Universities; the Embassy of Spain/Consulate General of Spain; Anselmo's Restaurant; Muriel's Jackson Square Restaurant; Kinko's; Law Offices of Robert M. Becnel & Diane Zink; Canadian Consulate General; Milling, Woodward, Benson, LLP; University of Chicago; Louisiana State Museum; Hotel St. Marie; Prince Conti French Quarter Hotel; St. James Florals; Peter T. McLean, Ltd.; Johnson Controls, Inc.; Louisiana Binding Services; Organ Historical Society; American Guild of Organists, New Orleans Chapter; French-American Chamber of Commerce; Omni Royal Orleans Hotel; Villefranche and Beaujolais Chamber of Commerce and Industry; and the Louisiana State University History Department Development Fund.

We are publishing these essays for the benefit of a larger public at the suggestion of many of the attendees at the Conference. The Louisiana Endowment for the Humanities and the Louisiana Historical Association have made this publication possible. The staff of the Center for Louisiana Studies at the University of Louisiana at Lafayette, led by Dr. Carl A. Brasseaux, took the electronic text through the publishing process and handled distribution on behalf of the Conference and the Louisiana Historical Association.

The Library of Congress, the Denver Public Library, The Amon Carter Museum of Fort Worth, the Putnam Museum of Davenport, Iowa, the Louisiana State Museum, The Historic New Orleans Collection, the Nevada Historical Society, the Oklahoma Historical Society, The Louisiana and Lower Mississippi Valley Collections, Louisiana State University Libraries, Dr. Colin McEvedy, Mr. James Crandall, Mr. Bruce Paulson, and Dr. Ross Frank provided illustrations, in many cases without fee. This help is gratefully acknowledged.

The opinions expressed are those of the authors and do not necessarily reflect the views of the Louisiana Historical Association, the Historic New Orleans Collection, the Louisiana Endowment for the Humanities, the Center for Louisiana Studies, or the editor.

Finally, a special word of thanks to the scholars who not only presented such dynamic and informative lectures at the Conference but who also generously revised those presentations and responded in a timely way to this editor's suggestions.

Part I
Contexts

Contexts

The first six essays provide "Contexts." Joseph Ellis's Keynote address reviews the basic political story of the Purchase and considers why, at the end of his life, Jefferson chose not to list the Purchase on his tombstone.

The next three essays form a subsection on international contexts. Sylvia L. Hilton examines Spain's international position in the late 1790s, the Spaniards' view of the inevitability of American expansion, and their reactions to the Purchase. David P. Geggus lays out the development of French interest (1789 to 1803) in recovering possession of the Purchase Territory from Spain and discusses the various factors commonly said to have influenced Napoleon's decision to sell. Gene A. Smith explores British Imperial interest in the Purchase Territory from the acquisition of West Florida in 1763 to the Battle of New Orleans in January 1815. These essays show that the European powers contested the ownership of the Mississippi Valley and the Gulf Coast and thus what the stakes were for the new American republic.

The fifth and sixth essays examine economic contexts that are useful for understanding the Purchase and the histories of its peoples. Because little is known about Saint-Domingue's pre-Haitian Revolution imports, Selwynn H. H. Carrington uses data from the trade between the thirteen continental colonies (in time the United States) and the British sugar colonies in the Caribbean during the 1770s to gauge the realism of Napoleon's idea that he could use the Purchase Territory and its 50,000 or so people (in 1803) as a supplier of foods and forest products to replace Saint-Domingue's dependence on the United States for those commodities. Daniel H. Usner, Jr. shows that patterns of livelihood and exchange in three different parts of the Purchase Territory were not at first affected by the Purchase although they were undergoing dynamic changes having other origins. He thus sounds a theme that appears in several of the essays that follow: that the Purchase made little initial difference to people living in the Territory.

Chapter 1

Jefferson and the Purchase

Joseph Ellis

There are several dramatic ways to describe it and just as many truly strange paradoxes about the place it has assumed in both Thomas Jefferson's legacy and historical scholarship in general. On the dramatic side, the Louisiana Purchase was the biggest steal in the history of real estate transactions, a third of a continent, probably the most fertile land on the planet, for $15 million, or less than four cents an acre. Economically, it created the conditions that made the United States self-sufficient in food and the agricultural superpower of the twentieth century. Politically, it was the most consequential executive decision in American presidential history, easily besting Harry Truman's decision to drop the atomic bomb in 1945. Strategically, it removed the threat posed by the major European powers from the western borders of the infant American republic, a threat that had existed throughout the revolutionary era and had led many European observers to presume that the emerging nation called the United States would quickly collapse into regional sovereignties and then be gobbled up among the world powers hovering at its edges. In short, it made the term "manifest destiny" another one of Jefferson's self-evident truths.

On the paradoxical side, Jefferson chose not to mention it on his tombstone as one of his proudest accomplishments. He also chose not to mention his presidency, in which the Purchase was his landmark achievement. The first national memorial to Jefferson, a grand arch sheltering his statue, was dedicated at St. Louis in 1913 and celebrated him as the founding father of the American West. But if you go to the Jefferson Memorial on the Tidal Basin and read all the lyrical passages on the polished plaques, you will see no words about the Purchase. His status in the American pantheon now derives its power from the magic words of the Declaration of Independence rather than his action as our first imperial president.[1]

The historical scholarship on the Purchase also exposes a paradox. Most of the books on the political and diplomatic history of the decision and its implementation are dated, over forty or fifty years old, largely because the reigning orthodoxy in the profession has been social history, which focuses on racial, ethnic and gender categories, the ordinary rather than the extraordinary, those diverse folks at the periphery rather than those dead-white-males at the center. Though my own professional predilections run against this grain, it nevertheless strikes even me as strange that the inhabitants of that vast territory Jefferson acquired have only recently attracted the attention of social historians dedicated to telling the different stories of that distinctive region before it was thoroughly assimilated into the predominant Anglo-American culture.[2]

The chief goal of this conference is to give new momentum to this burgeoning scholarship. My task, at least as I have been given to understand it, is to review the old story of Jefferson and the Purchase, perhaps to put the old wine in some new bottles along the way, and thereby to provide the political framework within which the newer voices and stories can proceed apace. Another less uplifting way to put it is that my purpose is to help you remember a story that you once knew, but have forgotten; or perhaps should have learned, but never did.

Let me begin with a new bottle designed to catch your attention because of its contemporary shape. A new president enters office after an extremely close and controversial election, in fact decided on the thirty-sixth ballot in the House of Representatives. Vilified in the press as a vapid, fatuous and dreamy-eyed pretender to power, who only won the election because of backroom shenanigans in one key state, he lacks a national mandate and is reviled by the most influential members of the Northeastern establishment. Then, early in his term, an unforeseen opportunity presents itself to galvanize public opinion and popular support. He seizes that opportunity boldly, makes it the defining feature of his presidency, isolates and eviscerates opponents who challenge either his decision or his authority to make it, and wins re-election by a landslide as the opposition party dissolves into utter disarray.

The analogy between Jefferson and George W. Bush is hardly perfect—no analogy ever is—but it does raise to relief the controversial character of Jefferson's ascendancy to the presidency and the political role the Purchase performed in consolidating his control. We need to remember that the president of Yale, Timothy Dwight, ordered all Yale graduates never to cast a vote for Jefferson or risk revocation of their degrees; that Henry Adams, in his monumental history of Jefferson's presidency, described his first year as "marked by an outburst of reciprocal invective and slander such as could not be matched in American history." William James once said that legislation in a democracy is "a business in which something is done, followed by a pause to see who hollers."[3] In Jefferson's case the hollering began right away, before he did anything.

The more harmless barbs made fun of his stated belief, published in *Notes on Virginia*, that the American West was populated by giant, woolly mammoths. But the sharpest accusations came from James Callender, who broke the Sally Hemings story in September of 1802, which dominated the New England press into the winter, only to be displaced the following spring by stories of negotiations in Paris to acquire New Orleans. We now know beyond any reasonable doubt that Callender's charges about a long-term sexual relationship with his mulatto slave were true, as were the charges that Jefferson had lied about paying Callender to libel John Adams in the recent election. The major reason these potentially damaging criticisms never did any serious political harm to Jefferson's presidency is that the looming acquisition, not just of New Orleans but of a vast expanse that effectively doubled the national domain, made the Hemings accusations seem irrelevant. He won re-election in 1804 riding a swelling wave of popularity, 162 electoral votes to 14.[4]

The Story

Let me now attempt to serve you some old wine without any bottle at all. By that I mean to provide a succinct narrative of Jefferson's role in the Louisiana Purchase without any interpretive accouterments to embellish the story. Such an effort, as we all know, is destined to fail, since telling a story without any interpretive convictions to guide and shape it is just as impossible as pouring wine without any bottle. That said, there is a virtue in placing the most salient and uncontestable historical facts on the table, establishing the narrative line, if you will, before proceeding to raise the edgier questions about what it means, whether it is a triumph or tragedy, and why Jefferson did not want it on his tombstone.

Although he himself never traveled further west than the Shenandoah Valley, Jefferson's proprietary interest in the Mississippi Valley and the vast expanse beyond it was long-standing. He shared the prevalent view that the Mississippi was America's major artery, as one pundit put it, "the Hudson, the Delaware, the Potomac, and all the navigable rivers of the Atlantic, formed into one stream." His several schemes for improving navigation on the Potomac were based on the romantic illusion, shared by most Virginians, that it offered direct access to the bounty of the American interior. A few months after he assumed the presidency, when James Monroe asked his opinion on a proposal to re-settle Virginia's freed slaves on western land currently owned by Spain, Jefferson observed that, true enough, Spain was a mere holding company, conveniently occupying the unexplored region until American settlers swarmed over the Mississippi. "It is impossible not to took forward to distant times," wrote Jefferson, "when our rapid multiplication will . . . cover the whole northern, if not southern continent, with a people speaking the same language, governed in similar forms, and by similar laws; nor can we contemplate with satisfaction either blot or mixture on that surface." By "blot or mixture" Jefferson meant that neither freed slaves nor Native Americans had any enduring role in his vision of the American West. The former should be exported to the Caribbean or Sierra Leone. The latter should be offered the opportunity to abandon their tribal hunting and gathering customs and integrate with the succeeding waves of white settlers. "We presume that our strength and their weakness is now so visible," he explained, "that they [Native Americans] must see we have only to shut our hand to crush them, & that all our liberalities to them proceed from motives of pure humanity only."[5]

And so even before Napoleon presented him with a heaven-sent opportunity to purchase the American Midwest, Jefferson already presumed it was destined to become part of the United States. Although he had obviously never read Frederick Jackson Turner[6], the Jeffersonian vision was Turnerian in two important ways: first, it regarded the West as the crucial region in shaping the future of the new nation; second, it was the place where the agrarian idyll could be regularly rediscovered, thereby postponing into the indefinite future the crowded conditions and political congestions of European society. It was the geographic version of the fountain of youth.

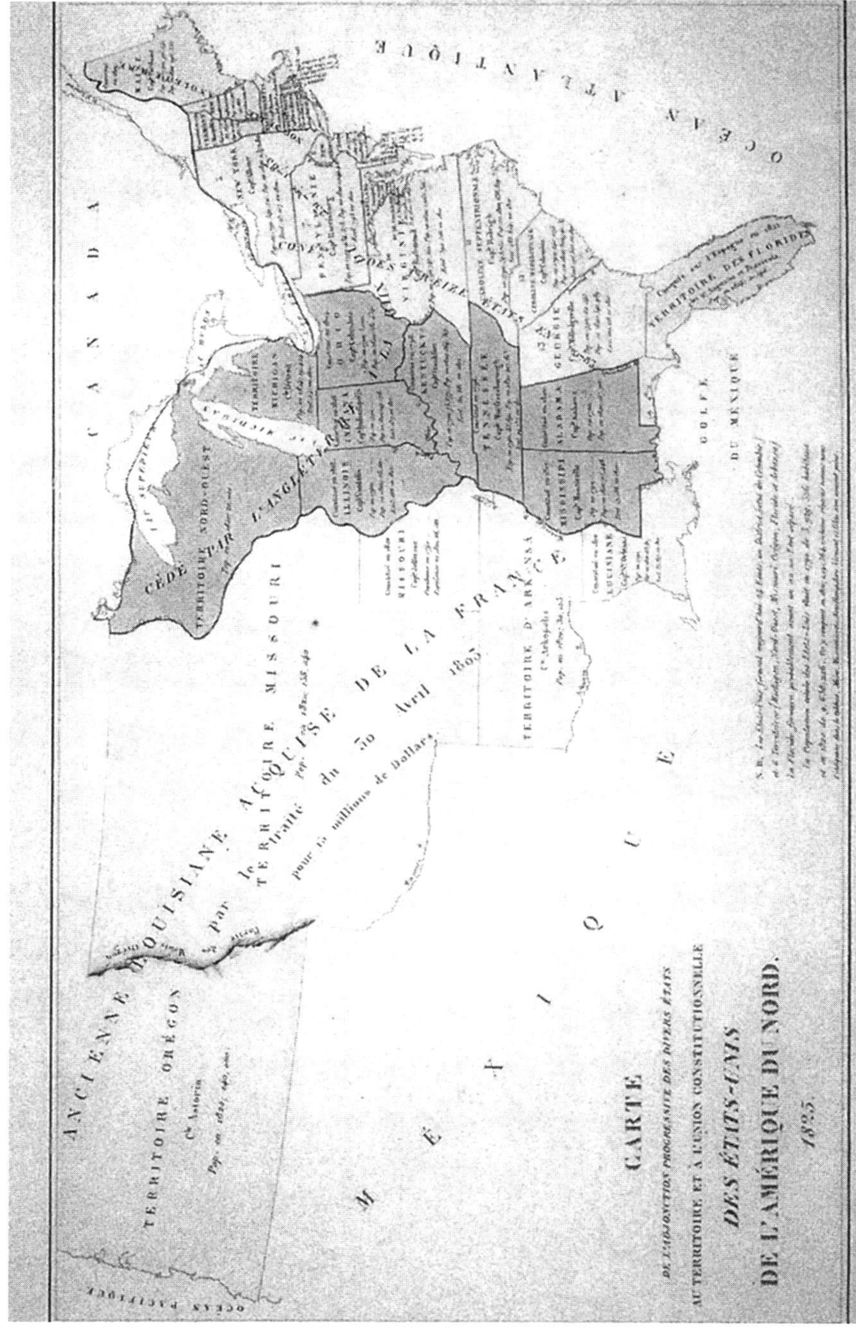

Figure 1. *The Louisiana Purchase* as defined by the Adams-Onis Treaty of 1819. The Historic New Orleans Collection, Accession 1970-7. Courtesy of the Collection.

Jefferson did have the opportunity to read James Madison's argument in *Federalist 10* and concurred with the Madisonian claim that expanding the size of the American republic actually reduced the risk of political instability by multiplying the number of factions or interest groups, which then balanced or checked one another. He was therefore immune to the fear of fragmentation prevalent among many New England Federalists, who worried that a more expansive version of the United States would split into several regional units in the European mode. In the Jeffersonian vision, the United States would not just integrate the West into the Union; the West would integrate the older states into a newer and ever-changing version of America. All in all, then, we can say that Jefferson's pre-Purchase view of the West was breathtakingly bold, deeply romantic and thoroughly racist.[7]

What became the great opportunity initially appeared as a great threat. In 1802 it became public knowledge that Spain, the chronically weak "sick man of Europe," had ceded its control over the ill-defined Louisiana Territory to Napoleon and France. Jefferson immediately wrote to Robert Livingston, the American minister in Paris, warning that French control of the Mississippi dramatically changed the strategic chemistry on the North American continent: "There is on the globe one single spot," Jefferson observed, "the possessor of which is our natural and habitual enemy. It is New Orleans. . . . Perhaps nothing since the revolutionary war has produced more uneasy sensations through the body of the nation." He then ordered James Monroe, currently serving as governor of Virginia, to drop everything and proceed to Paris. "The circumstances are such as to render it impossible to decline," he apprised Monroe, because "on the event of this mission, depends the future destinies of this republic." Jefferson gently shouldered aside his eminently capable secretary of state, James Madison, to take personal control of the negotiations. He drafted instructions authorizing Monroe to purchase New Orleans and as much of the Mississippi Valley as possible for up to $10 million.[8]

Historians have spilled a good deal of ink arguing about the person who deserves the lion's share of credit for negotiating the Louisiana Purchase. My own sense is that a contemporary remark by Edward Channing, the British foreign minister, captures the essence of the diplomatic situation: "Napoleon threw the province, so to speak, at Livingston, Monroe, Madison, and Jefferson; and they share between them—equally—whatever credit there was in catching it and holding it—that is all." It was fashionable for many years to tell the story of the transaction as a meditation on the potency of dumb luck. My view is that Jefferson deserves credit for immediately recognizing the huge stakes involved, and for being prepared to discard the former domestic priority of his presidency, which was debt reduction, as well as his own constitutional reservations about executive power (more on this shortly) and for responding so decisively when Napoleon rather impulsively decided to consolidate his resources on the European continent in preparation for the next round of the Napoleonic wars.[9]

But the immediate cause of Napoleon's decision should direct our attention to another influence—the insurgent slaves and malaria-carrying mosquitoes of Saint-

Domingue. Napoleon abandoned his dreams of a French empire in America when an expeditionary force of 25,000 French soldiers under the command of Charles LeClec, his brother-in-law, was effectively annihilated in savage fighting against the slave rebellion in Saint-Domingue led by the charismatic black Napoleon named Toussaint L'Ouverture. The original plan was for LeClec to suppress the slave insurgency, then proceed with his force to occupy New Orleans. Instead, Toussaint's army and malaria wiped out the French force, along with LeClec himself, prompting Napoleon to cut his losses in the western hemisphere. There is a rich irony here, because Jefferson, who had previously supported the French effort to suppress the slave rebellion in Saint-Domingue, then became the beneficiary of the French failure to do so in the form of Napoleon's decision to sell the entire Louisiana Territory. Word of the treaty's terms reached Washington on July 3, 1803, so that the celebration—it was regarded as providential—coincided with the anniversary of American independence.[10]

It quickly became apparent that the seizure of an empire required an imperial president. The famously inscrutable and unscrupulous French minister, Talleyrand, put it nicely: "I can give you no direction," he observed to Jefferson on the question of the province's boundaries, "you have made a noble bargain for yourselves, and I suppose you will make the most of it." This turned out to be an understatement. Back at Monticello in the summer of 1803, Jefferson studied the maps of the Gulf Coast and concluded that the southeastern border of French Louisiana was the Perdido River, near present-day Pensacola, and the southwestern border was the Rio Grande. Since no one in France knew the location of the Perdido or Rio Grande any more than the Potomac or Hudson, Jefferson's expansive interpretation of his new acquisition only ruffled feathers in Madrid, where the Spaniards objected to the entire sale, claiming that Napoleon was not empowered to sell their former colony, and that neither West Florida nor Texas were part of the deal. "We scarcely expect any liberal or just settlement from Spain," Jefferson observed to Monroe, but "whatever may be the views of Spain, there will be no difficulty in getting thro' with our purposes." In short, Spain's military and economic weakness rendered it powerless to oppose Jefferson's extravagant claims, which also envisioned the acquisition of Florida, "all in good time," a prediction that came true fifteen years later. Texas would take longer.[11]

Jefferson's expansive tendencies as a map-reader clashed with his narrowly defined notions of executive power and his well-documented opposition to the doctrine of "implied powers." He simply did not believe that the Constitution permitted the acquisition of foreign territory unless specifically granted by a constitutional amendment. His first instinct was to request Congress for just that, but he reconsidered when coded letters from Livingston suggested that Napoleon was having second thoughts. To pursue the cumbersome ratification process necessary for a constitutional amendment would place the entire Purchase at risk. After a few weeks of mental anguish over his constitutional scruples, Jefferson decided to abandon them. He confided to Madison that "the less we say about constitutional difficulties respecting Louisiana the better, and what is necessary for surmounting them must be done *sub silentio*." In effect, if the choice was between sustaining his strict interpretation of executive authority or doubling the size of the American republic, he chose the more pragmatic course, rationalizing that "to lose our country by a scrupulous adherence to written laws, would be to lose the law itself. . . ."[12]

He had already played fast and loose with the law earlier that spring while waiting to hear if the treaty had been signed. Jefferson's appointment of his personal secretary, Meriwether Lewis, to lead an expedition that would explore the Louisiana Territory and beyond has, for good reason, become a fixture in national mythology as the launching of one of the greatest adventure stories in American history. What is often ignored, however, is the awkward fact that the Lewis and Clark expedition was really a covert reconnaissance team formally authorized to go no further than the Mississippi basin, since the vast region west of that location still belonged to France and Spain. Jefferson acknowledged that the official charge to Lewis was designed to conceal the true destination, which was the Pacific, and the official description of the expedition as a scientific venture or a mere "literary pursuit" was intended to mask the mapping mission and the implicit presumption that this huge region was destined to become American soil.[13]

The ratification debate in the senate was perfunctory, one senator claiming that this geographically massive and constitutionally problematic piece of business received less scrutiny than "the most trivial Indian contract." Jefferson had leaked the rumor that Napoleon now regretted the decision to abandon his Franco-American empire, so any delay in making the treaty official risked ruining the whole transaction. Congress cooperated by passing enabling legislation that delegated all decisions about the provisional government in the Louisiana Territory to the executive branch. John Quincy Adams was one of the few senators to oppose the legislation, observing that it gave Jefferson more power over the residents of the territory than George III ever exercised over the thirteen colonies.[14]

Jefferson personally drafted the provisional constitution, although he wanted that fact kept secret. As he explained to Senator John Breckinridge of Kentucky: "You must never let any person know that I have put pen to paper on the subject. . . . I am this particular, because you know with what bloody teeth and fangs the Federalists will attack any sentiment or principle known to come from me, and what blackguardisms and personalities they make it the occasion of vomiting forth." The real reason Jefferson was so sensitive on the question became clear once the document became public. It made the Louisiana Territory a colony of the United States ruled by a governor appointed by the president and council of thirteen appointed officials that Jefferson called the "Assembly of Notables," thinking that the term might have an appealingly familiar ring to French residents accustomed to the aristocratic ethos of the *ancien régime*. John Quincy Adams mischievously asked whether Jefferson might wish to add a provision assuring the Louisiana colonists that they would not be taxed without their consent. Madison, whom Jefferson almost surely consulted about the provisional constitution, privately conceded that it would "leave the people of that District for a while without the organization of power dictated by the Republican theory."[15]

When a delegation from the territory came to Washington the following year to protest their status as unrepresented subjects, Jefferson refused to meet with them. The question they posed, after all, proved awkward for the man who had drafted the Declaration of Independence to answer: "Do the political axioms on the Atlantic become problems when transplanted to the shores of the Mississippi?" Jefferson's private response emphasized the temporary character of the provisional constitution and his clear conviction that "our new fellow citizens are as yet incapable of self government." Republican principles would eventually be planted, take root and grow in the Louisiana Territory, he believed, for the same providential reasons that "the empire of liberty" would extend to the Pacific. All in the fullness of time.[16]

The Missouri Epilogue

Strictly speaking, that is the end of the story of Jefferson and the Purchase. His attention shifted to other political and diplomatic problems in 1804. (If we wished to push the analogy with our current president beyond the breaking point, we could notice that one of those problems was the ongoing war with the Islamic terrorists of that time, the Barbary pirates. But that's another story.) There is an important epilogue, however, which occurs in 1819-1820, long after Jefferson had retired to his mountaintop at Monticello.

One of the rights that the delegation of protestors from the territory claimed in 1804 was the right of property, which they defined as the right to own slaves. Earlier in his career, as a delegate to the Confederation Congress in 1783, Jefferson had proposed legislation prohibiting slavery in all the western territories as a condition for admission as states, a proposal that failed by only one vote. By the time of the Purchase, however, his position on slavery in the territories had changed. It is difficult to locate the precise moment when the change occurred, because Jefferson preferred to avoid making public statements on slavery, and his private statements were consistently paradoxical, opposing it as a moral abomination in the abstract while insisting that the federal government lacked jurisdiction to outlaw slavery in the states, indeed lacked jurisdiction to make domestic policy of any sort at all. Peter Onuf, who has written the most recent and comprehensive account of the subject, argues that there was an inherent if elusive logic to Jefferson's thinking on this pressing question. My view is that his logic, if we can call it that, was both tortured and strained, and in fact seemed designed to sustain the contradiction that slavery violated the principles on which the American Revolution was based, but that there was nothing that he or anyone else who shared those principles could do about it. At the time of the Purchase, while he opposed the creation of a black homeland or reservation in the territory as a "blot," he did not oppose and implicitly endorsed slavery's extension into any and all western states entering the Union.[17]

The matter lurked beneath the surface of national attention until 1819, when the admission of Missouri into the Union provoked the first full-scale public debate. Jefferson objected to the debate itself, calling it—famous phrase—"a fire bell in the night," which he also heard as a "death knell of the Union." His lyrical lamentations on the Missouri question—it was an "act of suicide" and "treason against the hopes of the world"—followed naturally from his original premises about the role of the West, which was supposed to be America's safety-valve, the place where problems went to find solutions, had now become the breeding ground for the most ominous problem of all. More ironically, the precedent he himself set in acquiring and then governing the Louisiana Territory as an executive action had now become the constitutional grounds for those leaders of the anti-slavery cause claiming federal jurisdiction over the question of slavery in the territories. As John Adams put it: "that the purchase of Louisiana was unconstitutional or extra Constitutional I never had a doubt—but I think the Southern gentlemen who thought it Constitutional ought not to think it unconstitutional in Congress to restrain the extension of Slavery in that territory."[18]

Jefferson went to his grave clinging to his mystical belief in the magical powers of the West. "I still believe," he wrote in 1821, "that the Western extension of our confederacy will insure its duration, by overruling local factions, which might shake a smaller association." He also embraced the rather bizarre doctrine of "diffusion," the belief that the spread of slavery into the western expanse would reduce its virulence and eventually transform an untractable into a manageable problem. Adams, upon hearing that his old friend and political rival endorsed "diffusion," observed that it must be symptomatic of Jefferson's creeping senility, since the spread of a cancer had never before been regarded as a cure for the disease.[19]

We could pursue the thread of this story all the way to 1861, when it became the immediate cause of the Civil War. And we should probably make a pit-stop in 1858, where the Lincoln-Douglas debates provided the fullest rendering of the moral and political issues at stake, pausing long enough to notice that both Abraham Lincoln and Stephen Douglas claimed the mantle of Jefferson for their side. Douglas had the stronger claim on the Jefferson legacy, but Lincoln ultimately won the debate, and insisted on taking Jefferson with him into the history books. If the story began as a Jeffersonian saga about the mystical power of the West, it ends as a cautionary tale about the mystical power of the Jefferson legacy itself.[20]

An Interpretive Postscript

It should by now be reasonably clear why Jefferson did not put the Louisiana Purchase on his tombstone. He did not like conspicuous displays of power, especially by kings or executive magistrates, and the Louisiana Purchase turned out to be the most conspicuous display of presidential power in American history. The Purchase would probably have not happened if Jefferson had not behaved as an elected monarch, but his entire career from the Declaration of Independence to the Kentucky and Virginia Resolutions had been an ideological crusade against monarchical values, so his role in the Purchase was a total violation of his deepest political convictions. To make it worse, by the time he composed his own epitaph he realized that his greatest presidential achievement had sown the seeds of sectional division over slavery that were likely to blossom into a war that threatened to destroy the entire republican enterprise. These were not the kind of accomplishments he wished to advertise.

Was it a triumph or a tragedy? The juxtaposition of these options strikes me as naïve, and the advocates for any one-sided answer to the question need to nourish themselves on the two staple foods of all enduring works of history, which are irony and paradox. An unbridled celebration of the Purchase commits the sin of blind patriotism, which presumes that Jefferson's vision of the territory as white man's country was just as inevitable as he claimed. A multicultural critique of the Purchase commits the sin of mindless presentism, which presumes that our contemporary convictions about racial and ethnic diversity can be imposed judgmentally on the past because the political agenda of modern-day historians is more important than the intellectual and psychic make-up of long-dead folks, who can no longer defend themselves. The ideological geometry of both the patriots and the presentists is too linear to accommodate the twists and curves of either the Mississippi or Jefferson's mind.

My view is that Jefferson's role in the Louisiana Purchase was a triumph because it demonstrated, contrary to all of Jefferson's warnings against monarchy, that only a flamboyant display of executive power could make the American experiment with republican government work in great crises, a lesson that both Lincoln and Franklin Roosevelt learned and applied in subsequent crises. It was a tragedy because, for all of Jefferson's clairvoyance about the abiding weakness of Spain and the temporary vulnerability of France, he missed the even larger opportunity to address and resolve the two lingering contradictions of the American Revolution and the two acknowledged failures of the revolutionary generation. These were slavery and the fate of the Native American population.

It is not presentistic to characterize these contradictions as failures, because Jefferson and the other vanguard members of the revolutionary generation recognized and consciously acknowledged that the elimination of slavery and a just settlement with the indigenous occupants of the continent were moral imperatives dictated by the principles on which the nation was founded. The Louisiana Purchase represented an opportunity to end slavery in the territories and to use the revenues from the sale of western land to subsidize a program of gradual emancipation. It also represented an opportunity to provide a permanent and not just temporary home for those Native Americans who did not wish to assimilate into what Jefferson, rather ironically, called "an empire of liberty." His contemporary critics accused him of being excessively bold, the first American emperor. In retrospect, he was not bold enough to become the American liberator. As is usually the case, the triumph and the tragedy were joined at the hip; or more accurately, were inextricably linked together in the depths and shallows of that other vast expanse that was Jefferson's mind.

Chapter 2

Spanish Perspectives on the Louisiana Purchase: Imperial Responsibility and Diplomatic Realism

Sylvia L. Hilton

The Spanish Empire at the Turn of the 18th to the 19th Century

The first point we should bear in mind when considering Spanish perspectives on the Louisiana Purchase is that the Spanish government labored under a heavy burden of imperial responsibility. The vast Spanish empire was beset by multiple, complex, internal problems, which were responding only slowly to the modernising efforts of Spanish enlightened reformers. From Spain's global imperial viewpoint, Louisiana was to a large extent a liability. The metropolitan government considered it to be little more than a defensive barrier protecting the rich, more densely populated and Hispanicized provinces of New Spain. Louisiana's population, although growing fast, could not compete with the spectacular demographic growth of its American neighbour, and in any case the Louisianians' loyalty to the Spanish Crown was increasingly suspect. Last but not least, the province enjoyed privileges connected with trade and immigration that made it an anomaly within the empire, fostering undesirable economic dependencies (on France and the United States) as well as internal social and cultural tensions.

In its international relations, Spain had little room for diplomatic maneuver. Neutrality was a much-desired aspiration, but it was almost never a real option. European rivalries had created a diplomatic system that imposed the need to establish formal alliances. Spain was especially fearful of international isolation because of its multiple interests and vulnerable flanks in Europe and America. Consequently, throughout most of the 18th century Spain and France were united by successive 'family pacts', based on the supposed common interests of the Bourbon dynasty. Understandably, then, the French Revolution created a profound dilemma for the Spanish government. Spain had greater ideological and political affinity with the established order of Europe's legitimate monarchies, but Charles IV and his advisors continued to prefer the French alliance, because of British and American threats against the commercial monopoly and territorial integrity of the Spanish empire.

After failing to save Louis XVI's life, Spain entered briefly into a desperate cooperation with the European coalition against French revolutionary excesses and international proselytism. The war of 1793-1795 was a disaster from the Spanish point of view, not just because of losses sustained, but because it pushed the state into near-bankruptcy; a financial situation from which it was unable to recover, and which severely restricted the government's range of options in foreign and imperial policy. After returning to the French alliance under the treaty of San Ildefonso of 1796, Spain found it increasingly difficult to pursue an independent foreign policy, although this was not for want of trying.

Spain, Louisiana, and the United States

Meanwhile, the emergence of an independent sovereign power in America had greatly complicated Spain's imperial and international outlook. Spanish aid during the American war of independence was a reasonably auspicious start to Spanish-U. S. relations, although neither power was under any illusions concerning the interested nature of that aid. However, in their negotiations of 1786-1787 Spain's representative to the United States Diego Gardoqui and U. S. Secretary of State John Jay failed to reach an agreement on disputes arising from the peace treaties of 1782 and 1783. As a result, relations between the two countries were soured by frontier conflicts over Indian policies, trade and navigation on the lower Mississippi, and territorial limits.

Spanish government advisors had clearly foreseen American expansion and the Spanish retreat as early as 1777. They thought that these political developments would inevitably result from natural demographic and socio-economic processes, encouraged by the geographical and political conditions of North America. In that year, Secretary of the Navy Gonzalez de Castejón asserted: "Nothing will be able to contain a power which is independent in any part of the Americas in its perfectly natural ideas of expansion."[1] Some advisors thought that only internal divisions within the United States might frustrate or at least slow down the realisation of these predictions. For this reason they closely followed the evolution of early constitutional weaknesses and regional separatism, and the later development of divisive political partisanship, in the American confederation.

Consequently, Spanish policy in Louisiana and the Floridas was not designed in order to conserve these provinces indefinitely, but to delay their inevitable loss as long as possible by means of diverse defensive measures that were both pragmatic and economical. Diplomatic envoy Diego de Gardoqui was instructed in 1786 to keep Spanish demands to a minimum: "By these means, we might decently attend to our immediate need, and delay for a while the events that seem inevitable in the long run, that the Americans will take possession of all those lands to the Mississippi and the Ocean, not forgetting the Floridas; objectives that we can no longer doubt, without hallucinating, they intend to attain. And in any case we might be able to take advantage of this truce to place ourselves in a better position than it seems we are at present to stop them."[2] Thus, Spanish diplomacy toward the United States tended to adopt conciliatory tones, playing for time while avoiding any major conflict.

In 1795, battered by the war against France, bankrupt, and in fear of an Anglo-American rapprochement that might mean greater losses, Spain made important concessions regarding the pending disputes. By Pinckney's treaty of San Lorenzo, the United States obtained the northern part of West Florida, the right of free navigation on the Mississippi, and a three-year right of deposit at New Orleans. At the same time, the Spanish government had also decided to give Louisiana back to France as a way of involving French troops and colonists in the effort to contain American expansion. An initial agreement was reached in 1796, although the definitive conditions were not agreed until 1800 and 1801.

Manuel Godoy, the leader of the Spanish government, has been much maligned for his part in this decision, but he was not alone in thinking it might alleviate Spain's difficulties vis-à-vis the United States. The governor of Louisiana, Manuel Gayoso de Lemos, told the viceroy of New Spain in 1798: "I think that, although it would be risky, it would be less so to have the French in this province than to keep it as abandoned as it is, exposed to an easy conquest by the Anglo-Americans."[3] Indeed, despite some historians' criticisms of this move, it might have proved to be a brilliant one, if France had persisted in building its American empire. The retrocession was a gamble that did not pay off for Spain, but not even Napoleon foresaw the difficulties in Haiti that frustrated French plans in America.

Even before the retrocession became public knowledge, Spain had had ample warning that the United States would not look favourably on such a step. In July of 1802, the Spanish representative in the United States, Carlos Martinez de Irujo, wrote to the Foreign Secretary: "I am increasingly convinced that, although the two parties that divide this country have different political views, they are in agreement that U. S. interest requires the annexation of Louisiana and the Floridas."[4] In late 1802, American outrage at the sudden suspension of the right to store merchandise at New Orleans was so great that Spaniards were left with no doubts that the U. S. government would intervene in the event of any change in the status quo that might threaten American interests in the west.

Spanish Reactions to the Louisiana Purchase

The attitudes of the continental European powers regarding the Franco-American treaty of 1803 by which the United States bought Louisiana were of little importance. None of them had strong interests in America, or the naval capacity to operate effectively there. Consequently, Spain could not expect and did not seek their help. Only British attitudes had to be considered. Britain still had very great interests in North America, and might have taken steps to prevent the cession of Louisiana to France, but there was no chance of British aid or intervention to stop its transfer to the United States. Although not particularly pleased about U. S. control of the trans-Mississippi territory, the British government would not risk the recent and precarious Anglo-American rapprochement to defend British claims in that region, much less a rival power's nominal sovereignty rights on the basis of legal technicalities. Spanish watchers of international affairs had become more fearful of an Anglo-American understanding since Jay's treaty of 1794. Indeed, suspicions that Britain and the United States might reach some sort of agreement for cooperation was a constant factor in Spanish calculations during this period.

Spain had little legal margin for maneuver in 1803. No international law, agreement or treaty prohibited the transfer of colonial territory by sale, so any legal grounds that would permit the Spanish government to contest the Louisiana transaction had to originate in bilateral commitments. Spain and the United States might have negotiated an agreement that included reciprocal guarantees of territorial possessions. This idea had been suggested several times before 1803 but had not prospered. As a result, the Spanish government had to accept that American diplomacy was not bound by any bilateral legal obligations to Spain on that subject. Nonetheless, the Spanish legal argument was quite strong. The retrocession of Louisiana to France had been agreed subject to the condition of international (especially British) recognition of the kingdom of Etruria, in Tuscany, and evacuation of the French occupying troops. Spain was interested in this matter because the heirs to the Etrurian throne were the nephew and daughter of the Spanish monarchs. France had not fulfilled this condition and was, therefore, not the lawful possessor of Louisiana. In addition, in July 1802 French ambassador Gouvion St. Cyr had given in writing a solemn promise that Louisiana would never be alienated to any other power. This effectively invalidated its sale to the United States.

Specific Spanish responses to the Franco-American treaty of 1803 are best summarised on three fronts: responses to the French government; responses to the U. S. government; and imperial defensive measures.

In the first place, although the indignant rhetoric and high moral ground of Spanish protests might indicate otherwise, pragmatic realism actually ruled Spanish responses to the French government. Spain had entered into the Louisiana retrocession agreement more or less willingly. The territory had been bargained away; its loss was far from being a national disaster or tragedy. The option of war, therefore, was not even considered as a possible reaction to the Franco-American treaty.

The Spanish government might have taken advantage of French disloyalty to denounce the oppressive alliance of 1796, and declare Spanish neutrality in the imminent Anglo-French conflict, but this too was deemed impossible. Even half-hearted French support remained crucial to Spanish strategic imperatives. Secretary of State Manuel Godoy could not deny that, under the circumstances, Napoleon had obtained valuable benefits (both real and potential) in the treaty with the United States. Realistically, then, Spain's only viable option would have been to counterbalance the American offer with a more attractive Spanish offer. Spain did have resources that might have been used to persuade Napoleon to be more attentive to Spanish interests, but by that time Charles IV's advisors were unwilling to increase their already onerous commitments and concessions to France.

These considerations meant that the Spanish response to the French government had to rely on legal and moral arguments. These were put forward in extremely irate diplomatic protests, which were stated in the strongest language possible, in a tone of unqualified moral condemnation. Focusing principally on the sale of Louisiana as a betrayal of Spain's friendship and alliance, both in itself and in the fact that Charles IV had neither been consulted nor properly informed, the protest was accompanied by a detailed list of Spanish grievances and complaints. In this way the protest was used as a vehicle to convey a sense of Spanish distress at all the real and imagined damages that Spain had sustained in recent years, as a result of its close ties with France. Spanish bitterness against Napoleon was particularly inspired by the fact that the retrocession of Louisiana had only been contemplated in the first place as a means of involving French power in the containment of U. S. expansion, and French negotiators had freely used this persuasive argument in order to obtain Spanish acquiescence.

This indignation was not, however, devoid of other purposes. Despite its severely limited margin for maneuver, the Spanish government attempted to exploit its legitimate cause for complaint as a calculated reaction, in order to increase its moral leverage in other Spanish diplomatic endeavours. On the one hand, it still persisted in efforts to consolidate the international status and security of the Etrurian kingdom, and on the other hand, it was trying to gain some relief from French pressures generally.

Throughout the summer and fall, Napoleon and the French Foreign Minister, Charles Maurice de Talleyrand-Périgord, became increasingly impatient with Spanish lamentations. They responded with counter-accusations regarding Spain's generally uncooperative attitudes and conduct, while remorselessly urging Spain to take an active part in the war that had broken out in May. The Spanish government was desperate to stay neutral, but before long was faced with three equally odious choices: to join France in the war at once; to give Napoleon commercial privileges or monetary "subsidies," in exchange for which he would permit Spain to maintain an imperfect neutrality; or to refuse to cooperate at all and risk a French invasion of Spain. Even though there was no money in the public coffers, by the convention of October 19, 1803, the Spanish government promised to make monthly payments to Napoleon.

Meanwhile, French arguments did nothing to effectively contradict the claim that the sale of Louisiana was not legally valid, but barely veiled threats against the Etrurian throne and even against Spanish national security forced Charles IV's government to abandon its protest. Napoleon demanded that his ally accept the French right to dispose of Louisiana. Before the end of the year a verbal assurance was given, and on January 22, 1804, the Spanish ambassador in Paris, José Martinez de Hervás, confirmed to Talleyrand that Spain would not resist the transfer of that territory to the United States. In a matter of months, then, the Spanish discourse had evolved from outraged denunciation to reluctant acquiescence, and in the end to fearful appeasement.

Spanish leaders had not expected either the timing or the method of the American acquisition of Louisiana. It came as a nasty shock in Spain's relations with the United States. It is open to debate whether Jefferson would have gone to war over Louisiana under any other circumstances, but there is no doubt that he would have done so to uphold American rights under the treaty with France. War with the United States was unthinkable for Spain, as it would certainly put at risk the Floridas, Mexico, and the Spanish Caribbean. Godoy had originally justified the decision to abandon Louisiana on practical grounds, arguing that its retrocession to France would be a positive relief. It would no longer be necessary to find the money to cover the costs of administration and defence of such a vast, underpopulated and unproductive province. The absurdly long and remote military frontier would become shorter, and more easily supplied and reinforced. Economic and human resources could be redeployed to more pressing uses. New Orleans would cease to be a semi-legal back-door entrance to trade in other Spanish American markets. Imperial policies could be made more uniform, as the need to accommodate the peculiar social and cultural character of Louisiana disappeared. The Spanish representative in Washington, Irujo, pointed out that these reasonable, practical arguments did not become less true because the United States and not France took possession of Louisiana in 1803. So, again, the Spanish response was nothing stronger than a diplomatic protest, although when Irujo presented it to U. S. Secretary of State, James Madison, he did so in the firmest terms possible.

Although fully convinced that legality was on their side, the Spanish government held out little hope that the United States would let itself be restricted by technical considerations concerning France's right to sell Louisiana. Irujo, a seasoned observer of the American political scene, was not surprised when the Senate voted 24 to 7 to ratify the treaty, sweeping aside the scruples of constitutional and other legal purists. Jefferson then moved to take possession of the territory by force of arms, should Spain offer any resistance to the transfer. Alarmed by the possible repercussions of an American resort to arms, Irujo in turn sent urgent word to local authorities in Louisiana, the Floridas and Cuba to prepare for the possibility of war.

An interview with Madison in early November left the Spanish minister with no doubts about American intentions. "He has given me to understand very clearly", Irujo reported, "that if the governor of Louisiana does not hand over that province to the properly authorised person, they [the Americans] did not have time to enter into negotiations on the other side of the Atlantic." The United States would use force in defence of its rights, but Irujo warned that this would have other risks, saying: "if things go that far, they will also attack the Floridas and they will try to keep them as compensation for the expenses that they will say we caused them in order to take possession of a province which they say belongs to them."[5]

The Spanish government, in fact, took no steps to stop the formal ceremony of retrocession to France, or the transfer to the United States. Indeed, in the absence of competent French authorities in a few isolated settlements, local Spanish officials made the transfer directly to their American replacements. New instructions were sent to Irujo in early 1804, by virtue of which the Spanish diplomat informed Madison on May 15, that, notwithstanding its evident justification, his government had decided to formally withdraw its protest against the Franco-American treaty.

In sum, the Spanish responses to both France and the United States were restricted to diplomatic protests out of necessity. Spanish political realism dictated that the cause was relatively peripheral to Spain's national and imperial interests. Any stronger action would be too costly and fraught with grave risks. Nonetheless, efforts were made to minimise the damage. The key issue of concern was the vagueness of the Purchase's boundaries.

The Question of Boundaries

Even before the American purchase, the Spanish government had already shown concern regarding the boundaries of the retrocession to France. In May of 1803, the

Spanish commissioners for the retrocession to France, the Marquis de Casa Calvo and Manuel Salcedo, publicly declared that West Florida was a separate province and would therefore remain in Spanish possession. However, the American government had tried to acquire New Orleans and all or part of the Floridas (well before any thought of purchasing Louisiana) in reaction to the western outcry at the suspension of the U. S. right of deposit in the fall of 1802. Then, in 1803, when Livingston and Monroe inquired about the boundaries of Louisiana, the French government was deliberately unhelpful. As a result, the United States put forward extravagant territorial claims both to the east and to the west, based on the imprecise terms of the Spanish-French treaty of retrocession of 1800, which were simply carried over into the French-American treaty of 1803.

The Spanish government half expected Monroe to come to Madrid to negotiate the purchase of the Floridas. Consequently, at the same time that it vigorously maintained its protest against the Louisiana transaction, between July and December of 1803 it was debating the possibility of ceding the Floridas to the United States in exchange for the return of Louisiana. A number of governmental advisors recommended this line of action as the best means of containing the damage and establishing an unambiguous Spanish-American frontier along the Mississippi. The difficulties of maintaining the Floridas also recommended this option. Constant bickering with the United States was easy to foresee. Spanish influence over the Native Americans in the area had been much reduced since 1795, because most of the tribal lands had then come under U. S. jurisdiction. In any case, tribal friendship depended on the British fur-trade company that was headed by John Forbes, whose loyalty to Spain might not be as strong as that of his recently deceased predecessor, William Panton. The general state of commercial irregularity, economic dependency and relatively sparse population of the Floridas all remained unsolved problems. Finally, the adventurer William Augustus Bowles, who had mobilised hostile Indian forces against the Spaniards in the Floridas, had recently underscored Spanish vulnerability. Suspicions also lingered regarding his links to British backers and even American accomplices. His capture in June 1803 may partly explain the Spanish resolve to keep the Floridas after all. The final "positive decision" not to give up the Floridas was reached in mid-December and communicated to the U. S. government.

In the meantime, Congress passed the Mobile Act, authorising the President to form a customs district centered on the river and bay of Mobile. This elicited a suitably energetic new protest from Irujo, who made it clear that those territories belonged to Spain. This was followed up by a message from the Captain General of Cuba to the Spanish governor of West Florida informing him of the offensive articles of the Mobile Act and ordering him to prevent any American move into the province. By early 1805, Spanish diplomacy was being backed up by France. The French ambassador, General Turreau, told Madison, in the presence of Irujo, that West Florida had not been included in the original retrocession agreement, and that both parties had intended it to remain in Spanish hands.

The western limits of Louisiana gave the Spanish government even more cause for concern. Spaniards had been predicting American ambition to possess the riches of Mexico since the 1770s. In early December 1802, Jefferson told Irujo about his interest in sending an overland expedition to explore the Missouri and a route to the Pacific coast. However, the response from Madrid to Irujo's reports about preparations for the Lewis and Clark expedition was no more energetic than a brief note assuring him of royal approval of his well documented dissuasive reply. Otherwise, although the Spanish commandant at St. Louis was sufficiently surprised by their lack of Spanish passports to ask them to wait until he could receive orders, there was no attempt to prevent or intercept this expedition. However, during the next few years efforts *were* made to stop other American expeditions that might penetrate Spanish domains while exploring the Louisiana Purchase territory.

More worryingly, the United States soon claimed Texas as part of the Purchase. This prodded the Spanish government to reinforce the military preparedness of New Spain's frontier defense system, and to undertake a systematic search for documentary proof attesting to the historical existence and the boundaries of Texas as a separate administrative jurisdiction. Also in 1804 the Spanish government created a boundary commission to defend Spanish interests. Perhaps the most significant achievement arising out of initial Spanish responses to the Louisiana Purchase was the geographical survey of New Spain's boundaries which was carried out between October 1805 and February 1806, and which was of considerable scientific and diplomatic importance.

In 1804, Spain was dragged into the French war against Great Britain, and the following year lost its navy at the battle of Trafalgar. This made it all but impossible to effectively oppose American ownership of Louisiana, even if the Spanish government had been inclined to do so. On Christmas Eve of 1804, Irujo wrote to the Spanish Foreign Secretary: "I have little doubt that this government will take advantage of the calamitous circumstances in which unfortunately our nation finds itself, to continue its unjust claims regarding the limits of Louisiana."[6] The good news was that he did not think that the U. S. government would use force, but would try to purchase Spanish acquiescence to American demands. This prospect suggested that Spain's overall strategy of diplomatic fencing, tactical delays, and minor counter-claims might still be maintained. In other words, the Spanish withdrawal from North America would continue—but as slowly as Spanish diplomacy could realistically make it.

SUGGESTED READINGS

Cox, Isaac Joslin. *The West Florida Controversy, 1798-1813: A Study in American Diplomacy.* Albert Shaw Lectures on Diplomatic History. Baltimore, 1918. Reprint, Gloucester, Mass.: P. Smith, 1967.

Din, Gilbert C., ed. *The Louisiana Purchase Bicentennial Series in Louisiana History.* Vol. II, *The Spanish Presence in Louisiana, 1763-1803*. Lafayette, La.: Center for Louisiana Studies, University of Southwestern Louisiana, 1996.

Hoffman, Paul E. *Luisiana*. Colecciones MAPFRE 1492. Madrid: Editorial MAPFRE, 1992.

McDermott, John Francis, ed. *The Spanish in the Mississippi Valley, 1762-1804*. Urbana, Ill.: University of Illinois Press, 1974.

Weber, David J. *The Spanish Frontier in North America*. Yale Western Americana Series. New Haven: Yale University Press, 1992.

Whitaker, Arthur P. *The Spanish-American Frontier, 1787-1795: The Westward Movement and the Spanish Retreat in the Mississippi Valley*. New York & Boston: Houghton Mifflen Company, 1927. Reprint, Lincoln, Neb.: University of Nebraska Press, 1969.

________. *The Mississippi Question, 1795-1803: A Study in Trade, Politics and Diplomacy*. New York: C. Appleton-Century Company, 1934. Reprint, Gloucester, Mass.: P. Smith, 1962.

Chapter 3

French Imperialism and the Louisiana Purchase

David P. Geggus

The night before Napoleon Bonaparte made up his mind to sell Louisiana his war minister, Louis Alexandre Berthier, argued at length with him against such a move. He reminded the First Consul how colonies had made France wealthy and how Louisiana could compensate for France's past losses in India and those then threatening in the Caribbean. He called Louisiana potentially the most important of France's overseas possessions, both as an agricultural producer and as an outlet for the trans-Appalachian commerce of the United States. In the hands of others, it would be a commercial rival (even, Berthier somewhat fancifully asserted, for French grapes and olives). The minister, who had negotiated Louisiana's conditional transfer from Spain to France in October 1800, argued with more foresight that its value would increase, if ever a Panama canal were built. At the very least, he added, Louisiana could serve as a dumping ground for France's political dissidents.[1]

Why, therefore, should Napoleon abandon this vast tract of land that he had gone to the trouble of acquiring some thirty months before? Why did he override the advice of, not only his war minister, but his ministers of the navy and colonies, and of foreign affairs, and the violent opposition of his brothers, Lucien and Joseph (one of whom he drenched with bathwater, when he tried to argue him out of the sale during Napoleon's bathtime)?

Of all Bonaparte's territorial acquisitions, Lousiana was among the most ephemeral and inexpensive. If the few cents per acre of Jefferson's purchase have long been celebrated as a bargain, Bonaparte's essentially forced transfer from Spain had cost him no more than a few empty promises. Nor was this the first time France had parted with its lands on the Mississippi. In 1763, the Duke de Choiseul had given away without much remorse a far larger swath of territory to Spain and England. The factors that shaped his thinking still applied in 1803. Louisiana seemed vulnerable to British attack from the north and the south, and it cost its colonial rulers, French or Spanish, far more than it produced in revenue.[2] Moreover, it seems fair to say that none of France's rivals was very interested in adding it to their own empires. Spain, the colonial ruler in 1803, valued Louisiana mostly as a buffer to protect Mexico, in other words as empty space. Great Britain had, in 1797, refused a Spanish offer to exchange both Louisiana and Florida for tiny Gibraltar.[3] Indeed, Choiseul had once considered swapping Louisiana for Iceland.[4]

Despite the 1768 rebellion against Spain of Louisiana's Francophone colonists and their subsequent appeals to the French government, France displayed little interest during the closing years of the ancien régime in regaining the colony.[5] Only one piece of evidence suggests that the government wished at least to keep the possibility open. The treaty of alliance France made with the nascent United States when it entered the Revolutionary War in 1778 explicitly renounced any intention of regaining Quebec but made no mention of Louisiana. Nevertheless, there is no sign of the colony impinging on government policy until the French Revolution.[6]

Public interest in Louisiana increased early in the French Revolution, partly because the unpatriotic abandonment of its French settlers by an uncaring monarchy made good copy as a critique of despotic government. Historians generally have given most credit for reviving concern about the colony to a lengthy report drawn up in March 1789 by the French minister to the United States, the Marquis de Moustier.[7] Arguing that the colony's potential economic value to France warranted its "retrocession," or reacquisition, Moustier outlined two future roles for Louisiana. One was as a supplier of farm produce and lumber to France's Caribbean colonies. The other was as a point of access to the trans-Appalachian United States market for French merchants and manufacturers.

For most of the eighteenth century, the French West Indies dominated Atlantic trade in tropical produce. The booming colony of Saint-Domingue (modern Haiti) was the world's major producer of sugar and coffee, and a major source of indigo and cotton as well. This Caribbean success story had made the colonial losses in North America and India in the 1760s easier to accept. However, to the annoyance of French merchants and farmers, Yankee traders supplied an important part of the foodstuffs, timber, and livestock purchased by the plantation colonies[8] Moustier's plan was to develop Louisiana as a source of supply, and so keep more of colonial commerce in French hands. This meant greatly expanding a relationship that went back to the period of French rule and continued to grow in the 1780s under the slowly liberalizing rule of Spain, although Louisiana's contribution to French Caribbean commerce was extremely small.[9]

Moustier's second aim was inspired by the rapid growth of the U. S. population west of the Appalachians, whose natural outlet to world trade was the Mississippi. His hopes to use New Orleans as a point of entry for French manufactures were apparently unrealistic, because European goods reached the frontier more cheaply overland from the eastern ports than via the slow haul up the Mississippi.[10] Moreover, Moustier admitted, the very growth of the frontier population suggested that one day both banks of the Mississippi would fall under U. S. dominion. To this prospect the minister suggested two responses. Either France could use its control of the river to detach the trans-Appalachian settlements from the United States and combine them with Louisiana, as some residents of Kentucky then wanted, or it could accept the loss of Louisiana as inevitable but in the meantime reap the commercial profits it would bring. Since at least 1780, French and other commentators predicted an eventual U. S. expansion west of the Mississippi. Any French scheme for the retrocession of Louisiana, therefore, depended on taking possession before the west became irretrievably American. This awareness gave a sense of urgency to such schemes, which increased during the 1790s as Anglophone settlers poured into the Mississippi Valley.

Moustier's report marked a turning point in French policy. According to historian Alexander DeConde, the new French government, inspired by the minister's arguments and patriotic appeals from fellow revolutionaries in Louisiana, first raised the topic of retrocession with Spain in 1790.[11] Although quickly rejected by Spain, the issue became a regular theme in French diplomacy during the following decade, subject to variations imposed by the twists and turns in France's international relations.

French policy took an aggressive turn under the bellicose and idealistic Girondin faction, whose period of dominance (March 1792-June 1793) saw France become a republic and go to war against most of its European neighbors. The Girondins knew that westerners threatened to drive the Spaniards out of Louisiana and assumed that American fellow republicans would be willing partners in expelling the Spaniards in order to obtain free navigation of the Mississippi. Accordingly, Edmond Genet, the Girondin's minister to the United States, was instructed to encourage a secessionist movement in Louisiana. As soon as Genet reached the United States in April 1793, he began recruiting a private army of western frontiersmen to invade the colony. The French spoke of liberation rather than conquest, but left it unclear whether Louisiana would become independent or fall under French or U. S. control. Federalist hostility and the Jacobins' ouster of the Girondins soon doomed this policy.[12] However, subsequent regimes, although preoccupied with European affairs, did not abandon plans to regain Louisiana.

In the mid-1790s, Spain switched from being an enemy to being an ally of revolutionary France. The French now increased their diplomatic pressure for a retrocession of the colony. At the same time, relations with the United States steadily worsened. French seizures of American ships trading with France's enemies led the two republics into an undeclared maritime war (the "Quasi War") that lasted until 1800.[13] Moreover, the Jay Treaty (1794) that seemed to settle differences between England and the United States led many Frenchmen to suspect the two Anglophone powers were forming an alliance against them. This gave the Louisiana question a new urgency, for it appeared that Federalist warhawks like Alexander Hamilton might now seize the colony from Spain, France's ally. If, on the other hand, the French occupied New Orleans, they could put pressure on Washington by bottling up the Mississippi. Better still, they could permanently curb U. S. expansion. The French foreign ministers of the late 1790s, Charles Delacroix and Charles-Maurice Talleyrand-Périgord, both thought that the United States was an inevitable ally of Great Britain that had to be contained. Although Delacroix's interest in colonial affairs was somewhat limited, Talleyrand, who replaced him in July 1797, had developed a dislike for the United States during his two years' exile there and openly denounced U. S. expansionism.[14] Beyond this political importance, the economic promise of Louisiana seemed greater than ever. The takeoff of sugar manufacture in these years, which marked a major turning-point in local history, was apparently too small in scale to have much impact on foreign opinion. However, the booming population and trade of the trans-Appalachian region and the record flow of goods through New Orleans attracted attention from observers such as General Collot, a

French spy who traveled in the Mississippi Valley at this time. Also the need for replacing French West Indian dependence on U. S. suppliers was stronger than ever, as France and the United States drifted toward war.[15]

Notwithstanding this strength of motivation, France's leaders had to temper their desire for Louisiana with a need first to win and keep Spain as an ally. So, even as Spain slid into a subservient relationship to France, the war-distracted Committee of Public Safety and the Directory never felt strong enough to force Louisiana from the grasp of the Spaniards. As the price of peace in July 1795 (Treaty of Basle), Spain gave up little-valued Saint-Domingue rather than Louisiana, which the French would have preferred.[16] In the later 1790s, the Directory made several flimsy proposals to exchange various territories for Louisiana—Gibraltar, Portugal, part of Brazil, Tuscany and other parts of Italy—but none proved to be offers the Spaniards would accept. The Directory also showed a willingness to see Great Britain take Trinidad, Puerto Rico, or Louisiana, all Spanish possessions, in order to end the war.

It was against this background that the colonial ambitions of the French government shifted temporarily from the west to the east. Talleyrand argued that Egypt could replace the Caribbean as a source of sugar and cotton and would provide a shortcut to India, where henceforth France could again challenge the British.[17] The plan was enthusiastically seconded by the rising general, Bonaparte, who, as a result, spent most of 1798-99 empire-building in the Middle East.[18]

Some scholars have suggested that Bonaparte's Corsican origins predisposed him to favor a Mediterranean-centered policy, just as others argue that his wife's West Indian birth reinforced his interest in the Caribbean. More certain is that this question of east or west was strongly influenced by matters of war and peace. As the British navy controlled the Atlantic, whatever colonies France had or acquired in the Americas, it could not exploit them in wartime, since the sea-lanes were too unsafe. However, Britain's maritime reach was far weaker in the Mediterranean. So, as long as France and England were at war, it made more sense to switch to an eastern strategy. Unluckily for France, the destruction of Bonaparte's fleet at Aboukir Bay showed that British naval power was, even in the Mediterranean, an insuperable obstacle.

Defeated in Egypt, Bonaparte returned to France to seize power and reinvigorate plans for a new empire in the west. However, he never gave up dreams of oriental conquest, and early in 1801 he and the Czar Paul discussed sending a Franco-Russian army overland into India. Historians disagree to what extent the eastern and western strategies were alternatives or simultaneously pursued. The conventional view depicts the concentration on Louisiana and the Caribbean from 1801 to 1803 as an interlude between periods when the Asian strategy dominated. However, Yves Bénot, the leading left-wing historian of French colonialism, argues that Bonaparte simply refused to choose. Both projects were jointly pursued as part of a plan for world domination, and were symptoms of a chronic inability to confront reality.[19] There is no doubt that each strategy contributed to the failure of the other.

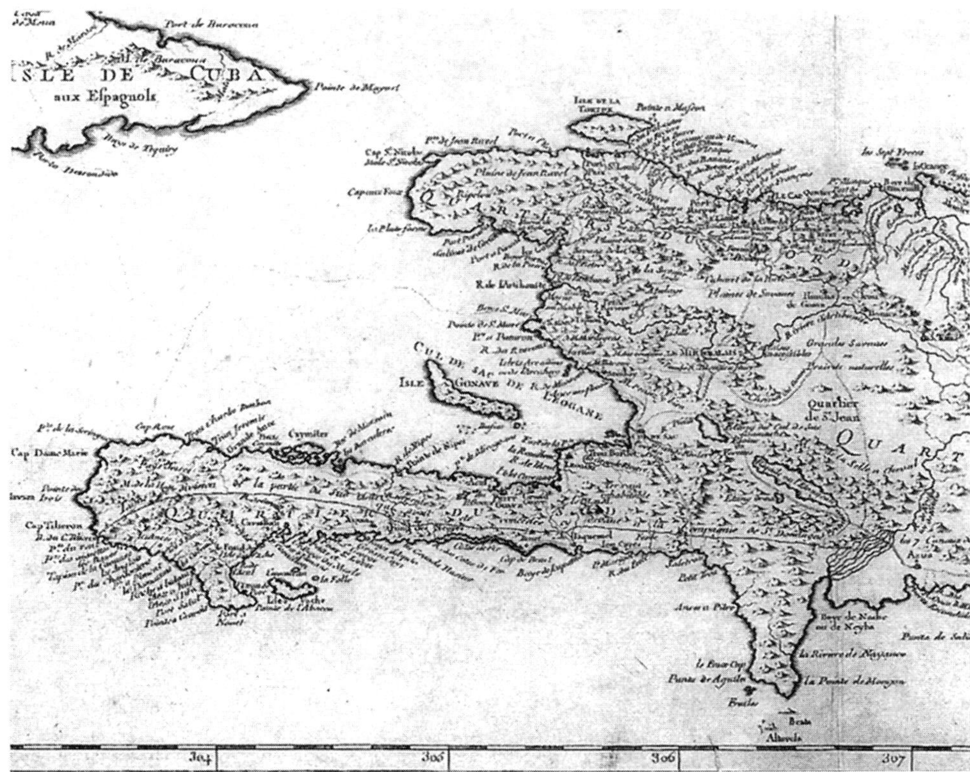

Figure 2. Guillaume de L'Isle, *Carte de l'Isle de Saint-Domingue, 1722*. Paris, Buache, 1745. Courtesy of Special Collections, Louisiana State University Library and the LOUISiana Digital Library.

Bonaparte's plans for Louisiana continued those of the Directory. Like previous regimes, he hoped to acquire Florida at the same time as Louisiana. Florida was to facilitate the defense of the Mississippi and more effectively hem in the United States. Together the two colonies would greatly strengthen the French position in the Caribbean. He wished to reassert metropolitan control in Saint-Domingue, the former power-house of the Atlantic economy and (at least by May 1802) to restore slavery and racial discrimination, which the Revolution had abolished.[20] Although Napoleon depended on U. S. commercial support to conquer Saint-Domingue, his secret aim was to restore mercantilist control and exclude U. S. trade from Saint-Domingue once France was in full control of it.[21] He showed no interest in Canada. Louisiana's role was to complement France's revived Caribbean empire, not to link up with a reconquered Quebec, as some American and English commentators feared.[22] Similarly, if Spain's decrepit empire beckoned, it could only have been in the long term. Bonaparte knew that American expansionists called Louisiana the highroad to Mexico, but Spanish silver mines do not seem to have been among his immediate priorities.[23]

Within a year of his seizing control of the French government, Bonaparte had extracted from Spain a conditional promise to retrocede Louisiana (Treaty of San Ildefonso, October 1, 1800) and in March 1801 the agreement was sealed by the Convention of Aránjuez. The First Consul succeeded where his predecessors had failed because of the Spanish king's respect for him and fear of his wish to garrison Spain, because of changes in Spanish ministers and their growing apprehension about U. S. expansion, and particularly because he had defeated Austria and gained in Italy the territory to be exchanged for Louisiana.[24] He had already (by the Treaty of Mortefontaine, September 30, 1800) made peace with the United States and, when Thomas Jefferson replaced John Adams as president, in March 1801, Franco-American relations looked set to become more friendly. In October 1801 peace preliminaries were signed with Great Britain, which enabled Bonaparte to send an army to Saint-Domingue. It sailed in December. Yet no French official would reach New Orleans until March 1803, just a month before Napoleon suddenly sold the colony.

This brings us back to our original question. Why, once the pieces of Napoleon's western design had thus fallen rapidly into place, did he abandon it in less than eighteen months? Some observers, like Dupont de Nemours, Jefferson's backchannel to the French government, thought Napoleon always intended to sell New Orleans, but evidently they were wrong, as the continuing, meticulous preparations for a Louisiana expedition demonstrate.[25] Other commentators have stressed that the design was never complete; the failure to force Spain to cede Florida together with Louisiana meant that the latter never could be adequately defended.[26] The point is important but, in light of the French continuation of their plans for Louisiana long after it was clear Florida was unobtainable, it is not a good explanation of why those plans were finally abandoned. Instead, scholars generally lean toward one of three explanations that center either on the United States, Great Britain, or Saint-Domingue.

As diplomatic historian Elijah Wilson Lyon put it in his classic study of the question, the success of Bonaparte's plan "depended on the friendship of the United States, peace with England, and the subjugation of St. Domingo." Of these three factors, Lyon and Alexander DeConde (more equivocally) accorded most weight to French fears of U. S. hostility to the retrocession.[27] Because U. S. hostility to retrocession was well known to the French government, this argument implies that the French believed that they could outmaneuver the Americans but that they suddenly changed their minds, influenced by French Minister L. A. Pichon's reports of U. S. bellicosity during the winter of 1802-3 (Pichon opposed the retrocession).[28] There is, even so, only limited evidence of French government alarm on this score. Yet it is a persuasive coincidence that news of warlike motions in the U. S. Senate (the "Ross Resolutions" authorizing the seizure of New Orleans) reached Napoleon two days before his final decision to sell.[29]

The American factor has by far the best claim of the three explanations of the Purchase to be considered its proximate cause. Among the benefits of the sale were the conversion of U. S. antagonism to friendship, the consolidation of a pro-French ministry in the White House, and the strengthening of the only maritime power that might eventually rival Great Britain.[30] On the other hand, historians who give priority to European factors argue that it was only the outbreak of war with Great Britain that forced the French to take the American threat seriously.[31]

Scholars who stress the Saint-Domingue factor make two arguments. First, they attribute the French failure to effectively occupy Louisiana to the delay and loss of resources caused by France's disastrous attempt to reconquer Saint-Domingue. The military quagmire that became the Haitian war of independence, it is argued, prevented Louisiana from being garrisoned and fortified, and its French population and Indian neighbors from being organized, as was planned, to resist external attack. The second argument is that the French defeat in the Caribbean at the hands of their former slaves rendered the whole western strategy pointless, because Saint-Domingue was the reason for Louisiana's retrocession. While French colonial historians have tended to downplay the connection between the Haitian Revolution and the Purchase,[32] it has been consistently emphasized by U. S. historians since the late nineteenth century, when Henry Adams wrote that "the prejudice of race alone blinded the American people to the debt they owed to the desperate courage of five hundred thousand Haytian negroes who would not be enslaved." Adams added that the black leader Toussaint L'Ouverture influenced the history of the United States as much as any European ruler.[33]

The first of these Saint-Domingue-related arguments is problematic, as several factors delayed the departure of troops for Louisiana. Some scholars believe that the Leclerc expedition sent to Saint-Domingue was meant to detach forces for New Orleans, when it could spare them.[34] However, we have no certain proof of it; such an order was not part of Leclerc's instructions or mentioned anywhere in his correspondence.[35] Perhaps it was conveyed orally (as maybe was the case with the restoration of slavery in Saint-Domingue), so as not to alarm the United States or the British. However, the later discussion of detaching troops for Louisiana from the expedition sent to Guadeloupe makes this questionable; the instructions were in any case top secret. Bonaparte certainly considered sending a separate expedition to Louisiana, even long before the Spaniards made the retrocession legal, for example in February and October 1801. Yet these projects were rapidly canceled. In the event, the First Consul preferred to wait until the paperwork arrived from Madrid, and this the recalcitrant Spaniards dragged out until mid-October 1802. Thereafter, logistical problems and winter weather kept the proposed expeditionary force immobilized in the Netherlands.[36] If the Caribbean crisis caused the diversion of troopships, it does not seem to have been responsible for the slow assembly of stores, or the storm damage, that delayed the Louisiana expedition into January, when it became icebound for some two months. Had there been no Saint-Domingue expedition, or if it had encountered only brief resistance, it is not certain Louisiana would have been garrisoned earlier.

As for the second argument, we do not know exactly when Napoleon gave up hope of success in the Caribbean. Perhaps it was in the first half of January, when he learned of General Leclerc's death (January 7) and shouted out at dinner (January 12) "Damn sugar! Damn coffee! Damn colonies!"[37] According to Yves Bénot, "there could be no further doubt about the inevitable disaster."[38] And yet, according to historian Gustav Roloff, Napoleon then pushed his colonial policy with increased energy. The reports from Saint-Domingue were "far from entirely hopeless." He sent extensive supplies and 15,000 more soldiers to the colony, and promised 15,000 more in the fall.[39] Treasury minister Barbé-Marbois recalled Napoleon slowed down the dispatch of reinforcements but did not change his plans. Above all, he continued to push for the departure of the Louisiana expedition at least until February 24.[40] The death toll in Saint-Domingue was certainly staggering, but one can hardly argue it foreclosed expansion in Louisiana any more than it foreclosed expansion in Europe.[41] Finally, the loss of Saint-Domingue did not necessarily mean Louisiana lost its purpose. Some contemporaries saw it as a possible replacement for the pearl of the Antilles.[42]

The official explanation generally given by Napoleon and Talleyrand for the sale of Louisiana was the imminence of war with England, which finally broke out in May. Lucien Bonaparte's memoirs leave a similar impression.[43] So do the recollections of the French minister who negotiated the Louisiana Purchase, François Barbé-Marbois.[44] Friction began building between Britain and France in late 1802 over their respective failures to carry out treaty obligations. The French retained troops in Italy and the Netherlands, contrary to the treaty of Lunéville, and the British kept Malta, contrary to the treaty of Amiens. Fearful of renascent French ambitions in Egypt and in Europe, the British began mobilizing in early March. This convinced a reluctant Napoleon, in the opinion of his apologists, that he could no longer avoid war.[45] Even historians who play down the British factor usually give early March as the date the First Consul probably "lost interest" in Louisiana.[46]

The resumption of a maritime war meant troops could no longer be sent either to Saint-Domingue or to Louisiana. Both colonies could be blockaded and, if Haitian independence was not already inevitable, it became so once assured of British naval support. Above all, Napoleon believed the British would quickly seize New Orleans, and that this required a complete about-face in policy. In his *Histoire de la Louisiane*, Barbé-Marbois suggests that the city could have been more easily seized by the Americans than the British, but he explains the First Consul's decision largely in terms of the British threat. Although his American counterpart in the negotiations, James Monroe, denied that the British factor alone could have influenced the question, Barbé-Marbois claimed that, by March 8, Napoleon already thought war inevitable and that any Louisiana expedition would be captured at sea. A month later, Napoleon's priority had become preventing the British from taking New Orleans. Sale to the United States would achieve this end and help finance the forthcoming war. According to Barbé-Marbois, Napoleon also hoped the Purchase would strengthen the ability of the United States to challenge Britain as a maritime power. [47] Some of those who minimize the importance of the British factor point out that an imminent seizure of New Orleans by Britain *did not necessitate* the sale of Louisiana, since captured French colonies were likely to be returned at the end of a successful war, as they had been in 1802. Others stress that, if the Haitian war of independence had not prevented the garrisoning of the colony, it could have held out against British or American foes, as was Napoleon's intention. More important, they argue it was not the renewal of hostilities in Europe that determined colonial policy, but failure in the Americas that persuaded the First Consul to abandon his western design and resume the struggle with Britain. Some add that European victories were needed to distract attention from defeat in the Caribbean.[48] In this view, Napoleon, not the British, was responsible for the breakdown of the peace of Amiens; he decided to risk war, not because of irremediable conflicts in Europe, but because, once he had written off Saint-Domingue, neither Louisiana nor peace with England was of use to him. Indeed, it is difficult to understand why Napoleon willfully antagonized the British by publishing in late January the Sébastiani report on Egypt, if he had not already decided to abandon the Caribbean and resume hostilities.[49] However, if he had truly written off Saint-Domingue at that time, one may wonder why he was sending 15,000 soldiers there, and also hurrying along the Louisiana expedition.

It is thus difficult to separate cause and effect in this seamless web of influences surrounding the sale of Louisiana. The three main factors, American, British, and Caribbean, mutually reinforced one another. The success of the black insurgents in Saint-Domingue was partly due to Jefferson's decision to continue supplying them, which was entirely due to his opposition to French plans for Louisiana. The likelihood of Jefferson's seizing New Orleans was greatly increased, both by the French army's difficulties in Saint-Domingue, and by the approach of war between France and England, just as the danger of losing Louisiana in a war with England was considerably magnified by the American threat.

If we indulge in counterfactual speculation, it is just possible to imagine any one of our three factors standing alone as a sufficient cause for the sale of Louisiana. But, in my view, none looks wholly convincing, or more so than the others. The safe, if not satisfactory, answer to the question of why Napoleon sold Louisiana is, therefore, "all of the above;" it grew out of a combination of developments in the United States, Europe, and the Caribbean. American, English, and Haitian nationalists can all claim a share of the credit. Jefferson handled the situation deftly but he also owed an ironic debt of gratitude to the British government he detested, to his Federalist opponents, who had called loudly for the use of force, and to those he called the "cannibals of the terrible republic."[50]

As for France, the reacquisition of Louisiana both cost little and ultimately yielded little, since the Purchase price was spent primarily on building a flotilla for an invasion of England that never sailed. The Purchase brought France 60 million francs ($11.25 million), less substantial brokerage fees, and the excusing of more than 20 million francs

($3.75 million) of debts to American merchants that Napoleon would never have paid anyway. The preparation of the Louisiana expedition cost about 2 million francs.[51]

France abandoned Louisiana just when Châteaubriand's best-selling novel *Atala*, and other celebratory publications were increasing public knowledge of the region but, as in the 1760s, the impact on public opinion appears to have been slight.[52] Saint-Domingue was lost almost simultaneously, and between 1803 and 1811, France was to lose all its colonies, at the same time, ironically, as the refugee diaspora from Saint-Domingue was giving a now American Louisiana its final veneer of Frenchness.

Chapter 4

Nexus of Empire: Louisiana, Great Britain, and the Struggle for North America

Gene A. Smith

While paddling down the Mississippi River some fifteen miles below present-day New Orleans in early September 1699, Jean Baptiste Lemoyne, Sieur de Bienville, suddenly encountered the twelve-gun English corvette *Carolina Galley*, struggling against the river's heavy current. Bienville and his associates were surprised to see an English warship on the river and knew they had to take action to prevent a further incursion. The blustering nineteen-year-old Frenchman convinced English captain William Bond to halt and to return downstream. Had Captain Bond ignored Bienville's warning and continued upriver, it is likely that the English would have developed close trade connections with the Chickasaw Indians and their allies earlier than they eventually did and could have established a powerful Mississippi Valley presence that would have allowed Anglo-American control over much of the trans-Appalachian interior. Instead, Bond heeded Bienville's warning rather than continuing upstream. As a result, France retained possession and control over the Mississippi Valley until 1763.[1]

This generally oversimplified and seemingly minor incident had great implications for the future of Louisiana and the Mississippi Valley. As Captain Bond departed, he threatened to return with additional ships and men and to settle the region. Yet despite that threat, the English made no concentrated efforts to establish a presence in the region until the end of the French and Indian War, even though the British Board of Trade had developed grandiose imperial plans to sweep across the interior of the North American continent. Instead England, France, and Spain continued struggling with one another for control of this unique nexus of empire. Too, the three empires competed for the support of southern Indian tribes as they tried to secure dominion over the Mississippi River basin.[2]

Historians of the United States have long related in colorful terms the significance of the Ohio River Valley and the Great Lakes for the development of North America. During the seventeenth and eighteenth centuries, France and England vied for control over the region and the Indians in their quests for continental hegemony. Not surprisingly, historians oriented to that struggle consider Louisiana, the Mississippi River, and the Gulf South of minor importance in the national story. This is amazing when one considers that this nexus of empire—stretching from Florida across to Louisiana—presented incredible opportunities for cultural, economic, and imperial interaction, as not two but *three* European nations, England, France, and Spain, as well as numerous Native American tribes all encountered one another in their attempt to define boundaries of control.[3]

From the late seventeenth to the mid eighteenth-century France and England fought a series of imperial wars in which they tried to gain control over the future development of the North American continent. And while it seemed by the 1750s that both nations had focused on the Ohio River Valley as the key to their future colonial developments, it was the Mississippi River that ultimately determined the fate of the continent. French colonial officials understood the geographical importance of the great river that connected their Canadian colony in the north with Louisiana and the Gulf of Mexico in the south and they worked to keep British influence in the region at a minimum. For example, the French governor-general of Canada in 1750, Admiral Comte de La Galisonnière, understood that the only way to prevent Anglo-Americans from seizing Canada, Florida, and Louisiana—"the bulwark of America"—would be to strengthen Canada's defenses and fortify Louisiana, because Canada, as he wrote, "will serve as the outwork of Louisiana." British officials also saw the Ohio and Mississippi Rivers as essential avenues for controlling the continent, and they worked to secure an economic advantage by providing weapons and inexpensive English trade goods to native tribes willing to form alliances.[4]

Although the Anglo-French struggle over Louisiana and the Gulf frontier ended with the 1763 Peace of Paris, another contest soon began, and this time it was between Spain and England. France transferred Louisiana west of the Mississippi (and the Isle of Orleans) to Spain in 1763 and the British secured control over the colonies of East and West Florida, colonies that together resembled a pistol with its barrel pointing directly towards the Mississippi River. Both the English and Spanish governments worked diligently after 1763 to strengthen their new possessions. Meanwhile Anglo-Americans flooded into the formerly French trans-Appalachian lands in the Ohio, Tennessee, and Cumberland river valleys, establishing forts and towns and soon appearing ready to move across the Mississippi River. In response to a 1771 war scare between England and Spain, General Thomas Gage even sent one thousand men to Pensacola for a proposed invasion of Louisiana; in effect Gage was loading the Florida pistol. Even so, Spanish officials in Louisiana vigorously promoted immigration, offered generous land bounties to Anglos, and actively recruited from diverse populations in their attempt to maintain political control over the region and improve its economic stability. As part of the same contest, the Spanish government also decided to provide secret support to the American rebels in their struggle against Great Britain, believing it would ultimately fragment Anglo-American power and ensure the security of Louisiana. By the end of the American War for Independence Spain had preserved her Louisiana colony and had expelled British forces from the Gulf Coast. The resulting 1783 Treaty of Paris returned the two Florida colonies to Spain, assuring that the Gulf of Mexico would be, at least temporarily, once again a Spanish lake.[5]

Even though British officials and military forces had been expelled from the Gulf frontier, British entrepreneurs and loyalists remained in the years after 1783. In the trans-Appalachian areas controlled by Native Americans, traders dispensed guns, blankets, and supplies in exchange for deerskins, sending them to British merchants who remained in Pensacola, St. Augustine, and the Bahamas. East Florida Loyalists worked to create an autonomous refuge in the St. Marys River area without the approval or support of either Britain or Spain. A similar scheme, briefly considered in 1782-83, would have used black and white Loyalists from West Florida to seize a haven for British Loyalists in Louisiana and land to compensate men whose property the American rebels had confiscated.[6]

Land speculation, loyalist relocation, Indian trade, and imperial ambition all converged in the Gulf South during the 1780s. British officials began looking more closely at the West, with the idea that the upper Mississippi Valley could become the southern boundary of Upper Canada. British policy strove to win the goodwill of frontiersmen without promising military aid, provided support and encouragement to Indians so they could protect their independence, and waited until the opportunity presented itself before trying again to secure Florida and Louisiana. By the late 1780s the latter seemed a distinct possibility as western Americans began discussing with British and Spanish officials the possibility of breaking off from the United States. British authorities also listened attentively to westerners wanting help in taking New Orleans. Spanish officials, meanwhile, established an intricate system of Indian alliances and begun actively intriguing with western separatists in Kentucky and Tennessee, hoping their efforts would keep the Mississippi River under Spain's control and keep Americans and the British at bay. For example, the enigmatic General James Wilkinson indicated to Spanish officials in 1787 that western Americans demanded navigation of the Mississippi River and that they even would ally themselves to their former enemy—Great Britain—to secure that right. Britain's reward, he indicated, would be the acquisition of Louisiana. Spanish spies sent from Philadelphia to the west reinforced Wilkinson's story when they reported British influence among the followers of James O'Fallon in Kentucky. James White also suggested that the Tennessee settlements would separate themselves from the fledgling United States if Spain would simply protect them.

The question of westerners' use of the Mississippi River and protection soon became moot because in 1790 the U. S. Congress created the Southwest Territory and in 1795 the U. S. and Spain agreed to Pinckney's Treaty, which opened the Mississippi River to American navigation. Even though these developments dampened separatist tendencies, British authorities continued working for a unified Mississippi Valley that could serve as a haven for Loyalists, be economically and politically controlled by Britain, and link Canada to the Gulf Coast.[7]

The 1790s brought new crises that seemed to affect directly the destiny of Louisiana. The May 1789 Spanish seizure of four British merchant ships at Nootka Sound on Vancouver Island brought Britain and Spain to the verge of a war that would have undoubtedly have seen fighting in the Mississippi Valley and in Louisiana. British troops in Canada could have easily moved down the Mississippi River and joined with naval forces from the Gulf of Mexico. And once British forces took Louisiana and the Floridas, many, including Francisco de Miranda, suggested that they move on to liberate Spanish America. In fact this scenario seemed too good to be true, as both Britain and the United States could secure what they desired if they simply worked together—the U. S. would get navigation of the Mississippi River and an outlet to the Gulf of Mexico, and Britain would gain control over the Mississippi Valley, permitting it to link Canada to the Gulf of Mexico.[8]

British Loyalists saw the Nootka Sound controversy as a golden opportunity to rejoin at least another part of North America to the British Empire. Since taking over as governor of the Bahamas in 1787, John Murray—the Earl of Dunmore—had supported several plans to retake Florida. In 1788 he had sent the self-styled director general of the Creek or Muskogee Nation, William Augustus Bowles, on an unsuccessful filibustering expedition into Florida. At the time of the 1790 Nootka Sound controversy Dunmore sent Bowles with a contingent of Creek and Cherokee chiefs to Canada to remind British officials there, including Governor Lord Dorchester (Guy Carlton), of the strategic importance of New Orleans and the Floridas. Bowles and his companions then traveled on to London, met with authorities at Whitehall, and encouragingly found British officials entertaining the possibility of military action in this nexus of empire; this was the first serious consideration of military action since 1783. Yet as it turned out, Spain ultimately gave in to British demands, thereby averting war and the loss of its colonies, for the moment.[9]

The peaceful settlement of the Nootka Sound controversy did not satisfy Bowles. While remaining in London he made it clear to British officials that his Indian allies would fight Spain, if necessary, to establish trade links with the British Bahamas. Such a proposition played directly into British hands and encouraged the support of Loyalists and dissatisfied frontiersmen in the American Southwest. Unofficial British support and encouragement of the Indians, Bowles insisted, would be the last British opportunity to secure control in America. It should not be overlooked. While Bowles did not gain all that he wanted from British officials, he did secure one important concession: Muskogee recognition and the right to bring Indian commerce via Muskogee ships to the Bahamas to trade for British manufactured goods. A Muskogee nation in the Old Southwest (roughly western Georgia, and all of Alabama and Mississippi) was one way for Britain to gain a toehold along the Gulf South.[10]

The episode with Bowles did not represent British imperial ambitions as much as it represented Bowles, Dunmore, and Dorchester's attempt to become political and economic leaders of the southern Indians. Bowles's rise to power would help undermine Loyalist Alexander McGillivray and the English trading firm of Panton, Leslie, and Company, both of which had worked with Spain to gain influence over the southern Indians. Once Spanish influence had been destroyed, a Bowles-and-Muskogee-dominated southwest could link with the British-dominated upper Mississippi valley to create a western economic buffer zone against an ever-expanding United States. Moreover, this British-controlled arc would look to New Orleans as it natural port of deposit.[11]

Bowles returned to Florida where he and his Seminole and Lower Creek supporters constructed a warehouse at the mouth of the Ochlockonee River and tried to control the Indian trade of the interior. Spanish officials and Panton, Leslie, and Company (Spain's official partner in the southern fur and deerskin trade) responded by attacking Muskogee commerce. Bowles retaliated in January 1792 by seizing Panton's warehouse at St. Marks, Florida, and then traveling to New Orleans to negotiate with Spanish officials. The Spaniards did not trust Bowles or his confederation, nor would they permit him to return and rally the Muskogee nation to continued depredations. They instead sent him as a prisoner to Spain where he arrived in June 1792, and then in 1795 transferred him to a more remote prison in the Philippines. Before too long he found his way back to Florida.[12]

After Bowles's forced departure, Scotsman Jack Kinnard attempted to control the rum, cattle, and cloth trade with the Lower Creeks. And although he experienced some short-lived success, Panton, Leslie, and Company soon drove him out of business, too. Ex-Loyalist George Wellbank also tried to revive Bowles's Indian trade and political networks. Basing his support and supplies from both Detroit and the Bahamas, he worked to unite the western tribes under a British protectorate that would stave off western American settlement and dominate the interior trade. While Wellbank gained a surprising number of converts among the Indians, Lieutenant Governor of Upper Canada John Graves Simcoe would not commit additional British resources because he feared the possibility of a war with the United States. Simcoe's decision proved wise, because General "Mad" Anthony Wayne defeated the Indians at the Battle of Fallen Timbers in August 1794, completely dashing Wellbank's plans.[13]

By 1794 the turmoil of the French Revolution in Europe had temporarily united Spain and England. Even so, the British still coveted Louisiana and closely watched European events to ensure that France did not attempt to regain its American empire. Simcoe also refused Louisiana Governor Baron Carondolet's (Francisco Luis Hector) proposal to act against an anticipated French and American attack.

This lackadaisical British support prompted Carlos IV's minister of state, Manuel de Godoy, to reorient Spanish foreign policy. During the summer of 1795 Spain secretly signed a peace settlement with France, leaving England to stand alone. Later that fall Godoy, now fearing that Britain and the United States would jointly attack Louisiana, negotiated the Treaty of San Lorenzo (Pinckney's Treaty) with the United States, an agreement that provided the Americans with free navigation of the Mississippi River, a deposit at New Orleans for three years, and established the thirty-first parallel as the boundary of the United States and Spanish West Florida. Godoy had given up the navigation of the Mississippi River and Spain's claim to the east bank above 31 degrees as a way to satisfy Americans and as a way to preserve Louisiana and the remainder of its North American Empire.[14]

The Treaty of San Lorenzo immediately satisfied most western Americans, stifled most separatist tendencies (including James Wilkinson's "Spanish Conspiracy") and helped to undermine Tennessee Senator William Blount's plans to seize Louisiana with a Tory and Indian force, supported by the British Navy. Former Loyalist Indian trader William Chisholm had recommended a similar plan. Apparently Blount and his partners had speculated heavily in western lands and wanted to sell those properties to British investors. While the renewal of war between France (with her Spanish ally) and England in October 1796 greatly depressed the land market, it also offered a reason for London to support an attack on Louisiana. Robert Liston, the British minister in Philadelphia, encouraged Blount's plans and passed the information on to Foreign Secretary Lord Grenville (William Wyndham) and the Ministry. Blount and Chisholm insisted, and Liston repeated to London, that the time had come for an immediate attack on Louisiana. Rumors abounded that French agents planned to seize Louisiana, free slaves, close the Mississippi River, and further depress western land values.

While Blount, Chisholm, and their associates worked through Liston to secure a commitment, other British operatives in the Old Southwest tried to enlist Americans. Among those approached were George Rogers Clark in Kentucky and Revolutionary War General Elijah Clarke in Georgia. They were asked to lead expeditions with British aid against St. Louis, New Orleans, and Santa Fe. According to Governor Simcoe, once Britain had taken New Orleans and opened the Mississippi River to British commerce, the remainder of the trans-Appalachian west would immediately fall into British hands. Still other correspondents of the Ministry maintained that land prices would also increase.

Even though these possibilities provided powerful motives for British policy-makers, Grenville and other members of the Ministry refused to attack Louisiana and Florida. Such an attack, planned and launched from the United States, might provoke an Anglo-American conflict and threaten Canada. Moreover, by 1798 the U. S. and France teetered on the brink of war and that possibility would permit Britain to ally with rather than fight with the United States. An Anglo-American alliance could certainly deny France a foothold in North America, and perhaps permit either Britain or the U. S. to seize Louisiana and Florida from Spain. In fact, denying France territory in North America, obtaining commercial control over New Orleans and the Mississippi Valley, and linking the Gulf Coast with Canada constantly influenced British thinking in the years before 1799.[15]

By 1800 William Augustus Bowles had escaped his confinement and with British assistance had made his way back to Florida. His renewed Muskogee nation again captured Panton's St. Marks store, as well as a nearby Spanish fort, and Muskogee ships again preyed on Spanish commerce. Britain had also learned that Spain had agreed to transfer Louisiana to France for concessions in Europe. Bowles thought that the British would soon be forced to take Louisiana and perhaps Florida, if for no other reason than to protect their Canadian colony from Napoleon's France. Yet the general European Peace of Amiens between March 1802 and May 1803 convinced British officials instead to wait and watch. By the late spring of 1803 England and France had resumed fighting and news about another Louisiana transfer had found its way to London. The U. S. purchase of Louisiana, financed by British capitalists, confirmed that no British expeditionary force would be going immediately to the Gulf of Mexico. News of the transfer of Louisiana from Spain to France and the anticipated occupation of New Orleans by the United States ultimately sealed Bowles's fate. While at an Indian council in May 1803 a party of Upper

Creeks captured Bowles and turned him over to Spanish officials, who took him in chains to Havana, where he died in December 1805.[16]

Bowles's capture, which coincided with the Louisiana Purchase, ended an era of active British involvement in the Old Southwest. Even British merchants and traders operated on a smaller scale thereafter as the fur and deerskin trade began playing out, soon to be replaced by the cotton trade. Aaron Burr possibly courted British support for his separatist or imperialist schemes in 1804-06; he constantly told his followers, in any case, that British money and warships from the Gulf of Mexico would join them at New Orleans. But this did not happen, and his exact plans still remain a mystery. The Kemper brothers, especially Reuben, and other revolutionaries in West Florida initially looked to the Bahamas for support of their cause. But in the fall of 1810, the American government annexed Baton Rouge and West Florida, claiming that the district was included in the Louisiana Purchase. Thereafter British merchants maintained close commercial ties with West Florida, but the Ministry did not commit resources or send people because British interests were focusing on the rest of Spain's American empire. In fact, Spanish American trade was becoming far more important to England than the deerskin trade of the Old Southwest.[17]

During the years following the Purchase British diplomats, traders, and raconteurs still tried to exercise influence over colonial policy concerning North America. Thomas Douglas, the fifth Earl of Selkirk who had been nominated in 1806 to succeed Anthony Merry as the British minister to the U. S., developed an elaborate plan to establish a British settlement in the Louisiana Territory even though he had preached the importance of trade and markets over political sovereignty. Meanwhile British military and naval officers still explored the possibility of operations against Louisiana. During the 1790s military plans had called for seizing the land between New Orleans and Pensacola, including Mobile and the Louisiana Florida Parishes, to protect the Canadian territories to the north. A successful campaign would have permitted the British to create a series of western North American colonies linking Canada to the Gulf Coast while also frustrating Napoleon's ambitions for a New World empire. And while the American purchase of Louisiana ultimately removed the immediate French threat to Britain's plans for the Old Southwest, it did not assuage English concerns that Louisiana, and its control over the Mississippi River, still remained the key to British possession of Canada.[18]

Once the war with the United States began in the summer of 1812, British policymakers and military officers were quickly reminded that the fate of Canada ultimately lay along the Gulf Coast. During the later fall of 1812 Sir John Borlase Warren, British commander of the North American Squadron, proposed a diversion against New Orleans to relieve the American siege of Canada. A year later Warren called again for his country to make "a vigorous attack to the southward in taking possession of New Orleans and bringing forward the Indians and Spanyards [*sic*] . . . and a division of black troops to cut off the resources of the Mississippi."[19]

During 1813 other officers made similar suggestions for a British victory. Naval Capt. James Stirling, concluding that Louisiana was "very open to attack," sent to the First Lord of the Admiralty, Viscount Melville, a detailed memorandum on the geography of the region. The conquest of Louisiana by British forces supported by Indians, blacks, and "displeased" Spaniards would, according to Stirling, place the trans-Appalachian west "at the mercy of Great Britain." Likewise Admiral Henry Hotham, the commanding officer at Bermuda, suggested that "the place where Americans [were] most vulnerable [was] New Orleans," and an attack there would "check [American] operations against Canada."[20]

By the spring of 1814, when Vice-Admiral Alexander Forrester Inglis Cochrane replaced Warren as commander of the much-reduced North American naval station, he recommended to the Admiralty that a small force of regulars, Indians, black slaves, Baratarian pirates, and disaffected citizens could "take possession of N. Orleans by which we should have considerably weakened the [American] efforts against Canada." Cochrane's plan, virtually the same as Warren's from a year earlier, apparently resonated strongly with the Lords of the Admiralty at this time because the government approved Cochrane's plan for an attack and appointed General Robert Ross as the army commander. However, Ross died in a September 1814 attack against Baltimore.[21]

British policy-makers expected the southern campaign to be overwhelmingly successful. Even the Duke of Wellington, who had refused to accept a command in North America, anticipated that his brother-in-law, General Sir Edward Michael Pakenham, would capture New Orleans. Once it had been secured, Wellington insisted that it should be held for the future. The British ministry unquestionably wanted to occupy New Orleans and the entire Gulf Coast because that would give it continued influence with the Indians and runaway slaves, permit it to continue promoting western disunion from the United States, and provide an important link with and greater protection for Canada.

Cochrane wanted to co-opt the support of Jean Lafitte and his Baratarian supporters, to rally the southern Indians to his cause, and to enlist runaway slaves within his ranks as he had done during the Chesapeake campaign. If successful, these efforts would bring Cochrane the support he thought he needed to gain control over New Orleans. Instead Lafitte joined with Jackson, who had defeated the southern Indians at the Battle of Horseshoe Bend in late March 1814. Jackson also guaranteed a full pardon to slaves who helped defend New Orleans and promised a monetary and land bounty to those "sons of freedom"—or free blacks—who joined his cause. In fact, Jackson ultimately denied to Cochrane and the British an important source of much-needed local manpower. The resulting British defeat on January 8, 1815, south of New Orleans at the Plains of Chalmette all but shattered British plans for Louisiana and the Gulf Coast.

In early February 1815, before news of the Treaty of Ghent had arrived in the Gulf or before the treaty had been ratified, British forces did capture Fort Bowyer, which guarded the entrance to Mobile Bay. This easy victory provided British forces with a renewed foothold along the Gulf Coast from which they could march overland against Louisiana.

Yet before they could secure the city of Mobile, news arrived indicating that the war had ended. The restoration of peace between the U. S. and Britain in late February 1815 completely dismantled and finally ended all British plans for securing Louisiana, the Gulf Coast, and Mississippi Valley, and linking them to their Canadian provinces.[22]

The conclusion of the War of 1812 and defeat of Napoleon marked an end to an era that had begun in 1783. Although the British worried about the fate of Canada, they did not try again to assume France's role in North America. Afterward British traders declined in importance as lands on the southern and western periphery of the U. S. succumbed to American control. The Indian confederations inhabiting those areas disintegrated. Even American separatists, who had once thought of dismantling the country, now looked to populate and develop Thomas Jefferson's "Empire of Liberty." British agents had intrigued along the southwestern frontier and the British government had expended considerable effort to build alliances against France, Spain, and the United States, all to no avail. Thus, what began as a seemingly unimportant event in 1699 along the Mississippi River flowered into a full-scale attempt to shape this important nexus of empire along the American frontier. For Great Britain in the end, as in that beginning, the result was failure.[23]

SUGGESTED READINGS

Alvord, Clarence Walworth. *The Mississippi Valley in British Politics: A Study of the Trade, Land Speculation, and Experiments in Imperialism Culminating in the American Revolution*. New York: Russell and Russell, 1959.

Braund, Kathryn E. Holland. *Deerskins and Duffels: The Creek Indian Trade with Anglo-America, 1685-1815*. Lincoln, Neb.: University of Nebraska Press, 1993.

Burt, A. L. *The United States, Great Britain, and British North America: From the Revolution to the Establishment of Peace after the War of 1812*. New York: Russell and Russell, 1961.

DeConde, Alexander. *This Affair of Louisiana*. New York: Scribner, 1976.

Latour, Arsène Lacarrière. *Historical Memoir of the War in West Florida and Louisiana in 1814-15: With an Atlas*, expanded edition. by Gene A. Smith. Gainesville Fla.: The Historic New Orleans Collection and University Press of Florida, 1999.

Owsley, Frank L., Jr. and Gene A. Smith. *Filibusters and Expansionists: Jeffersonian Manifest Destiny 1800-1821*. Tuscaloosa, Al.: University of Alabama Press, 1997.

Usner, Daniel H., Jr. *Indians, Settlers, and Slaves in a Frontier Exchange Economy: The Lower Mississippi Valley Before 1783*. Chapel Hill: Published for the Institute of Early American History and Culture, Williamsburg, Virginia, by the University of North Carolina Press, 1992.

Wright, J. Leitch, Jr. *Britain and the American Frontier, 1783-1815*. Athens: University of Georgia Press, 1975.

_______. *William Augustus Bowles: Director General of the Creek Nation*. Athens: University of Georgia Press, 1967.

Chapter 5

Caribbean Economic Perspectives on the Louisiana Purchase

Selwyn H. H. Carrington

The Louisiana Purchase is probably the most significant transfer of property that took place at the beginning of the nineteenth century. It seems to be the first occasion that a territory of such colossal size was sold by one nation to another. The purchase marked "a decisive epoch of general history and of American history in particular."[1] This vast territory, with many climatic regions, was immediately incorporated into the territorial structure of the United States, which during the previous century and a half had emerged as the primary producer and trader of numerous commodities for the West Indian part of the Atlantic economic system. French Saint-Domingue, in particular, prior to its revolution, imported much of its food and some forest products from the thirteen colonies and then the United States. U. S. trade statistics show that in the five years, 1789-1794 (October 1 to September 3), U. S. exports and re-exports to the French West Indies (not just Saint-Domingue) averaged $3,751,720 per year, rising to a war-driven average of $6,063,889 in the eight years following (1794-1802).[2] In view of these numbers, the question I will consider here is how realistic was Napoleon's plan to use the Louisiana Purchase Territory (then Spanish Louisiana) as a substitute source of those commodities for a revived French Saint-Domingue?

As is well known, the French Revolution inadvertently helped to produce a revolution in Saint-Domingue, France's prize colony and the mainstay of its Caribbean economic system in the decades preceding the uprising in France. Unwilling to accept this loss, Napoleon attempted to revive France's American colonial empire by sending his brother-in-law General Charles Victor Emmanuel Leclerc with 35,000 men to recapture St. Domingue from Toussaint L'Ouverture, the leader of the Haitian freedmen who was ruling central Saint-Domingue in the name of France. At the same time, Napoleon pushed the Spaniards to retrocede Louisiana, which he planned to use as a supplier of foods and forest products to replace the United States, then, as earlier, a principal supplier of those commodities to Saint-Domingue. However, LeClerc failed because disease and the brutal ferocity of the war with L'Ouverture's generals Dessalines and Christophe (following L'Ouverture's arrest) destroyed over two-thirds of the French soldiers as well as uncounted numbers of Haitians. The British, pursuing their own vain attempt to seize the colony, later captured the remainder of the French force.

The defeat of France in Haiti destroyed Napoleon's dreams of the restoration of the Old Antilles and their lucrative trade. His acquisition of Louisiana from Spain also lost its luster and the territory became "a superfluous dependency, costly and annoying." As a consequence, Thomas Jefferson, the third president of the United States, was able to negotiate the purchase of the territory.[3]

How realistic was Napoleon's plan to use Louisiana as a supplier of foods, lumber, and other goods that could replace Saint-Domingue's dependence on the United States for those items? While no clear answer can be given because we lack complete statistics for Saint-Domingue's commerce before 1790 and the Haitian Revolution, we can gain some insight by examining the relationship between the British West Indian sugar colonies and the thirteen continental colonies that became the United States. Jamaica, in particular, is instructive because it was second to Saint-Domingue in the production of sugar. Such an examination will indicate how large a volume of foods and forest products (lumber, barrel staves, etc.) and other products might have been required *and* what a French Louisiana would have had to buy from Saint-Domingue if it were to serve as a replacement for the United States. The United States was both a supplier *and* a customer of the British West Indies and Saint-Domingue, receiving rum, molasses, sugar, coffee and some minor items like ginger in payment for the goods it sent south. To help ground this comparison in facts, we will also look at some of the few trade statistics we have for Saint-Domingue's imports via the free port at Môle Saint Nicolas, a trade that was heavily in American hands almost from its inception in 1765.

We should begin by recognizing that as early as 1700 Louisiana had a small trade in lumber, staves, shingles, pitch, tar, peas and other vegetables with the French West Indian colonies especially Guadaloupe and Martinique. The scale of this trade grew over time, but was never very large. Clarence Gould has noted that given "the small population of Louisiana, the volume of the trade it carried on with the Windward Islands from about 1738 to 1763 was remarkable. From one to nine ships [mostly schooners] are reported almost every year, and usually there was one or more to Guadeloupe."[4] Trade with Saint-Domingue was carried on during these voyages. Although Gould thought that the Spaniards cut off this trade, we know that after a brief interruption at the beginning of their rule in Louisiana, they permitted it.[5] Moreover, from the beginnings of French Louisiana, propagandists portrayed La Louisiane as *potentially* a cornucopia of grain and other foods. This idea, which we know was later realized when the upper Midwest became the breadbasket of the world, was reinforced for Napoleon's contemporaries by the Marquis Moustier's manuscript memoir of March 1789 and Jacques-Pierre Brissot's *Nouveau voyage aux États-Unis* (Paris, 1791).[6] Moustier, in particular, spread the idea that Spanish Louisiana, in French hands, could supply all of Saint-Domingue's needs and, in addition, provide an avenue for French manufactures to reach the U. S.'s western settlements.

Potential is one thing, reality is another, as Robert Livingston, the U. S. minister to France in 1802 emphasized in a pamphlet that refuted Moustier's ideas.[7] What can we learn about the realism of Napoleon's plan for Louisiana by studying the U. S.-British West Indies trade? The data we will examine come from the decade before the American Revolution, a period with which I am familiar. So long as we keep in mind that we are using it as a model or proxy from which to gain insight into the realism of Napoleon's scheme, it can serve our purpose.

Because the European colonial plantation system was based on a monocultural slave society, it became dependent on external supplies of provisions and lumber. The thirteen American colonies emerged during the seventeenth century as the sources of every class of foodstuffs, live stock and lumber consumed on the Caribbean islands. During the eighteenth century, British West Indian commercial intercourse with the mainland colonies worked well, and despite a series of wars in the Caribbean during the eighteenth century, the weaknesses inherent in this artificial monocultural slave economy were overlooked. Europe did not produce significant quantities of the categories and quality of the commodities that the Caribbean slave societies required. Hence, from the establishment of the plantation system in the Caribbean, the sugar islands relied almost solely on the continental colonies for their sustained economic growth; and the growth and prosperity of the British islands became indispensible to the agricultural, industrial and commercial development of the mainland colonies. The British West Indies provided the northern agriculturists with a steady and reliable market for their provisions; the New England fishermen with an outlet for their inferior grades of fish; the lumber-men of the middle and southern colonies with a secure market; and American farmers with the best eighteenth century market for their coarse salted beef and pork, as well as livestock. In addition, the New England shipping industry with its numerous artisans was kept in steady employment, building and repairing ships for the West Indian trade, including the slave trade. Indeed, after the middle of the eighteenth century, the North Americans supplied the islands with captive Africans, boards, joists, planks, shingles and complete frames for buildings; staves, heading and hoops for casks for sugar and rum; fish, flour, biscuit, rice, beans, dried peas, maize, salted beef, salt pork, livestock, tobacco, lamp oil, candles, soap, wax, tallow and pitch for domestic consumption; horses, cattle and oxen for plantation uses; and a small quantity of manufactured goods such as hats, shoes, iron bars, house frames and household furniture.[8] The manufactured goods worried colonial officers such as Lieutenant-Governor Stuart of Dominica who sent a complaint on this matter to the Earl of Dartmouth, Secretary of the Colonies in 1773, pointing out that this trade in manufactures was contrary to the interests of the British.[9] The Earl of Dartmouth acknowledged that the increased importation of captive Africans and manufactured goods from the thirteen colonies deserved very serious considerations but that he could take no punitive action until Parliament passed legislation to resolve the matter.[10]

Although each British North American colony contributed to the needs of the sugar colonies, certain continental colonies controlled a majority of the exports to the islands. The New England colonies supplied most of the lumber, shingles, staves and hoops, and as a result of their trade with Newfoundland, Nova Scotia and Canada, these colonies also supplied almost five-eighths of all the fish consumed on the islands. Of the total of 21,271,995 feet of lumber imported into the British West Indies from North America in 1771, the New England colonies supplied over two-thirds. They sent half the shingles, about one-third of the staves and nearly all the hoops. Of the total amount of bread and flour exported to the West Indies, Pennsylvania sent slightly less than two-thirds. The rest came from Virginia, New York and Maryland.[11] Of the 75,000 barrels of beef consumed in the islands annually, the American colonies supplied about 14,000 barrels.[12] Of the 15,129 barrels and 9,651 tierces (one third of a pipe) of rice imported into the British islands in 1771, 13,308 barrels and 7,967 tierces were sent from South Carolina. The majority of horses, oxen and other livestock reaching the islands came from the New England colonies.[13]

The annual value of North American products exported to the British and foreign West Indies in 1770 was £844,178, of which the majority went to the British islands.[14] Sales to just the British West Indies averaged £745,000 for the three years immediately preceding the American Revolution, and included the cost of freight, which was approximately £245,000.[15]

Jamaica's share of this trade was substantial, as befitted its role as the physically and economically largest of the British sugar colonies. In 1770 Jamaica took approximately one-third of some articles exported by the continental colonies. For example, of the 14,500 barrels of beef sent to the sugar colonies annually, Jamaica imported some 7,903 barrels. On the average during the 1770s, Jamaica annually imported 29,674 barrels of flour, 6,557 barrels and 3,450 kegs of bread, 6,479 tierces of rice, above 15,000,000 staves, shingles, and headings, 6,197,322 feet of boards and large quantities of other articles.[16] In 1774 the value of American products sent to Jamaica was put at £177,746. According to the estimates of a Jamaican planter, the value of North American exports to Jamaica in 1775 was approximately £210,000.[17] Detailed statistics of the chief articles imported into Jamaica for the years 1768-1774 are available and show conclusively the extent of Jamaican reliance on American supplies.

The statistics just reviewed give some indication of the food and lumber requirements of the British sugar colonies and their sources of origin, ca. 1770. An indication of what Saint-Domingue consumed comes from one year's data, August 31, 1769 to August 31, 1770, on the imports of Môle Saint Nicolas, then newly operating as a free port open to non-French shipping. Officals recorded the importation of 9,606 barrels of flour, 599 barrels of biscuit (hard tack), 866 barrels of salted beef, 964 barrels of other salted meats, 2,484 casks of dried cod and 244 cases of "green cod," 846 barrels of dried vegetables (beans, peas, etc.), 422 barrels of maize, 755 casks of rice, and certain other items, all worth 1,517,519 *livre,* which at a bit more than five *livre* to the U. S. dollar amounted to some $305,000. Imports continued to run at that value into the 1770s, although the mix was different, with wood of all sorts becoming a major item (ca. 1 million *livre* per annum) followed closely by live animals.[18] Keep in mind that these are only a part of Saint-Domingue's imports.

Whether from Saint-Domingue itself or by implication from the trade of the British West Indies (which is better documented), the figures on imports ca. 1770 suggest the scale of what Louisiana would have had to produce to meet the demands of a fully restored sugar economy on Saint-Domingue, which at its peak had produced nearly as much sugar as all of the British islands combined. In so doing, the figures suggest how unrealistic Napoleon's vision was, at least in the short run *unless* it could draw on the production of Ohio, Kentucky, and Tennessee and even then the short fall might have been dramatic. For example, in February to July 1790, Spanish officials recorded 4,904 barrels of flour, 261 barrels and 34,000 pounds of salted meat, 35 barrels and 500 pounds of butter coming into New Orleans from the American settlements.[19] Even if twice those amounts arrived, they were very little compared to the Atlantic coastal exports just noted for the British Islands. By 1803, of course, the quantities of foods coming down the Mississippi had increased, but probably still would have fallen far short of the requirements of a revived Saint-Domingue. And it must be recalled that much of the flour and other foods coming down the Mississippi were consumed in New Orleans.

Turning now to the other side of the coin: how the British sugar islands paid for the foods and forest products they received from the thirteen continental colonies, we see more evidence of the unreality of Napoleon's plan, again, in the short term.

In 1770 the total value of the imports into the thirteen colonies from the foreign and British West Indies was estimated at £949,656, two-thirds of it from the British West Indies.[20] Rum imports from the British islands amounted to approximately 45 per cent of this total, and were rising. Molasses was the next most valuable article, amounting to slightly over £181,800; but only seven per cent of this was taken from the British islands; most of the rest came from the French colonies, especially Saint-Domingue, and was distilled in New England into rum. The sugar imported from all the Caribbean (6,544,700 pounds) was valued at £165,641; all but £49,070 came from the British islands. The coffee valued at approximately £15,259, except some £44 worth, was taken from the British colonies. Jamaica shipped 589 casks of coffee in 1768, but 2,816 by 1774.[21]

The value of British West Indian products bought by the Americans was slightly under that of British West Indian imports from America.[22] So closely balanced was the trade that in 1775 Jamaican planter Edward Long estimated that if the Americans refused to take Jamaican sugar (then exported to the thirteen colonies to a value of £45,780 as part of a total of exports to them amounting to £178,675), the deficit in trade against that island would have to be retired in bills of exchange drawn upon merchants in Britain because there was never enough money on the island to meet even that small of a deficit. "If on the other hand," he stressed.

> the Americans should continue to take this Quantity of Sugar, no Balance [would] remain to be paid by . . . [Jamaica]. But there would be a mutual equal liquidation of commodities, without any blame on either side.[23]

In some years, however, when natural disasters forced the planters to import greater quantities of American provisions and lumber, the British islands had a trade deficit. In 1774 Jamaica had one amounting to £17,532.[24]

As was true for the quantities of goods shipped to the British West Indian sugar colonies and the few statistics we have for Saint-Domingue, so these figures for the continental colonies' imports from the British West Indian colonies suggest how unrealistic Napoleon's idea was—in the short term at least—that Louisiana could replace the United States as Saint-Domingue's supplier of food and lumber. The complement to such supply was buying enough sugar, rum, coffee and other products to more or less balance the books, at least if the British colonial experience is a guide. Louisiana's population in 1803 was about 50,000 souls (about half slaves), mostly concentrated around New Orleans. That number was hardly likely to consume hundreds of thousands of pounds of sugar, thousands of pounds of coffee, and lesser amounts of other products (such as ginger). Moreover, after 1795 the major plantations around New Orleans had been converted to sugar production, mostly for export. The planters, Francophone though many of them were, would hardly have willingly given up that profitable enterprise for the sake of French Imperial policy.

But assuming for the moment that the Purchase Territory *had* become French in 1803 and increased its production of foods and forest products even if not to the full extent of a revived Saint-Domingue's demand, it does not appear how a French Louisiana—absent a massive population growth (unlikely in view of the history of French colonies in the Americas)—could have avoided running an enormous trade surplus with Saint-Domingue, defeating a major part of all colonial schemes: that a colony produce a surplus for the mother country, or at least not a continuing payments deficit. Nor, as Livingston pointed out in 1802, were the U. S. western states (by then containing several hundred thousand inhabitants and growing rapidly) likely markets for French manufactured goods and wines, items whose sale *via* a French Louisiana might have helped balance the latter's books. Americans in the west had little taste for French wines and had cheaper goods coming to them over the Appalachian Mountains. The movement of goods in bulk up the Mississippi was still an extremely slow and costly enterprise. The steamboat had not yet been invented.

In sum, our review of the trading relationship between the thirteen continental colonies and the Caribbean, and in particular the British Sugar colonies (notably Jamaica), suggests—but obviously does not prove because it is a proxy for the still-to-be-determined actual numbers—that the Purchase Territory in French hands could not have provided the quantities of foods and forest products required by a revived French Saint-Domingue. That is, as Livingston had correctly argued, a French Louisiana could not have been a substitute for the United States. Nor would a post 1803 French Louisiana have been able to balance a trade in foods and forest products by consuming a corresponding value in sugar, molasses, and coffee, the principal products of pre-1789 Saint-Domingue. Napoleon's vision of a complementary Louisiana and Saint-Domingue relationship was unrealistic.

Chapter 6

Patterns of Livelihood, Networks of Exchange: Economic Life Inside the Louisiana Purchase

Daniel H. Usner, Jr.

Coupling the word "economy" with the phrase "Louisiana Purchase" in the same sentence gives people good reason for anticipating—even for dreading—what is to come. Never one who hesitates to disappoint his audience, however, I will avoid the predictable listing of achievements and improvements that constituted the successful trans-Mississippi expansion of the United States after 1803. The tendency to generalize about commercial and agricultural development across this vast space, in fact, inhibits asking the very questions about economic change that interest me the most when I consider the acquisition of Louisiana by the United States. Those questions, about the patterns of livelihood and networks of exchange operating among people who inhabited Spanish Louisiana at the dawn of the nineteenth century, should not be reduced to some kind of background for later development.

Here is the familiar story. Virile and energetic Anglo-Americans began to filter into Louisiana during the last quarter of the eighteenth century, infiltrating a society that lacked economic vigor. The city of New Orleans and settlements west of the Mississippi River had been colonized by Frenchmen and Spaniards whose effeminate and lazy behavior could not possibly subdue such a vast wilderness. Bourbon despotism and Roman Catholicism inhibited development, causing the colonial populace to be complacent and in the way of commerce generated by American pioneers in the trans-Appalachian West. The acquisition of Louisiana by the United States accelerated the inevitable displacement of Creoles by Anglo-Americans and the welcome emergence of a dynamic economy in the Mississippi Valley. Resistance and resentment among French-speaking people steadily diminished, with the Battle of New Orleans serving miraculously as a unifying force in some versions of the legend.

The endurance of this economic story is largely due to its versatility. It initially served as a justification for territorial expansion and political domination, fitting the Louisiana Purchase into the larger narrative of American progress. U. S. Army captain Amos Stoddard described a quaint indolence among French people living along the Mississippi River. "While the English Americans are hard at work, and sweat under the burning rays of a meridian sun," wrote Stoddard, "they will be seated in their houses, or under some cooling shade, amusing themselves with their pipes and tobacco, in drinking coffee, and in repeating the incidents of their several perambulations over distant lakes and mountains."[1] Over time the tale of carefree Frenchmen confronted by ambitious Americans became a useful way to distinguish Louisiana from the rest of the United States. Exotic origins of an anomalous culture, we cannot forget, generate booming business for tourism and even provide a convenient excuse for corruption, at least here in New Orleans.[2]

The great departure from a static past sparked by the Louisiana Purchase will no doubt persist in popular narratives and public perceptions, but recent historical scholarship on various fronts should nevertheless cause some doubt about its accuracy and survival. Looking either at literature on American Indians in the trans-Mississippi West or at works focusing on colonial Louisiana, one can no longer accept the common assumptions about pre-Louisiana Purchase life west of the Mississippi River. But let us not underestimate the obstacle. In the skillful hands of great American historians like Francis Parkman and Frederick Jackson Turner, the trans-Mississippi West became one of the most potent metaphors of otherness in the American mind—a wasteland still waiting to be conquered and occupied, improved and developed. Through the eyes of Parkman, even St. Louis was viewed as a place "which to our forefathers seemed remote and strange, as to us the mountain strongholds of the Apaches, or the wastes of farthest Oregon." The Missouri River, through Parkman's eyes, was "born among mountains, trackless even now [1851], except by the adventurous footstep of the trapper—nurtured amid the howling of beasts and the war-cries of savages, never silent in that wilderness." In this picture of the region purchased by Thomas Jefferson from Napoleon Bonaparte and the French symbolized the deferment of progress. "Boon companions of the Indians," in Turner's words (1896), "they ate and drank and sang and fought side by side with their savage brothers, married with them and took up their life. The gay, adaptable Frenchman was no wilderness conqueror."[3]

A century after Turner wrote these words, historians view the trans-Mississippi West differently. The Mississippi Valley, Great Plains, American Southwest, and Pacific Coast have become less remote and strange to historians of early America. The English Atlantic seaboard is sharing attention with Spanish, French and even Russian colonial regions as well as with American Indian societies, and the contest among European empires is being examined closer to the ground than ever before. For understanding economic life inside the Louisiana Purchase, all of this is consequential. Where empires competed for alliance and trade with Indians, economic relations were generally inclusive. Accommodation and cross-cultural exchange occurred, although not without intermittent and selective violence. Once a single imperial power attained control over a region, economic relations became more exclusive. Subjugation and displacement replaced negotiation and coexistence. Opposition to the construction of sharper boundaries by communities still interested in older forms of livelihood and exchange, however, often persisted during and after the transformation.[4]

Under the influence of economic anthropology and European economic history, many historians have been taking traditional forms of livelihood and exchange more seriously. Almost everywhere before 1800, changes in what Fernand Braudel called material life occurred sporadically. Routine and continuity prevailed. Toward the end of the eighteenth century, however, a great divide was being crossed at a few places and the consequences would be felt globally after 1800. Change began to drive economic life, and calculation and vigilance took over. Karl Polanyi called this the "great transformation," by which economies previously submerged in social relationships became societies ruled by the market system.[5] Life inside the Louisiana Purchase is best examined, therefore, on its own terms. When this is done, we become curious about what persisted as well as what did not. We might even wonder more about the desirability, than about the inevitability, of United States expansion. The regions encompassed in the vast Louisiana Purchase were extremely diverse. This has been too readily overlooked. So to illustrate my points, I will briefly describe three very different places.

Given the composition of the population living inside the Louisiana Purchase, it should be no surprise that the political economy of this region in 1803 was still dominated by American Indian patterns of subsistence and networks of exchange. Unfortunately it continues to be difficult for Americans to take Indian economic activity seriously (with or without casinos). This was certainly not the case for many non-Indians who actually inhabited the newly formed territories of Orleans and Louisiana at the dawn of the nineteenth century. Woodlands, Prairie, Plains, and Mountain peoples comprised a Native American population of approximately one quarter million in the Purchase area. (Keep in mind that another half million Indians inhabited the Pacific Northwest, California, the Great Basin, and the Southwest.) The non-Indian population inside the Louisiana Purchase did not exceed fifty thousand people (37,000 in lower Louisiana and 10,000 in upper Louisiana).[6] Directly and indirectly this relatively small colonial populace in Spanish Louisiana was still connected to Indian economics, mostly but not exclusively through the trade in animal skins.

With or without ties to colonial markets, American Indian economic life was complicated and dynamic in ways that historians have only recently come to understand. Let us glimpse at a group that was rather remote from the territory's non-Indian settlements and outposts. The Flatheads, calling themselves Ootlashoots, lived (and still live) in the Bitterroot River Valley, amidst the headwaters of both the Columbia and the Missouri rivers. These Salish-speaking villages were positioned at an important economic gateway, one linking Great Plains with Pacific Northwest peoples. From the west, the Flatheads acquired salmon, salmon oil, baskets, bows, abalone earrings and incised dentalium. With these goods and their own products, they traded to the east for pipestone, manufactured pipes and pottery, and corn. Over the course of the eighteenth century, European-introduced items filtered into this indigenous trade network, as the Flatheads raided and traded for horses from Shoshones and provided them to Blackfeet and Crows who in turn introduced them to guns.

Well into the nineteenth century, Flathead village life revolved around an intricate cycle of hunting and gathering activities. A seasonal pattern of livelihood lay at the foundation of material and spiritual life, but it was by no means backward or static. The eighteenth century demonstrated how this age-old system could effectively assimilate new influences and adapt to outside forces. Camas, other roots and plants, small game and fish—all gathered in the local valleys during the summer—continued to comprise the main diet of Flathead people, while buffalo hunting west of the Rocky Mountains supplemented their diet. With the adoption of the horse for traveling and hunting, the buffalo became more important to the native economy. Historians have been paying closer attention to the internal and external impacts of this change, and so we now better understand how everything from the role of women to conflict between nations was affected. The spread of smallpox epidemics, particularly in the 1760s and 1780s, caused devastating losses of life and debilitating setbacks to livelihood. Nevertheless, the Flathead people proved to be resilient in their productive capacity and versatile in their trade ability.

Before the Lewis and Clark expedition reached Flathead country, Canadian fur companies were forging trade ties with the Flatheads and other Rocky Mountain and Columbia Plateau tribes. By 1795 a Flathead trade party visiting the Mandans on the Missouri River had caught the attention of Pierre-Antoine Tabeau. David Thompson's establishment of Salish House on Clark Fork in 1809 ensured that the Flatheads would trade principally with the Northwest Company for some time to come. This was the overall trend in trade development all along the Missouri River as far down as the Mandan and Hidatsa towns. The Louisiana Purchase did not preempt or reverse the Canadian merchants' expansion of their exchange relationships with American Indians from the Great Plains to the Pacific Northwest. It would take decades for U. S. companies to replace their presence in the far West.[7]

Traveling hundreds of miles to the mouth of the Missouri and visiting a place better known as a gateway, the town of St. Louis just down the Mississippi presents another example of the economic complexity that pre-dated the Louisiana Purchase. St. Louis was established during the 1760s in the midst of older colonial settlements comprising the Illinois country. Thanks especially to the works of Carl Ekberg and Morris Arnold, we have recently acquired a fuller understanding of how agriculture and commerce developed in the central and upper Mississippi Valley during the eighteenth century. French villages on both banks of the Mississippi produced substantial volumes of grain and livestock, while some residents focused more on trade with nearby Indian communities. The prevailing pattern of livelihood there was based on nuclear villages with open fields and common pasturage. St. Louis originated as a trade and administrative post, but it quickly became surrounded by arable fields subdivided into longlots and a commons for livestock and firewood. At both Ste. Genevieve and St. Louis, wealthier inhabitants employed African-American slaves on larger fields. By 1791 slaves comprised thirty percent of these two towns' total population of 2,111. During the 1790s Spain was encouraging Anglo-Americans and American Indians to migrate from U. S. territory into upper Louisiana. The mix of economic activities available to these newcomers helped maintain notable stability and continuity, although ominous pressures on lands and resources were instigating sporadic conflicts with indigenous communities.[8]

Of course the St. Louis area at the beginning of the nineteenth century is best known for its pivotal place in Indian trade. Before the town was founded in 1764, French trade with Great Lakes and upper Mississippi Valley nations already operated as a vital network of exchange. Many of the horses, mules, and cattle initially acquired by colonists in the Illinois country had reached them through a chain of trading and raiding among Native Americans that reached all the way to Spanish New Mexico. The steady expansion of trade in furs drew a growing number of French men into the kinship systems of Central Siouan peoples along the lower Missouri River and its tributaries. This was a mixed economy indeed, where the exportation of profitable products for the trans-Atlantic market resulted largely from American Indian customs of marriage and exchange. Even as economic life in and around St. Louis became increasingly commercial, successful merchants like the Chouteaus and Gratiots needed to mobilize family relationships originating between Indian women and French traders.

Recent studies by Tanis Thorne and Jay Gitlin have awakened us to the complexity of social and economic interaction in this part of the Louisiana Purchase, confronting forcefully the dominant stereotype of French-Indian relations. Strong family ties and versatile bicultural identity facilitated commercial exchange and growth. The most important economic development toward the end of the eighteenth century was an intensification of competition over Indian trade, especially with the Osages, by companies based in Canada, Louisiana, and the United States. Indian communities consequently suffered mounting political instability, while small traders of mixed ancestry faced tightening restrictions on their activity. A fluid and illicit movement of goods across imperial boundaries had been targeted by the Spanish government for some time, but the Louisiana Purchase reduced this issue to one between U. S. and Canadian companies. French merchants of various backgrounds adapted rather well to Americanization and continued to dominate the St. Louis trade system for a long time. For Indians, métis, and poorer French inhabitants of the region, the sudden change from Spanish to American rule was less disruptive than the gradual shift away from the fur trade as companies leaped over them for more western sources and as land development accelerated at the local level.[9]

For our third scene of livelihood and exchange inside the Louisiana Purchase, let us travel way down the Mississippi River to present-day Donaldsonville, Louisiana. Then still a distributary of the "Big Muddy," Bayou Lafourche flowed into the Gulf of Mexico just west of the most populous settlements in colonial Louisiana. Occupied by the Chitimachas for most of the eighteenth century, this waterway and its adjoining lands had become a crucial link in the exchange economy of the lower Mississippi Valley. Deerskins, livestock, and foodstuffs were transported through a web of intercultural relations whose intricacy matched that of the bayous and wetlands routinely crossed by native villagers and colonial traders.[10]

The political economy of Bayou Lafourche was significantly influenced by the migration of Acadians to Spanish Louisiana beginning in the 1760s. While colonial authorities originally situated many Acadian immigrants on land along the Mississippi, more and more preferred moving as far west as the Vermilion River. Demands on small farmers for militia duty and levee construction, as Carl Brasseaux has capably explained, combined with pressures from more prosperous settlers to motivate Acadian movement into the less populated backcountry. The accelerated growth of plantation agriculture and slavery, which involved incoming Anglo-Americans as well as French and Caribbean Creoles, infringed on small-scale farming and face-to-face exchange. To escape some of this pressure, many Acadian settlers steadily established these preferable economic practices along Bayou Lafourche and places farther west.

These Acadians, it is important to underscore, were not running away from economic changes or challenges. As they established their modest farms along Bayou Lafourche, with five arpents (one arpent is 192 feet) or so of frontage, their mix of crops included marketable corn, rice, vegetables, and cotton. Fishing, gathering, and herding also produced occasional surpluses for commerce. Control over economic resources and activities was the issue, and the conversion of more labor and land to the production of cotton and sugar, especially after 1800, put Acadian independence in jeopardy. But their own quest for separate space was far from benign. Houma and Chitimacha Indians in south Louisiana needed to defend their livelihoods against Acadian pioneers. Conflict between peoples with similar livelihoods intensified, as Indians committed acts of banditry in protest. Acadians' interaction with African-Americans also deteriorated for a combination of reasons: large-scale plantation slavery threatened the exchange economy, mounting prospects of slave rebellion instilled racial anxiety, and of course some Acadians became successful planters themselves.[11]

Amidst these social and economic changes, the Louisiana Purchase hardly seemed important. In fact, the rift between small producers like most Acadians and a rising planter class of various origins was far more significant than the exaggerated clash between Creoles and Anglo-Americans. After all, as historians Sarah Russell and Peter Kastor have recently demonstrated, plantation development in south Louisiana actually depended upon cooperation between French and Anglo families as land and slaves were being purchased in ever growing amounts. By the 1820s even the alluvial soil along Bayou Lafourche would be reached by sprawling sugar plantations.[12]

This sketch of three different regional economies inside the Louisiana Purchase only begins to identify points worth further consideration. Traditional patterns of livelihood and networks of exchange, still meeting the needs of many inhabitants in the early 1800s, were neither simple nor static. Production for outside markets had been moderately affecting society and culture, but change did not undermine autonomy and choice. Merchants and governments still exerted limited control over the everyday life of most people. With or without the Louisiana Purchase, however, these regional economies were being pulled into, or perhaps were attracting, wider economic forces of change. Economic conflicts erupting before the Louisiana Purchase would take a long time to be resolved; economic changes also predating 1803 might take generations to play themselves out. Perhaps they would not be fixed or finished at all. That the Louisiana Purchase marked a great political divide is a certainty. What this meant for the economic life of many inhabitants across the territories is not. The economic transformation would provoke from the trans-Mississippi West continuing strategies of adaptation and resistance yet to be explored.

Part II
The Peoples of the Purchase and Their Histories

The Peoples of the Purchase and their Histories

The second group of essays, "The Peoples of the Purchase and their Histories," largely consists of paired essays, with each pair roughly dividing the story of a particular sort of person at 1803. Patricia Galloway and Susan Allison Miller discuss the history of Native Americans from before the European invasion of the Mississippi Valley until almost the Civil War. Galloway shows that, contrary to the cardboard stereotypes still too common in our collective memory, Native peoples had been successfully responding to and creating changes in their physical, social and technological environments for millennia before Europeans and Africans appeared in the Mississippi Valley, and continued to do so after they did. As a member of the Tiger Clan and Tom Palmer Band of the Seminole Nation, Susan Allison Miller challenges the reader to rethink the meaning of the Purchase with her essay "Those Homelands You Call the 'Louisiana Purchase.'" She chronicles the ways in which the colonial powers and the United States ignored Native rights, especially during and after the Purchase.

Peter H. Wood and Celia E. Naylor-Ojurongbe discuss the African-American or Black experience in the Purchase Territory, from the 1520s to ca. 1860. Wood looks at the growth of slavery in the Territory and highlights the multiple roles of enslaved Africans during the colonial period. Naylor-Ojurongbe discusses the early National period and finds that slavery, and black exclusion laws, existed in the "free" parts of the Territory after the Missouri Compromise of 1820. She also highlights individual Blacks whose stories show the difficulties that free persons of color faced, and overcame.

Europeans in the Purchase Territory are the theme of the late Glenn R. Conrad's review of the French-speaking population and Light T. Cummins' review of Spaniards and Englishmen in the period after Spain gained control of Louisiana in 1763. Conrad asks why the Francophones never had a unified political voice after 1803 and explores some of the possible reasons. Cummins looks at how Spain attempted to control Louisiana by, among other things, allowing Anglo-Americans to settle in it, ironically paving the way for its easier absorption into the United States after 1803.

Johanna Miller Lewis and Lucy Eldersveld Murphy tell us the hardships that women endured on the post-Purchase Mississippi Valley frontier (Miller Lewis) and how they played vital roles in bridging the social and other distances between ethnic groups and forming networks to overcome the relative isolation of frontier life (Murphy). Miller Lewis notes that by the time Americans began to move into the trans-Mississippi West, especially into Arkansas, expectations about frontier life and women's social roles had changed from those common among the first generations of frontier women east of the Appalachians. The result was that women moving to an often primitive frontier endured great emotional as well as physical hardship. Murphy calls attention to Sacajawea as an especially instructive example of the importance of women in the frontier story but goes on to show the various means by which frontier women wove together communities from collections of strangers. The presence of women, she suggests, often made the difference between relative peace and open hostility among males of different ethnicities.

Turning to a different aspect of the history of the peoples who came to inhabit the Purchase Territory, Andrew R. L. Cayton and Peter J. Castor examine how the Euro-Americans, at least, came to define and affirm a common sense of "Americanness." After showing how concerned Americas were in 1803 about national unity in a republic spread over half a continent, Cayton suggests that passionate, emotional patriotism became the sign of "attachment" to the nation. Aaron Burr failed that test; Andrew Jackson exemplifies it. Kastor shows how the Francophones and other residents of the Territory of Orleans used the rhetoric of "attachment" to overcome other Americans' suspicions of their fitness for citizenship and gain acceptance as members of the nation.

Finally, Hans W. Baade and Randy J. Sparks examine two other aspects of the lived experience of post-1803 residents of the Purchase. Baade examines the persistence of the Civil Law in Louisiana (the state), attributing it to French lawyers who used the American jury system and the Francophone population of the area to impress their law on the land. Sparks presents a sweeping examination of the presence and growth of Protestant religious groups. Whether they were the Lutherans of the German Coast in the early French period or the late colonial and post-1803 Baptists, Methodists, Anglicans and Presbyterians, Protestants were a minority in Lower Louisiana, growing in numbers only slowly before 1860, and often most rapidly among persons of African descent.

Chapter 7

Indians of the Lower Mississippi and Trans-Mississippi to the End of the French Regime

Patricia Galloway

Introduction

When Eric Wolf wrote his groundbreaking book about colonialism, *Europe and the People Without History*, he did not mean to suggest that non-European peoples had no history, but that Europeans defined them as such because non-Europeans' ideas about their pasts were not recognizable to Europeans as "history."[1] Similarly, Johannes Fabian, in *Time and the Other*, pointed out that non-Europeans were considered by Europeans to be somehow stuck in the past. Such a "denial of coevalness," he argued, not only made non-European colonized people into useful metaphors for earlier stages of European cultural development, but also solidified the notion that non-Europeans did not belong in a modernizing world.[2]

European history was seen as the only "real" history and Europeans as its only effective actors. Thus Amerindians have been included in natural history museums as anthropologized specimens and in histories as part of the introductory geographical setting chapter, while their ongoing history has been excluded from the historical museum and the main part of the historical text. That this situation has not changed much should be recognized in the fact that even histories explicitly devoted to Native groups are most frequently told from the European outside, looking in at the self-presentation that Native people adopted for outsiders' benefit.

Generally, though, historians have abandoned Native history to archaeologists. Archaeology depends upon material remains to construct sequences in terms of changing patterns in artifact clustering, either in geographical distributions or vertical strata of cultural deposits, or both. Although in many and perhaps most cases these sequences do have a substantial temporal element, they also depend dialectically upon classifications imposed upon the artifacts themselves. Hence they are built upon categories just as firmly Western as are the temporal notions they are said to help define. In the hands of archaeologists patterns of artifact and settlement change became exemplars for schemes of cultural evolution, structured upon technology. In the end archaeology inevitably built its sequences backward from a European-dominated present, echoing the nineteenth-century European framing of progress in terms of stone, bronze, and iron ages and of hunting-gathering, herding, and agriculture. This progression always terminated in European excellence and guaranteed that non-Europeans would be judged primitive and backward by comparison. Hangovers from this kind of thinking still haunt a more postmodern archaeology.

As Native scholars have begun to intervene in and take control of the discourse about their own history, both history and archaeology have been awakened to their biases. Thus to write a thing called "history" about the Native past at all is problematic at the present decolonizing juncture, and central to any such effort must be an emphasis on seeking to hear the voices that have been so long silenced. The first step in this direction requires that we recognize the problems presented by the documentary, material, and oral archive on which historical writing is based, as well as the control of that archive. If North American Native peoples are recognized as fully equipped with an historical tradition, then we are compelled to ask how we may understand that tradition and take it into account.

It is a commonplace today to deride the exceptionalism of earlier United States historiography, the assertion that the American ethnogenesis was morally privileged in some way. Yet in the context of cultural contact and comparison, every people's history is exceptional and unique—and so are those of the Native groups Americans came to call "tribes." For the lands that would be the southern part of the Louisiana Purchase, I shall attempt briefly to show how.

Amerindian Advent

Amerindians were the human explorers and settlers of the last unsettled continent on the globe: the first pioneers of the Americas. Whether their time is measured in thousands of years or is considered "ancient," as peoples they emerged in truth from the earth of the Americas because it was that earth with its unique ecological complement that shaped them as they shaped it. Their science mastered its environments as they discovered what was safe to eat and how to hunt and eventually manage the unique animals they encountered. They made whole cultures from global cooling and warming episodes. Their technology mastered travel modes across the length and expanse of the continent.

These pioneers of more than ten thousand years ago hunted the dramatic Pleistocene megafauna—giant sloths and beavers, sabertooth tigers, bison, and mammoths—as long as they and the cold of a waning ice age lasted (although they also undoubtedly hunted smaller mammals and gathered foods as well). There is no real knowing how much impact their hunting had on these animal populations, which were probably more strongly affected by climate changes to a warming and drying trend that in its turn favored the expansion of the human population as well as the alteration of the environment.[3] With the warming in climate came a gradual increase in sedentariness. People continued to hunt seasonally but began to establish permanent living sites based upon the collection and eventually the cultivation of squashes and oily seed-bearing plants like sunflower and sumpweed. In the South, archaeologists have come to understand during the last twenty years that large populations and even monumental architecture marking centers for periodic gatherings came about remarkably early—as early as 4000 BC—without agriculture.

Nevertheless a significant cultural development was the arrival, apparently from Mexico via the American Southwest, of another and more important seed: maize. Celebrated in Native tradition as the gift of the Corn Mother from her own body, maize was cultivated and owned by women. This crop, which began to be popularly grown around AD 900, revolutionized Native life in the Americas as life in west Asia had been changed by wheat and in Africa by millet. Maize enabled the further expansion of populations and compelled their concentration on lands appropriate to its cultivation.[4] Because these lands were those of large alluvial valleys, the great river valleys of the continent's center saw the emergence of increasingly highly organized populations. Their leaders' power began to be significant enough not only to extend trade and communication far and wide but to raise much larger communal structures upon the landscape: the so-called "mound-builders" of AD 1000-1500.

Anthropologists refer to these organized populations as chiefdoms because of the conventional nomenclature applied to their leaders. The largest of them, that centered on the enormous and complex city in the continental center now called Cahokia, was a vast polity, and its leader was certainly much like a king. By the European fourteenth century there was a significant number of such polities, each quite distinctive in the style if not the overall manner of organization of its culture. Across the central and southern part of the continent there were many varieties of this "Mississippian" set of practices, manifesting enormous and tiny civic-ceremonial centers and sophisticated and countrified settlements. Most of these societies recognized the importance of women's fertility and work on the land by organizing their genealogy and landholding on the maternal principle. They organized their ceremonialism around the events of the agricultural year.

These polities did not coalesce into a single nation. Instead they rose and fell on their own timetables, driven by population growth and resource exhaustion. Eventually many of them proved to be somewhat fragile in their dependency upon multiple annual crops and abundant seasonal game. This dependency proved particularly dangerous when another spell of climate change, the so-called Little Ice Age that preceded and coincided with the period of European exploration and early settlement, made maize crops too uncertain to support large populations in close concentration. Cahokia's decline took place in the late thirteenth century, when its population dispersed; others lasted longer, into the fifteenth and even sixteenth centuries, to be seen by early European explorers.[5] But the movements of peoples as a result of these changes are well embedded in the origin histories of many modern Native American groups.

European Advent

To say that 1492 changed everything is of course true: chaos theory has taught us that a single butterfly can do that. Native peoples had been trading, negotiating, and warring literally for millennia with Native Others, had abundant traditions for doing these things, and had already themselves changed their ways many times. But two significant additional sources of change were introduced by Europeans, both of them to have serious, even calamitous implications: Old World microbes and European technologies. As is now well-known, Europeans brought with them an array of diseases, from smallpox to malaria to measles, all products of the crowding of large populations and thus extremely dangerous to Native groups also so concentrated. These diseases were the quite unintended passengers that proved most powerful in the often slow-motion European conquest of the Americas. Further, Europeans also brought with them weapons technologies superior in potential killing power, transportation technologies with a longer reach, and technologies of communication and governance that could enable a more detailed control than that possessed (or even desired) by the polities they found. When, beyond all expectation, they encountered a populous continent that lacked those kinds of coordinated technologies Europeans enjoyed a certain advantage from them. In neither case, however, did these two engines of change, diseases and technologies, have complete immediate effect. Native people were on the whole healthier to begin with than Europeans, and were highly proficient in their own technologies of war, transportation, communication, and governance. What they brought to the confrontation was powerful enough in its own way to change European practice and thinking, if not to overcome them.

The impact of the European arrival was not immediate for the Louisiana Purchase region, unless we accept with Henry Dobyns that the 1519 smallpox epidemic carried to Mexico by Cortés was able to spread among Native people as far as northern Mexico, Texas, and the lower Mississippi River valley.[6] Since Native people across the entire continent had well-developed communication routes, including the Caribbean islands, it was certainly possible for word of the coming of strangers to run on ahead of their actual appearance, but certainly not at Internet speeds. More likely, it would take a year or more for news to be passed across the continent, more if it had to cross ethnic boundaries where there was active warfare. All of these characteristics lessened the chance for the spread of acute diseases, but news could travel even if the messenger died.[7] Thus it is not perhaps surprising that early efforts to explore the Gulf Coast by sea were met with something less than enthusiasm by Native peoples, as Pánfilo de Narváez found in 1528. It has been suggested that possible Spanish slaving along the coast, reflected in Ponce de León's efforts on the Florida peninsula but otherwise unrecorded, might account for this caution. What the Narváez expedition saw along the Gulf Coast was the widespread and varied exploitation of fisheries. What it encountered was the Native people's mistrust. Alvar Núñez Cabeza de Vaca and the other survivors of the expedition, making their way into the interior after being cast away on the south Texas coast, observed the seasonal patterns of resource extraction of large groups of hunter-gatherers in northern Mexico, peoples who had clearly not heard of the coming of strangers.

It does not seem that many people in the interiors, even had they heard of it, had taken in the potential significance of what was going on along the coasts: it might not have seemed unusual to hear about odd things being seen in foreign lands. They got a rude awakening when the Hernando De Soto expedition made its way through the southern interior from 1539 to 1542 and Francisco Vázquez de Coronado marched from New Mexico to present-day Kansas in 1541, nearly meeting Soto. Soto came with a colonizing equipage of 600 men, a herd of pigs, and riding horses, all living things capable of carrying disease. Coronado brought men and horses as well, and was in a position to set up conditions for a trade in horses that would have its own dramatic impact on the Plains and the South.

Both Spaniards came with the intention of discovering extraordinary riches. Although there were gold deposits here and there in the regions they saw, neither Soto nor Coronado found them. Soto hoped to find large populations that could be enslaved or laid under corvée tribute by means of the physical control of their leaders. This did not work either. Everywhere Native stratagems of resistance thwarted both of them. A good part of their failure can be attributed to the Native communication networks already mentioned. On several occasions Soto seized "chiefs" only to find that clothes did not make the man and he had been fooled by a volunteer. Both Soto and Coronado were literally misled by guides willing to sacrifice their lives. So although the sixteenth-century Spanish expeditions into the Purchase lands did indeed encounter impressive centralized polities that they dearly hoped to be able to dominate, they did not succeed in doing so. After Soto had died in the attempt, his lieutenant Luis de Moscoso led his men westward, only to find thinly populated lands beyond the strong and numerous Caddo groups that they dared not treat with less than politeness. The Spaniards were glad to make it back to the Mississippi and escape with their lives. Although Tristan de Luna followed Soto to the Mobile-Pensacola area some years later in an effort to make a settlement, Luna's attempt was no more successful, even if it suffered less loss of life.

Protohistoric Intermission

From the 1560s to the last quarter of the seventeenth century the lands of the Purchase were essentially left alone by Europeans, and we must depend on the evidence of oral tradition and silent objects buried in the earth to tell what happened. Clearly European-precipitated changes took place. Spanish expeditions had left behind human wastes in their camps, a few human escapees, and numbers of animals all along their routes. Although the diseases potentially transmitted might not have been acute, they certainly had the potential to add significantly to the disease load of Native peoples all across the South and the trans-Mississippi, weakening populations for disease outbreaks once European contact resumed. In addition, although Spaniards made no more attempts for the moment to tackle the deep North American interior, they continued to travel, stop, and make contacts along the coast of the Gulf of Mexico, their "Spanish Sea," and push missions outward from St. Augustine so that acute diseases could continue to be spread to Native contacts. The impact of Old World diseases, it has been argued, was to precipitate serious "virgin soil epidemics" in populations that had not previously experienced those specific diseases and had no immunity to them. Population losses of 60%-90% have been mentioned, and clearly demographic disaster of such magnitude would have destroyed most functioning social structures.

But the material evidence of archaeology and the emergence of powerful new groupings of Native people in our region stubbornly suggest that losses were not everywhere so serious, being worst where riverine access was easier, and that some polities or polity fractions survived intact enough to attract to themselves other less intact groups. There was a great deal of population movement and consolidation during this so-called "proto-historic" period of only marginal contact with Europeans, movement and consolidation reflected in archaeological remains and traditional migration accounts. Confederacies like the Creek and Choctaw east of the Mississippi and the Caddo to the west emerged into history from populations that had been variably stressed by disease.[8] What Europeans saw in the late 1700s were groups with distinct "villages," "divisions," or "races" that were organized in more or less loose confederations for mutual defense and marriage partnering, groups spread usually along contiguous watercourses or ecological zones. Egalitarian in a general way, these confederations were still often led by men who sometimes inherited their rank. They shared out some ceremonial functions in such a way as to cement their linkages, and the relations between segments could be articulated in terms of formal ranking, with their previous historical relations to one another providing precedents. These groups were therefore usually less centrally organized than their constituent elements had been before. The Natchez were the exception that proved the rule because, in contrast to other groups, their core population remained on its land base. The people who lived in these groups had of course not forgotten how to hunt, fish, gather, or grow maize. They had also retained traditions of governance and religious beliefs that became the underpinnings of organizations that would prove to be impossible for Europeans to master politically and resistant to European religious proselytizing.

Return of the Repressed

Although English and Spanish settlement along the eastern seaboard of North America and the Florida peninsula were well established by the seventeenth century, it was not until the French explorations at the end of that century—Father Jacques Marquette and Louis Joliet in 1674 and Robert Cavelier, Sieur de La Salle, in 1682—that a permanent European presence began to be established in the Mississippi Valley. The French explorers discovered new conditions compared to what Soto had seen, the results of the migrations and confederations just discussed. They also discovered peoples who were perfectly aware of the growing pressure of Europeans on the borders of their regions. European threats were working now through Native peoples they had armed, and the peoples of the interior were cautiously interested in developing alliances themselves with Europeans who would be willing to provide support for defense.

La Salle participated in welcoming ceremonies and made alliances all down the Mississippi River, running into opposition only among the Chitimachas and allied Natchez on the lower river. La Salle's abortive settlement on the Texas coast in 1685 failed at least partly because the dispersed populations of the coastal region saw it as an intrusion into a barely supportive environment. These Native people eventually killed most of the survivors. After La Salle's death attempting to reach the Mississippi by striking off northward, the men in that expedition took advantage of the hospitality of Caddoan people of east Texas. Some remained among them while others were aided by neighboring Caddo groups to travel northward to the French post that Henri de Tonti, La Salle's partner, had established in 1686 on the Arkansas River among the Quapaw.

Tonti's post contained only of a few voyageurs, but it began to open a window on the Quapaw, who would become firm allies of the French, and to permit a better view of their Tunica and Koroa neighbors. Tonti himself explored further west in 1690 in search of La Salle, and Spanish awareness of the French intrusion in the area led to the establishment of short-lived missions among the Caddo in the same year. The picture was elaborated when in 1699 Pierre Lemoyne, Sieur de Iberville, brought an expedition to follow up on La Salle's effort and explored the coast and up the Mississippi River, and in 1700 when Louis Juchereau de Saint-Denis explored the Red River and established a firmer French acquaintance with the Caddo. From then on the Caddo would be able to exploit the interests of two European nations.

All these French explorations revealed that the banks of the lower Mississippi were dominated by a few larger groups—Quapaw, Tunica, and Natchez—surrounded by or interspersed with many allied smaller tribes like the Yazoo, Ibitoupa, Taposa, Koroa, Grigra, Tioux, Chitimacha, Houma, Bayougoula, Mongoulacha, and Acolapissa. Immediately to the east of the Mississippi, Tunicas and Natchez dominated from north to south; further east, the north was dominated by the Chickasaw and the south by the emergent confederacy of the Choctaw, while Choctawan Pascagoulas and Siouan Biloxis were living on rivers debouching along the coast. To the west of the lower Mississippi the three divisions of the large Caddo confederacy dominated most of western Louisiana, eastern Texas, and southwestern Arkansas, while the Quapaw controlled the lower Arkansas River valley. All of these groups knew of one another and from time to time traded and warred in shifting constellations.

For Europeans breaking in upon a dynamic situation, the picture became confusing quickly. Especially the so-called "small tribes," most of them remnants of larger groups decimated or displaced by disease, were moving around and contesting settlement areas with one another. This unsettled condition was probably due both to the contestation for farming and hunting lands and fisheries and to the movements of larger tribes, set off perhaps by the pressure of the Iroquois wars. Both Quapaw tradition and linguistic evidence suggest that the Dhegiha Sioux Quapaw came downstream to their Arkansas home, possibly after first being pushed southwestward on the Ohio River. They in turn probably pushed the Tunicas southeastward before them, across the Mississippi into the Yazoo Basin, where they had established a center of power by the time of French contact.[9]

The French, as the dominant European power, represented a godsend for the Native peoples of the region, another and possibly generous new European nation that promised trade for western tribes and help for eastern tribes against the English. They brought trade goods that peoples of the region already knew of and wanted to have, particularly the guns of which they were already victims. The Chickasaws had been contacted by the English in the 1680s, and had begun carrying out slaving expeditions to serve a market in

South Carolina. Iberville had found that Choctaws and Quapaws, as well as the smaller tribes of the lower Mississippi and Mobile delta, were suffering from these raids, were eager for French assistance, and were willing to assist the French in making the modest settlements they said they wanted. Initially, all went very well, as the small French outposts along the coast of the Gulf of Mexico and settlements around Mobile Bay demanded very little of their hosts and the tribes were provided with guns to defend themselves. Even a faction of the Chickasaw sought French alliance and trade.

Yet in the interior and among the Native peoples there was considerable turmoil as the impact of growing European contacts, however distant, began to be felt. As early as 1706 the Tunica were driven out of the lower Yazoo valley by the pressure of English-Chickasaw slave raids. They settled south of the Natchez opposite the mouth of the Red River. There they were able to take and maintain control over the Red River regional trade in salt and horses. Meanwhile the Taensa, formerly dwellers on the west side of the Mississippi above the Natchez, departed and with French assistance moved eastward to settle in the Mobile River delta.[10] It is interesting to observe that both of these groups had had French missionaries just at the turn of the eighteenth century, Father Antoine Davion for the Tunicas and Father François-Jolliet de Montigny for the Taensa. Both remained French allies thenceforth.

English-supported slave raids ceased for two reasons: Indian slavery became uneconomic and a localized Yamasee rebellion in Carolina against the English in 1715 cut it off. While the English were looking the other way, as it were, the French took the opportunity to establish a firmer footing with strategically-located forts. They had already established Fort St. Jean Baptiste among the Natchitoches Caddo on the Red River in 1714 (though it was countered by the nearby Spanish mission of Los Adaes founded in 1716).[11] Now they built Fort Rosalie at Natchez in 1716, Fort Toulouse among the Alabamas in 1717, and Fort St. Pierre at the Yazoo River forks in 1718. But these forts were not necessarily built to guard the Mississippi River against the English, nor to assist with the exploitation of mines in the Illinois country, even though English attacks from the east came in 1708 and 1712, and an English agent was captured among the Indians on the Mississippi in 1713. They were also built to monitor and control activities of Native groups.

In 1716 an incident between the Natchez and the French revealed the internal factionalism that the influence of competing Europeans could create. The new French governor, Antoine de La Mothe, Sieur de Cadillac, had refused the Natchez calumet ceremony and offended Natchez leaders in 1715, while ordering Jean Baptiste Lemoyne, Sieur de Bienville, to erect a fort among them. Before Bienville could act, the Natchez were accused of the murder and robbery of four Canadian voyageurs on their way to the Illinois. At the same time the French trade house was also plundered, and Bienville then had to undertake a punitive expedition. Camped among the friendly Tunicas, he lured

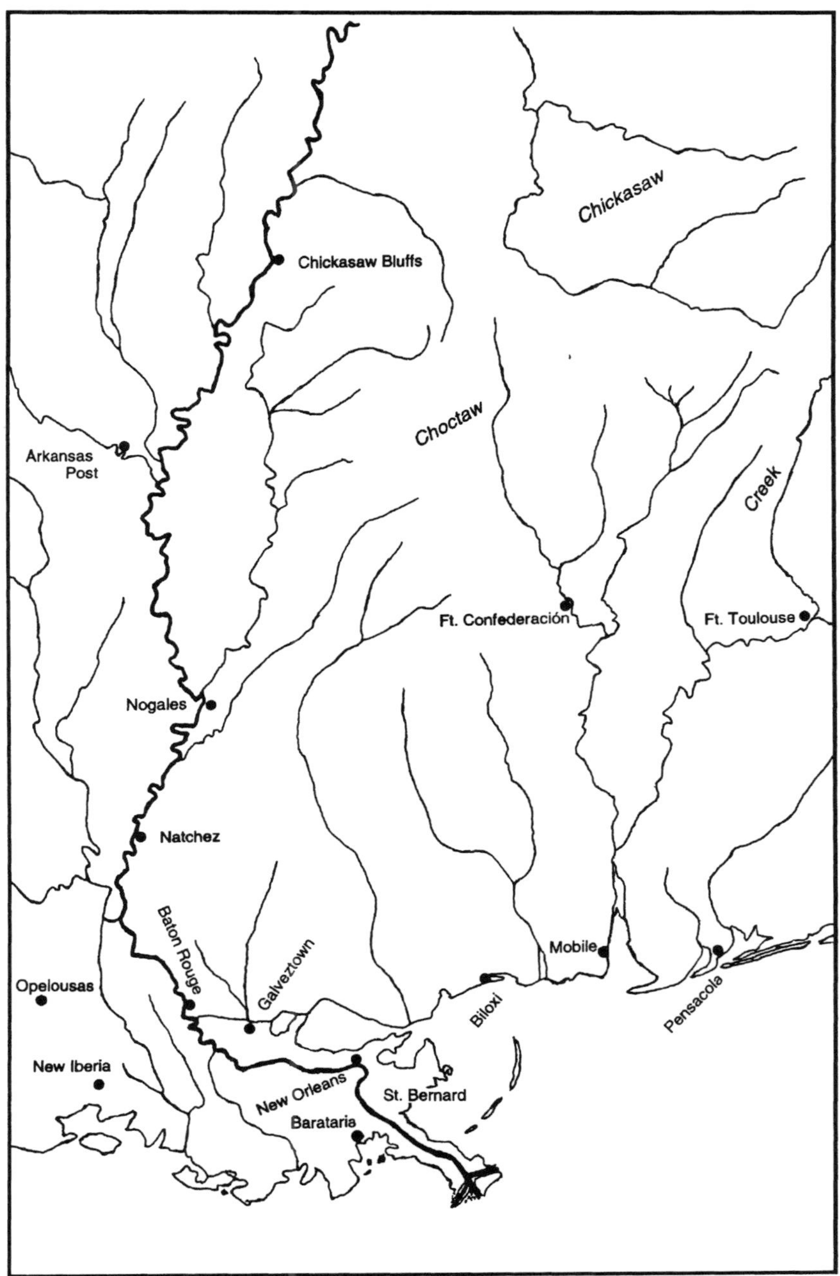

Figure 3. Colonial posts and settlements.

Natchez chiefs to his temporary fort and captured them, executing those he found to be responsible for the deaths. Although the English-allied Terre Blanche Sun had escaped, Bienville succeeded in obtaining return of the stolen goods and assistance in constructing the fort, probably from those Natchez more disposed toward alliance with the French. It seems reasonable to believe that English incentives might have been responsible for the attack.

But this was just the beginning of difficulties for the Natchez, not the end. In France the Crown farmed out the Louisiana colonial effort to the speculative colonizing ventures of the Company of the West under the direction of John Law. In 1718 preparations began for the foundation of a new capital at New Orleans. A second French trading post was established further up the Red River among the Kadohadacho Caddo in 1719. In the same year French immigrants began to arrive on the Gulf coast, poorly supplied and in desperate need of assistance from Indian allies. It was soon found that the lands of the Natchez region were by far the most fruitful for the agricultural enterprises—tobacco and indigo—planned for the French concessions, and the largest French settlements were made there, served by the labor of the first African slaves to be brought to Louisiana.

The Natchez granted the French land on usufruct terms, but the settlement of such a large number of people eventuated in friction. In 1723 a French soldier killed a Natchez elder and another disturbance ensued. Clearly the resentment it stirred did not fade away, especially when the post commander, Detchéparre (Chepart) moved in 1729 to exploit Natchez land for his own benefit and that of his patron, Governor Etienne Périer. By that time the leading French partisans, Tattooed Serpent and the Grand Village Great Sun, were dead. When Detchéparre demanded a specific piece of land that included what he judged to be an abandoned mound site, the Natchez asked for time to harvest their crops. They took the time to organize—perhaps with the help and encouragement of the English—an uprising that might have originally included all the tribes of the Yazoo and the Choctaw and Chickasaw. In the event, when the Natchez under guise of hunting to provision the French settlement seized all the French guns, killed the men, and took the French women and children hostage, they also had the assistance of the enslaved Africans who had worked the French farms. The French responded violently.

The Natchez fled both west and east. One segment was hunted down on the Red River and sent to the French Caribbean as slaves. Another group escaped to the Chickasaw and were taken in by them to form their own village.

The diaspora of the Natchez changed the balance of Native power in the lower Mississippi region. It enhanced the importance to the French of the Tunica and Ofo on the east bank of the Mississippi and of the Quapaw and Caddo on the west bank. It brought ruin in the form of Quapaw attacks on the Yazoo, who had joined the Natchez in revolt and killed French soldiers and settlers at Fort St. Pierre. The Chakchiuma, who had stayed out of the revolt, were nevertheless forced to retreat from the Yazoo River to join the Choctaw and then the Chickasaw. Finally, the Natchez flight attracted French warfare against the Chickasaw in 1736 and 1740, into which the Choctaw were drawn as participants in spite of their deep traditional relationship and ongoing marriage alliances with the Chickasaw. The Chickasaw themselves were rent by factional strife as a result, since not all Chickasaws were happy to welcome the Natchez. Eventually many of the Natchez moved once again to become the Notchee of South Carolina. For a time it looked as though one segment of the Chickasaw might break off and settle among the Choctaw. Further, factional rivalries evident among the Choctaw before and during the Chickasaw wars broke out in open civil war in 1746, a war incited by French demands for restitution after the killing of three Frenchmen. This internecine struggle did not end before some 800 individuals, several of them important leaders, had been killed, but the divisional structure of the confederacy survived.

In the years leading up to the Seven Years' War, much European attention was focused to the east, on the French-English rivalry. Yet westward, the fur trade was booming and the Caddo and Tunica were prospering with it as middlemen, so much so in the Tunica case that the burials of their leaders came to be astoundingly rich with French trade goods. The Quapaw further north moved their villages because of a flood in 1748, and the following year persuaded the French to move their fort also after a Chickasaw attack. The Choctaw continued low-level hostilities with some of the Upper Creek towns, traded with the Chickasaws' English traders when French trade goods ran low, as they did in the late 1750s, and continued to war on the Chickasaws at other times on behalf of the French. The Chickasaw remained clients and allies of the English.

Conclusion

Over the period from roughly 1500-1760, then, it is possible to trace in the southern region of the Purchase a wide range of trajectories that historic polities took in reaction to contact with Europeans. The Siouan Quapaw, after their move into the Valley, made early alliance with the French and suffered for it through population diminution. The Caddos' confederated segments, which had drawn together prior to European contact, later dispersed to exploit their environment more effectively through the fur and horse trades. The Natchez began as the most authoritarian polity. They took in refugee bands of Koroa, Grigra, and Tioux when their own population declined, but fell afoul of the French in defending their right to control their own sacred spaces. They ended destroyed: enslaved in Saint-Domingue or in diaspora in Tennessee or the Carolinas. The Choctaw as a protohistoric confederation of some four disparate but related peoples were able to maintain their alliance even through civil war, possibly because of their relatively remote location. The Chickasaws absorbed Natchez, Yazoo, and Chakchiuma, but themselves still were driven to partial exile.

In no case was any group, however major, untouched. But no group had been untouched at its origin; no group had escaped climatic changes and shifts in subsistence regimes long before the coming of Europeans. Native America had changed with European colonialism, but as of 1760, in the lands of the Purchase, Native people and Native polities still held the balance of power.

Chapter 8

Those Homelands that You Call the "Louisiana Purchase"

Susan Allison Miller

Patricia Galloway has discussed North American indigenous peoples in the southern part of the Louisiana Purchase, especially the area now occupied by the states of Louisiana and Texas. Her narrative ends at 1760. This paper takes up the narrative in that year and extends the discussion throughout the western drainage of the Mississippi River onto the Great Plains, northward to the U. S.-Canadian boundary, and westward to the crest of the Rocky Mountains.

The International Community of the Western Drainage, 1760

By 1760, the highly organized mound-building chiefdoms, best known for sites that they occupied in river valleys in the East approximately 1000 to 1500 AD, were gone. They had existed also in the woodlands west of the Mississippi River nearly to the margin of the Great Plains. Until shortly before the arrival of Coronado in 1541, for example, ancestors of the Caddo and Wichita people lived in complex communities in the Red River and Arkansas River drainages of present western Louisiana and Arkansas and eastern Oklahoma and Texas. In the Arkansas River drainage, at the site known today as Spiro Mounds in eastern Oklahoma, Caddoan ancestors developed an important regional center from about 850 to 1450 AD.[1] There, specialists coordinated a regional ceremonial practice and a far-flung trade that reached the Gulf Coast, central Texas, the Midwest, the Appalachian Mountains, and Florida. At the historic peak of the center's development, the people of surrounding villages were governed by elites who headed a hierarchical regional government. From their choice location on a major river road, they controlled much of the important trade between the Woodlands and the Plains.

In 1760, the Caddo and Wichita peoples were still there in the western woodlands and the eastern Southern Plains; still planting corns, squashes, and beans in the riverine floodbeds, still hunting and gathering foods in the woods and grasslands, still engaging in trade between Woodlands and Plains, and still conducting elaborate religious ceremonies. They had decentralized their government and residential pattern but had retained some of the regional governmental structure of the chiefdom. And like many other peoples of the western drainage, their cultures were changing in response to European influences.

Scholars argue conventionally that Europeans introduced horses and horse culture to the Americas. Many tribal intellectuals dispute that belief on the ground of traditional narratives in which horses predate Europeans here. The conventional scholarly position is that by 1760 Spanish horses had been passing from Spanish to Indian hands for generations. Spaniards had been ranching on the Rio Grande since the early 1600s. People in the Pueblos on the northern Rio Grande acquired horses from Spaniards and traded them to

Apaches and Jumanos from the Plains. Apaches and Jumanos, in turn, traded horses to Caddos and Wichitas to their east. Thus by the late 1600s, Caddos and Wichitas had horses; and soon their relatives, the Pawnees, on the Platte River system of the central Plains had horses, too. The horse invigorated the ancient trade that crossed the Plains and passed through the Caddos and Wichitas to the woodlands.[2]

Elsewhere by 1760, two sets of peoples unrelated to the Caddos, Wichitas, and Pawnees had migrated up the rivers from east to west onto the central Plains. The Iowa, Missouria, Winnebago, and Oto peoples speak closely related languages and share origin narratives. The Omaha, Osage, Ponca, Kansa, and Quapaw peoples are similarly related to each other. They had been moving down the Ohio and Mississippi rivers and up the Missouri and other rivers of the western drainage, establishing farming towns along the way.[3] They had acquired horses through the Southern Plains trade.[4]

Related to them are the Mandans and Hidatsas, who had arrived farther north on the Plains in an earlier migration. Mandan towns of earth-covered houses had been at the Great Bend of the Missouri River (now in central North Dakota) since about 1000 AD. The Hidatsas (also known as Minitarees and sometimes mistaken for the Atsinas—who were also known to the French by the pejorative "Gros Ventres") had arrived later, about 1600. Another related people, the Crows, lived farther upriver (in present Wyoming). By the time French traders arrived in 1738, the Sahnish people, known as Arikaras to their close relatives the Pawnees, had moved northward on the Plains and settled on the Missouri down river from the Mandans and Hidatsas.[5]

Long before the arrival of Europeans, the Missouri River was a major trade route, and the Mandan, Hidatsa, and Sahnish towns were important commercial centers. They produced large crops of maizes, beans, and squashes and traded those for goods that passed along the Missouri and for processed bison products and other goods brought in from the Plains by people from communities that followed the herds. By 1760, French fur traders based in St. Louis were involved in the Mandan-Hidatsa-Sahnish trade. Assinboines and Plains Crees, coming from the northeast to trade with the Mandans, Hidatsas, and Sahnish, brought goods obtained from British traders of the Hudson's Bay Company. The Crows may have introduced horses into that market in the mid-1700s.[6] Soon Cheyennes, Arapahoes, Kiowas, and Plains Apaches were coming from the central and Southern Plains with Spanish horses from the Southwest. In sum, by 1760 with guns coming in from British traders, horses from Spanish and Pueblo herds, and indigenous products from peoples within a wide radius, the Mandan-Hidatsa-Sahnish trading center was in an economic boom.

Elsewhere in the mid-1700s, the Blackfeet, the real Atsinas, and the Crows on the west-central Plains got the horse, not from the Plains network, but from the ancient trading route through the Rocky Mountains from the northern Rio Grande.[7] The Kiowas got the horse from the Crows.[8] According to their origin narrative, they had moved down into the Crow country from the Yellowstone country on the eastern slope of the Rocky Mountains (in present-day Montana).[9] In 1760, they were beginning the southward migration on the Plains that Scott Momaday narrates so beautifully in *The Way to Rainy Mountain*.

The Cheyennes had gotten the horse on the Cheyenne River in the 1750s and by 1760 had entered the Plains from the upper Mississippi Valley. Later, in the 1790s, they were to meet the Arapahoes in the Black Hills and form an alliance that endures to this day. The Arapahoes and the Atsinas entered the Plains from the northeast and northwest, respectively. All three groups—Cheyennes, Arapahoes, and Atsinas—speak languages related to that of the Anishinabe people (also known as Chippewas or Ojibwas).

The Numunuh people (or Comanches) are relatives of the Shoshones from the Great Basin. In the late 1600s, they had been on the northern Plains and had moved into the southern Rocky Mountains, where they acquired the horse and horse culture from the Rocky Mountain Ute people. Early in the 1700s, they moved down the Arkansas River Valley onto the Plains. By 1760, they had pushed the Apaches to the western margin of the Plains and were in Texas, participating in the Caddoan trade and harassing Spanish colonists.[10] By the 1770s, Comanches and Kiowas would be supplying horses to the north-central plains, the southeastern prairies, and New Mexico itself, where they created their own market by raiding for horses.[11] They would become so significant in taking and selling captives that the Americans would label the entire package the "Comanche trade."

Also by 1760, the Lakotas, still east of the Missouri River, were yet to acquire enough horses to move fully onto Plains. Both Richard White and Gary Anderson have refuted the long-held belief that Anishinabe people drove the Lakotas out of the area just west of the Great Lakes and onto the Great Plains. Scholars now agree that after the Lakotas got the horse, economic opportunity drew them to the Plains. With their Dakota-speaking relatives to the east, they formed a trading chain that carried Plains products to the Great Lakes and European trade goods to the Plains.[12]

According to scholars' convention, the arrival of the horse in Native America set off a transportation revolution. Suddenly, communities that had depended on bipedal and canine transport could travel faster and farther, and that meant that they could range farther from the rivers and springs into the often very dry grasslands; and they could carry more and heavier belongings. Before the horse, the bison herds had provided to varying degrees for all communities on and near the Plains, including sedentary farmer-hunter-gatherers such as those along the Missouri River and communities that followed the herds with dog-drawn travois. With the horse, communities could exploit the herds more thoroughly. By 1760, many disparate cultures that had adopted the horse were converting rapidly to economies based on bison products, agriculture, gathered resources, and trade. The historian Pekka Hamalainen is reconceiving the horse factor in Plains Indian history, basing his analysis on the size of an indigenous people's horse population, limiting ecological factors, economic and military factors, and cultural factors. He finds, for example, that adoption of the horse "destabilized subsistence cycles, wrecked grassland and bison ecologies, created new social inequalities, upset gender relations, and undermined traditional political hierarchies," so that the adaptations were unstable and only the Lakotas had long-term success.[13]

Figure 4. Pamplin Cheyenne-Arapaho Ledger, Plate WX by Short Horn. Courtesy of Morning Star Gallery, Sante Fe, New Mexico, and the Plains Indian Ledger Art Digital Publishing Project (http://plainsledgerart.org).

Like the horse, pathogens of the eastern hemisphere arrived before people of the eastern hemisphere on many parts of the Plains. By 1760, waves of epidemic diseases were entering the western drainage of the Mississippi River along with the European trade. Their effects would become increasingly pronounced over the next hundred years.

Each of the indigenous societies of the western drainage, like societies everywhere, claimed an area of land as its homeland. Those homelands were not vaguely defined, but, rather, were understood clearly by all peoples of the region. Landforms such as rivers and mountain ridges described the boundaries. Scholars believe that neutral buffer zones were often in place between neighboring peoples' lands. Maps by the nineteenth-century geographer Charles C. Royce depict indigenous land cessions in the area now occupied by the United States (figure 5).[14] The maps show indigenous homelands nested snugly against each other just as were the European nation-states of the time and as are the national claims of today all over the world.

Land claims of indigenous peoples were and remain based in ancient historical narratives that encode the laws, values, histories, and protocols of a society. Each indigenous people had and has a set of such narratives. In *The Way to Rainy Mountain,* the Kiowa N. Scott Momaday recounts such narratives among his people. One can learn to read indigenous narratives, often labeled "myths" or "legends," for that kind of knowledge.

Further, each indigenous nation had its own legal system, its own tradition of diplomacy and more, all grounded in the nation's sovereign status. The European nations, and, later, the United States, recognized the sovereignty of the indigenous nations by making treaties with them. A recent definition of sovereignty is found in Article 1 of the Montevideo Convention on the Rights and Duties of States, an international agreement that took effect in 1934 and to which the United States is a signatory. The Montevideo Convention reads in part,

> The state as a person of international law should possess the following qualifications: (a) a permanent population; (b) a defined territory; (c) government; and (d) capacity to enter into relations with the other states.

The legal historian John R. Wunder argues correctly that according to the criteria of the Montevideo Convention, the American indigenous peoples "have been sovereign nations for centuries and continue to be under international law."[15] So a community of nations occupied the western drainage of the Mississippi River in 1760. Contrary to the stereotype of "warlike tribes," they were in constant diplomatic interaction with each other. Their agreements comprised a body of international law; and indigenous law was the law of the land in those homelands that you call the "Louisiana Purchase."

The Doctrine of Discovery and the Western Drainage, 1803

When officials of various European nations laid claim to indigenous lands in North America, they ignored the tribal and international law that obtained in those countries. Scholars explain the arrogance of colonial Europeans as the product of beliefs in the superiority of European peoples and their ways of life. I do not know that belief in one's superiority is an acceptable motive for violations of law. Scholars also argue that Europeans rationalized their violations of the law of the land in the Americas with the argument that their single masculine deity was the only deity, that all lands of Earth belonged to him, and that he wanted only his followers to have the indigenous homelands.

With those principles in mind, European jurists and theologians devised a rather precious rationale within their own international law: the Doctrine of Discovery. In one thread of the development of that doctrine, a religious leader within a European religious organization, the head of the Church of Rome, improvised religious doctrine to control the exploitation of the lands allegedly discovered by Christopher Columbus in 1492. In 1493, Pope Alexander VI issued a decree or "papal bull" known as *Inter Caetera II*, drawing an imaginary line from the North Pole to the South Pole one hundred leagues west of the Azores and the Cape Verde Islands (just off the western coast of Africa) and guaranteeing to Spain title to all lands west of that line that did not belong to a Christian king or prince on Christmas Day, 1492. That is much as if the Nineteenth Generation

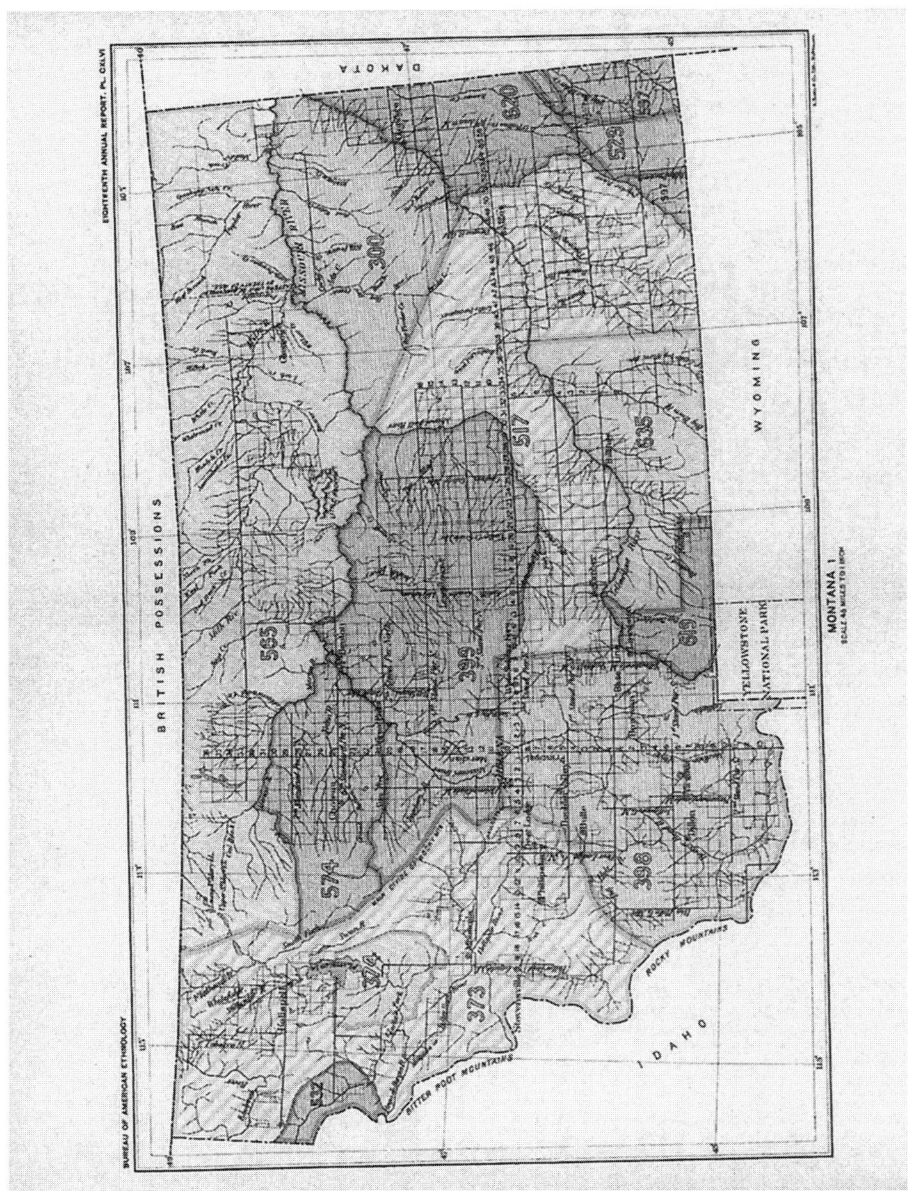

Figure 5. *Lands of Native Peoples. Montana I.* From Charles C. Royce, *Indian Land Cessions in the United States*, in Smithsonian Institution Bureau of American Ethnology, *Eighteenth Annual Report* (Washington, D. C., 1899). From the collection of the Geography and Map Division, Library of Congress.

Keeper of the White Buffalo Calf Pipe, a Lakota named Arvol Looking Horse, granted someone else title to your house on the ground that you don't follow the Pipe.

The Pope's principle that rights of Christians override rights of other people broke from the legal tradition of Roman law and European common law, which upheld land title based on continuous occupation and use from time immemorial. Within that tradition, title to unoccupied lands, which were termed *terra nullius,* was available to the first nation to discover them. To accommodate their desire to acquire the indigenous homelands of the western hemisphere, Europeans had to deal with the reality that the American lands were already occupied, so they redefined *terra nullius* to mean land occupied by people who did not use it as Europeans did.

The mechanism by which the alleged discovering nation might acquire lands from an indigenous nation was a provision in the Doctrine giving the alleged discoverer the sole right to acquire the land from its indigenous owner, should that owner wish to sell. Note how that provision denied the rights of indigenous nations to choose their own trading partners. The Doctrine developed in various other directions for hundreds of years. Ultimately, it cast Indian people as children unable to govern ourselves effectively and therefore needful of governance by Europeans.[16]

When the United States broke with Great Britain, it kept the latter's claim to rights under the Doctrine of Discovery. By the time John Marshall had installed the Doctrine in U. S. case law in 1823 in the U. S. Supreme Court decision *Johnson v. McIntosh,* the United States had already been using it as the framework of its policy towards the indigenous nations.[17] The Doctrine as applied in the western hemisphere sets up a religious discrimination; it denies indigenous nations the rights deriving from continuous occupation of lands (rights that people in or from Europe enjoy); it subordinates the rights of nations whose economies are based in indigenous economic activities; it purports to legitimate the violation of indigenous nations' sovereign rights to determine their own trading partners; and it denies the full humanity of indigenous persons.

That brings us to the Louisiana Purchase. The European claim to the western drainage had passed from Spain back to France. In 1803, the United States bought France's claim to Louisiana. From the perspective of American History—the history of the people of the United States—the "Louisiana Purchase" was the acquisition by the United States of the western drainage of the Mississippi River. To the American mind, the agreement between the United States and France to transfer ownership of that huge area was a legitimate treaty between the only interested legitimate parties. That event began what the people of the United States view as the "opening" of that area to American settlement.

When viewed from perspectives of North American indigenous peoples, however, that episode has an entirely different appearance. From perspectives in which Christians do not have more rights than other people, European culture does not confer rights that override those rights of indigenous nations deriving from continuous occupation of their lands; Europeanness does not override the rights of indigenous nations to engage in indigenous economic pursuits, choose their own trading partners, and govern themselves without interference; Europeanness does not confer immunity on its carriers from the legitimate legal controls that indigenous nations extend across their own lands; and no European deity owns the lands of indigenous America—from such perspectives, the Louisiana Purchase was an agreement between nations that had no legitimate claim to the lands in question but, rather, ignored the legitimate legal interests of the nations whose lands were involved. The Louisiana Purchase was a conspiracy to violate the controlling law of the land in the western drainage.

U. S. Colonialism in the Western Drainage

People in the western drainage had changed their lifeways in response to colonization by France, Spain, and Britain but have found that U. S. colonization takes a more pervasive form. Throughout the nineteenth century, people in the western drainage felt increasing pressure from the U. S. population. Increasingly, that pressure degraded indigenous economic bases and displaced indigenous communities. As communities lost access to food or were torn from their homelands, conflict among them increased. Meanwhile, throughout the nineteenth century, the microbial colonists, however unintentionally, supported the U. S. colonial project.

Richard White is probably correct in his assertion that history would have been different, and tribal nations would have kept more of their homelands, if the epidemics had not done so much damage.[18] He refers to the West in general, but the generalization appears to hold for the Mississippi River's western drainage. There the crippling effects of eastern hemisphere diseases on the community of nations can be glimpsed in the following list that comes predominantly from Henry Dobyns' survey of North American epidemics of the eighteenth and nineteenth centuries and David Wishart's study of their effects on tribes of the middle Missouri River region. Smallpox had struck Texas tribes in the 1750s. Influenza was throughout the region in 1761. Smallpox struck Texas tribes again in the mid-1760s, and measles in the mid-1770s.[19] Around 1800, smallpox decimated the entire population of the western drainage. It killed more than half the Omahas, for example, and the survivors had to burn their town of earthlodges and disperse in small parties.[20] More smallpox epidemics struck the Plains in 1815-1816 and 1831-1834. The latter epidemic killed 5,000-6,000 Pawnees, reducing their population by half. It was said that some of their towns were so devastated that dogs disposed of the remains of the dead.[21] Another 1,750 Pawnees died in epidemics and warfare from 1835 to 1840. Cholera killed at least 180 Omahas in 1835. In 1837-1838, smallpox struck the Mandans, sparing fewer than fifty of their 1,600 people.[22] Smallpox was epidemic on the Plains twice in the 1840s. In 1849, gold seekers from the United States spread cholera along their route to California.[23] Cholera devastated communities of Kiowas and Comanches on the Southern Plains.[24] Twelve hundred thirty-four more Pawnees died in six months of cholera and starvation. Smallpox hit the middle Missouri again in 1851[25] and spread across the Plains in the 1850s, again in the 1860s, and again in the 1870s. In the 1890s, it spread into Oklahoma from California.[26]

While the Americans were colonizing the indigenous lands of the western drainage, epidemic diseases removed entire generations from indigenous nations.

Also overrunning the western drainage during the nineteenth century were American settlers. Officials of the United States often had to scramble to stay ahead of the American settler population and uphold the U. S. government's claim to an exclusive right to deal with the indigenous nations. Scholars are divided over the question of whether U. S. Indian policy has been a series of differing policies or a single policy with a single goal and a series of tweaks. I am in the single-policy camp, where discussion has centered on the nature of the goal of that single U. S. policy. Some scholars have argued that the goal has always been assimilation of the indigenous people into the U. S. population. Others argue that the goal of U. S. Indian policy is the exploitation of the resources of the indigenous peoples. *Exploitation of resources* is correct.

The better to avail Americans of indigenous resources, the United States retained the practice of making treaties with indigenous nations as Great Britain had done. Treaty-making conformed to the Doctrine of Discovery and therefore allowed the U. S., in its pursuit of indigenous resources, what has come to be known as plausible deniability when its acts are considered in light of the international law of the eastern hemisphere. Treaty-making may seem like a fair and balanced procedure, but it is open to a variety of frauds. Coercion, for example, has often forced nations to treat unwillingly. Suborning of tribal leaders by threat or bribe has undermined a long list of negotiations. Substitution of puppets for authentic indigenous leaders has occurred throughout the history of American colonization. The bait and switch con also shows up regularly.

Even before the U. S. acquired the European claim to the western drainage, American officials envisioned those western lands as a place to resettle indigenous people living east of the Mississippi. That idea grew into the Indian Removal Policy. The best summary of Indian removal is still Arrel M. Gibson's in his textbook on Indian history, published more than twenty years ago.[27]

By 1825, the U. S. had treaties with Osages, Quapaws, Otoes and Missourias, Kansas, and other nations for large areas of their homelands comprising present-day Arkansas, Missouri, and Iowa.[28] Americans expected those tribes to be satisfied on small areas of their previous homelands, but their indigenous economies, founded on farming, hunting, and gathering, would not work in such limited areas. Therefore, people sought food outside the new tribal limits, and as traditional uses of resources became increasingly difficult, raiding for resources became increasingly attractive.

American officials intended those lands acquired by treaty for the resettlement of eastern tribes. Even as the procedure was being implemented, however, American settlers were trying, often successfully, to occupy the same lands. In the case of the Kickapoos, an 1819 treaty assigned them to new lands in present-day Missouri, but that land was in an area already designated "Missouri Territory" and undergoing what American historians call "state formation." Two years later, the Kickapoos were competing with covetous citizens of the State of Missouri for the Kickapoo land and resources, and soon the Kickapoos lost that land and had to move again. Cherokees and Choctaws in the area that became the State of Arkansas had similar experiences. Settlers used their votes to influence the U. S. political process in their favor and terrorism to force indigenous neighbors to quit indigenous lands. In Missouri and Arkansas, groups of settlers burned Indian towns, broke into Indian homes, stole Indian livestock, and poached game on Indian lands. If Indians tried to use the American legal system, courts acted in favor of the criminals. If Indians protected their property with force, settlers called that an "Indian war," and the U. S. sent troops to punish the victims of the crimes. That is a pattern that played out in various ways throughout the implementation of Indian Removal, as different branches and agencies of the U. S. bureaucracy conducted competing policies.[29]

In 1825, imagining that the land from the Mississippi Valley east to the Atlantic would be enough for American settlers, President Monroe and Congressional supporters set aside an area for Indians encompassing the area bounded by the western boundaries of Arkansas, Missouri, and Iowa; the Platte River, the crest of the Rocky Mountains, the Arkansas River, the one-hundredth meridian, and the Red River. They called that the "Indian country" and, later, the Indian Territory. The Choctaws, Cherokees, and Kickapoos left Arkansas and Missouri voluntarily and moved into the Indian Country.[30]

As this policy was implemented, people with homelands in the resettlement zone felt its destructive effects. American commissioners arrived to make treaties to "extinguish" the limited Indian title that John Marshall's interpretation of the Doctrine of Discovery acknowledged. Should an indigenous people decline to give up its lands, American military units were on hand to ensure compliance. American officials called that "making peace." The American military buildup intimidated the Osages into moving onto the lands assigned them in the treaty of 1825[31] and the Caddoes, Wichitas, Kiowas, and Comanches into making treaties from 1835 to 1837. The Quawpaws had given up their land in Arkansas in 1824 and agreed to live among the Caddoes. They were culturally unlike the Caddoes, however, and the merger did not work out. Impoverished, some of them signed a treaty in 1833 to move to land in present-day Kansas and others dispersed among Cherokee and Comanche communities. None of the treaties had long-term benefits for the indigenous parties.

Meanwhile, the United States was seeking treaties with indigenous nations east of the Mississippi River whereby those nations would cede their lands and resettle in the Indian country. People are not eager to give up their homelands, so the U. S. resorted to dirty tricks to conclude those treaties. My people, the Seminole Nation, rejected an extorted treaty and fought an extended war of resistance before most of us were forced to relocate in present-day Oklahoma.

The relocations were not voluntary. They were brutal, forced travel during which the old and the weak died in shocking numbers. In one particularly egregious case, beginning on August 28, 1838, in Marshall County, Indiana, several hundred Potawatomis, followers of the chief Menominee who had signed no treaty ceding his people's land, were decoyed into an ostensible council and surrounded and held at gunpoint by one hundred Indiana volunteers. As the Oklahoma historian Grant Foreman tells the story,

> [General John] Tipton then proceeded to the church, where other Indians were engaged in worship, and made his presence known by firing guns, surrounding the church, and making prisoners of the people within. . . . When evening came and they did not return home, others were sent out in search of them and they too were made prisoners. All of them were held under guard while troops were scouring the reservation for others and destroying their houses.

More than 850 of Menominee's people were set upon a forced march to Kansas. Foreman quotes their priest Benjamin Marie Petit:

> On September 4, 1838, they were lined up, some afoot, some on ponies, followed by the wagons, and all heavily guarded with guards at the rear with bayonets, which were often used to keep the weak ones in the procession. Before starting the torch was applied to their village, so that they might see their homes destroyed and they would not want to return. When all was in readiness, this grewsome [sic] procession, nearly three miles long, like a funeral procession, which in reality it was, started on its final journey. It was a very sickly season. The sun was hot and the road was dusty. They drove down the Michigan road to Chippewa on the Tippecanoe [River] where they camped the night of the fourth. Here their cup of sorrow was made to overflow. They wished to take their dead with them, and when this was denied, they had to leave them at the roadside or camping ground; hence every camping ground was a burial ground.
>
> In making preparations for this expedition it was thought a picnic by the volunteer guards, many of whom were turned away, but at the end of the first day, twenty of the troops, heat-sick, stole twenty of the Indians' ponies and deserted the command.[32]

Then for six astonishing pages Foreman quotes and summarizes the journal kept by the white conductor of that party during the period September 4 through November 5, 1838. In somber entries covering sixty-three days, the deaths of twenty-eight children are recorded, along with deaths of numerous adults.[33] Typically of the removal parties, this Potawatomi party was infected with typhus and suffered a total of forty-two deaths along the way.[34]

That Indiana case suggests something of the real scope of Indian Removal. Americans tend to recall Indian Removal as the experience of five "tribes" in the Southeast during one presidential administration and one decade, the 1830s. Its full description, however, involves at least fifty distinct peoples, many from an area north of the Ohio River reaching to Wisconsin, Minnesota, and Michigan and as far east as New York, and others from the present-day western states of Kansas, Nebraska, Texas, New Mexico, Arizona, Colorado, California, and Oregon. Rather than ending with the 1830s, the policy was effected in its most virulent form during the Civil War and continued through at least the 1870s. Arguably, the United States' forced relocation of Navajos in their land dispute with the Hopis is a late-twentieth century case of Indian Removal.

William E. Unrau estimates that by 1846 "approximately 10,000 persons [of the northeastern tribes] . . . had been forcibly settled in the eastern third of the future Kansas." Those tribes included the Ottawas, Delawares, Kickapoos, Miamis, Potawatomis, Sacs and Foxes, Shawnees, Chippewas, Kaskaskias, Peorias, Pianksashaws, Weas, Wyandots, and the Munsee and Stockbridge bands of New York.[35]

Then, from 1854 to 1871, the indigenous nations of Kansas and Nebraska again had to deal with pressures to cede their lands and undergo relocation. Railroads wanted rights of way through their lands, and because railroads need customers, they also wanted American settlers on those lands. About half the tribes of that area, such as the Pawnees and Poncas, underwent relocation to the area of present-day Oklahoma, and the others, such as the Omahas and Kansas Kickapoos, adjusted to severely reduced lands.[36] "Too often it is forgotten," write H. Craig Miner and William E. Unrau in *The End of Indian Kansas,*

> that between 1854 and 1871 there was accomplished a second major removal of Indians in America, and yet, by comparison to the first—the one inaugurated during the Jacksonian era—virtually nothing from a serious, documentary point of view is known about it. . . . Kansas, which became a United States territory when not one square foot of it was legally available for public ownership, presents a complex and unusual case. Yet its pattern affected more Indians and occupied more government time than the celebrated exploits of the military against the more warlike western tribes—a hackneyed theme that has prompted whole volumes on single campaigns.[37]

Indeed American historians have given thorough attention to military exploits against "warlike" tribes. Such stories were playing out in the northern extreme of the western drainage in the 1850s. American immigrants were provoking trouble on the lands of the Dakota peoples (better known to Americans by the pejorative label "Sioux," which came from an Anishinabe word meaning "snakes"). U. S. officials were beginning to implement the reservation policy on the north-central and west-central Plains. In the Treaty of Fort Laramie of 1851, the various Dakota peoples, the Mandans, Sahnish, Crows, Assiniboines, Cheyennes and Arapahoes accepted reservations.

On the eve of the U. S. Civil War, the indigenous nations of the western drainage had made room, however unwillingly, for more than fifty others from east of the Mississippi River. Each of the nations had taken a major hit to its economic system, but each still occupied common (or "communal") lands, conducted public affairs in the ancestral language, framed its government in indigenous institutions, and maintained the ancient relations with the spirit world. Their very survival was drastically threatened, however, and their circumstances would continue to deteriorate for several more generations.

Chapter 9

From Esteban to York: African Americans in the Purchase Territory During Three Centuries

Peter H. Wood

In 1776, the year that Thomas Jefferson drafted the Declaration of American Independence, not even the farsighted Virginian himself could forsee all that lay ahead for the colonists who openly challenged British rule. He certainly could not imagine that twenty-seven years later, as the president of a new republic, he would purchase the entire Louisiana Territory and double the size of the United States. As an innovative participant in the Enlightenment era, Mr. Jefferson loved numbers. So it seems fitting, as we acknowledge the bicentennial of his 1803 Louisiana Purchase, to begin with some population numbers, and to start in 1776—the other year that will always be associated with his name.

Later, the periodic national census that Jefferson had advocated would help to compile clear figures for the newly acquired territory, as its population spiraled upward during the next two hundred years. But no formal census data are available when we go back to the year 1776. Indeed, we are only beginning to develop a general grasp of the demographic picture for parts of North America during the eighteenth century.

According to recent estimates, roughly 51,000 people resided in the area that is now Mississippi, Louisiana, and East Texas in 1776. Over half (more than 28,000) of the inhabitants of the area were Native Americans: Choctaws, Chickasaws, Caddos, and others. But there were also more than 12,000 Europeans (primarily French and Spanish) and over 10,000 Africans, mostly concentrated along the lower Mississippi.

By 1790, the population of the same lower Valley region was approaching 75,000 people, but the growth was uneven. The Indian population had remained virtually unchanged, as refugees from eastern nations offset deaths from war and disease. The white population had jumped sharply, to at least 21,000, and the African-American population (black and mulatto, slave and free) had grown fastest of all, more than doubling in fifteen years to exceed 24,000.[1] Such numbers are suggestive, and they are forcing many Americans to consider for the first time what this audience already knows: that the Louisiana region was a crucial part of North American history long before President Jefferson purchased it for the United States.

Indeed, such numbers are gradually prompting us to revise the way we think about the entire unfolding of American history. As historian Colin Calloway has recently written, "Instead of viewing American history as the story of a westward-moving frontier—a line with Indians on one side, Europeans or Americans on the other—it might be more appropriate to think of it as a kaleidoscope, in which numerous Europeans, Africans, and

Indians were continually shifting positions."[2] This multi-colored kaleidoscope is older than we realize.

In 1533, the Spanish conquistador, Hernán Cortés, exploring the Pacific coast of northern Mexico, encountered the Baja peninsula. He presumed that it was an island, and he called it "California," a name drawn from a travel romance that had been published in Spain a quarter of a century before. That popular text featured a fanciful island in the New World, known as California and inhabited by a race of black Amazons. "Know that to the right hand of the Indies was an island called California, very near to the region of the Terrestrial Paradise, which was populated by black women [*mujeres negras*], without there being any man among them."[3]

By 1533, when Cortés named the Baja peninsula for this imaginary empire of the black Amazons, at least one real African had already reached the American West. Remarkably, we even know his Spanish name: Esteban—or Stephen, in English. He was one of 400 soldiers and servants who disembarked near Tampa Bay on Florida's west coast in 1528. The party's commander, Pánfilo de Narváez, hoped to explore the Gulf coast and discover another rich kingdom, comparable to the Aztec empire that Cortés and his men had toppled earlier in the same decade.

Narváez, however, proved hopelessly incompetent in the face of difficult conditions. Cut off from their supply ships and confronted by strong Indian opposition, most of the officers and men, both European and African, died in the wilderness or in a desperate attempt to reach the coast of Mexico aboard homemade rafts. At least fifteen, including Esteban, washed up on the coast of east Texas and survived for a time as slaves among the coastal Indians. Another who survived was Alvar Núñez Cabeza de Vaca, who had been the expedition's second in command. Sometime in 1535, Esteban and two Spaniards joined Cabeza de Vaca in a desperate trek that took them across the Southwest and then southward in western Mexico toward Guadalajara.[4]

The four travelers reported seeing large Indian pueblos in the Southwest that the Viceroy of Mexico took to be the fabled Seven Cities of Cíbola. So in 1539 he dispatched an exploration party northward, with Esteban as the guide. But Spanish slave raids had turned the Indians of western New Mexico against the intruders, and when Esteban was killed by the Native Americans, the party retreated back to Mexico.[5]

Technically speaking, Esteban probably never set foot in what would someday become the Louisiana Territory. But at the time of his death in New Mexico in 1539, other Africans, accompanying other Spaniards, were preparing to make their way into the Mississippi River Valley.

Two armies of transatlantic newcomers, each numbering in the hundreds, probed the North American interior. The party of Hernando De Soto moved northwest from Florida as far as western Arkansas, and the expedition of Francisco Vásquez de Coronado moved northeast from Arizona, all the way to central Kansas and northern Texas. The two competing enterprises searched in vain for cities of gold that would rival Peru's Inca empire seized by Francisco Pizarro in 1533. The two parties came within 300 miles of each other, in what would later become the Louisiana Territory.

One journal of the Coronado expedition mentions black participants in the course of describing a hail storm that hit the party on the plains of northern Texas. "While the army was resting," the account states, "a tempest came up one afternoon with a very high wind and hail, and in a very short space of time a great quantity of hailstones. . . ." The men attempted in vain to shield the horses with their armor, but "there was not a horse that did not break away, except two or three which the negroes protected by holding large sea nets over them. . . ."[6]

We know that Africans also took part in De Soto's expedition. When he landed on the Florida coast in 1539, his army included roughly 600 people—soldiers, priests, artisans, cooks, and servants—and some were Africans.[7] Before the army entered the Mississippi Valley, one of these Africans—"Gómez, a negro belonging to Vasco Gonçalez who spoke good Spanish"—defected from the invasion force and went to live with the Native Americans. He absconded with the Indian cacica, or queen, of the town of Cofitachequi. According to informants, "it was very certain that they held communication as husband and wife."[8]

Later in the grim De Soto odyssey, other Africans also remained behind, and some of them may have fathered children. At one Indian town, according to a chronicler of the expedition, "there had remained a Negro named Robles, who was sick and unable to travel. He was . . . entrusted to the cacique who very willingly and affectionately took upon himself the task of caring for and curing him. We have included an account of these details," the chronicler added, "so that when God, our Lord, shall will that that country be conquered and won, an effort may be made to see whether some trace or memory remains of those who thus stayed among the natives of that great kingdom."[9] If these early African visitors left any offspring behind, their descendants must have blended into the Indian communities of the American South over the course of six or eight generations.

After the expeditions of Coronado and De Soto, it was nearly 180 years before additional Africans entered the Mississippi Valley in any significant numbers. They came by sea, in chains, to the fledgling French colony of Louisiana. The first two French slave ships from the Bight of Benin arrived in 1719, a full century after the arrival of Africans in the English colony of Virginia.

The Louisiana colony had been struggling to survive for two decades since its founding in 1699. Labor remained exceedingly scarce, and provisions were chronically in short supply. The immigrant workers being shipped from Europe had little agricultural experience. Mortality was high, morale was low, and official oversight was characterized by corruption and neglect. A majority of European newcomers died or returned to Europe within a few years of their arrival. Although some Native Americans had been enslaved, their numbers were also declining rapidly. So not long after John Law's Company of the West took control of the colony in 1717, would-be planters turned to the importation of Africans in an effort to develop a profitable colony.

Between 1719 and 1721, eight ships brought 1,900 Africans to Louisiana. More than half died within several years of arrival. But more shipments followed, almost all coming directly from the coast of Africa, and almost all bringing people identified as Bambaras, taken from the interior of West Africa's Senegambian region.[10]

Between 1723 and 1729, the Company's ships brought 2,650 more people from Africa, mostly from Senegambia. As the white population sagged through death and departure during the 1720s, the colony's black population rose steadily. By the end of the decade some 3,600 African men and women were being forced to work in Louisiana. But conditions were extremely unstable, and a series of upheavals between 1729 and 1731 dislocated the slavery system almost as soon as it began.

Most of the Africans who survived the middle passage during the 1720s had been put to work clearing land along the Mississippi to grow tobacco and indigo. The labor was hard, the environment strange, the food meager, and the climate sickly. Parcels of strangers lived cramped together in crude and isolated barracks. Soon, they outnumbered the European inhabitants by roughly two to one, which prompted fearful white owners to impose harsh discipline. Possible alliances between Africans and Indians became a special source of fear among nervous officials. From the outset, historian Dan Usner points out, "Indian villagers were offered bounties of munitions and alcohol for capturing and returning runaways."[11]

But despite these efforts to divide and conquer, Native Americans often sided with the African newcomers. Many Indians had been enslaved alongside blacks; some had intermarried; and Indians and Africans often escaped bondage together. In 1728 the governor worried that if these so-called "maroons" established a refuge for additional runaways, planters would be unable to keep control. Then, as tobacco production encroached on the sacred lands of the Natchez, they prepared to resist, and rumors spread among black workers "that they would be free with the Indians."[12]

In November 1729, the Natchez launched their attack, killing more than 200 whites (over one tenth of the colony's entire French population) and taking captive some 300 enslaved African women and men. The French quickly mobilized a counterattack, using Choctaw allies to destroy Natchez villages and drive the Indians off their land. Some Africans accompanied the Natchez when they were dispersed; others committed suicide rather than return to bondage.[13]

If anything, the turmoil surrounding the Natchez Revolt only inspired further black resistance. In the summer of 1731, authorities in New Orleans uncovered an elaborate plot among Bambara slaves from Senegal. Supposedly, they intended to kill the French settlers while they attended mass, burn down the town, and liberate the colony. The leader proved to be a trusted African named Samba Bambara who had worked for the Company of the Indies as an interpreter in Senegal and an overseer in Louisiana. He was broken on the wheel along with some of his co-conspirators, and a woman implicated in the plan was hanged while armed colonists looked on, fearful of more unrest. Not surprisingly, rumors soon surfaced regarding a plot, real or imagined, to kill all the whites

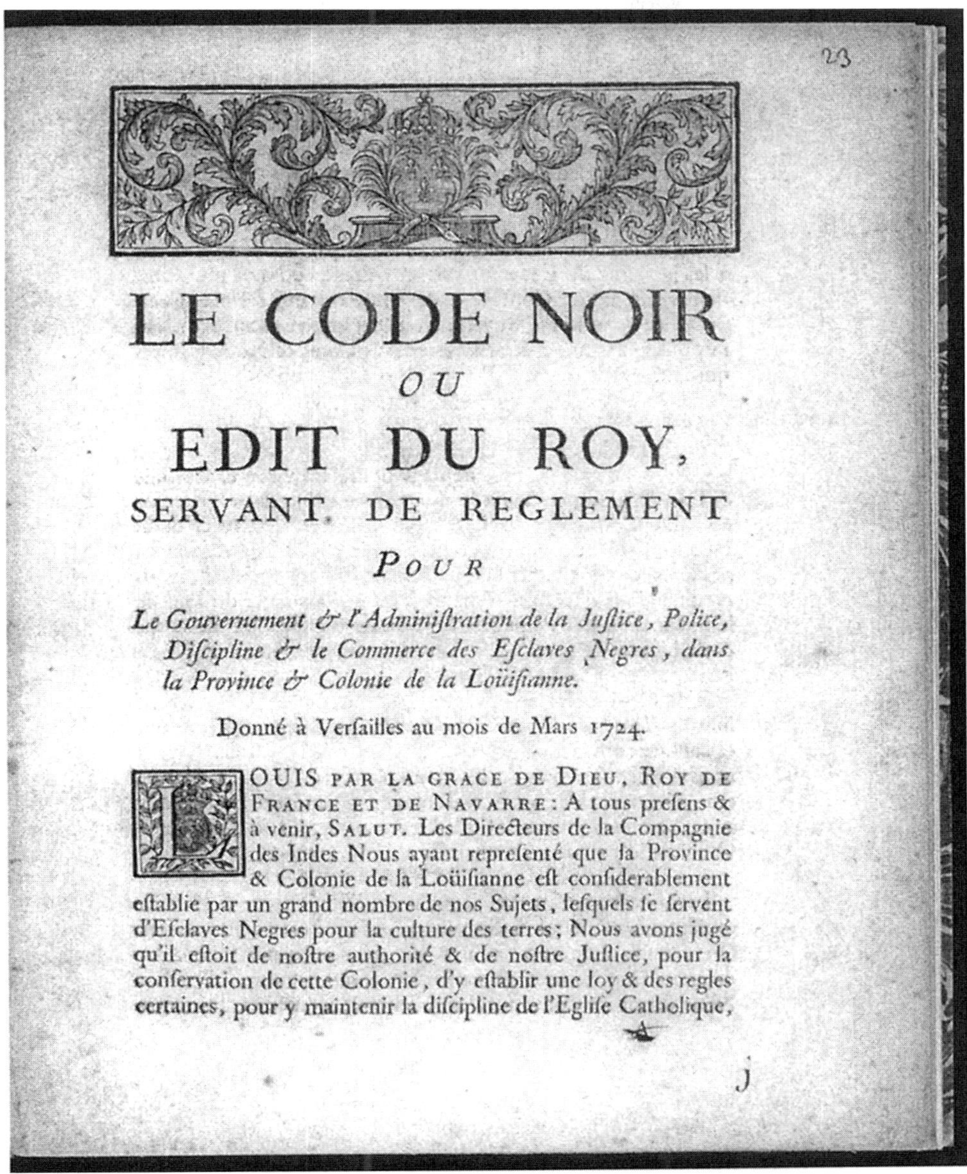

23

LE CODE NOIR
OU
EDIT DU ROY,
SERVANT DE REGLEMENT
POUR
Le Gouvernement & l'Administration de la Justice, Police, Discipline & le Commerce des Esclaves Negres, dans la Province & Colonie de la Loüisianne.

Donné à Versailles au mois de Mars 1724.

LOUIS PAR LA GRACE DE DIEU, ROY DE FRANCE ET DE NAVARRE: A tous présens & à venir, SALUT. Les Directeurs de la Compagnie des Indes Nous ayant representé que la Province & Colonie de la Loüisianne est considerablement establie par un grand nombre de nos Sujets, lesquels se servent d'Esclaves Negres pour la culture des terres; Nous avons jugé qu'il estoit de nostre authorité & de nostre Justice, pour la conservation de cette Colonie, d'y establir une loy & des regles certaines, pour y maintenir la discipline de l'Eglise Catholique,

Figure 6. First page, *Code Noir*, 1727. The Historic New Orleans Collection, Accession 82-158-RL. Courtesy of the Collection.

on Christmas Eve. A haughty Company official shrugged off the idea, but reported that "the riffraff of this city are alarmed to the point where all the little settlers are on guard and go to midnight mass armed like Don Quixote."[14]

The upheaval of 1729 to 1731 changed the direction of Louisiana culture in a variety of ways. Other historians have written at length about the distinctive society that emerged over the remaining years of the eighteenth century, and we now know far more than I can relate in a brief essay. But let me simply spell out half a dozen significant and interconnected developments that gave rise to a slavery colony unlike any other in North America.

First, the African slave trade was brought to an abrupt halt for more than a generation. Most southern slave societies began with small numbers of relatively assimilated "Atlantic creoles" until this so-called "charter generation" gave way to greater numbers of slaves imported directly from Africa. In Louisiana the opposite was true, as an initial influx of enslaved men and women directly from Africa was then followed by a long period of creolization. The effort to bring a full-blown slave society into being on the banks of the Mississippi in the single "bubble" decade of the 1720s had backfired, primarily because of the stiff opposition posed by the Africans themselves.[15]

No dominant and profitable staple crop emerged, and for decades the economy stagnated. Slave owners turned to the production of livestock, naval stores, lumber, and barrel staves. Lacking the wealth to import new workers and realizing that their slave labor force would have to reproduce itself naturally, they conceded the need for improved living conditions. Reluctantly, the French loosened the controls over their slave regime. To cut costs, slaves were allowed to grow their own gardens. Black overseers became commonplace instead of whites. Marriages were encouraged; miscegenation became common; and the free people of color increased steadily in number.

Despite a labyrinth of laws and restrictions, Africans in Louisiana experienced considerable, if grudging, autonomy in daily life. Many had access to regular free time and occasional money, to horses and boats, to knives and guns. Indeed, one of the most striking developments was that the frontier practice of arming blacks to fight, which died out rapidly in such English colonies as Virginia and South Carolina, expanded in Louisiana into an accepted and important tradition. Loyal slaves had helped in suppressing the Natchez uprising, and a free black militia would be cultivated in the second half of the century to help fight Indian enemies and foreign empires, and to suppress slave uprisings and maintain order.

Even more distinctive, perhaps, is the decidedly urban nature of Louisiana society. "In 1763," writes historian Ira Berlin, "fully one-third of the white population and one-quarter of the black population of Louisiana resided in and around the capital city, and an even larger proportion of both lived within a day's boat ride of the city."[16] All these developments, taken together, help explain the emergence of a vibrant and distinctive black creole cultural tradition in early Louisiana, even under the most trying conditions. Indeed, we could easily stay here in New Orleans and roam around Congo Square. But instead, I want to turn our attention briefly upriver.

Almost as soon as a sizeable African-American community took hold in the lower Mississippi valley, blacks also began to appear much further upstream. They were part of the grand French strategy to establish forts in a wide arc from the Great Lakes to the Gulf Coast. Trading posts and Catholic missions would secure the loyalty of Native Americans. New settlements would allow the French to exploit rich farmland, explore for mineral wealth, and block expansion by the English colonies further east. In 1717, France transferred jurisdiction over the Illinois Country from Canada to Louisiana, and in 1719 the French erected Fort Chartres in southern Illinois, between the recently established missions of Cahokia (1697) and Kaskaskia (1703).

In 1720, a year after the first slaves reached Louisiana, some of these Africans arrived in Illinois country. The entrepreneur Philippe Renault had the slaves row themselves upriver to Fort Chartres. There they were to construct Renault's nearby settlement, called St. Philippe, and to work in his proposed mines. More black workers would follow. In 1721, Governor Jean Baptiste Lemoyne, Sieur de Bienville, noted that forty newly-arrived Africans had been assigned "to row the boats that will ascend to the Illinois Country."[17]

The sparse records from Illinois Country reveal that by 1732 one hundred sixty-eight Africans made up more than one third of the area's population. In 1752, the non-Indian community consisted of 768 French and 445 enslaved African men, women, and children. A decade later, there were 600 whites and 500 blacks living at Kaskaskia. When the Paris Peace Treaty of 1763 conceded Illinois and much else to the British Empire, many of these French and Africans moved across the Mississippi into Upper Louisiana (nominally controlled by Spain) where they helped to found the fur-trading village of St. Louis. By 1776, blacks made up thirty percent of that new town's growing population.[18]

African Americans continued to arrive in St. Louis from all directions after the American Revolution. In 1800, for example, Jean Baptiste Pointe Du Sable—part French, part African—sold his holdings on the shore of Lake Michigan, where he had founded the trading post that would become Chicago. He died in 1818, just north of St. Louis, in St. Charles, Missouri. He was buried in the Roman Catholic cemetery there, where his grave was rediscovered in 1991.[19]

No such grave has ever been found for York, the Virginia-born slave and companion of William Clark who also passed through St. Louis. Indeed, his death remains a mystery. York seems to have been born in the early 1770s, the son of Old York and Rose, two slaves belonging to John Clark, whose own sixth son, William, was born in 1770. Roughly the same age, the two boys grew up together, hunting and fishing along the Rappahannock River. In 1784, the Clark family migrated from Virginia to Kentucky with their slaves, and York became the body servant of young William. Eventually, at John Clark's death in 1799, York became William's personal property.[20]

We know that York played an integral part on the famous expedition, living and working so closely with his master that Clark listed him sometimes as "2nd self" in his journal.[21] We also know that during the two-and-a-half-year trip he drew awe and admiration from Indian groups in the Northwest that had never seen "a black man before."[22] The Native Americans called York "the big Medison." When he was ordered to dance at a Mandan village, Clark reported that it "amused the Croud Verry much, and Somewhat astonished them, that So large a man should be active."[23]

The explorers named several natural features after York (on the Upper Missouri and the Yellowstone), but his name was left off a list of those who had served in the expedition and deserved compensation. His relations with his owner worsened in the ensuing years, and in November 1808 Clark wrote to his brother Jonathan that if York should attempt "to run off, or refuse to perform his duty as a Slave, I wish him Sent to New Orleans and Sold, or hired out to Some Sevare Master untill he thinks better of Such Conduct."[24]

It seems that York was hired out to a man from Louisville and then eventually was granted his freedom, before disappearing from the record. He may have died of cholera in Kentucky, or, just conceivably, he may have returned to the West and lived among the Crow Indians in north-central Wyoming. When a mountain man named Zenas Leonard visited a Crow community in 1832, he reported that, "In this village we found a Negro man, who informed us that he first came to this country with Lewis and Clark."[25]

In conclusion, two things strike me regarding early African-Americans in the Louisiana territory. First, we have been making enormous strides in exploring the black history of early Louisiana in recent years, thanks to the outstanding work of Daniel Usner, Gwendolyn Midlo Hall, Thomas Ingersall, Sylvia Frey, Jack D. L. Holmes, Robert McDonald, Hans Baade, Virginia "Ginger" Gould, the late Kimberly Hanger, Paul Lachance, Thomas Fierhrer, James McGowan, and many others. And there are people here today who are carrying on and expanding this tradition. You know as well as I do that important work remains to be done.

My second point also relates to writers of history, and it stems from reading once again about Esteban and York. While they lived in utterly different worlds, both have had a similar fate in the hands of generations of historians. After long years of neglect, they were brought forward in the late nineteenth century, only to be stereotyped and belittled in both history and fiction throughout the first half of the twentieth century. But by the 1960s, their stock began to rise rapidly. Since then, two generations of eager revisionists have turned the negative stories about these two men upside down. In fact, understandably, zealous authors have sometimes gone far beyond what the record dictates to mythologize each into a cardboard superhero who could do no wrong. We are only now beginning to take a deeper interest in their actual lives and to gain much-needed perspective on the situations in which they lived.

As we come to know the context for the accomplishments of Esteban and York, we may then be able to gain greater access to thousands of other Africans and African-

Americans and to build an appreciation for their difficult lives in the Louisiana region before Thomas Jefferson's purchase. Their numbers were not large. But their determination was extraordinary, their culture was vital, and their descendants are numerous. Hopefully, it is a story that we shall all be able to understand more fully, and respect more deeply, in the years ahead.

Chapter 10

Born a Slave, Born Free and "To Go Free": African-American Experiences in the Louisiana Purchase Area During the Antebellum Period

Celia E. Naylor-Ojurongbe

The history of the Louisiana Purchase territory, particularly the antebellum transformation of specific areas to United States' territories and then to states, significantly shaped the lived experiences of African Americans, both enslaved and free during the antebellum period. Partially as a result of this movement to statehood and Anglo-Americanization, some of the area's African-American denizens experienced a change from living within somewhat fluid, intercultural communities to more fixed hierarchical structures based firmly on racial ideology.

Louisiana, the State

The story of the changing position of enslaved African-Americans and free people of color (the *gens de couleur libres*) in Louisiana before and after 1803 is one that still evokes controversial and emotional exchanges between scholars.[1] My comments about Louisiana will highlight a few areas of inquiry that still remain unexamined or neglected, specifically in relation to African-American experiences.

Antebellum Louisiana was a tripartite society composed at the highest level of European-Americans and White Creoles, free people of color (including Creoles of Color) at the next level, and African-American slaves at the lowest level. In order to maintain social order and control, as Judith Schafer's stellar work illustrates, the laws of antebellum Louisiana reinforced the distinction between these separate populations.[2] Yet, even as the courts of Louisiana attempted to maintain distinctions between Whites, free people of color and slaves, in some ways they also facilitated the passing from one group to another—specifically the transformation of slaves to free people of color.

Although the French Louisiana's *Code Noir* of 1724 outlawed slave self-purchase, under the Spanish slave laws derived from the *Siete Partidas*, slaves had the right to self-purchase or *coartación*.[3] When in 1806, the Louisiana territorial legislature passed a new *Black Code*, it prohibited self-purchase on the grounds that slaves were not permitted to own property and thus could not purchase themselves. Slaves in American Louisiana could not force their owners to sell them; however, if their owners agreed to sell their slaves in this manner, a legal and binding contract for freedom was permitted. Although these cases were exceptional, they were unknown in other slave states.[4] The new code also required judicial authorization for manumission. In these cases, a slave had to meet two requirements: the slave had to be a minimum of thirty years old and also had to have a four-year record of good behavior prior to the manumission.[5]

After the Louisiana Purchase, the three segments (sometimes referred to as "castes") of Louisiana society became even more separate and distinct due to the escalating restrictions placed on manumission and growing discrimination against free people of color.[6] The existence of slaves and slavery in Louisiana not only affected the status and rights of slaves, but also the position and "place" of free people of color. Studies—such as the work of the late Kimberly S. Hanger—focused on the elaborate and complex lives of free people of color are furthering our understanding of the peculiar challenges confronted by free-born and freed people of color, as well as what Hanger describes as a group consciousness among Creoles of Color. More remains to be done on the ways Creoles of Color differentiated themselves from slaves and, in some cases, attempted to emulate the racialist ideas of the time by practicing racial endogamy.[7]

With the burgeoning interest and scholarship on women in the African diaspora, it is not surprising that one particular area of growing interest centers on the lives of Creole of Color women.[8] The forthcoming dissertation of Mary W. Williams explores the societal regulation of sexuality and the disposition of "property" in Louisiana from 1770-1830.[9] The dissertation-in-progress of Tamara McNeill argues that the race and class identities of Creoles of Color were constructed through the development of a gendered tripartite caste system.[10] Shirley E. Thompson's forthcoming book (*The Passing of a People: Creoles of Color in Mid-Nineteenth-Century-New Orleans*) emphasizes the social and political identities of Creoles of Color in New Orleans.[11] She, for example, examines notions of property and propriety in direct relation to male Creole of Color responses to the institution of plaçage (the extra-legal unions/liaisons or common law marriage between Creole of Color women and White men). The work of Mary Williams, Tamara McNeill and Shirley E. Thompson will undeniably usher in even more studies on the "place" and experiences of Creole of Color women.

The significant presence of free people of color in Louisiana has created a growing body of scholarship regarding this population; however, a similar trend in relation to Louisiana slaves has been virtually nonexistent. Except for Joe Gray Taylor's *Negro Slavery in Louisiana* (1963), Ann Patton Malone's *Sweet Chariot: Slave Family and Household Structure in Nineteenth-Century Louisiana* (1992), and a few dissertations in the last decade, slave culture in Louisiana still remains a crucial area of future research.[12] Although Taylor presents an account of the work lives of slaves as dictated by the demands of cotton and sugar plantations, the daily "private" lives of slaves and the world they created are relatively unexamined in his text. For instance, Taylor only briefly mentions and dismisses African "remnants" of spirituality.[13] The retention of African-based spiritual beliefs in Louisiana, particularly the adaptation of Yoruba-based cultural and religious practices, would be an especially fruitful area of investigation (particularly in light of the 1809 influx of refugees from Saint-Domingue). Katherine Olukemi Bankole's recent dissertation on West African survivals in antebellum Louisiana begins to unravel some of the necessary work in this area.[14]

As the question of slave resistance continues to demand further consideration in the Americas, so too should the expressed opposition of Louisiana slaves to their enslavement attract a significant amount of scholarly attention.[15] Junius Peter Rodriguez, Jr.'s dissertation, "Ripe for Revolt: Louisiana and the Tradition of Slave Insurrection, 1803-1865," presents Louisiana's vulnerability to slave unrest, as well as the legacy of slave insurrection in this region.[16] Additional examinations of the range of Louisiana slaves' responses to their subjugation would be especially useful in enhancing our understanding of Louisiana slaves and slavery in general. The focus should be not only on slave revolts in Louisiana (for example, the slave revolt of 1811 in St. John the Baptist Parish involving over five hundred Blacks), but also on other manifestations of slave resistance.[17] The available archival sources in this area (including slave narratives, newspapers and private collections) await scholars with innovative ideas about Louisiana's slave culture.

The Rest of the Purchase Territory

Although often the focal point of the Louisiana Purchase, Louisiana is, in fact, only part of the story. The status of African Americans in the other territories of the Louisiana Purchase area was shaped by the presence, absence or toleration of the peculiar institution. Congressional measures like the Missouri Compromise of 1819-1820 and the Kansas-Nebraska Act of 1854, dictating the expansion or restriction of slavery, affected the very fabric of society in a number of the Purchase Area territories.[18]

Although "Kansas" evokes visions of mass Black migration and "exodusters," the Black presence there was not numerically significant before the onset of the Civil War. The 1860 census enumerated 359 free Blacks and 266 mulattoes out of a total Kansas population of 107,204.[19] In 1860, 99% of Kansas's inhabitants were White settlers (both proslavery and free-soil), who set their sights on Kansas to further their personal and political convictions.[20] Overshadowed in national memory by "Bleeding Kansas," the actual struggles and lives of Blacks in antebellum Kansas remain an untold story.

The "free" territory of Nebraska, often described as the decidedly "free" counterpart of Kansas in the 1850s, was in fact home to African-American slaves.[21] In 1854, the first territorial census enumerated a total of 2,732 non-Native Americans in Nebraska, including thirteen slaves.[22] On December 5, 1860, Nebraska Territory was not only a home for a few African-American slaves, but it was also a site for at least one documented slave auction.[23] Indeed, some of the territorial legislature's first measures restricted Black rights and citizenship and attempted to exclude Blacks from residence.[24] Yet, in 1859, the territorial legislature in Omaha passed a law prohibiting slaveholding in the territory.[25] Sharing borders with Kansas, Missouri and Iowa, Nebraska also became an active passage on the Underground Railroad.[26] Although certainly not "Bleeding Kansas," the presence of free and enslaved African Americans in Nebraska contributed to uneasy contradictions and debate in the Nebraska Territory.

Nebraska was not the only territory that claimed freedom and exclusion simultaneously. Due to the provisions of the Missouri Compromise, slavery was proscribed in Iowa. Even so, slavery and slaves filtered into Iowa Territory. Established on July 4, 1838, Iowa Territory was certainly not the home of a substantial number of slaves. The 1840 census of Iowa indicated there were sixteen slaves (all residing in Dubuque), 172 "free colored persons" and 42,924 whites in the Territory of Iowa.[27] Due to the mere presence of Blacks, Iowa's first territorial Legislative Assembly (from November 1838 to January 1839 in Burlington) endorsed its own "Act to Regulate Blacks and Mulattoes and to Punish the Kidnapping of Such Persons." This act required free people of color to file their certificates of freedom before being allowed to reside in the territory and to post a $500 bond.[28] It also entitled slave-owning visitors to stay in Iowa with their slaves and in effect secured their property. The act further outlined a process for slaveholders to reclaim ownership of a Black or mulatto slave.

As this act directly pertained to restrictions on "free" persons of color and the protection of White slaveowners in Iowa, it was of limited assistance in the case of Rachel, an African-American woman who, although born a slave, sought to procure her freedom in Iowa. On May 2, 1839, Thomas S. Easton of Burlington petitioned the Iowa Territorial Supreme Court for a writ of habeas corpus. [29] Easton had bought Rachel in New Orleans at a slave auction on June 27, 1835 and then moved to Burlington. In his petition Easton stated that Rachel was "wrongfully, illegally and fraudulently held in custody and detained" by David Hendershott, Burlington's mayor. Both Mayor Hendershott and Rachel appeared in court on May 6 declaring that she "voluntarily" remained at the mayor's residence."[30] As a result of their actions, the next day Easton filed another petition claiming that Rachel was indeed his "proper goods and chattel" and should be returned to him. At 9:00 a.m. on May 8, all parties appeared before Charles Mason, Chief Justice of the Supreme Court of the Territory of Iowa. Easton decided to retract his petition. Judge Mason then ruled in favor of Rachel and ordered that she be released from custody. One local newspaper, the *Iowa Territorial Gazette*, stated: "It has been decided by Chief Justice Mason, at the present term of court, *that Slavery cannot exist in Iowa*. This decision settles the question at least for the present."[31] The newspaper's provocative statement did not reflect the reality entirely; it was primarily a promise of things to come.

Although Rachel's case was complicated by Easton's presence, the case of free people of color or hired slaves also appeared in the Iowa courts. On July 4, 1839, the first birthday of the Territory of Iowa, the Supreme Court of the Territory of Iowa presented its first published opinion—*In the matter of Ralph (a colored man) on Habeas Corpus*.[32] Ralph was born a slave in Virginia around 1795. In 1832, his owner, Jordan Montgomery, moved his family, including his slaves, from their home in Kentucky to an area near Palmyra in (northeastern) Missouri. This move, however, was not a particularly productive one for the Montgomery household. By 1834, Jordan Montgomery had signed a written contract with his slave Ralph agreeing to sell his freedom to him. The cost of Ralph's freedom was $500, with a $50 additional payment for his hire. Ralph was allowed to earn this money however he could, in effect becoming free although not yet paid for.

Ralph, like many others during this time, decided to try his luck in the lead mines in Dubuque, Iowa, approximately 300 miles away from Palmyra. Ralph, and other African-American slaves, believed that Iowa territory was a viable place to live a "free" life. Ralph's plans for a free life, however, were complicated by the passage of the "Act to Regulate Blacks and Mulattoes." Because of his declining finances, Jordan Montgomery decided to use the 1839 act to reclaim Ralph as his slave.

At 8:00 a.m. on July 4, 1839, the Supreme Court of the Territory of Iowa heard Ralph's case. Basing its decision on the Missouri Compromise, the court's ruling that day clarified Ralph's position in the territory. The court stated: "'The master who, subsequently to that Act [Missouri Compromise], permits his slave to become a resident here, cannot, afterwards, exercise any acts of ownership over him within this Territory. The law does not take away his property in express terms, but declares it no longer to be property at all. . . . We think, therefore, that the petitioner should be discharged from all custody and constraint, and be permitted to go free.'"[33]

Iowa represents one of many states in the Louisiana Purchase with contradictions. Although Ralph was able "to go free," in subsequent years the Iowa courts ensured that they would abide by the fugitive slave laws of the United States.[34] When, in 1846, Iowa achieved statehood, discriminatory laws reflected Iowa Territory residents' anti-Black stance. Exclusionary practices prevailed, including the continual rejection of Black male suffrage and a ban on free-Black immigration.[35] Despite the state's exclusionary laws, the Iowa free-Black population increased from 333 in 1850 to 1,069 in 1860.[36]

One of the reasons why delegates at Iowa's constitutional convention in 1844, and Iowa's state legislature in the 1850s, attempted to limit African-American immigration concerned the region's geographic location. Partially because of its proximity to the slave state of Missouri, Iowa became part of the Underground Railroad. Some Iowa residents regularly jeopardized their position within their communities in order to provide shelter, food and other forms of assistance to fugitive slaves. At the same time, due to the significant number of Iowa residents with anti-Black sentiments, the Territory of Iowa was for the most part a stop along the freedom trail and not the final destination.[37]

Minnesota's antebellum history, like that of its neighbor Iowa, reflected the reality of an African-American slave presence within a "free territory." In 1820, the establishment of Fort Snelling (located in southeastern Minnesota) encouraged European-American settlement in this region. Officers stationed at Fort Snelling brought their African-American slaves with them to their new post.[38] Perhaps the most famous Fort Snelling African-American resident was Dred Scott.[39] In addition to slaves of officers at Fort Snelling, Minnesota Territory also included slaves whose owners vacationed there during the summer months. Constructed in 1856-1857, Winslow House, a five-story limestone hotel by the St. Anthony Falls, attracted southern slaveholding families from Alabama, Mississippi, Louisiana, Tennessee and Missouri. Southern families traveled in style in steamboats up the Mississippi River to spend their vacation at the popular Minnesota summer resort.[40] Even though Minnesota's 1857 constitution included the prohibition of slavery in the state, businesspeople in St. Anthony eagerly welcomed their southern, slaveholding brethren and relied on their support of Minnesota's economy.

The conflict between Minnesota's constitutional position on slavery and the economic need for southern tourists came to a head in the summer of 1860. Only three years after the Dred Scott decision, African-American slave Eliza Winston's appeal for freedom in a Minnesota district court yielded an entirely different result.[41] The court's ruling in favor of Eliza Winston supported Minnesota's state laws and ignored the Supreme Court's Dred Scott decision. For months after this case, groups of White citizens in Minnesota harassed and attacked abolitionists and any supporters of Eliza Winston.[42] The conflicting views in this case regarding the position of Minnesota's Black residents mirrored the ongoing tensions within the state over Black rights, including Black male suffrage and the integration of Minnesota's public schools.[43]

Although the promise of freedom, no matter how precarious, in Iowa and Minnesota certainly appealed to some African-American slaves, others simply seized upon the potential of remarkable moments and events. The discovery of gold in 1858 at Cherry Creek (part of current day Denver) attracted persons from other territories and states, including free Blacks and slaves. The discovery of gold in Colorado motivated free and enslaved African Americans to migrate to the area in search of freedom, independence and economic opportunity. In his 1860 account of the 1859 Pikes Peak gold rush in Colorado, Albert Deane Richardson, a *New York Tribune* reporter noted that "Ethiopian Sam . . . is still the slave of Judge Elmore of Kansas. . . . The judge has permitted him to come to Pike's Peak, upon his agreement to pay twelve hundred dollars for himself as soon as he can accumulate the money." Ethiopian Sam's wife, Richardson stated, was "formally a slave of the Rev. 'Tom Johnson' of the Kansas Shawnee Mission; but from her earnings as a laundress saved and paid six hundred dollars for her freedom."[44] Certainly, Ethiopian Sam and his wife were not alone in their search for freedom "in the diggings."

Free and enslaved African Americans have not been one of the major, or minor, focal points in studies of the development of mining towns in Colorado or in other mining areas. Yet, one of Colorado's cherished pioneers is slave-born Clara Brown.[45] (figure 7) Born a slave in Virginia sometime between 1800 and 1806, she finally purchased her freedom in 1856.[46] She arrived in Denver in June 1859 and then moved on to Central City in the midst of the gold rush frenzy. Having worked as a laundress, Brown opened one of the region's first laundry businesses. Brown's business thrived in the mining town. She used her earnings to invest in her community, especially in the area of real estate. Brown also became the first Black inductee into the Society of Colorado Pioneers.[47]

Figure 7. *Clara Brown*. By permission of the Denver Public Library, Western History Collection, Z-275.

Declarations of Clara Brown's initial success in Colorado, however, may camouflage aspects of Colorado Territory's discriminatory practices. As was the case for Iowa and Nebraska, the Colorado territorial legislature also embraced exclusionary laws related to African Americans, including the prohibition of interracial marriages, Black suffrage and Black attendance in public schools.[48]

If responses to the "slavery question" differed in the states of Missouri, Kansas, Nebraska, Iowa, Minnesota and Colorado, in the case of Texas, the question of slavery was embedded within international politics and struggles over national sovereignty. Texas, often described as one of the South's footholds of slavery, represents one of the areas within the Purchase Area that changed dramatically during the antebellum period. In September 1821, news of independent Mexico's antislavery stance traveled throughout the United States offering what for some fugitive slaves had been seemingly unattainable: freedom.[49] African Americans, free and enslaved, crossed into Mexico's "free" land, especially the Mexican province of Texas (particularly eastern Texas) with hopes of freedom and land ownership.[50]

Land in Texas attracted European-American slaveholders as well. Some from the southeastern United States believed Texas was an ideal place to reproduce and extend chattel slavery. In 1822, Missourian Stephen F. Austin, "the Father of Texas," established the first legal settlement of Anglo-Americans in Texas.[51] By the fall of 1825, there were 443 bondspeople in Austin's colony alone, including 69 families in a total population of 1,800.[52] Even though slaves were present in Texas, the Mexican government had not issued an absolute decision on slavery. That changed when on March 11, 1827, a final declaration on slavery was included in Article 13 of the Constitution of the recently created state of Coahuila and Texas. It stated: "From and after the promulgation of the Constitution in the capital of each district, no one shall be born a slave in the state, and after six months the introduction of slaves under any pretext shall not be permitted."[53] Due to the new state's decree on slavery, Anglo slaveholders were forced to become creative about the classification of their slaves. European Americans worked within the constraints of the debt peonage system in Mexico. As a result, individuals who had been slaves in the South became indentured servants for life in Mexican Texas. A few Anglo-Texans even imported slaves from Africa through Cuba.[54]

On March 2, 1836, Texas declared its independence and in subsequent weeks adopted a constitution. Texas's new constitution wholly reflected the views of southern-born Anglo-Texans. It bestowed citizenship rights on all persons except Africans and the descendants of Africans and Indians. In an effort to exclude free Blacks from the new republic, the Constitution forbade free persons of African descent from residing permanently in the republic without the consent of the Texas Congress.[55] As a result, the freedom promised to Blacks by the independent nation of Mexico in 1821 disappeared fifteen years later. By their actions, Anglo-American Texans conveyed their intolerance for a free-Black presence within the new republic of Texas.

Having successfully recreated the "peculiar institution" within Texas, Anglo-Texans focused on expanding their property and profits within the new state. Texas, the home of 3,000 African-American "servants" in 1835 by 1840 included 12,570 slaves in 26 out of 32 Texas counties. An 1847 state census of Texas reported 102,691 Whites, 295 free Blacks and 38,753 slaves.[56] The first U. S. census of Texas in 1850 presented an even larger population of 58,161 slaves (and only 397 "free colored" people) out of Texas' total population of 212,592.[57] The state included 182,566 slaves by 1860—almost one third of the entire population of the state.[58] Texas (or *Tejas*), the Spanish pronunciation of a Caddo Indian word meaning "friends" or "allies," was neither friend nor ally to Black residents within its boundaries.[59]

African Americans and Native Americans

Although Texas' history provides one source for Mexican-American and African-American alliance and discord, perhaps one of the more interesting, yet often neglected, topics of interest in the Louisiana Purchase territory is that of African-American and Native American relations. Within the Purchase area, these interactions ranged from the adoption of Blacks into Native American communities to the enslavement of African Americans by Native American nations.

There has been limited historical analysis, in particular, of the relationships between African Americans and Native Americans involved in the fur trading economy in the current states of Missouri,[60] Colorado, Minnesota, Nebraska, Wyoming, Montana, and the Dakotas. Historians mining records involving the fur trading economy have highlighted several people of African descent who had significant involvement in this trade.[61] Notable fur traders of African descent include the slave Pierre Bonga and his son George Bonga; both were associated (by marriage) with the Ojibwa nation in Minnesota.[62]

Travelers' accounts of Colorado document the presence of African-American slaves working in Colorado's fur-trading center at Bent's Fort.[63] The African American most often mentioned in relation to Colorado fur trading is James Pierson Beckwourth (figure 8). Born a slave in Virginia in 1798, Beckwourth's father and owner relocated to Missouri in 1810. In the 1820s James Pierson Beckwourth trapped in various locations including Idaho and Wyoming. While in these areas, he developed and honed his skills as a hunter, trapper, interpreter and trader.[64]

It is not simply coincidental that the men mentioned here married Native women.[65] Marriage between African-American fur-traders and Native American women no doubt helped to cement relations between these fur traders and Native American nations. Even though these unions could have been grounded in loving relationships between the individuals involved, they also, for the fur traders, provided avenues of access into Native American fur-trading networks. An unwritten chapter in this region's historiography is certainly the involvement of African-American residents in the fur-trading economy.

Figure 8. *James Beckwourth*. By permission of the Nevada Historical Society, Las Vegas.

Enslaved and free African Americans not only contributed to the thriving fur trade in the Louisiana Purchase territory, but also facilitated the reestablishment of Native American communities in one particular region. The Louisiana Purchase provided an opportunity for the federal government to relocate a significant number of Native Americans from east of the Mississippi to an area west of it. Some Native Americans, however, made this journey with the assistance of their African-American slaves. As a result, the position of African Americans and the question of slavery were not only issues in U. S. territories that included a White majority, but also in one territory that represented a Native American majority—Indian Territory (present-day Oklahoma).

The examination of African-American enslavement by Native Americans has been for the most part focused on the Five Tribes: the Cherokees, Creeks, Choctaws, Chickasaws and Seminoles.[66] By the turn of the nineteenth century, slavery within the Five Tribes had become an integral aspect of life in these nations. What began as the trading of Indian slaves primarily due to warfare evolved in the eighteenth century into the enslavement of people of African descent.[67] When members of these five nations were forcibly relocated in the 1830s to Indian Territory, many Indian slaveholders took their slaves with them. Only a small percentage of Native American slave owners among the five nations owned over one hundred slaves; the majority of Native American slave owners operated small farms with under ten slaves. By 1860, African-American slaves in Indian Territory comprised 15% of the residents in the Cherokee Nation, 14% of the residents in the Choctaw Nation, 18% of the residents in the Chickasaw Nation, and 10% of the residents in the Creek Nation.[68] In addition to the slave population, there was also a small population of free Blacks living among the Five Tribes.[69]

Although clearly the property of Native Americans, slaves of African descent who were born and raised among the Five Tribes also understood their connection to these nations in terms other than enslavement. For some slaves of the Five Tribes their identification with Native American nations was embedded within their cultural, racial and national identity.[70] The interviews of ex-slaves of Oklahoma conducted in the 1930s provide evidence of the remarkable socio-cultural connections between African-Americans and Native Americans in Indian Territory.[71] Ex-slaves of the Five Tribes described how wearing Indian garb, preparing native meals, speaking an Indian language and even being a herb doctor or medicine woman significantly shaped their sense of themselves and their relationships to Indian communities and nations.[72] Their construction of their lives among Native Americans resulted in tangible and appreciable blood/familial, cultural and national connections with specific native communities. Even after the Civil War, African-American freed people in the Five Tribes attempted, with some success, to become recognized members of these nations. In fact, as a result of the Dawes Act of 1887, most enrolled freedpeople of the Five Tribes received land allotments in Indian Territory (figure 9).

Figure 9. *Chickasaw Free Persons Filing on Land Allotments, ca. 1889-1901*. By permission of the Oklahoma Historical Society, Photo Number 3759.

Summing Up

African Americans in search of socio-political freedom and economic opportunity looked to various territories within the Louisiana Purchase area as an answer to their dreams of freedom. Many were able to navigate from one area to another in order to assert or reclaim their freedom. Some succeeded with the assistance of Black and White "conductors" along the Underground Railroad. For others, dreams of freedom were thwarted by the realization of racial injustice on the "frontier." They discovered that even "free" territories were not havens for freedom; rather, their presence in some areas was restricted, confined and in some cases barely tolerated. Nonetheless, enslaved and free people of African descent carved out lives for themselves and their families in slave quarters, in "free" communities and even on the run and, by so doing, they have left an indelible mark on the Louisiana Purchase territory's history.

Chapter 11

The Louisiana Purchase and the Francophones of Louisiana

Glenn R. Conrad

This conference on the Louisiana Purchase and its aftermath affords me the opportunity to suggest to younger historians the need for a detailed examination of the French community's lack of significant political cohesiveness in the face of this monumental event and the political and social developments in Louisiana that followed it during the nineteenth century. In the pages that follow, I will suggest some of the dimensions of this seeming paradox.

For the casual observer, it is easy to conclude that because the Francophones entered Louisiana under roughly similar circumstances in the two centuries between 1700 and 1900 they shared a common cultural outlook and as a result formed a cohesive Gallic culture on the Gulf Coast best labeled "French Louisiana." Such a culture, one would reason, should have been capable of providing a political and economic reaction to the Purchase and its aftermath that would have been meaningful throughout most of the nineteenth century. A more studied examination of Louisiana Francophones, however, reveals that for the first two centuries or so of their shared Louisiana experience, the several French-speaking communities maintained only loose, sometimes antagonistic relationships with one another. So often they interacted not as Gallic brothers but more like peevish distant cousins. This situation resulted from the fact that the various groups spent sufficient time elsewhere, in broadly dissimilar environments, to develop peculiar subcultures—their own ways of life—which they transported to Louisiana and jealously protected for generations. Their only apparent cultural linkages were their Roman Catholic faith, be it nominal or not, and their language.

Most French-speakers who migrated to Louisiana can be categorized as adventurers, exiles, or refugees. Although they arrived from dissimilar environments, most had shared similar traumatic experiences: war, revolution, social upheaval, the frontier, and man's inhumanity to man. For many, these experiences produced psychological scars that persist until today. Thus Louisiana Francophones, although sharing a cultural genesis, erected social barriers to protect their recollected ways of life (as lived elsewhere) and built class ramparts to guard their idealized visions of their futures. In doing so, they sought to offset not only the cultural onslaughts of a strange land teeming with non-French-speakers but also to isolate themselves from the misunderstood cultural mores of their Gallic kinsmen. As the first two centuries of the Louisiana experience unfolded, these social barriers became psychologically institutionalized and remained, well into the twentieth century, prime considerations in any interactions between Louisiana Francophones.

There are, for students of French Louisiana, four varieties of Gallic culture in the state. First, immigrants coming directly to Louisiana from France in the first half of the eighteenth century developed a strain. Second, inhabitants of eastern Canada developed a culture between 1605 and 1755 that the Acadians conveyed to Louisiana. Third, refugees from the Saint-Domingue revolution introduced a strain that evolved in the French West Indies during the eighteenth century. Fourth, political and social exiles carried nineteenth-century French culture to Louisiana.

The initial wave of Francophones in Louisiana, coming between 1700 and 1765, breached the wilderness, opened the frontier, and spread itself thinly across the broad Mississippi Valley. This group was, however, largely unprepared physically or psychologically for the cruel world of the frontier that taunted their spirit of adventure.[1] The goal of many of these immigrants, whether they were from France or Canada, was to reap the wealth of the Indies, and return home to an aristocratic lifestyle. But the consequences of events on the Plains of Abraham (the British capture of Quebec, 1759) and later the storming of the Bastille (July 1789) altered forever the daydreams of these adventurers.

As the first half of the eighteenth century slipped away, the dreams of the colonial survivors, frequently punctuated with nightmares, took on the dimensions of reality.[2] Gradually, agricultural pursuits were substituted for exhausting and fruitless expeditions in search of Cibolan wealth. Colonists began to congregate in definable limits and villages arose, most importantly the entrepôt of New Orleans.[3]

Within three or four decades of the founding of New Orleans in 1718, the pioneering agricultural units to be found along the Mississippi River above and below the city underwent a metamorphosis. Farms began to take on the characteristics of tropical plantations, especially after the introduction of slave labor and its persistence thereafter as a method of production.[4]

The rise of a plantation economy, with its social consequences for master and slave, generated a new strand in the social fabric of the Louisiana frontier, an incipient colonial aristocracy. The Louisiana environment was subtly transforming the European values of the colonists and effecting among them a cultural metamorphosis from Frenchman to Louisiana Creole.[5]

Into this budding world of the Louisiana Creole, there unexpectedly arrived a group of northern Francophones, the exiled Acadians. Largely an unlettered peasant society, the Acadians embraced a distinct subculture born of one hundred and fifty years in the frozen world of Canadian winters, on the rocky soils of maritime districts, and in a relatively quiet realm of virtual social isolation.[6]

The Acadians, forced from their home of 150 years by an imperial contest that meant little to them, became wanderers and as such added still another dimension to their New World adventure.[7] This fiercely independent yeomanry experienced years of psychological and cultural degradation in the English Atlantic colonies, in France, and in Saint-Domingue. In each of these strange worlds, the Acadians perceived stark evidence of the danger to the human spirit inherent in the cultural clash of a majority and a minority.

It is no wonder, then, that Acadians continued their travels, seeking a place where they might preserve and project their way of life, be it real or imagined, as it had been in Acadia. That way of life had been unmistakably pastoral, incorporating values more akin to those of the sixteenth-century's Age of Faith than to those of the aristocratic eighteenth-century's Enlightenment.

The Acadians' odyssey brought the first large contingent to Louisiana in February 1765.[8] There on the broad coastal plain, they found their promised land. There, too, they found splendid isolation from the antagonistic world of the eighteenth century. There, in the tangled wilderness of the bayou country and on the broad, empty prairies, they found shelter for themselves from the strange lifestyle of their Creole kinsmen.[9] During the two decades that followed the arrival of the first of these exiles, fully three to four thousand Acadian kith and kin made their way to Louisiana.

The explosion of racial warfare in the French colony of Saint-Domingue in the late eighteenth century impelled thousands of refugees directly toward Louisiana, or to Louisiana after a brief sojourn in Cuba, Jamaica, or several American east coast cities. This exodus was unusual, for in addition to the white planter aristocracy, their minions, and their black slaves, hundreds of planters of mixed race, the so-called *gens de couleur libres* or "black Creoles," and all who found themselves within their social and economic orbit, were also forced from their century-old cultural milieu by the Haitian rebels.[10]

For the most part, the Saint-Domingue refugees were members of a sophisticated provincial aristocracy or were part of the service-oriented bourgeoisie, both groups having maintained strong ties with the metropole while evolving their peculiar West Indian Creole culture. That lifestyle, together with their social affinity for Louisiana Creoles, sufficed to allow these island Creoles to permeate the world of the Mississippi planter class and their urban commercial counterparts. Indeed, the rapport between these two Creole elites was so strong that it is possible, beginning in the early nineteenth century, to speak simply of "the Creoles."[11]

Finally, beginning with the French Revolution and Age of Napoleon and perhaps terminating in the aftermath of the Franco-Prussian War, thousands of French immigrants poured into Louisiana, carrying with them their nineteenth-century cultural baggage. Mostly identifying with the middle class, these newly-arrived Francophones settled in New Orleans, by then the commercial capital of the South, or fanned out across the state, establishing themselves in the smaller towns. Like all good bourgeoisie, they opened shops and joined their non-French counterparts in the embrace of Victorian values.[12]

With this exposition as background, the question can be asked: Did these culturally disparate French-speaking groups, at the time of the Louisiana Purchase and the years that followed, forge a common, a synthetic, Louisiana Gallic culture that went beyond their religion and their language to embrace a political response to the coming of the Americans?

The answer is that they did and they did not. That they did was a result of class consciousness among Creoles and the Foreign French; that they did not was reflected in the near absence of Acadian thought in the elitist Creole agenda between 1804 and the Constitution of 1812. Professor Warren Billings has noted:

> President Jefferson's arrangements for the Territory of Orleans ignored Creole concerns and appeared to break faith with the Treaty of Cession. Territorial Governor William C. C. Claiborne's hostility to things Latin consequently heightened the clamor for statehood among native Louisianians who saw in early admission the means of checking the intrusion of American influences upon their customs, their language, and their law.[13]

With these concerns in mind, a delegation of Creoles went before Congress in 1804 to request immediate statehood. Their plea was rejected and the Territory of Orleans was born. Five years later Creoles in the Territorial Legislature, with the help of some prominent Americans, again petitioned Congress for statehood, which was finally forthcoming in 1812.[14]

Before that, however, a state constitution had to be drafted and approved by Congress. The Creoles and Foreign French, with a sprinkling of Americans, met in the Constitutional Convention to produce the Constitution of 1812. (As an aside, 26 of the 45 convention delegates were Creoles or Foreign French. Only one Acadian name is found in the roster of delegates.) Whether this constitution was "aristocratic" and thus favored the Creole planter class and mercantile princes of New Orleans or was greatly similar to the constitutions of other states entering the Union at that time, the fact is that it allowed the Creoles to hold sway over Louisiana for the next 33 years or until adoption of the Constitution of 1845. By the 1820s and 1830s there were growing signs that the Creoles would abdicate their leadership role to the growing number of Americans, rather than contest the political ascendancy of the Americans in coalition with the Foreign French and the Acadians. The majority of Creoles preferred to return to the "subtleties of good living which derived naturally from their noble lineages." Rather than haggle with the crude Americans in the legislative forum, they much preferred "enjoying the balls and the dances, betting heavily at the table or perhaps at the cockpit, endlessly smoking . . . [the] inevitable cigar, whiling away hours over [their] beloved dominoes, busying [themselves] with the demands of . . . [a] close-knit family life."[15] Afterward, the Creoles did forge business contacts with the small town and rural Francophones, but gave little or no thought to forming an alliance with these groups to contest the political ascendancy of the Americans.

Apparently the Creole planters were unaware of the sweeping political changes of the nineteenth century brought on by the American and French revolutions, especially the concepts of republican government. Instead, they seemed determined to bring to perfection a lifestyle that they had engendered in earlier times on the banks of the Mississippi or on the plains of Saint-Domingue. What they were fabricating was their conceptualization of a pre-revolutionary French provincial aristocracy that included a world of black slaves and peasant Acadians.

By the 1850s the New Orleans Creoles were becoming beleaguered by other ethnic groups seeking their fortunes in the metropolis of the South. Provincial in outlook, the Creoles were in no way prepared to compete for leadership with the Americans and Foreign French.

Then, a decade later, the world of the planter aristocracy exploded as a result of the great American ideological contest and its attendant civil war. Staggering up from the social, political, and economic debris of war and Reconstruction, the Creole remnant entered a half century or so of cultural stagnation that ended early in the twentieth century in the dispersal and integration of their society into the mainstream. Their role as spokesmen for Louisiana Francophones, never over-arching, was terminated and today lives only in the realm of family tradition or in commercialized cultural myth.

The nineteenth-century French immigrants, those whom Professor Joseph Tregle calls "The Foreign French," were probably the best equipped group of those under examination to formulate a Gallic cultural synthesis in the post-Purchase period. They were for the most part political expatriates sufficiently imbued with nineteenth-century concepts of nationalism to understand the political and economic consequences of a politically articulate Francophone populace. They possessed the intellectual capacity to create a *parti français* composed of Creoles, Acadians, and themselves.

Only to a minor degree, however, did the nineteenth century immigrants formulate a program designed to bring Louisiana's Francophones together. Acting spasmodically, the immigrants formed a few fraternities, organized scattered literary societies, and launched a French or bilingual newspaper here and there. But, unlike other ethnic and racial groups in post-Civil War Louisiana, the Francophones did not use such organizations and literary outlets to grind their political axe. Possibly many Creoles regarded such organizations and literary outlets as being beneath their social status, while most Acadians would have regarded them as bewildering.

A reason for the immigrants' inaction in this regard is not difficult to find. The immigrants were, basically speaking, middle class, living in the typical middle-class havens of the western world: cities and towns. In these settings they discovered that their values were carbon copies of those of their American, German, and Irish neighbors. Moreover, these Frenchmen regarded themselves as being the economic and social equals of the rest of the community, and they were accepted as such. They did not see themselves as organizers of, or participants in, a *parti français*. Indeed, after a generation or two, the immigrants were flowing gently into the American mainstream.

Finally, we come to the Acadians. If, as noted, these people came to Louisiana determined to preserve and protect a set of values honed during 150 years in Acadia, they certainly succeeded. Throughout the remainder of the eighteenth century, during the nineteenth, and into the twentieth they preserved, with some significant exceptions, their pastoral lifestyle in the bayou country and prairies of south Louisiana. Thus the Acadians, in more-or-less cultural isolation, were disregarded, overlooked, and often denigrated by the

Creoles, the immigrants, and eventually by Americans. (Parenthetically let me say, it is regrettable that some contemporary Acadians engage in American-bashing for the loss of their cultural heritage, when, in fact, their Gallic kinsmen, through lack of political and economic unity, contributed greatly to the disappearance or transformation of that heritage.) No one, therefore, could have reasonably expected the Acadians to forsake the haven of "New Acadia" to undertake a leadership role in organizing a *parti français*, despite the fact that two Acadians were elected governor of Louisiana during the antebellum era.

Thus, it is possible to conclude that a French political synthesis in Louisiana to address the *fait accompli* of the Louisiana Purchase and matters subsequent to it could not be forged given the disparate social, economic, and political backgrounds of Louisiana Francophones.

Chapter 12

"In Territories So Extensive and Fertile": Spanish and English-Speaking Peoples in Louisiana Before the Purchase

Light T. Cummins

It is my purpose today to talk about Louisiana during one of its briefest historical eras, the period from the mid-1760s until 1803, during which time the province was a colony of Spain. Louisiana's Spanish period witnessed vibrant growth, remarkable expansion, and a conspicuous progress that have left indelible influences on the modern state. This was especially the case regarding the creation of a distinctive ethnic diversity; that is, an historically identifiable colonial complex that clearly rivaled in durability and sophistication those elsewhere in North America. Although a complete analysis of the lower Mississippi Valley as such a region is beyond the limited scope of this paper, it can be noted that one means whereby the Spaniards helped to forge this area into a well-defined colonial complex was social control.

Spain had no choice upon receiving Louisiana after the Seven Year's War but to implement and maintain a determined social control over the colony. Social control, as used in this context, is—as sociologist Joseph S. Roucek has noted in his seminal work on the subject—"the collective term for those processes . . . where one group determines the behavior of another group" in order "to stabilize society and to provide a means for orderly and continuous adaptation and change."[1] In Louisiana, Spain used two methods to achieve this social control.

Spain's efforts to maintain social control involved the firm establishment of Spanish political, economic, and social institutions along the lower Mississippi in an effort to bring order and structure to an increasingly varied population and the expansion of that population with persons of various ethnicities, making it even more diverse. Spaniards found and added to a unique blend of Euro-African norms in Louisiana in areas such as colonial government, art, architecture, economic development, society, culture, and religion. The ethnic parameters of this Louisiana colonial complex expanded during the three decades of Spanish sovereignty to include Acadians, Canary Islanders, French refugees from the Haitian Revolt, a considerable number of African slaves and, notably, the addition of English-speaking settlers in larger numbers. Spain encouraged the inclusion of this English-speaking population as an additional means of maintaining social control in Louisiana. This defensive colonization became a tool whereby Spain could hopefully hold the province in the face of threatening international encroachments. In short, the immigration which Spain fostered in Louisiana became a means of social control because it diffused social, cultural, economic, and political power among different groups of settlers. The result was the creation of a unique colonial complex that was neither French, Spanish, Anglo-American, nor African, but a combination of all of them.

Spanish colonial administrators in Louisiana faced, from the very moment that Spain received the colony at the Peace of Paris in 1763, the difficult and daunting task of governing a colony whose population was predominately non-Hispanic, whose governmental institutions were not those of Spain, and whose geo-political situation guaranteed that Louisiana would be a crossroads of many conflicting interests. Governing the colony was an almost overwhelming task because relatively few Spaniards ever came to the colony and many of those who did were sojourners in the category of governmental officials, military officers and soldiers, or other public servants.

The efforts of the Spanish government to maintain social control in this colonial atmosphere can be seen, by way of example, in the actions of several royal governors who served in the colony. Antonio de Ulloa, Spain's first governor in Louisiana, was a renowned naturalist and scientist, a founder of the Natural History Museum in Madrid, a member of the British Royal Society, and the first scientific researcher to identify platinum as a distinct metal. It is somewhat ironic, therefore, that Ulloa's tenure as governor of Louisiana ended in disaster and disgrace when an unruly mob of protestors drove him from the colony. The collapse of his administration, however, had an unforeseen result: social control became the center piece for Spain's governmental emphasis in Louisiana. It would be accomplished both by coercion and co-option.

General Alexander O'Reilly was the first of Spain's administrators who left a lasting mark on the history of Louisiana. He used coercion when he arrested the leaders who had revolted against his predecessor, Antonio de Ulloa. Several of them received the death penalty, while others paid with long prison sentences. O'Reilly, however, also used co-option in creating a workable system of social controls for Spanish Louisiana. Students of law and jurisprudence know that he promulgated the famous Code O'Reilly, which blended the influences of Spanish law with French procedure to create the lasting singularity of Louisiana law.[2] He also addressed an additional series of political and legal matters that dealt with such diverse concerns as land owning and slavery in Louisiana. His land regulations of 1770 changed the basic structure of property acquisition in Louisiana. This decree outlined the process whereby land grants were to be made, set procedures for land owning, and institutionalized a system permitting provincial administrators to began making a substantial and increasing number of land grants. As one historian has noted of this decree: "Its provisions represented a liberality of land grants that would not be seen in the United States until the Homestead Act of the 1860s."[3] The Code O'Reilly also outlined the basic provisions of slave holding that would give a distinctive character to that institution in Louisiana. O'Reilly abolished the previous French *Code Noir*, substituting in its place the Spanish laws on slavery that harked back to *Las Siete Partidas* that were promulgated in the 1260s. These laws were more humane than those of France, and later of the United States. "Overall," as historian Gilbert C. Din has noted, "Spanish law came down strongly on the side of slaves who sought freedom and against their masters who tried to prevent it."[4] O'Reilly also turned his attention to governmental structures. It was he, for example, who created the singular Louisiana local political units of the parishes, a uniqueness that remains until the present day. He also dissolved the French Superior Council and instituted the Cabildo as New Orleans's municipal governing body.

Although he governed in Spanish Louisiana for only a scant seven months, General O'Reilly engaged in numerous other activities that left their mark on the colony. He ordered the taking of the first accurate and impartial census in 1769. He improved relations with Native Americans while he also attempted to stop British smuggling along the lower Mississippi River. He was also the first administrator, but most certainly not the last, who attempted to bring order to New Orleans's teeming and colorful urban life when he issued decrees to regulate taverns, bars, inns, billiard parlors, and public houses. O'Reilly also organized the Louisiana militia. And not least, he undertook a series of public improvements that included levee and road construction.

O'Reilly's successor, Luis de Unzaga y Amezaga, began to exercise administrative power as Louisiana governor at the time of O'Reilly's departure in March 1770. "He exhibited many characteristics of a pacifier," one historian has written of Unzaga, "having skills as an organizer, a calm temperament in decision making, evenhandedness, and a methodical nature that sometimes frustrated subordinates who sought quick and expedient action."[5] He proved to be the perfect sort of governor to bring tranquility to Louisiana while he continued to implement policies of social control. During his tenure, Unzaga strengthened the Spanish judicial system instituted by O'Reilly. He opened a public school at New Orleans. Unzaga had a commitment, as well, to increasing the colony's trade connections. The commerce of Louisiana, for that reason, greatly expanded during the period of his leadership, although an upswing in smuggling—especially with British merchants in nearby West Florida—was an unintended result of his liberal commercial policies. Governor Unzaga also had to deal with the opening phases of the American Revolution and the impact that this conflict had on the lower Mississippi. As Louisiana governor, he permitted rebel expeditions to take refuge in the city while he unofficially sanctioned at New Orleans the pro-American activity of Oliver Pollock, who would eventually receive a formal appointment as the agent of the Continental Congress in the Crescent City.

It was Unzaga's successor as governor, Bernardo de Gálvez, who dealt with the military pressures in Spanish Louisiana that the British colonial revolt created. Gálvez, as a member of a powerful and well-connected family at court in Spain, put Louisiana on a sound military footing starting in 1777 when he took office. The governor also showed overt sympathy for the American rebels while he treated the British as traditional enemies, which they had always been to the Spaniards. Once Spain entered the war as a belligerent in 1779, Bernardo de Gálvez won a series of military victories over the next three years that conquered all of British West Florida. Gálvez's contributions, however, were not limited to his exploits during the American Revolution. He paid particular attention to maintaining social control over Louisiana's increasingly diverse population. His administration witnessed the settlement of New Iberia and the strengthening of Louisiana's fugitive slave laws.

Gálvez's successor as Governor of Louisiana, Esteban Rodriguez Miro, assumed office at New Orleans on an interim basis during the American Revolution while Gálvez, still holding the appointment as governor, was absent from the colony conducting his military campaigns. Miro officially became governor in 1785 and remained on the job until 1791. It was during these years that the demographic pressure of an expanding United States began to be felt in Spanish Louisiana. Like his predecessors who faced a Francophone majority, Miro also adopted social control policies, clearly favoring cooption rather than coercion. He promulgated land distribution policies that sought to control the influx of English-speaking settlers into lower Spanish Louisiana, especially in the Natchez District, as a "counter-colonizing" measure. He welcomed all Anglo-American settlers who would pledge loyalty to Spain in exchange for ownership of land. It is impossible to overestimate the historical importance of this action on Miro's part. It was Miro's idea in 1785 and 1786 that the potential rivalry between Spanish colonial authority and Anglo-American frontier folk could be resolved by trading land for national loyalty. Miro's policy set in motion an ever-increasing immigration of Anglo-Americans into the lower Mississippi Valley. All of these English-speaking settlers signed loyalty oaths to the King of Spain in exchange for land and the promise of a new life on it. Beyond this rather momentous impact on the development of Louisiana history, Miro also shaped the colony further by negotiating treaties with the Native Americans of the area, holding a series of congresses at Pensacola and Mobile. He also became involved in the frontier intrigues of General James Wilkinson, that roguish frontier rascal who schemed to make the western part of the United States independent and ally it with Spain. Miro put the American general on the Spanish payroll as a spy and informant. Miro saw his arrangements with Wilkinson as part of the larger scheme to settle English-speaking immigrants on the lower Mississippi in Spanish territory.

Miro's successor, François-Louis Hector, the Baron de Carondelet, replaced Miro as Louisiana governor in 1791, continuing in effect all of his predecessors' policies and programs of social control. This was especially the case regarding immigration of English-speaking settlers into the colony. Like Miro, Carondelet sought to attract new migrants from both Europe and the United States, hoping to convert them into loyal Spanish subjects in exchange for land. But unlike his predecessors, he had to deal full force with the social control issues that the French Revolution of 1789 created in Louisiana. In the face of this revolution, the Francophone European majority in Louisiana manifested varying degrees of sympathy or revulsion for events in France. Carondelet, a monarchist by inclination, worked to defend Louisiana against what he saw as revolutionary sedition. This became a very real problem for the Louisiana governor when a group of New Orleans residents sent representatives to France to express support for the revolutionary cause. Carondelet took stern measures to stamp out what he styled "Jacobinism" by augmenting the number of royal troops stationed in the colony and by requiring loyalty oaths from residents. He also engaged in a series of arrests and banishments. He worked to place in positions of local government and militia command only those residents who rejected the French Revolution and supported Spanish hegemony. Carondolet's problems with revolutionary fever did not come only from the problems in Louisiana relating to the French Revolution. The difficulties associated with the Haitian slave revolt on the island of Saint-Dominque also threatened the social control of Spanish Louisiana throughout his period as governor.

Carondelet believed that the cruelty of the Saint-Domingue planters toward their slaves had been a key cause of the 1791 revolt eventually led by Toussant L'Ouverture. He thus decided to regulate slave affairs in Louisiana to the end of preventing the sort of abuses along the Mississippi that he felt had been endemic in the French West Indies. He also sought to improve the lot of free Blacks in the colony as part of this process. Although a laudatory policy by modern standards, Carondelet's attempt to liberalize slave conditions had the opposite effect because slaves in some areas of Louisiana began to challenge their masters' authority and engage in other obstreperous behaviors. This caused the governor to retreat from his previously proclaimed policy and issue stern proclamations. Such actions on his part were no doubt a contributing factor to unrest among the slaves of the Point Coupée district north of Baton Rouge in the mid-1790s. Although historians have subsequently debated about how real the Point Coupée Slave Conspiracy was, Governor Carondelet and the Louisiana planters had no such doubts in 1795. They were convinced that the Point Coupée district harbored disloyal slaves who threatened the safety and security of the colony as they supposedly organized for revolt. The governor swiftly sprang into action as Spanish officials arrested sixty supposed slave conspirators. Twenty-three of them were executed and their heads hung on poles along the river as a warning to future conspirators, while the remaining slave prisoners received forced labor sentences under the most harsh of conditions. This was social control at its most coercive. Carondelet's fears about the influences of the French Revolution, coupled to his concerns about organized slave insurrection, resulted in his issuing a comprehensive set of policy codes and slave regulations in 1795. "The new code established," one historian has noted of Carondelet's edict, "a draconian slave regime under which all Blacks were subject to the complete authority of any and all whites, regardless of which whites owned them."[6]

These slave regulations made the lower Mississippi a more attractive destination for French West Indian planters, who brought their slave gangs to Louisiana in order to escape unrest in the Caribbean. This refugee population brought a distinct brand of French Creole culture to Louisiana that permeated the entire province by the time of the Louisiana Purchase. As one scholar has noted: "many of the strong French cultural influences so visible to Anglo-American residents during the early statehood period existed due to the influx of recent immigrants from Saint-Domingue, who were still in the process of becoming acculturated to Louisiana, especially at New Orleans."[7] In addition, this immigration gave the institution of slavery in Spanish Louisiana at the close of the eighteenth century a distinctly West Indian flavor that it had not previously had, and which would endure well into the American period.

By the time Carondelet departed from Louisiana, the role that the province played in the Spanish colonial system had begun to change. The mid-1790s witnessed the rise of Napoleon in France and the entrance of an independent United States onto the stage of European diplomacy. These changes came in the face of a decline in the internal stability of the Spanish government following the death of King Charles III in 1787. The new Spanish King, Charles IV, presided over a court in Spain at which corruption and debility became the order of the day. Louisiana, as a Spanish possession, increasingly became a pawn in the diplomacy of the 1790s even as it suffered disastrously from a decline in governmental vitality. Partly for that reason, the final years of Spanish Louisiana after Carondelet lacked the strong and decisive leadership that characterized much of the early era of Spanish social control along the lower Mississippi.

By the closing years of the 1790s, the enduring impact of Spanish rule had become apparent; namely, there existed a population of pronounced ethnic diversity in the colony. This was the great legacy of Spanish attempts at social control in Louisiana. The government of Spain, from the time of Ulloa to the closing of the eighteenth century, encouraged immigration into Louisiana and the total population increased five fold. Few of these persons, however, were Spanish-speaking. Instead, new groups came to the Mississippi Valley, including Canary Islanders (who spoke Spanish), Acadians, French West Indians, and–most importantly–English-speaking settlers. As well, a significant number of new arrivals were African or African-American slaves who came with no choice in the matter. Since the influx of slaves was tied directly to the expansion of agriculture, it is not surprising that the increase in the size of the slave population accounted for approximately one-half of the total demographic growth in Louisiana during the Spanish period. All of this immigration made Louisiana increasingly diverse in its society and culture, with a provincial population in 1803 of about 50,000 people. New Orleans had about 10,000 of them. This immigration also fragmented and isolated the social, political, economic, and cultural power of the Francophone population.

The increasing number of these migrants changed forever the nature of the lower Mississippi Valley. This was most certainly the case for the English-speaking population. In effect, these English-speaking settlers fostered a demographic movement that preordained the Louisiana Purchase. This Anglo-American population, which constituted a significant segment of the colony's inhabitants by 1803, came mainly from three sources. First, a number of them arrived on the lower Mississippi early in the period of Spanish domination as merchants and traders who secured permission to reside in Louisiana, especially at New Orleans. Many of these English-speaking inhabitants, including persons such as Oliver Pollock and Daniel Clark the elder, were Irish or Scots-Irish Roman Catholics, hence the Spaniards accepted them. Second, a considerable number of English-speaking people were residents of conquered British West Florida and subsequently became Spanish citizens of Louisiana. Third, the largest number of English-speakers in the colony resulted because of immigration into Louisiana from the United States. They were frontier folk and planters who appeared in the Mississippi Valley in ever increasing numbers as the eighteenth century moved towards its end.

The Spanish policy of welcoming English-speaking settlers into Louisiana if they declared their loyalty seemed a prescient solution to problems of social control. Spain found in these people a source, at the least, of theoretically loyal colonists who could further Louisiana's stability while they served as a possible counterweight to the Francophone majority. With Miro's policies starting in the mid-1780s, various entrepreneurs and potential land agents began appearing at New Orleans with proposals to sponsor the migration of Anglo-Americans into Louisiana. One of the most ambitious, the Frenchman Pierre Woves d'Arges, actually traveled to Spain where he appeared at court in order to seek permission to bring 1,500 English-speaking United States citizens into Louisiana where they were to become Spanish subjects. This French entrepreneur argued that these settlers would constitute a defensive bulwark which could hold the colony under Spanish control in the face of potential United States territorial expansion. They might also provide a needed economic boom to the colonial economy. The court approved d'Arges's ambitious plans, although circumstances eventually determined that he would never implement his scheme. Nonetheless, others took advantage of such opportunities. By the mid-1790s, Carondelet had worked with various land agents in order to encourage American immigration into Louisiana. The Marquis of Mason Rouge, for example, received a large grant of land for such purposes. Others, including Joseph Piernas, Louis de Vilemont, William Murray, the Baron de Bastrop, George Morgan, and Moses Austin, received grants of land for the settling of English-speaking immigrants all along the river from the Baton Rouge area northward to St. Louis. All of this caused Thomas Jefferson to observe that he wished "a hundred thousand of our inhabitants" would take advantage of these opportunities.[8]

Many of these English-speaking settlers in Spanish Louisiana quickly began to play significant roles in the life of the colony. Indeed, the governmental records of the province contain numerous examples of the considerable commercial and agricultural activities of these people, many of whom amassed considerable financial fortunes and established family dynasties that lasted well into the nineteenth century and, in some cases, beyond. This was especially so in the Natchez District and in the Felicianas, where Spanish colonial documents make numerous mention of such families including the Percys, the Williamsons, the Russes, the Lovels, the Pollocks, and the Joneses. Evan Jones, by way of example, can be mentioned as an individual success story in this regard. He first came to the lower Mississippi Valley in 1765 as a West Florida merchant. He took an active role in the life of the British colony, serving in the Provincial Assembly which met at Pensacola. He, like hundreds of others, remained in Louisiana after the American Revolution, becoming a Spanish subject. In the mid-1780s, Jones moved his residence to New Orleans, where he lived in a home on present-day Bienville Street. Governor Miro, as he did for all of these English-speakers in Jones's circumstances, reconfirmed all British landholdings with new, valid Spanish titles, thereby ensuring that Jones remained a wealthy man. He served during the 1790s in the colonial militia of Spanish Louisiana while he represented the United States along the lower Mississippi as the American Vice Consul at New Orleans. With the Louisiana Purchase of 1803, Jones was elected to the New Orleans City Council and served as a Director of the Bank of the United States.

Many other English-speaking Louisianans during the Spanish period had life stories similar to Evan Jones's. These included, among many others, Daniel Clark, the younger, James Mather, James Jordan, Oliver Pollock, and Thomas Pollock. Of these, Daniel Clark the younger had become perhaps the richest person in Spanish Louisiana by the time of the Purchase in 1803. Young Clark came to the Mississippi Valley in 1786 to join his uncle, Daniel Clark the elder. The older Clark was already a successful merchant at New Orleans. Young Clark, once in the colony in the late 1780s, proved to be very successful in the export of Louisiana trade goods while he invested heavily in land along the Mississippi from New Orleans to Natchez. He also profited greatly in the slave trade. Daniel Clark's land-holdings eventually numbered in the hundreds of thousands of acres, with one tract along the Ouachita River alone comprehending over 200,000 acres. The Clark fortune eventually produced one of Louisiana's most prolonged and complicated legal disputes that involved the unsuccessful efforts of Myra Clark Gaines across much of the nineteenth century to gain clear title to many of these holdings.

The point to be drawn from the foregoing discussion of English-speaking migration into Spanish Louisiana is a simple and valid one for the historian. The Anglo-Americanization of Louisiana began several decades before the Louisiana Purchase of 1803. Indeed, by 1803, the process was a demographic reality that had only to be translated into a political reality by the Louisiana Purchase. These Anglo-American, English-speaking Louisiana citizens were more than an opening vanguard of settlement, they were the settlement itself and they made Spanish Louisiana the first frontier of expansion after the American Revolution.

The net result of these considerations regarding Spanish- and English-speaking peoples leads to the conclusion that the colonial rule of Spain in Louisiana had a profound impact that can still be seen today in the modern state, especially in its economic, social, cultural, and racial diversity. Even today, the vast and beautiful land which is Louisiana still resonates to historical rhythms that began during its relatively brief existence as a Spanish colony. Jefferson himself acknowledged this when he reported the Louisiana Purchase to the Congress in 1803. He said: "On this important acquisition, so favorable to the immediate interests of our Western citizens, so auspicious to the peace and security of the nation in general, which adds to our country territories so extensive and fertile and to our citizens new brethren to partake of the blessings of freedom and self-government, I offer to Congress and our country my sincere congratulations."[9] In reality, however, Jefferson misplaced his congratulations. They were instead owed to the Spanish colonial administrators whose efforts during the previous thirty-five years to maintain social control created a distinct and enduring, late eighteenth century colonial complex that blended different peoples into a single territorial province of striking ethnic diversity. It was that diversity, as much as the additional territory acquired by the United States, which made the Louisiana Purchase so remarkable as a seminal event in this nation's history.

Chapter 13

"I am left aloan to struggle in a cold and selfish world": The Settlement Experiences of Women in the Lower Mississippi Valley

Johanna Miller Lewis

In May of 1859 Mary Owen Sims wrote in her diary:

> My time has been so multifariously employed that I actually have not had time to write. I have hired out two of my Negro men and discharged the overseer; and keep one of the men at home and the women and children farm it. Myself this year I live quite alone, no white soul on the place save me and the children. They all grow very fast so I have to devote a good portion of my time to instructing them. I felt very solicitous for their future. As for myself, I feel that the sunshine of my days had passed and oh how lonely I do feel. At times I feel as though I was cut off from all sympathy of my kind; at least as far as sympathy and congeniality of feeling is concerned I feel perfectly isolated—those whom I most looked to for advice and protection have proved false and I am left alone to struggle in a cold and selfish world. . . . It has often been a source of regret to me that my daughters were not sons: a man can change his station in life but a woman scarcely ever arrives at a more exalted station than the one she is born in. If we except those whose minds are masculine enough to cope with men—there are very few of our great women who are not in some degree deficient in those feminine qualities that makes woman lovable. But a woman whose mind is superior and whose feelings have been cased in a more exquisite mould to be compelled to associate with coarser minds who cannot understand her is compelled to feel lonely.[1]

Writing on the eve of the Civil War, Mary Owen Sims did not find Arkansas a habitable place for women. But how typical were Mrs. Sims' experiences?

This essay will try to answer that question by comparing the experiences of women who settled the southern frontier east and west of the Mississippi River. Did settlement become easier as the frontier moved west and settlers could benefit from the experience of others? Or, did the rising standard of living in the east make the settlement experience of starting all over again more difficult? In order to answer these questions, it will be necessary first to place the specific experiences of women in the trans-Mississippi West into the larger context of Frederick Jackson Turner's frontier thesis and the stages of westward movement in American history.

Almost from the moment of the settlement of Jamestown in 1607, Anglo-Americans moved west. The desire for space and the availability of land compelled colonists to blanket the land between the Atlantic Ocean and the Appalachian Mountains by 1763 when King George III's Proclamation forbade his American subjects to cross the mountains. This first phase of settlement to the Appalachians took five generations of colonists approximately a century and a half to accomplish.

While the American Revolution put a temporary damper on the westward movement, at war's end frontiersmen such as Daniel Boone were ready to lead the new citizens of the United States across the Appalachian Mountains to the lands known as Kentucky and Tennessee and across the Ohio River into the Northwest Territory. As historian Malcolm Rohrbaugh has noted, the settlement of the trans-Appalachian frontier differed from that of the eastern seaboard for three major reasons: the settlers were in "hostile" Indian territory; a veritable "land ocean" of trees, mountains, and swift moving streams separated them from their homes and established institutions; and they had the settlement experiences of the first colonists in America to draw upon in times of crisis.[2] Even so, in no small measure because of the assistance provided by the federal government's 1787 Northwest Ordinance, only three generations were needed to occupy the area between the Appalachian Mountains and the Mississippi River, a geographic region twice as large as the thirteen colonies it took five generations of colonists to settle.[3]

By 1800, Americans wanted to move even further west. For the preceding two decades farms located on the fertile lands of Ohio, Tennessee and Kentucky had produced a growing agricultural surplus that local markets could not always absorb. For a true market economy to develop in these new territories, farmers needed a reliable regional market in which to sell their agricultural products. With the Cumberland and Kentucky rivers feeding into the Ohio River and then the Mississippi, the logical market was New Orleans. However, numerous barriers prevented New Orleans from becoming that logical market, not the least of which was that the land west of the Mississippi did not belong to the United States. Consequently, commercial trade down river progressed slowly until 1795 when an unexpected United States diplomatic victory opened the Mississippi to transport the surplus commodities of the trans-Appalachian frontier to the world. Thomas Pinkney's treaty also established the right of deposit for American goods at New Orleans.[4]

But the biggest boost for westward movement came with President Thomas Jefferson's Louisiana Purchase in 1803. Suddenly, the west was a whole new world for Americans seeking land and opportunity—the geographic size of the United States literally doubled and the Mississippi River became the nation's first super highway. The addition of territory west of the Mississippi offered Americans not just land, but, as events showed, a settlement experience quite different than that east of the river.

Before delving into the settlement experiences of women in the trans-Mississippi West, and in particular in Arkansas, it will be helpful to review Frederick Jackson Turner's frontier thesis. Written at the "close" of the frontier in 1890, Turner argued that as Americans moved westward, the new environment gradually weakened their inherited European culture and forced them to create new institutions and new values appropriate for a new nation. Democracy, nationalism, and individualism all took form on the frontier and contributed to the development of a unique American character.[5]

The increasing speed with which market economies, local and state government, churches, and educational institutions sprouted on the frontier, not to mention the widening of the electorate, suggests that Turner's thesis appears to hold true—even for women. But does a closer examination of women's settlement experiences on the frontier, and the southern trans-Mississippi frontier in particular, show that they really improved over time? It's difficult to tell even when consulting primary sources, although a tentative answer does emerge.

For instance, when William Byrd II, a member of the Virginia gentry, traveled to the North Carolina backcountry in 1728 to survey the dividing line between that colony and Virginia, he was appalled to find

> the wretchedest Scene of poverty I had ever met with in this happy Part of the World. . . . the distemper of laziness seizes the men oftener much then the Women. These last Spin, weave and knit, all with their own Hands, while their Husbands, depending on the Bounty of the climate, are sloathfull in everything but getting of Children. . . .[6]

Almost a century and a half later when visiting Arkansas, German writer Frederick Gerstacker noted that

> the women who shared the loneliness of the forests with their men . . . are subject to even greater hardships and more severe privations than the men, who are endowed by nature with inborn strength and endurance. The pioneer, accustomed since childhood to weather and storm, moves into the wilderness with his ax and rifle and makes a home there where no human foot has ever trod. . . .
>
> In a lean-to of rough-hewn logs, protected on only three sides from wind and rain, the woman lives not days or weeks, but months or sometimes even years under conditions that would destroy the health of a European. The cold, damp earth is her floor, the wide lonely forest her domicile. No neighbor visits her; the nearest lives perhaps half a day's journey away.[7]

Gerstacker's portrayal of the trans-Mississippi West suggests that the frontier was not the positive experience for women that Turner believed. Why?

Like the seventeenth century colonists before them, the women and men described by Byrd in 1728 *expected* to start from scratch when they settled a new area. And while they may sound a bit desperate, later settlers to the backcountry sensed the challenge of the wilderness and arrived with a sense of destiny. For women especially, another important characteristic of the colonial frontier was the absence of a rigid society and its accompanying rules. Social and class divisions still existed but survival was what mattered. When necessary, society granted women (single women and widows in particular) enough legal and economic autonomy, as well as social space, to support themselves and their children.[8]

Not too surprisingly, when the next generations set out for the frontier they drew upon the experiences of their parents and grandparents to make the settlement process proceed more smoothly. Historians generally agree that the settlement of the trans-Appalachian frontier also benefited from the extensive religious, social and political institutions earlier pioneers created. Early settlement in Kentucky and Tennessee, for example, took place while they were still counties of Virginia and North Carolina, respectively. Consequently, the county governments handled land surveys, deed registrations and other civil and criminal matters before chaos took over. Religion too found a new life on the frontier, providing settlers with a stronger faith through the revivals of the Second Great Awakening.

Historian Joan Cashin ably demonstrated the experiences of women on the early nineteenth century southern frontier in her book, *A Family Venture*. Cashin chronicles the movement of families from the "Old South," namely Virginia, North Carolina and South Carolina, to what is sometimes called the "Old Southwest" or Kentucky, Tennessee, Alabama, and Mississippi. She found that the younger sons of planters in the Old South frequently married and moved west (with a financial stake provided by their fathers) to begin life as planters of the new staple crops of cotton and sugar. The settlement process was a replication, in much less time, of the staple crop, plantation economy supported by slave labor developed in the Chesapeake Bay region and Carolina low country during the colonial era.

Men found the move west an exciting opportunity that carried hopes of financial success and personal independence. Their wives, unfortunately, found the move both *disruptive* in forcing them to stop living the lives to which they were accustomed and *destructive* by removing them from their one constant source of strength, their extended families of origin. Cashin argues that migration was "a family venture" because men and women both took part in it, but they went to the frontier with competing agendas. Men wanted to strike out on their own with their close-knit immediate families and become successes, while women wanted to continue their extended kinship networks and recreate them on the frontier. Until the migrations of the 1820s, both men and women agreed on the importance and value of family. When men appeared to reject their family connections during the 1820s in favor of pursuing wealth, the resulting tensions and resentments felt by husbands and wives became deep divisions over the fundamental aspects of family life.[9]

The decision to migrate west was an easy one for young men who wanted to be as successful as their planter fathers, and who believed that the Old Southwest offered the only available fresh and fertile land on which to grow cotton at a time when there was unprecedented demand for cotton on the international market.[10] These restless souls frequently decided to move west without ever consulting their wives. When men did try to inform their wives, they did not tell them very much. North Carolinian Sarah Gordon Brown told her son, "He [her husband] says he is going to move but makes no farther preparation and none of us know what he is going to do."[11]

Leaving the east coast for the Old Southwest meant not just leaving one's extended family but packing up the essentials of the household and plantation, slaves and animals included, to make a hard journey west. For these reasons and others, wives equated migration with death. In letters and diaries women compared the two losses so frequently that it is sometimes difficult to tell the difference between "departed" relatives who had died and others who had migrated. For example, Louisa Cunningham mourned the loss of her beloved sister whom "providence has then seen fit to remove away from us." It was "a circumstance at all times melancholy and distressing—sundering apart those near and dear ties which so long has bound [us] together."[12]

After spending weeks if not months traveling over dusty roads and traversing numerous streams and rivers to get to their new homes, women had to face the material deprivations of the initial phases of settlement. The conditions they found on the frontier frequently shocked planter women: tents, lean-tos, and one-room log cabins replaced large, comfortable well-furnished homes. In addition to dealing with dank, dirty and badly lit interiors, women had to perform the kind of manual labor that their grandmothers had done in colonial days. If they were lucky, they might have acquired some of the necessary skills from elderly relatives or even sisters or in-laws who had already moved to the frontier.[13]

Women settling the nineteenth century Old Southwestern frontier faced a much different frontier than their colonial foremothers had. As the United States matured, society began to make clear distinctions between the world of men and the world of women. Some of the most significant differences placed on women stemmed from new ideas and expectations assigned to them by virtue of their sex. The idea that men, as heads of households, had to provide for their families was not a new one, but the idea that women were agents of civilization and keepers of morals in the home was. Women became completely dependent on their husbands, and to become a wife and mother was the highest calling in life. Despite the fact that this "cult of domesticity" developed in response to industrialization, all women were expected to follow it; moving to the frontier was not an adequate excuse to abandon one's duties.[14]

In sum, women on the antebellum Old Southwestern frontier faced the daunting process of trying to carve a new home out of nothingness while keeping up appearances. For young wives this situation could easily spell disaster. Unlike their husbands, young women did not get to experience a phase of semi-dependency between childhood and marriage. While their brothers and fiancés sought higher education, traveled at will, transacted business and engaged in a multitude of activities to prepare them to become autonomous heads of households, young women remained dependent and under the control of their parents until they married and became dependent on their husbands. Marriage marked an increase in social status for women, as did child bearing and running the household, but it removed any hope of autonomy.[15]

Thus while the settlement of the trans-Appalachian frontier became somewhat easier for men because governmental bodies and property laws were in place, it became more difficult for women because of the new expectations that society placed on them. As Joan Cashin noted, Turner's thesis was a double edged sword: for men, the opportunity to start from scratch was positive; for women, the abandonment of their family combined with the expectation to continue their domestic and maternal duties with little to no support, was negative to the point of destruction.[16] If the frontier settlement experience for women went from good to bad between the east coast and the Mississippi River, exactly what would happen when settlement of the trans-Mississippi West commenced?

In 1803 the Louisiana Purchase expanded the scope of the frontier almost beyond recognition and confirmed the desire of the United States government and people to continue moving west. The Mississippi River—the trade lifeline of a frontier people—now fell safely within the boundaries of an expanding nation.[17]

What lay across the Mississippi River? A land and a people who belonged to a different empire, from a different century. Unlike the westward pattern of settlement followed in the British American colonies and then the United States, in the early eighteenth century the French settled the upper Mississippi River Valley from New France by moving west up the St. Lawrence River and across the Great Lakes to the headwaters of the Mississippi and settled the lower Mississippi by moving inland from the Gulf Coast.[18] Content to claim the land for their sovereign and to civilize the natives through the Catholic Church in the late seventeenth century, early settlements, especially in the north, consisted of missionaries, trappers, and the Indians who chose to live among them. If growth and progress warranted, the King might send over some aristocrat with a military cadre to govern in his absence. Unlike the English preference to "make the world English" one settlement at a time, the French were content to blend in with the native population. Trappers commonly married native women, missionaries built churches and schools, and government officials set up housekeeping as they would have in France. In the lower Mississippi Valley, settlement was more like that in the Anglo-American South, with rudimentary plantations and small farms, but without the economic dynamism. Any mention of women in histories of early Louisiana revolves around the importation of marriageable French women to the colony in 1717 and the founding of the Ursuline school for girls in 1727.[19]

The Mississippi River may have been a lifeline for transporting agricultural bounty from north to south, but frequent flooding kept the settlements located directly on it to a minimum. Instead, in southern Louisiana, French, German and Acadians settled on the streams, rivers, and bayous near the Mississippi. Staple commodities provided the basis for expansion and prosperity, and the French (and, increasingly the Americans) of Louisiana began the large-scale cultivation of cotton and sugar. The French planters had experimented with cotton and sugar toward the end of the eighteenth century, and soon thereafter the cultivation of both spread along the Mississippi River as far north as Baton Rouge. Cotton also moved slowly inland, where the rich alluvial soil and ready transportation of this region offset the dangers of flood, disease, and isolation. As cotton cultivation gradually moved north into Arkansas (to the Arkansas River), planters replaced the trappers (*coureurs de bois*) and French culture began to wane.[20]

Elsewhere in Louisiana, and despite the Louisiana Purchase in 1803, the French influence remained large. New Orleans was its hub. New Orleans grew increasingly important as a cross-section of the western world and the western country. Supported by a vast and growing hinterland already undergoing a transition to staple crop agriculture, an increasing market for cotton and sugar, and the demand for both created by a general European war, New Orleans was transformed from a colonial frontier village into a world port. By 1810 probably something on the order of a quarter of the population of the Louisiana Purchase lived in New Orleans and its immediate environs.[21]

The overwhelming French presence in New Orleans and along the lower Mississippi, as well as the considerable influence of the Catholic Church in Louisiana, led the federal government to abandon ideas of organizing the territory along "American" lines. Territorial governor W. C. C. Claiborne noted in 1804 that while "the people of Louisiana are . . . honest and . . . attached to the American Government . . . they are uninformed, indolent, [and] luxurious."[22] Too, Louisiana retained its distinctive European flavor through its system of French civil law while following English common law in criminal cases.[23]

For women this situation was an extraordinary turn of events. Unlike their American counterparts east of the Mississippi suffering under the cult of domesticity, Louisiana women (those in the Territory of Orleans and then the state) remained individuals throughout their lives. They retained their maiden names, inherited property separately from their husbands, and had the right to write a will without their husband's permission. Such autonomy for married women was unheard of, especially when instead of primogeniture Louisiana's system dictated that daughters and sons inherited real property "by equal shares and without distinction by sex." Women's legal status and economic power, combined with a considerably more laissez-faire attitude toward race and sex, allowed for a vastly different female experience in Louisiana.

The "Americanization" of the trans-Mississippi West commenced with increased migration to the region north of Louisiana following the War of 1812. As it had been for generations past, the land was the lure, and military bounty lands for veterans in Arkansas also attracted prospective settlers to the western country. A prosperous economy, rising prices for staple agricultural products (especially cotton), an egalitarian banking system, and a democratic political philosophy added to the inducements. From the Mississippi and all its tributaries people disembarked and headed inland as far as their ambitions, inclinations, and supplies would take them. Their trade and contact with the outside world, especially in commerce, continued to focus for several decades on the great waterways.

Unlike the first inhabitants of Louisiana and the Old Southwest, most of these migrants to the western country were small farmers, not French planters or American want-to-be planters. Many small settlements in the western country consisted of these families of farmers and artisans, as well as the occasional doctor and lawyer, living in sufficient proximity to help one another and to meet for social activities.[24] Their wives and daughters supplied "a civilizing influence" and contributed to the domestic economy on the frontier. In Louisiana, the Acadians lived a similar, but not identical, lifestyle, preferring the pre-capitalistic values of their ancestors to the "transitional" economic ideals of the antebellum small farmer.[25]

While the Great Migration of 1815 turned much of the frontier South to cotton cultivation, Arkansas did not benefit from it. The *Gazette* commented in 1819 that Arkansas had plenty of lawyers but needed more farmers. The lands were good—"as rich as human avarice can desire"—yet immigrants were few. Lands that could have supported cotton cultivation lay vacant due to dangerous watercourses, flooding, and titles clouded by old Spanish claims. The energetic, aggressive agriculturalist did not go to Arkansas; he took his capital and went to Alabama, Mississippi, or Louisiana.

So, while women east of the Mississippi labored in their role of plantation mistress, and women in Louisiana enjoyed a French inspired society, what was life like for women in Arkansas? Simply put, the early settlement of Arkansas resembled the pre-Revolutionary colonial southern backcountry more than it did the trans-Appalachian West. Immune from the innovations of technology and market forces, most Arkansans hunted, trapped, grazed livestock, and generally pursued a lonely, solitary, self-sufficient existence.[26] For women, frontier Arkansas must have been brutal.

German traveler Frederich Gerstacker described the following scene in one of his *Tales from the Backwoods*.

> [the pioneer's] wife . . . lies all night long on the hard ground listening to the woeful howling of the wolves and the shrill cry and mournful wail of a lone panther. . . . But just as some men always allow themselves to be led by others and so never become self-reliant and independent, so it is with women. The normally weak nature of the woman waits only for the opportunity to discover its inner strength, and then she becomes suddenly very active and decisive. Even though up until that time she may have relied entirely on the strength and protection of someone more robustly built, now she courageously looks after her frightened children . . . [and] takes care of her daily duties.[27]

Despite the looming presence of the harsh frontier and the lack of amenities, Arkansas women apparently made their moves west positive ones. Letters and diaries show that Arkansas women shared only one important characteristic with their counterparts in the Old Southwest: anxiety at being separated from their families in the East, as documented by Maria Toncray Watkin's comment, "O the sorrow of heart I felt at parting with my sister's children who are as dear to me as my own—Farewell, dear Ones."[28]

Rather than dwell in their isolation and complain about missing their families, Arkansas women recognized that contact with other women—kith or kin, literate or illiterate, wealthy or poor—could make their lives tolerable. Arkansas women sought personal contact with other women whenever possible, through visiting and sharing labor, church meetings or community gatherings. Shortly after her family's arrival in Arkansas Mrs. Watkins wrote, "I met with a widow woman very clever. She appeared to sympathize with me in leaving Dear Friends behind and coming to this wilderness of Sorrow."[29]

While they may not have crossed racial lines, the white women of Arkansas relaxed their sense of propriety to obtain female companionship. Their ability to cure their own sense of isolation through seeking out others made Arkansas women replace the separate woman's world of the frontier found east of the Mississippi with an invisible women's culture in the midst of a masculine world.

Chapter 14

Women and Networks in the Upper Mississippi Valley and Northern Louisiana Purchase

Lucy Eldersveld Murphy

On August 11, 1805, Meriwether Lewis and three companions were wandering among the Bitterroot Mountains of Montana in the western reaches of the Louisiana Purchase in search of Shoshone Indians, from whom they hoped to purchase horses to take them across the mountains and to the Columbia River. Dressed in elk skin garments and browned by the sun, Lewis worried that he looked more Indian than European. The four men had left the rest of their party behind, and had begun to despair. Having left Sacajawea, their Shoshone "interpretess" and guide, at the main camp, Lewis hoped to communicate at any initial encounter by sign language, supplemented by the few words of the Shoshone language he had learned from her.

The first member of the tribe to reveal himself, a man on horseback at a distance of "about 200 paces," witnessed a bizarre spectacle. Lewis flapped a large blanket at him, held up "some b[e]ads, a looking glas and a few trinkets," and, when the Indian turned to leave, began shouting at him. According to Lewis, when the horseman began to retreat, "I now called to him in as loud a voice as I could command repeating the word *tab-ba-bone,* which in their language signifyes *white-man.*" Although—or perhaps *because*—Lewis pulled up his shirt sleeve to demonstrate his whiteness, the Indian "suddonly turned his ho[r]se about, gave him the whip[,] leaped the creek and disapeared in the willow brush. . . . "[1] Lewis was sorely disappointed.

Although she was not physically present at this encounter, Sacajawea's influence is clear. She had led the Lewis and Clark expedition to the neighborhood of her tribe of origin; she had taught Lewis to communicate with signals and a word, which both warned her tribespeople, and informed them. Sacajawea, an invisible presence in this initial encounter, was the link between people who would soon come into contact again.

Was Sacajawea having a little fun at Lewis's expense? He believed he was communicating in the local vernacular, but he also was certain that the Indians would be delighted to make his acquaintance if they discovered that he was "white." More likely, the Shoshones viewed Lewis's ethnicity and "color" with ambivalence and suspicion. Sacajawea probably knew this, and induced Lewis to perform in a particular way and to announce his Euro-American ethnicity so as to warn (if not entertain) her friends, while offering them the chance for contact.

Two days later, Lewis and his party spotted "two women, a man, and some dogs," who waited for the sojourners to approach them, but ran off when Lewis began shouting "*tab-ba-bone*," at them.[2] Much vexed, Lewis and his party walked on until they happened to surprise three Shoshone women. In Lewis's words, "they appeared much allarmed but saw that we were to[o] near for them to escape. . . . They therefore seated themselves on the ground, holding down their heads as if reconciled to die. . . ." Lewis gave them some beads and other trinkets. Then he and his companions used sign language to persuade the women to lead them toward the Shoshone camp.

The other Indians had reported Lewis and his strange behavior, however, and at that moment sixty mounted Shoshone warriors were galloping at full speed toward the intruders, but the women's presence with the explorers brought them up short. The women's intervention averted a violent encounter. The Shoshone men were soon embracing Lewis and his companions and bringing them home to smoke for peace.[3]

As was so often the case in successful nineteenth-century cultural encounters, women mediated in potentially difficult situations. These women convinced the warriors that the Lewis party was harmless, showing off the gifts that had created a kind of social obligation for hospitality on the receiving end. The three Shoshone women who mediated the encounter between Lewis and the warriors served as *links* between the two groups.

Six days after the Indians discovered Lewis and his party, the Shoshones were again growing suspicious as they awaited the arrival of Clark and the rest of the men. Finally, as tensions mounted, the Clark party arrived. Sacajawea with her baby and her husband Toussant Charbonneau led the group, and according to a companion, when she spotted the Shoshones waiting ahead, she "began to dance and show every mark of the most extravagant joy, . . . sucking her fingers . . . to indicate that they were of her native tribe. . . . the Indians . . . sang aloud with the greatest appearance of delight."[4]

Captured by the Hidatsas five years earlier, Sacajawea had long been away from friends and relatives, so on arrival at the Shoshone camp, she immediately began "renewing among the women the friendships of former days." One of the explorers recorded that, "just as we approached [the camp] a woman made her way through the crowd towards Sacajawea, and recognising each other, they embraced with the most tender affection." Soon, she was called away to interpret for a [men's] council, and as she recognized Cameahwait, the chief, as her brother, she "jumped up, and ran and embraced him . . . weeping profusely."[5] Here, Sacajawea reconnected with her family and community. That she was personally overjoyed by this, we can certainly understand.

The importance of Sacajawea's relationships was larger than her individual story. She linked her employers and their associates with the tribe in complex and interesting ways. Sacajawea, was a center, a hub (one might say) from which links radiated, through which people connected with each other. Oddly enough, the moment at which she created these ties came after she herself had been separated from her people for five years, the moment at which she was reunited with them. As she was *personally* mending the connections with her networks of origin, she wove them into a larger web with her newer connections: her husband, child, employers and traveling companions.

Overview of Women's Roles

These encounters between the Shoshones and the explorers illustrate many of the key themes of women's history in the Louisiana Purchase and the upper Mississippi Valley during the early nineteenth century: migration, danger, cultural encounters, discovery, diplomacy, trade and ceremony. And especially the ways women's networks tied people and their many experiences together.

Most nineteenth century women of all racial and ethnic groups were part of large and small social networks, families, clans, tribes, ethnic groups, churches and voluntary organizations of various types. Some were forced into coercive relationships as well. More than simply *members* of these interconnected associations, they frequently served as links connecting one group with another, sometimes, like Sacajawea, even as focal points where multiple connections converged.

These varied ways that women linked groups and individuals were especially important during the nineteenth century because it was a time of racial contestation for the Americas. As this graph, adapted from Colin McEvedy's *Atlas of World Population History* shows, after thousands of years as the western hemisphere's majority population, Native Americans became a minority overall in the late eighteenth century (figure 10). However, it was not until the middle of the nineteenth century that Euro-Americans became a majority. It is no accident, then, that the strongest conflicts of the first century after the Louisiana Purchase were race-related: Indian removal, the extension of slavery, the Civil War, and the Plains Wars. Often, the controversies and the accommodations occurred on the cultural and racial divides, where interracial relationships blurred distinctions, prejudices were fluid, and human contacts teetered precariously between appropriation and generosity, assimilation and exile. To all of these conflicts, the Louisiana Purchase region was central. So, too, were the experiences of the women who created, tended, and rewove the mesh of human relationships (or became ensnared in them) in the upper Mississippi Valley and Louisiana region. Here waves of people arrived, encountering those who had come before, altering the dynamics of society, economy, polity, and gender.

Native American Women

Throughout the region and the era, and across racial and ethnic groups, women *linked people to one another*. As daughters, mothers, sisters, and wives—and as community members—women of all racial and ethnic groups connected people in networks of mutual aid and communication. Women created ties between their brothers, sisters, children, parents, and friends, husbands, and other associates. Often, for Indian women in the nineteenth century, their kin, husbands, friends, and neighbors were of different tribes, ethnicities, and cultural backgrounds, so they strove to mediate among them. Sacajawea, for example, established diplomatic relations between her brother, a Shoshone chief, and Lewis and Clark, representatives of the United States. Her husband was a French Canadian fur-trade worker, her son a bicultural Métis. In addition, Sacajawea's mere presence

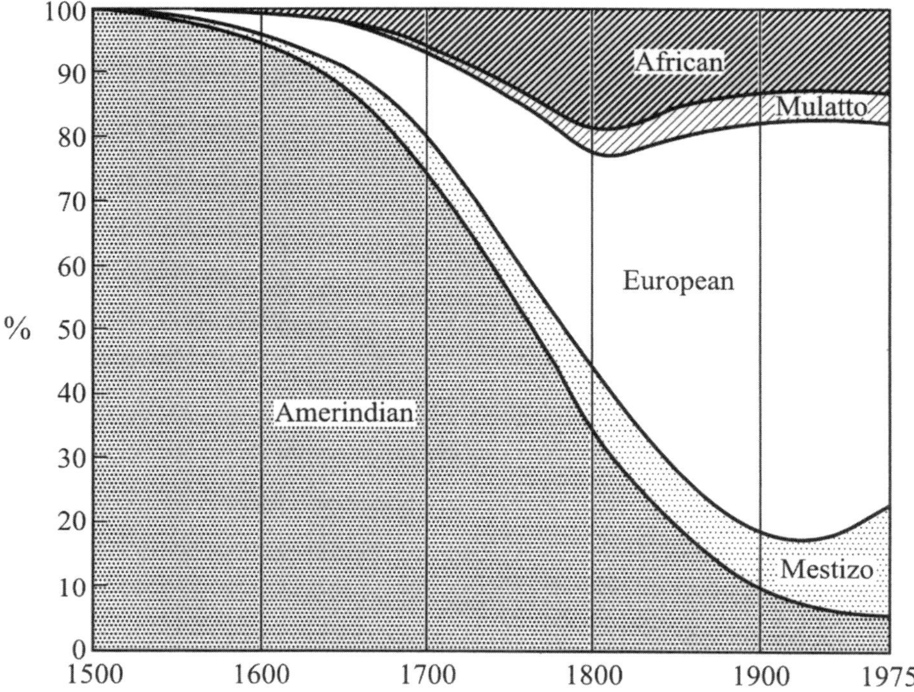

Figure 10. *The Americas, Ethnic Structure 1500-1975.* Redrawn from Colin McEvedy and Richard Jones, *Atlas of World Population History* (New York: Facts on File, 1978), Figure 4.7. Courtesy of Colin McEvedy.

in the Lewis and Clark party demonstrated the peaceful motives of the expedition to observant Indians. According to scholar Clara Sue Kidwell, Sacajawea's role as cultural mediator was not unique. Kidwell argues that "there is an important Indian woman in virtually every major encounter between Europeans and Indians in the New World."[6]

Sacajawea's story also demonstrates the ways that kinship could mitigate the effects of personal disasters. She adopted her nephew, whose parents had perished, probably due to violence or disease. Women of all racial and ethnic backgrounds knew that kin ties could create the safety nets that might help them cope with the transitions and tragedies of disrupted frontiers.[7]

Marriages like Sacajawea's were one way to create ties. Unlike many ethnic groups, Indian peoples in Purchase territory (particularly its northern areas) approved of—and even encouraged—intermarriage. During the fur-trade era, traders learned that their Native customers expected them to marry local daughters, creating bonds of obligation to their in-laws and their communities. Native wives became interpreters who learned and taught both their own Native families and their husbands about each other's expectations and cultures. Their bicultural Métis children grew up to continue the patterns of mediation. One such Métis child, for example, was Nancy McClure.

Nancy McClure's life illustrates both the ways that women, especially Native women, could link communities and the ways they could use those connections to mediate disputes and even prevent or minimize violence. She was the daughter of a U. S. Army officer and a Dakota Indian woman, born in Minnesota territory in 1836. Her parents' relationship, and her birth, linked the army with the Dakota community. She was bilingual (in English and Dakota), went to a mission school, and after her parents' deaths lived with her Indian grandmother. A great beauty, she attracted much attention during the 1851 gathering to negotiate a treaty at Traverse des Sioux, Minnesota. Her marriage to fur trader David Faribault was recorded by artist/traveller Frank Blackwell Mayer. This marriage linked her, her relatives, and her friends with the old Francophone fur-trade families of Wisconsin who were moving northward into Minnesota. During the Dakota Revolt of 1862, she used her bicultural status to save the lives of four people from the wrath of *Indians* fed up with the cruelties of U. S. government agents and policies, and to protect two of her Native relatives from equally vengeful *white* soldiers.[8]

Many other Indian and mixed-race Métis women worked to create networks which could smooth relations between their own people and the immigrants who would later call themselves "pioneers." One such "well known and highly respected" woman was Komick, whose background was Odawa, Ojibwe, and French. She lived with her white husband Henry Tourtillott in Oconto, Wisconsin, in the middle of the nineteenth century.[9] According to her granddaughter, Komick always introduced herself to new families that settled near them. She would help them make gardens, put up clothes lines, show them berry patches. . . . She and Aunt Catishe (Figure 11) both had small pox when they were younger, so when white families got it, they would both go in and help take care of people. Komick spoke English, French, Odawa, Menominee, and Ojibwe, skills that helped her to weave ties between various members of her changing community.[10]

While many Native and Métis women created ties to newcomers, they often maintained connections with their Native kin and relatives as well. Marguerite LePage LeClaire, for example, was a Métisse related to a prominent Mesquakie family and married to the Potawatomi Métis interpreter Antoine LeClaire who was stationed for many years at Rock Island (figure 12). Marguerite received a substantial land grant at the request of her Indian relatives at the time of the removal treaty of 1832, a grant which helped her family to become wealthy and prominent as founders of the city of Davenport, Iowa.[11] Afterwards, according to a local historian writing in 1910, "delegations of the Sac and

Figure 11. *Catishe*. Courtesy of Bruce Paulson, Suring, Wisconsin. Following the death of her son, it appears that in sorrow Catishe scratched his image from the photograph. (Editor's Note: this image has been digitally enhanced from the original tintype.)

Fox Indians visited her place every year, where they were always made welcome, entertained as long as they wished to remain, and when leaving, always carried away as a free gift what necessaries they required—corn, flour, etc."[12] Anglo uneasiness about having Indians in town might be calmed by knowing that they were associates and relatives of Marguerite LePage LeClaire and that she was keeping an eye on them. Many other Native and Métis women living on transitional frontiers remained in touch with distant Indian communities and welcomed, fed, and sheltered visitors. Some, like Hononegah Mack, a HoChunk (Winnebago) woman married to an Anglo fur trader, moved out of their own homes and into the guests' wigwams during the visits.[13]

African American Women

For African American women, however, ties of kinship were more vulnerable and those of friendship harder to forge across racial divides. Slaves were born into a dual system in which human relations might be either a source of strength—as in the love of families—or a vicious obligation. Even free blacks were affected by this dual system.

For *free* black women, the networks of human relations often threatened to become snares of deception. The proximity of slave and "free" territories, and the ambiguous nature of African Americans' status in Illinois and Minnesota, made free people and their families vulnerable. During the 1820s, roughly one hundred African Americans were among the 3,700 migrants to the lead region along the Mississippi River in northern Illinois and southern Wisconsin. Some were brought or sent there as slaves in spite of the Northwest Ordinance's prohibition of slavery.

Free blacks risked being ensnared by unscrupulous whites. For example, Mary DuPee was a poor, single, but free black woman who in 1830 found a temporary home for her two daughters with a white man named James Neavell at a mining town appropriately called New Diggings. When she married Leonard Bryant the following year, Neavell would not release the children, so Mary and her new husband brought suit in court to get them back.[14] Polly Crocket was born free but kidnapped as a child in Illinois and sold as a slave in Missouri. In 1844 she used the courts to obtain her freedom and that of her daughter, Lucy Berry Delaney.[15] There were many other cases like hers.

One of the first documents recorded in Crawford County, Wisconsin, suggests the ambiguity of blacks' legal status. Among the land records was an affidavit sworn in 1828 by Patsy, "(a woman of colour) heretofore indentured agreeably to the laws of Illinois Territory," swearing that "I do hereby voluntarily and of my own accord agree to go with the said Mrs. Street to Prairie du Chien or wherever else she may wish to reside, and to serve her in the capacity of a servant . . . my going with Mrs. Street . . . is of my own free will and accord. . . ."[16] Indentured servitude laws of Illinois were devices to perpetuate involuntary labor, so we must wonder how voluntary Patsy's employment and migration and connections to Street really were.

Figure 12. *Marguerite LePage LeClaire*. By permission of The Putnam Museum of History and Natural Science, Davenport, Iowa.

Laws on both sides of the Mississippi River connected African Americans with whites against their will in coercive networks. In spite of the coercion, however, black women sometimes constructed connections that could be protective. For example, when Nat, the black proprietor of the "Snowball Hotel" in Galena, beat his wife in 1828, knocking her down, a group of black women intervened. According to the local newspaper, the fight "produced an alarm amongst the inmates of the house, and Nat was soon surrounded with a trio of his sable countrywomen, the clatter of whose tongues disturbed the whole neighborhood." He was arrested.[17] The battered landlady had a group of other African-American women to thank for protection, even if it was the court system that punished her husband. But if both friendships and the justice system protected black women from abusive husbands in Galena, Illinois, across the Mississippi in Missouri, the law did not protect them.[18]

Slavery imposed a dual set of obligations on African-American lives. Although the love of kinfolk could mitigate the harshness of a chaotic world, kinship also influenced decisions about whether to try to escape. Elizabeth, a young slave woman in St. Louis, upon being sold down river to Natchez about 1830, said farewell to her brother William Wells Brown. He later recalled, "As soon as she observed me, she sprung up, threw her arms around my neck, leaned her head upon my breast, and without uttering a word, burst into tears." After taking a few moments to compose herself, she urged William to take their mother and flee.[19]

After William and their mother were captured making their way across Illinois, the older woman was sent to New Orleans to be sold. As they parted, she urged William, "Now try to get your liberty! You will soon have no one to look after but yourself." Their separation was wrenching, but he was able to escape alone, and later wrote of his experiences.[20]

Mothers might also be sold away from *infant* children and wives from husbands. Hired out to a slave trader, Brown remembered a slave mother with a fussy baby only a few weeks old among a group of slaves traveling overland for sale in St. Louis. Because the child's cries irritated the trader, he took the infant from its mother, gave it to a white woman who had boarded the travelers, and forced the mother to go on without her child. "I saw this woman crying for her child so piteously, a shudder, a feeling akin to horror, shot through my frame." This memory haunted him for a very long time.[21]

Ironically, abuse and coercion often made mothers of African-American women. For example, Brown knew from his mother that he was "a near relative" of his master. In addition, his memoir relates the story of Cynthia, "a quadroon, and one of the most beautiful women I ever saw. She . . . bore an irreproachable character for virtue and propriety of conduct." Cynthia was kept as a "mistress and housekeeper" at the farm of a slave trader by the name of Walker, who threatened her if she did not cooperate. When Walker eventually determined to marry a white wife, he sold Cynthia and their four children.[22] Sadly, *these* kinship connections amplified *her* vulnerability. Rather than being protective, these links made Cynthia and her children a hindrance to their master-father in his efforts to "purify" his lineage. Another example was equally tragic. On June 23, 1855, a slave known simply as Celia, killed her abusive master, Robert Newsom, in Callway County, Missouri. He had raped her repeatedly since purchasing her at the age of fourteen, and he was the father of her two children. Pregnant again when he attacked her, she hit him with a stick in self-defense. After a trial, she was executed by hanging.[23]

While the coerced ties between slave women and their masters could cause much anguish, there were moments when cross-racial connections could lift people out of the morass of slavery. In both Illinois and Missouri, some whites were willing to assist African-American women and men. Both Mary DuPee and Polly Crocket had the assistance of "liberty-loving whites" (as one writer called them) willing to help them gain access to the legal system as a means of protecting their liberty. So, too, did Celia in Missouri, although it did not save her life.

Elizabeth Keckley, a slave living in St. Louis, is another example of how white assistance occasionally worked. A successful dressmaker in the 1850s who had been supporting her master's family by hiring out her services as a needlewoman, she convinced her master to allow her to purchase herself and her son. A number of her customers—wealthy white ladies—helped to gather the $1,200 required for freedom. In this case, the links reached across the racial divide. (Keckley would go on to become Mary Todd Lincoln's personal dressmaker and to write a famous memoir.)

Euro-American Women

Ties of affinity or kinship were centrally important to Euro-American women as well. Although the stereotyped image of the "pioneer" was of a lone white man, a rugged individualist like Davy Crockett, hacking his way through the screaming wilderness alone, recent scholarship has demonstrated that people on the farming and town frontiers included families and tended to settle in groups.[24] For many migrants, kinship determined their destinations and helped them to adjust to new surroundings. White women often traveled with family groups.

Emily Austin was probably typical of many Euro-American migrants into the Louisiana Purchase during the middle of the nineteenth century. She moved *twenty times* between her 1813 birth in Tioga County, Pennsylvania, and 1882 when she published a memoir of her life as a Mormon farm wife, and later, a Methodist widow who worked as a nurse, teacher, and milliner. Her wanderings took her to eight states and eighteen communities, including six settlements in the Louisiana Purchase region. In most of her migrations, she went to stay with relatives, including a sister, a brother, relatives of her husband, her mother, and later her daughter (figure 13). This type of "chain migration" was common both for those journeying within the United States and for immigrants from other countries.

Austin's first foray into the Louisiana Purchase region began when, as Emily Coburn, she joined her sister and brother-in-law as some of the earliest converts to the Mormon religion. These three joined the Mormon migrations to three locations in Missouri, where, in 1833 she married Clark Slade, the first of a series of four husbands. After the Latter-day Saints were chased out of Missouri by intolerant neighbors, the family fled to Pittsfield, Illinois. They tried tenant farming, with little success. By 1842, Emily was a twenty-nine-year-old widow with five children under the age of ten. She soon moved to Nauvoo, the new Mormon settlement, to be near Clark's relatives. Later moves took her to be near her brothers in eastern Ohio and western Pennsylvania, to her mother in Madison, Wisconsin, and to be near adult children. She worked whenever possible as a milliner making fashionable bonnets, but could also work as a nurse, teacher, or seamstress. While she was migrating, so too were other family members in a common pattern of grouping and regrouping, so that when one location became unsatisfactory, her network of relatives provided a range of options. In a way, Emily Austin's kin network served also as a road map.[25]

Other Types of Networks

In addition to family connections, women wove ties to each other through work groups, churches, voluntary organizations and community projects. Women of all ethnicities enjoyed working together. Ojibwe women gathered wild rice together. Many Cheyenne women worked together to assemble the hides for a tipi.[26] Quilting parties were popular on many frontiers. Native and Métis women organized and managed maple sugar production in the early spring, while men assisted. Laundry went faster when eight arms did the work.

In the same way that working together enhanced their economic productivity, women's religious associations connected them to their communities and enhanced their authority. Native and Métis women such as Therese Schindler and Madeleine LaFramboise served as catechists for the Catholic church, teaching fundamentals of doctrine to Native neighbors, particularly to women. Women like Berenice Menard Chouteau and Marguerite LePage LeClaire supported and encouraged church building.

Priests were often dismayed by women's authority in Native and French Creole communities. For example, Madame Chouteau, matriarch of an important fur-trade family, supported Father Roux's efforts to develop a congregation at the fur-trade community at present-day Kansas City in the 1830s until he crossed the line and challenged her authority. Father Roux tried to outlaw the community's weekly dances and feasts, many of which Madame hosted. According to historian Tanis Thorne, Madame Chouteau "was offended. Roux . . . assert[ed] his authority over her by quoting from St. Paul. . . . Undaunted, she replied that Roux should refrain from condemning such harmless entertainments." In the end, Madame prevailed over Roux, who did not understand that the parties were, in Thorne's words, "cohesive community events," that is, *network builders*.[27] Of course, many women worked cooperatively with established denominations to initiate new church congregations and schools. Mother Philippine Duchesne, who established schools in St. Charles and Florissant, Missouri, is just one example.

By the middle of the nineteenth century, women organized not only in support of church and educational programs, but also around causes such as temperance, women's rights, and abolitionism. For example, Charlotta Pyles of Keokuk, Iowa, was an abolitionist ex-slave who, with her freed family members, worked to buy other kin their freedom, did public speaking for the cause in the East, and made her home a stop on the Underground Railroad. Clearly, she served as a link in several different but related

Figure 13. *The Family of William W. Montgomery, Burlingame, Kansas, ca. 1895*. Courtesy of Jim Crandell, Pasadena, California. *Back row*: Grace Laveta, Alfretta May, Emily Blanche, William Henry, Ralph Bryan; *Front row*: Esther Annetta, Sara Francis (née Slade, daughter of Emily Austin Slade, mother of the children), William Walker Montgomery (father of the children), Wayne Lyman, Rolia Slade.

networks: an extended family, a national group of abolitionists, and the shadowy world of activists helping fugitives to escape from slavery. She was also half Seminole, so she may have had other Native connections.[28]

During the Civil War, many women would organize Ladies Aid Societies as local affiliates of the Sanitary Commission. By the end of the nineteenth century, women's clubs and groups such as the Women's Christian Temperance Union gave women the networks they needed to make important changes in their communities.

Conclusion

The nineteenth century was a momentous era for the people of the Louisiana Purchase, a time of inter-cultural contact, migration, and social, economic, and political change. Because the United States acquired the Louisiana Purchase, waves of migrants from the eastern U. S. and from Europe pushed westward, forcing encounters between peoples of different backgrounds during the important demographic shift from the ages of indigenous majority, through a nineteenth-century transitional phase, before slipping into the relatively recent era of Euro-American control (see figure 10). Within and between groups, women built safety nets, tended kinship connections, and wove coalitions to cope with the challenges.

The popular image of Sacajawea is of a woman pointing west, but in reality she was a woman offering one hand to easterners, another to westerners. Some have criticized her as one whose efforts assisted in the whites' conquest of the Indian west, but her role—like that of most women—was more complex. Like many other women, she lived in a network of family connections, but also linked people of different groups, promoting cautious but peaceful interactions. For Sacajawea and many other women, the ties of kinship and affinity might be disrupted by war, capture, migration, work, and systems of racial hierarchy. Those who came after could not prevent many disasters—such as the suffering of slavery, violence, sickness, and land appropriation—but their networks could work to bind up the wounds of grief, share the joys and labor of daily life and community building, pick up the pieces when lives were broken and tying them up again.

Chapter 15

"Relations of Blood [and] Affection": The Origins of Patriotism in the Age of Jefferson

Andrew R. L. Cayton

For those Americans who consider the contours of our history, the role of the Louisiana Purchase in our national narrative is generally a happy one. Because it doubled the physical size of the United States, the acquisition of the vast domain that included much of the western drainage area of the Mississippi River holds a place of pride in a still powerful story of Manifest Destiny. Although more sensitive to the plight of American Indians and Mexicans, more aware of the ecological consequences of expansion, more thoughtful about alternative models of social development than their predecessors, most Americans nonetheless continue to assume the inevitability of the expansion of the United States.

In popular culture, the Louisiana Purchase matters specifically because it reconciles American cross-purposes, our impulses toward liberty and empire, freedom and power, consent and coercion. It confirms our national self-image as a republic expanding benignly, bringing the gospel of freedom to people long deprived of its incalculable benefits. We *purchased* Louisiana; we did not *conquer* it. The United States was an imperial aggressor in the Northwest Territory in the 1790s, eastern North America in 1812, Florida in the late 1810s and 1830s (against the Seminole and Miccosuki peoples), Texas and Mexico in the 1840s, the South in the 1860s, the Plains in the 1860s and 1870s, and Cuba and the Philippines in the 1890s. The Louisiana Purchase, like the Adams-Onis Treaty of 1819, by which the United States acquired Florida from Spain, serves to counteract that imperial image; it supports a story of a free people accepting land freely sold to them and, as important, of people freely choosing to become citizens of the republic.

It is no news that many historians have devoted their careers to undermining this happy tale. The problems are so familiar that mere mention of them reminds us of the contradictions inherent in the expansion of the republican empire. The Corsican who sold Louisiana to the United States in the name of France was himself a usurper who ruled through coercion rather than consent and who had extorted the region from an unwilling Spanish government. Moreover, Napoleon Bonaparte, having abandoned a plan to occupy Louisiana, was happy to rid himself of the vestiges of France's once considerable North American empire because of the cost in treasure and lives of an interminable attempt to suppress the Haitian independence movement.[1] All Europeans were playing with territory to which their claims were tenuous at best, certainly among the American Indians who unintentionally had made those claims plausible through alliances, commerce, and warfare. The scene so brilliantly invoked by Henry Adams of Bonaparte discussing the cession of Louisiana in his bath lays bare the frivolous banality of Europeans toying with people in whom they were interested only to the extent that they impinged on European concerns.[2] No wonder the popular vision of the explorers Meriwether Lewis and William Clark as agents of the possibilities inherent in human discovery and human perseverance exists in uneasy tension with our knowledge of the destruction wrought in their wake.[3]

Yet in our eagerness to revise the role of the Louisiana Purchase in the creation of the American empire, we sometimes lose sight of the extent to which contemporaries shared our concerns. If the great challenge of the twenty-first century for the American empire is to prosper in a global world of diverse peoples and interests, to stay true to republican principles without compromising them in the cause of empire, it differs only in scale from the challenge faced by President Thomas Jefferson and others in 1803. To them, the Louisiana Purchase was a momentous event in a series of episodes that added up to a story that had less to do with the expansion than the survival of the United States of America.[4] Cognizant of the contradictions inherent in an empire of liberty, in a continental democracy larger and more diverse than almost any other nation in the world, they were most interested in the question of how to create a nation that was more than the sum of its constitutions and borders.[5]

Nation-states were nothing new in the early nineteenth century. But they were more self-conscious. The commercial, cultural, and biological exchanges promoted by the European intrusion into the Americas and beyond had fostered a stronger sense of national distinctiveness. The contacts that broke down some barriers and promoted a degree of tolerance also had encouraged a more elaborate discussion of the sources and pervasiveness of difference. Indeed, the interaction of human beings in the Atlantic World was as much as about "us" as it was about "them," the celebrated "other" whose primary role was to nudge people into thinking about who they were by rejecting who they were not.[6]

The leaders of the American republic, created in colonial rebellion and nurtured within a federal political structure, faced a variation on the novel theme of nationalism. They had to create a nation quickly, for they had gambled their future on the ability of massive numbers of people participating as citizens in a huge political family. Religion and language, the building blocks of European nations, divided them; monarchy was unacceptable; folklore was limited. More, the republic was born in revulsion against the particular. Committed to a universal cause, explaining resistance to Great Britain as an assertion of the rights of man, of the liberty of local communities versus the tyranny of metropolitan governments, Americans assumed that the United States was the *summa* of human experience. The sheer size of the new nation was as daunting as its cultural diversity. Even within the rubrics of Protestantism or the English language, variations proliferated. The question of unity preoccupied Americans. What organized the peoples and regions of the United States into a whole? Territorial borders established limits and constitutions offered infrastructure. Alone, however, they were nothing more than the outlines of a nation; they did not create a sense of community.

Nowhere was this issue more pressing than in the Ohio and Mississippi Valleys. From the 1770s through the 1810s, trans-Appalachia was the cockpit of North America, the area in which most people assumed the future of the republic would be decided. Inhabited by tens of thousands of American Indians, from the Shawnees, Miamis, and Delawares south to the Creeks, Cherokees, Choctaws, and Seminoles, it attracted hundreds of European agents, soldiers, merchants, and speculators and was literally overrun with American citizens. Trans-Appalachia was a world of nearly continuous warfare, of raids and counter-raids that do not fit into the neat chronological boundaries of nationally defined wars. It was a world of schemers and adventurers, of endless possibilities and plots, a world in which James Wilkinson, the commanding general of the United States Army, George Rogers Clark, and Andrew Jackson flirted with the Spaniards, looking to advance themselves by cutting the best possible deal. It was a world in which the future was uncertain and sovereignty always at issue, a world in which all kinds of permutations seemed as likely one week as they seemed unlikely a few weeks later.

Who would govern trans-Appalachia? What would it look like fifty years hence? Would it be a multi-racial world? Would Indians and Americans co-exist? Would the French and/or the Spaniards remain major players? Would the considerable influence of British officials and merchants continue to grow? Would it become a separate nation or a series of nations? Or would the demographic advantage of the United States, with a population growing at well over thirty percent in the 1780s, triumph? And if it did, would Americans "become a distinct people" and constitute "a formidable and dangerous neighbor [?]"[7]

In exploring these issues, historians have tended to focus on questions of security and commerce. Assuming that tough-minded self-interest motivated trans-Appalachians, they implicitly suggest that national loyalty followed economic interest. The Washington Administration won the loyalty of many in the Ohio Valley in large part by reducing the threat of Indian attacks and implementing the development plans of the territorial ordinances of the 1780s. The battle of Fallen Timbers in August 1794 and the Jay Treaty with Great Britain and the Treaty of Greenville with Indians the next summer established the legitimacy of the republic west of the Appalachians.[8] In the same year, Pinckney's Treaty obtained a three year right of deposit at New Orleans, thereby stymieing some of the separatist tendencies created by the Confederation's fumbling of the Mississippi issue in the 1780s.

In this scenario, the key to attaching people to the United States was control of the river. The loyalty of trans-Appalachians hung in the balance as long as the Spaniards or the French (to whom the Spanish government conditionally ceded Louisiana in 1800) controlled the Mississippi and the port of New Orleans. No wonder then that Jefferson was so eager to acquire New Orleans; in many ways, the Louisiana Purchase climaxed two decades of efforts to establish the authority of the United States in trans-Appalachia. Once the republic controlled the Mississippi, its control of the heart of North America was all but inevitable.[9]

My purpose is to complicate rather than quarrel with this narrative of American expansion. My contention is that it involved an emotional as well as commercial dimension, rooted in a desire for people to choose to become Americans by mixing personal and national interests so thoroughly that it was impossible to tell the difference between them. Self-interest dictates loyalty as much as drainage dictates destiny. But patriotism consists of devotion to a nation based on an understanding of it as a grand extension of personal interest which is as much an emotional as a rational calculation. The issue in Jeffersonian America was how to nurture such a commitment, and in a romantic, democratic empire such as the fledgling United States, that necessarily included more than matters of commerce and diplomacy. It depended on a choice informed and confirmed by emotional attachment.

President Jefferson revealed the tone of the larger conversation in talking about the people of the North American interior. "The future inhabitants of the Atlantic & Missipi States will be our sons," he wrote, people with whom Americans had "relations of blood and affection." Jefferson claimed to be happy to leave their future in their hands. "[I]f they see their interest in separation, why should we take side with our Atlantic rather than our Missipi descendants? It is the elder and the younger son differing. God bless them both, & keep them in union, if it be for the good, but separate them, if it be for the better."[10] The United States could court them and shape the context with treaties and armies. But the ultimate decision was theirs.

National security depended on the decisions of thousands of individuals to identify with the republic as a whole. Purchasing Louisiana was a beginning, but it was only a beginning. Jefferson accorded voluntary attachment pride of place throughout his public and personal life.[11] The United States had "the strongest Government on earth" because it was "the only one where every man, at the call of the law, would fly to the standard of the law, and would meet invasions of the public order as his own personal concern."[12]

While this attitude may have existed more in the Jefferson's mind than in those of his fellow citizens, it was nonetheless the cornerstone of his national faith. The president most directly explained the process of attachment when considering the future of American Indians. He instructed Meriwether Lewis "to acquire . . . knolege . . . of the state of morality, religion & information" among Indians to that it would be easier "to civilize & instruct them" by adapting to their "notions & practices." The United States would be "neighborly, friendly & useful."[13] As important, Jefferson insisted to Indiana Territory Governor William Henry Harrison, that it was "essential to cultivate their love." Yes, commerce was the surest means to making Indians financially and then literally dependent on the United States, and power should always be held in reserve ("they must see that we have only to shut our hand to crush them"). But Jefferson preferred choice.[14] A republic created by force or diplomacy was a shell, a nation with borders but without meaning, a fleeting legality rather than a permanent community.

Moreover, emotional attachments, many suspected, were ultimately more reliable than pragmatic ones. Like people throughout the Atlantic world, Americans in the early republic were obsessed with questions of character. Unsure whether men were honest in their commitments, they were in search of ways to test them. Emotional outbursts, while dangerous, were windows on true selves. The sentimental eighteenth century had privileged the restraint of passion and the apotheosis of men who seemed without emotion, most notably, George Washington. But by the early nineteenth century, romantic passion was more acceptable socially and more desirable politically. If uncontrolled emotion could lead men into dark places and destroy family and community, bursts of passion could also demonstrate commitment. In their private lives, middle-class white Americans were revising common conceptions of courtship and marriage. The growth of the ideal of companionate marriage was predicated on the notion that a union made by consent rather than decree was more likely to serve the common good. Just as Americans considered the mysteries of attachment in their private lives, so, too, they pondered them in public.[15]

Nowhere was there a greater need for a reliable guide to human behavior than in the maelstrom of the Ohio and Mississippi Valleys, a world where deception and deceit were rampant, where loyalties shifted as much as the currents of the rivers, where men seemed guided solely by economic and personal interests. By opening the Mississippi, removing the French, and distancing the Spaniards, the Louisiana Purchase eliminated alternatives to the United States. But the Purchase, while gratifying, could not create the attachment needed to guarantee the loyalty of people west of the Appalachians.

Few people were as optimistic as Thomas Jefferson. Federalist John Routledge of South Carolina was particularly grim about "the purchase of a trackless world" which "must result in a disunion of these States."[16] Critics worried about the size and diversity of the United States, and the acquisition of citizens who became Americans by incorporation rather than birth or naturalization. However heartfelt the celebrations of the Purchase by the people of New Orleans, they remained "Frenchmen, Spaniards, and Americans" linked less by love of country than by "love of liberty and order."[17] Alas, lamented a Louisiana newspaper in 1811, "the great mass of the population" in the city of New Orleans considered the Fourth of July "a day of mourning rather than joy."[18]

In the Age of Jefferson, passion became the test, and the bedrock, of patriotism. If reason reveals interests and commerce channels them, loyalty depends on feelings. Men of passion were somehow trustworthy, for good or ill, precisely because they were intense. Let me look at this process in the lives of two famous Americans, Aaron Burr and Andrew Jackson.

In 1805 and 1806, Aaron Burr, the former vice-president of the United States and murderer of Alexander Hamilton, roamed the Ohio and Mississippi Valleys talking of a filibustering expedition toward territory claimed by the vice-royalty of New Spain. The prospect of a war with Spain, a nation few considered formidable, meant that everywhere Burr went, important men at least listened.[19] In its mixture of wealth and glory, Burr's adventure was only the most infamous of countless schemes. Yet Burr, the bad boy of the founding fathers, the villain who serves as a foil to his more popular brothers, merits the term "conspirator" and was tried for "treason."

Burr is the villain of our piece because he was an anachronism, an eighteenth-century gentleman with an eighteenth-century sense of empire and power. A cosmopolitan figure, a man at home in salons and comfortable with women, a father who encouraged his daughter to read Mary Wollstonecraft, a founding brother whose primary commitment was to himself, although in a genteel fashion, Burr was a restless and refined man who sought adventure in no small part to keep boredom at bay. He had the unusual quality of being a good listener. Where others concentrated on persuading others by the force of their words or personality, Burr obtained the same object by listening well, by finding "so much more meaning in your words than you had intended. No flattery was more subtle."[20] Beguiling, he was easily beguiled. Such was his nature. By instinct and training secretive and reserved, he was friendly without being revealing. Rarely did Burr seem emotional; rarely did he lose control. And, ironically, his mastery of himself made him seem less and less genuine.

Burr was interested in the United States as a vehicle for the fulfillment of his own ambition, not because he identified with the republic. He was in it but not of it. Whatever his exact plans in the Mississippi Valley, if he ever had any, he was undoubtedly motivated by a sense of himself as a gentleman adventurer seeking fame and fortune through an expedition against the Spaniards in Mexico.

In exile in Europe after his 1807 trial for treason, Burr was literally a man without a country, out of place in a romantic world of national sentiments that made no sense to a man who took pleasure in the company of women, especially if they were well-read and intelligent, but was almost never so foolish as to fall in love with them. Aaron Burr was, by design, not genuine. An enigma to us as well as contemporaries, he is forever hidden behind an eighteenth-century façade. We never see the real Burr any more than we ever understand the real purpose of his conspiracy.

When Burr talked of the United States, he did so dispassionately, if not unintelligently. Doubtful of the success of the republican experiment, he was suspicious in 1810 of the intensity of American citizens in their commitment to "license that it calls Liberty. The American nation is singularly jealous of the privilege that it has to depose at will those who govern; and these latter are, in effect, only the slaves to the passions of the multitude."[21] But it was less his ideological perspective than his studied distance, his refusal to engage emotionally, which disqualified him to be an American hero. He made men cry during his brief farewell address to the United States Senate on March 2, 1805. The vice president described his conduct as presiding officer as an effort to ensure "the dignity of the situation in which he stood" and he urged members to "cherish . . . habits of order and regularity." The Senate he saw as the last bastion of the United States and its Constitution.[22] Burr's speech produced tears, despite considerable distrust of the man who had killed Alexander Hamilton. Samuel Latham Mitchill later reported that he had "never experienced any thing . . . so affecting. . . . My colleague, General Smith, stout and manly as he is, wept as profusely as I did. He laid his head upon his table and did not recover from his emotion for a quarter of an hour or more." Even an unsympathetic journalist sarcastically commented that the speech was "so *pathetic* as to draw *tears* from *some* of the senators."[23]

The occasion was a consummate Burr performance, and a revealing one as well. It demonstrates the importance of emotion even in the United States Senate. It testifies to both Burr's considerable charisma, and his emotional reserve. He did not want to commit himself. Typically, the vice president left no record of his address and we have little information about his demeanor. We have no idea what he intended to do, or how he felt; we only know the impact he had on others. Burr was an American in name only. No wonder that attachments to Burr, including ours, were as fleeting as his attachment to the nation.

We think differently of Andrew Jackson of Tennessee, an ambitious, unrefined bully, a truly dangerous man, whose primary interest was in the greater glory of Andrew Jackson. The future tribune of American democracy, like many of his peers, was eager to attach himself to whatever government would best serve his interests. Jackson had no consistent, or thoughtful, ideological position other than self-protection. He was, and would remain, willing to develop loyalty out of personal interest. By 1806, Jackson knew that the United States was the most powerful player in trans-Appalachia. Racing to extricate himself from his association with Burr, he intensified his commitment to the American republic.

Unlike Burr, Jackson was an openly emotional man. While he worked to control his passions, he succeeded only intermittently. He wept, raged, insulted, and fought, often with impunity. Nothing was more prominent in his character than his determination to achieve his goals and punish his enemies. Jackson asserted himself; he did not insinuate himself. When he tried to flatter, he sounded false and he knew it. Not for him the behavior of an American aristocratic courtier. If he followed the etiquette of the duel, he also engaged in full-fledged, impulsive brawls in the streets of Nashville. If Jackson manipulated his notorious temper, its impact was always noisy and intimidating.[24]

Jackson was the antithesis of Burr, and so was his relationship with the United States. In the first decade of the nineteenth century, Andrew Jackson attached himself to the republic. He began to care about it, fell in love with it, by blending personal and national identity. If Jackson and his peers considered themselves American patriots, it was not because they were loyal to a national government but because they embraced the romantic idea that the United States was a collection of men like them. Patriotism amounted to a defense of their personal honor writ large. If Spaniards had taken an "insulting position" within the Louisiana Territory and had acted in ways "degrading to our national Character," then the pursuit of glory in the defense of the United States was "a laudable ambition." Merging private and public concerns, they would find "one voice" in the cause of "defending our national dignity & liberties."[25] Patriotism was what separated soldiers from supporters of Aaron Burr, those "*adventurers*" pursuing an "illegal project and enterprise."[26] Never mind that the goals of "adventurers" and patriots were similar: to seize territory and win fame and fortune in the doing. Patriots were not "*disappointed, unprincipled, ambitious* or *misguided individuals*."[27]

As these men came to equate their personal ambitions with national ambitions, their ever more virulent hostility to Indians helped them define a collective sense of American patriotism as much as the rituals of a republican political culture nurtured in Philadelphia and Washington, D. C. Reassured by the presence of an enemy whose savagery justified their ambitions, the angry young men of Tennessee described themselves as "inocent Citizens" and "victims" of "the ruthless hands of Savage barbarity" incited by European agents who have "deprived us of our fellow Citizens, of our Brothers our wifes & our children and [of] the influence that gave it birth."[28]

Fighting barbarous Indians helped Jackson and others construct the United States as something more than a government, as a people united in a defense of liberty rooted in religion, tradition, and race. Common cause against Indians gave legitimacy to ambitious passions, controlled dangerous factionalism, and created, Jackson said, "one sentiment" about the importance of their "attachment to the federal compact." "[A]ll must feel the injuries we have received, all must be determined to resist them, let us then, sir, with one heart and hand declare to the world, that firm determination . . . to go to any length with the government of our country, in defense and support of the nation's rights and independence."[29]

War, which finally came formally in 1812, was an opportunity to defeat the British, remove Indians, and intimidate the Spaniards, a chance to bring to an end decades of intermittent border wars. How, Jackson demanded of the Tennessee militia, could "we, who have clamoured for war, now skulk into a corner?" At stake was the character of the United States. For this was to be "an american war," which meant that it was not about "the ballance of power among an assasin tribe of Kings and Emperors," but about the defense of the rights and reputation of men of liberty. Justified in their righteous rage, Americans would "seek some indemnity for past injuries, some security against future aggressions, by the conquest of all the British dominions upon the continent of North america." They were "*a free people compelled to reclaim by the power of their arms the rights which god has bestowed upon them*."

Developing a conception of war as a struggle between different kinds of people, the alliances between Europeans and Indians that had defined North American politics were now evil as well as useless. It was time to end decades of discord in eastern North America by sorting out lines of authority and drawing borders, both territorial and cultural. It was time, Jackson told Tennessee volunteers in July 1812, to seize the opportunity to extend "the boundaries of the Republic to the Gulf of Mexico" and defeat the Creeks, the Shawnees, and "the blacks at Pensacola," as well as the British.[30] In short, it was time "that *all* our enemies should feel the force of that power, which has indulged them so long, & which they have, so long, treated with insult."[31]

Critical as commerce was in attaching trans-Appalachia to the United States, it was just one dimension. The process of nation-building was as mystical as it was pragmatic, a blend of interest and emotion. Unlike Burr, Jackson thought of himself as an American publicly and privately. His romantic conception of patriotism had less to do with what governments did or did not do than with imagining a voluntary association of people who had decided that they were alike because they were not barbaric Indians or despicable Spaniards. In sum, while the Purchase constructed the territorial borders of the United States in the Age of Jefferson, conquest facilitated the construction of a romantic nationalism around a network of patriarchal brothers defined by race, religion, and place. More often than not, the men who dominated the nineteenth-century North American republican empire would be those men who felt most strongly that they and their nation were one and the same, now and forever.

Chapter 16

An Identity by Any Other Name: Attachments in an Age of Expansion

Peter J. Kastor

Professor Drew Cayton's essay has given me a national context within which to operate, and has provided the word that will frame my essay. That word is attachment, and I introduce the word here as a way of suggesting that I am giving this paper under false pretenses. Look at the title of the panel. Look at the title of my own paper. The word "identity" appears front and center. And yet I want to argue today that the word identity is so fraught with problems that it not only loses its usefulness, but actually gets in the way of understanding how people in Louisiana responded to the Louisiana Purchase. So instead I will use "attachment" because that's the word I find most effective when talking about how Louisiana related to the rest of the United States.

The question I will discuss today may sound parochial and specific: how did people in Louisiana react to the Louisiana Purchase? But I would like to take this question as a point of departure for considering how people throughout the United States talked about what it meant to be an American and what it meant to be a nation. I cast the topic in this light for a variety of reasons. First, I specifically *do not* want my discussion of Louisiana to be parochial. Too often that's the case. A lot of Louisiana's history has been written to answer very specific questions about local development. The result: a world that seems so corrupt, so unusual, so definitively aberrant that Louisiana suffers in scholarly isolation. I would like to retrieve Louisiana from this intellectual back alley, not only by situating it within a national debate, but more importantly by arguing that Louisiana proved critical to the most important questions emerging in North America at the turn of the nineteenth century. For as people throughout North America argued about what it meant to be American and what it meant to be a nation, the people of Louisiana provided the ideal case study.

As a result, the best way to understand how Louisianians responded to the Purchase is to include people in other states and especially people in Washington, D. C. It was in the efforts to build linkages between these locales that people attempted to define Louisiana's fate. And the word people used throughout this conversation was "attachment." They used this term—and I use it today—because it casts a much wider net than "identity." When we use "identity," we usually refer to the abstract connections between individuals and larger societies. We particularly focus on individual feelings. Do people *feel* connected to the rest of the country? Do they *feel* they are Americans? And of course, when those connections get confused, we ask if people *feel* an identity crisis. While those connections between the individual and the national were important at the time of the Louisiana Purchase, they were hardly the only thing that people discussed. People were equally concerned with political, administrative, commercial, diplomatic, and legal connections. This was the case in large part because they operated before the word "identity" had even entered the public vocabulary with meanings similar to that of the current use of that term.[1] "Attachment" therefore keeps the discussion of Louisiana more grounded, for attachment was the word people used at the time.

Attachment would also provide Louisianians with exactly what they wanted. In the years following the Purchase, the quest for Louisiana's attachment gave its white residents the ammunition to overcome particular problems they associated with their colonial past. Put simply, nobody proclaimed they were "American" more loudly than white Louisianians. But establishing themselves as Americans depended in large part on their skillful use of the language of attachment, an idiom that had emerged in the context of empire and revolution in North America. So while the majority of Louisiana's residents might continue to speak one language—French—that was at odds with the English language that most American elites spoke, Louisianians and Americans had another language—attachment—in which they all became quite fluent.

On a final introductory note, I need to explain my terms. I use "Louisianians" to refer to those people who lived in Louisiana before 1803 and who found their nationality transformed by the Louisiana Purchase.[2] Likewise, the Americans to whom I refer were the predominantly Anglophone citizens of the United States from outside Louisiana. I realize these labels would be something of an insult to many Louisianians in the early nineteenth century who so forcefully argued that they, too, were Americans. By the 1820s few people would question whether Louisianians were also Americans. In the first two decades after the Louisiana Purchase, however, nobody was so certain.

Finally, the "Louisiana" I discuss is both the current State of Louisiana and its jurisdictional predecessor, the Territory of Orleans. To those of you who, like me, have come to New Orleans from places like St. Louis, I apologize now for leaving you out of my story. My reasons are simple: it was within what became the State of Louisiana that people saw the greatest threats to the Union. And it was attachment in all its forms that offered a solution to those threats.

Let me also reveal the premise that sets the stage for my discussion of attachment. Whites and free people of color in Louisiana welcomed the Louisiana Purchase. While free people of color eventually had reason to question the benefits of the transfer, whites remained resolute. White Louisianians made almost no effort to become French subjects (the assumption that so many now often bring to their discussion of the Purchase), nor did they resist federal sovereignty in any substantive way. By contrast, the greatest assaults on the federal hold on Louisiana came primarily from slaves and, to a lesser degree, from Indians and white Americans. Why this would be the case occasionally related to identity, but always related to attachment.

As other speakers in this conference have shown, white Louisianians had seen regimes come and go, and they responded in kind. By 1803 most of them had actually been raised within the Spanish empire, and much as they may have retained various French customs, their understanding of their relationship to a larger world emerged from their status as residents of an underdeveloped frontier that had known various European masters.

The residents of Louisiana responded accordingly to these circumstances. White Louisianians resented imperial policies during the eighteenth century that prevented their integration into larger economic and social networks, whether those policies came from Paris or from Madrid. Although white Louisianians never declared independence as did their neighbors in the British colonies east of the Mississippi, they nonetheless rejected the sort of jurisdictional inequality that characterized imperial systems.[3] White Louisianians did so in no small part because they were aware of the rhetoric generated by the revolutions in the United States and France, especially arguments about equality, whether for individual citizens or geographic entities.[4] They also received scattered indications of the emerging rationale for union within the United States. Not only did this take a constitutional form, but part of the argument for a strong Union rested on the argument that despite local differences and local loyalties, all Americans shared a unified commitment to republican government.[5]

Then came news in the summer of 1803 that France had sold Louisiana to the United States. Louisianians responded in ways similar to residents throughout the frontiers of North America. Fundamentally pragmatic in their outlook, they sought the means to connect themselves to larger networks in ways that would deliver specific benefits. Does this mean that preserving local cultural customs did not matter to white Louisianians? Of course not. But it does mean that, given a choice between the two revolutionary regimes, the American model seemed both more appropriate to their circumstances and less dangerous than the French. While many Louisianians felt a cultural affinity toward France, they also recoiled at what they considered the excesses of the French Revolution. Already eager for greater political opportunities, white Louisianians worried about stories of how the revolutionary regime crushed its critics. Louisiana Catholics were likewise concerned about new restrictions on the Church. Finally, because the regional economy depended on slave labor, white Louisianians were terrified by efforts in Paris to end the slave trade and because the revolt in Saint-Domingue suggested just what could happen when slaves adopted the ideology of revolution.[6]

So in 1803 Louisianians believed they faced unprecedented possibilities. They hoped federal rule would expand political opportunity, eliminate the uncertain property title (both in slaves and in land) that characterized the colonial period, and reinforce racial supremacy.[7] They were particularly pleased with the wording of the Louisiana Purchase, which guaranteed that "the inhabitants of the ceded territory shall be incorporated in the union of the United States," and that they would enjoy "all the rights, advantages and immunities of citizens of the United States."[8] Louisianians grasped at this promise with a vengeance, immediately claiming that they were, in fact, Americans, and should be treated as such.

Figure 14. Bror Thure de Thulstrup, *Raising of the American Flag: Louisiana Transfer Ceremonies*, 1903. Louisiana State Museum No. 01793. Courtesy of the Louisiana State Museum. Loan of the Louisiana Historical Society.

The response was hardly welcoming. Many Americans still considered territorial expansion a fundamental threat to the Union. Indeed, the Jefferson administration had specifically rejected any plans to acquire anything beyond New Orleans and the Gulf Coast, and only purchased such a vast area of land in 1803 because the French had made it clear that they would sell nothing less.[9] Beyond the matter of *geographic* expansion was the equally troubling question of *demographic* expansion. Critics throughout the United States claimed that the Louisianians might be citizens in the eyes of the law, but they were nonetheless aliens in fact. As New York Congressman Jonathan Miller stated, "I was born in Virginia, sir, and I have not yet lost some of my Virginia feelings. . . . I cannot see why we should expect the people of Orleans to act and feel differently."[10] Unlike other immigrants, the Louisianians had not undergone the naturalization process which was supposed to teach newcomers how to participate in a republican polity. That they spoke French or Spanish or that they were Catholic—seemingly the most obvious forms of difference—was less important to most Americans than the fact that the Louisianians seemed unfamiliar with republican government. Language and religion were indeed important, but political culture mattered more. This concern applied to Federalists and Republicans alike because, despite other areas of dispute, members of both parties were convinced that the United States faced internal and external threats which might destroy the Union.[11] When Louisianians complained about the initial form of territorial government, for example, a Congressional committee concluded "only two modes present themselves whereby a dependent province may be held in obedience to its sovereign State—force and affection." Louisianians got what they wanted in large part because federal officials concluded that co-opting white Louisianians was the only viable policy.[12]

White Louisianians responded to American hostility and doubts by claiming that affection was sufficient and that white Louisianians possessed affection in abundance. In 1807, a territorial legislature dominated by Creoles and émigrés from France and the French Caribbean wanted the rest of the nation to be "assured of the attachment and Devotion of the Citizens of this Territory to the Government of the United States."[13] In the July 4, 1810, issue of the *Louisiana Courier*, an editorial by "Americus" used the occasion to describe incorporation in very familiar terms. "The great anniversary of our national independence has again returned with its crowded blessings and attach us more firmly to our native soil, and raise our veneration for those illustrious worthies who planned our freedom, as well as support our cause in the cabinet by their counsels, and in the field by their valour."[14]

These efforts proved effective. By February 1812, John Prevost, previously a territorial judge in Louisiana, reflected the attitude of many American observers when he informed his friend, Secretary of State James Monroe, that "no member of our community has more uniformly discovered a sincere attachment to the government of the States [than Louisiana]."[15] He wrote in the midst of the debate in Congress over Louisiana statehood, and he shared the opinion of the men in both the House and Senate. Federalists and Republicans might disagree over whether Louisiana should be a state, but they articulated that disagreement from a shared conviction that the attachment of white Louisianians was a prerequisite for joining the Union. The question they had to debate was whether that attachment was real. A majority in Congress agreed that it was, creating the State of Louisiana in April 1812.

But there was more to the discussion of Louisiana statehood than the feelings of white Louisianians because attachment had other meanings that were no less important. It was not sufficient for Louisianians to "feel" they were Americans. White Louisianians and federal policymakers had long since agreed on the numerous forms of attachment that they wanted to see. They had to extend a republican political system west of the Mississippi while establishing a civil government that would protect Louisiana against the threats of foreigners and non-whites. As far as federal policymakers and white Louisianians were concerned, attachment included the geopolitical attachment of Louisiana to the United States, the attachment of human property to its owners, and the commercial attachment of Louisiana within national trade networks. To this end, white Louisianians and federal policymakers together set out to build an institutional apparatus that would preserve attachment in all its forms.

The institutional mechanisms of attachment were varied. The Jefferson and Madison administrations kept the largest concentration of peacetime troops in Louisiana to defend its attachment against the foreign threats that American policymakers perceived from Britain, France, and especially from Spain as well as the domestic danger of slaves, Indians, and disgruntled whites. New Orleans officials built the first uniformed police system in the United States as a further safeguard against slave revolt.[16] Federal policymakers and reform-minded white Louisianians attempted to build a system of public education that would train Louisianians in the principles of American politics. This effort proved to be a dismal failure, but more enterprising Louisianians created a host of private academies in the 1810s, all the while claiming that they were promoting attachment by training white Louisianians in the commercial, linguistic, and social skills they would need to thrive as citizens of the United States.[17] Finally white Louisianians and federal policymakers together hammered out a legal system which, while unlike that of other American states and territories, nonetheless provided a basis for civil behavior while imposing new restrictions on slaves and free people of color.

I end my list of institutions with the law because Louisiana's unique legal system has usually stood as the greatest sign of resistance by white Louisianians. But the core of that legal system—the Civil Digest of 1808—was only one of a series of public documents that overhauled Louisiana's legal system in ways designed less to preserve local culture than to integrate Louisiana into an American commercial community and to advance racial supremacy. What legal tradition would serve as the basis of that system might be subject to debate, but the need for reform was not.[18]

A critical thing to remember is that these very political debates—whether lovefests like the Louisianians' claims of devotion or angry disputes when Louisianians considered themselves ignored—were themselves means of creating attachment. Whether amiable or angry, a national conversation was just that: a conversation. To white Louisianians and to Americans, creating that conversation through letters, through newspapers, and through political participation would all make attachment a reality. Consider the case of Eligius Fromentin, a former French priest who became a leading figure in territorial and state politics. Fromentin campaigned vigorously on behalf of James Madison in 1812, only weeks after Louisiana became a state, to the point of publishing a pamphlet claiming "it is high time" for frontier residents to be heard. "Let us hear, once more, this New-Orleans Washingtoninan," was the condescending remark from a Pittsburgh pamphleteer who supported Dewitt Clinton, the president's most threatening opponent. What the pamphleteer did not mention (or perhaps did not realize) was that this sort of debate was exactly what the Louisianians wanted. With each exchange Louisiana became a more entrenched participant in the national political dialogue.[19] Nor was this process of forging networks limited to national politics or to public statements. In 1817, for example, the New Orleans City Council dispatched one of its members as an unofficial lobbyist to the East Coast, where he was supposed to establish contacts in other municipalities as well as Washington, D. C.[20]

Louisianians also decided that Americans themselves could provide an effective means to establish Louisiana's influence. Voters in Louisiana sent only one Louisianian (the Frenchman, Fromentin) to serve a full term in either house of Congress. The rest were Americans, mostly transplanted Virginians and veterans of the territorial regime. This outcome was not the result of ethnic voting, for Louisianians commanded majorities in both the electorate and the legislature. It was instead a tactical decision designed to maximize the new state's power in the national capital. The Americans who represented Louisiana would arrive with their power already established, unlike even elite Louisianians who, for all their local power, were outsiders in Washington.[21] These political attachments were only reinforced by an emerging set of kinship connections as families from the American and Louisianian elite began to intermarry in ways that only contributed to an already byzantine system of relations among leading Louisianians (William C. C. Claiborne, who served as governor throughout Louisiana's territorial period and became the state's first elected governor, actually married *two* Creoles).

These forms of contact only grew as Louisianians and Americans confronted external tests from foreign powers, slaves, Indians, and white Americans, all of whom challenged attachment along the lines that white Louisianians and American officials hoped to impose. The most famous threat actually remains the most elusive. Ongoing research is showing just how difficult it is to determine what Aaron Burr intended to do in 1806-1807. But the *reaction* was certainly clear. Members of the Jefferson administration certainly believed that the former vice-president had formed a conspiracy to advance a separatist scheme in Louisiana. The threat proved short-lived. Federal troops soon captured him, and (more importantly) white Louisianians ignored him. Burr only mattered to white Louisianians when they could use him to advance their claims of attachment. The strategy worked so well that members of Congress used the events of 1806-1807 to argue for statehood in 1811-1812. "When some citizens of the old States forgot the love every honest heart owes to his country," Nathanial Macon explained, the Louisianians "showed their attachment to the Union by the readiness with which they lent their aid to repel them. To make them a State would make the attachment still greater."[22]

Greater threats to attachment than Burr came from Indians, slaves, and foreign powers in ways that directly overlapped. Nowhere was this more true than on the borderlands between American Louisiana and Spanish America. The Louisiana Purchase failed to provide clear boundaries. Not only did these circumstances generate unending disputes between the United States and Spain, but they also created tremendous opportunities for Indians and slaves. Indians on the borderlands found that the very danger of international conflict also provided the ideal circumstances for Indians to manipulate. The Caddo Indians in the West and the Choctaw Indians in the East both successfully preserved their autonomy by holding the United States hostage, promising not to side with Spain so long as the United States did not demand the subjugating attachment that had characterized federal policies in other parts of the Union.[23]

While Indians pressed their own terms on the United States and Spain, runaway slaves disappeared into the borderlands. Claiborne warned the Marquis de Casa Calvo, a former governor of Spanish Louisiana who remained in the area after the transfer of power, that "if the protection be offered by the Commandant of Nacogdoches to a Single Slave deserting the service of his master, the consequences . . . will be injurious to the citizens of the United States, and may tend to disturb the good understanding between our two nations."[24]

The greatest assault on the attachment of slaves to their masters came in January 1811, when an army of slaves (estimates of its numbers varied from 150 to 500) marched on New Orleans in what may well have been the largest slave revolt in U. S. history. In the winter of 1810-1811, the troops and senior public officials who spent much of their time worrying about slave revolt were away from Louisiana's plantation district, attempting to consolidate federal sovereignty east of the Mississippi.[25] "An express gave up the alarm," observed Captain John Shaw of the United States Navy. "The whole city [of New Orleans] was convulsed, and the confusion which prevailed was general. . . . I have never before been witness to such general confusion and disarray."[26] The British invasion of Louisiana in the winter of 1814 and 1815 provided slaves with one final opportunity to secure their freedom in large numbers.

On the borderlands, in the slave revolt of 1811, and during the British invasion, slaves rejected the sort of attachment that whites hoped to build. They exploited moments of international crisis, when attachment seemed to be its weakest. All of these events reminded whites that removing foreign threats and preserving white supremacy were mutually reinforcing activities.

The British invasion actually seemed to prove the benefits of attachment in all its forms. After all, what could have been a better test of the attachment of Louisiana to the United States that the arrival of a massive foreign armada? The British certainly hoped to capitalize on the situation. They concluded that the slave revolt and white resentment would make for an easy invasion. They implored white Louisianians to overthrow "the *american usurpation in this country*." They invited slaves to flee their plantations and sought alliances with Indians.[27] As events showed, the British were mistaken about the situation, and their expectations now seem laughable given the lopsided American victory at the Battle of New Orleans. But they operated from the same logic as their American opponents. British strategists, American policymakers, and white Louisianians considered attachment essential. The question in 1815 was just how strong those attachments actually were.

In the years after 1815, whites struggled to finish the process of building attachments that would consolidate things locally while extending their influence nationally. Indians, slaves, and free people of color suffered accordingly. The civil and military apparatus prevented another slave revolt similar to the 1811 uprising, while legal changes created a host of new obstacles for slaves who hoped to secure their freedom through legal means. White supremacy also dashed the hopes of free people of color, who initially believed that their own claims of attachment might create new opportunities. Finally, with the federal hold on Louisiana's borderlands secured by the Transcontinental Treaty in 1819 (also known as the Adams-Onís Treaty), Indians lost the autonomy they had known since 1803.

I am not trying to suggest some ironic counterpoint to the tremendous benefits that white Louisianians found after 1803. To the contrary, I want to emphasize that the benefits of whites and the suffering of non-whites were mutually dependent. Perhaps more important for what I am discussing today, they also reflected the different meanings of attachment.

Looking back from the 1820s, white Louisianians and federal policymakers could take considerable pride in their achievements. They had preserved a union based on republican government and white supremacy against considerable dangers. And this test had been a long time coming. Since 1776, people had wondered how much territory and how many people the republic could incorporate. While many still doubted that the United States *should* expand, few doubted that it *could*. And Louisiana had shown the means to that expansion. Attachment seemed to validate the notion that a union of affection would be more effective than a union of force, at least when it came to white settlers.

The governor of Louisiana, a Creole named Jacques Philippe Villeré, said as much in 1819 when he proclaimed Louisiana a member of the "American family."[28] His metaphor was appropriate. People throughout the United States spoke of their Union as a family. Frontier residents in particular liked to invoke this idea, because it assumed equality and affection, rather than the inequality and distance that was a reality in so many empires. And what possessed stronger attachments than a family? The only question was how to classify Louisiana. Was it the eccentric uncle? The oddball aunt? The prodigal son? Perhaps so. By 1820, Louisiana still seemed unlike other states. Yet it certainly seemed attached. It was American.

SUGGESTED READINGS

Cayton, Andrew R. L. *The Frontier Republic: Ideology and Politics in the Ohio Country, 1780-1825*. Kent, Ohio: Kent State University Press, 1986.

Dargo, George. *Jefferson's Louisiana: Politics and the Clash of Legal Traditions*. Studies in Legal History. Cambridge, Mass.: Harvard University Press, 1975.

Gitlin, Jay. "Children of Empire or Concitoyens?: Louisiana's French Inhabitants." *In The Louisiana Purchase: Emergence of an American Nation*, ed. Peter J. Kastor, 23-37. Landmark Events in U. S. History Series. Washington, D. C.: CQ Press, 2002.

Gleason, Philip D. "Identifying Identity: A Semantic History." *Journal of American History*, 69 (1983): 910-31.

Kastor, Peter J. "'Motives of Peculiar Urgency:' Local Diplomacy in Louisiana, 1803-1821." *William and Mary Quarterly* 3rd. ser., 58 (2001): 819-848.

Lewis, James E., Jr. *The American Union and the Problem of Neighborhood: The United States and the Collapse of the Spanish Empire, 1783-1829*. Chapel Hill, University of North Carolina Press, 1998.

Morgan, Edmund S. "Slavery and Freedom: The American Paradox." *Journal of American History*, 59 (1972): 5-29.

Onuf, Peter S. "Liberty, Development, and Union: Visions of the West in the 1780s." *William and Mary Quarterly* 3rd. ser., 43 (1986): 179-213.

Russell, Sarah. "Ethnicity, Commerce, and Community on Lower Louisiana's Plantation Frontier, 1803-1828." *Louisiana History*, 40 (1999): 389-405.

Waldstreicher, David. *In the Midst of Perpetual Fetes: The Making of American Nationalism, 1776-1820*. Chapel Hill: University of North Carolina Press for the Omohundro Institute of Early American History and Culture, Williamsburg, Virginia, 1997.

Chapter 17

The Legal Heritage of the Louisiana Purchase

Hans W. Baade

Introduction

We are meeting today in a cosmopolitan city of an unmistakably European character, within walking distance of French- and Spanish-language judicial and notarial archives. The heritage of France and Spain is apparent in street names, architecture, geographical terms, the culinary vocabulary as well as its substance, and popular habits even, or especially, after dark. Many of us keep coming here in good part for some (or all) of these reasons, and Europeans like myself feel instinctively and immediately at home. My homing instinct, in particular, is also due, in good part, to the fact that my Lady, the Civil Law, is alive and well in these parts.

All of this has something to do with the Louisiana Purchase. My assigned task is to discuss the legal heritage of that momentous event, consummated on December 20, 1803, at New Orleans and a few months thereafter at St. Louis in what is now Missouri. I divide my topic into four segments, starting with the traditions established or confirmed by the Purchase itself and proceeding from there through the traditions then in place to the peculiar legal history of Orleans Territory and the present State of Louisiana. I conclude with some speculations as to why all of this happened here as it did.

The Precedent of the Purchase

The Constitution of the United States does not authorize the acquisition of territory by treaty, and this was well known in 1803. The precedent then set by the Treaty with France and by subsequent implementing legislation was that the United States could indeed acquire territory by treaty (as it did subsequently from Spain, Mexico, Russia, Spain again, and Denmark) but that such acquisitions had to conform to basic principles of United States constitutional law and of international law. In short, the United States acquired the public domain of the former sovereign but undertook to respect existing private property rights. It guaranteed religious freedom but not the rights of the previously established church, and it undertook to grant full citizenship to the inhabitants of the Purchase territory upon admission of these territories to statehood. This curiosity was due to the fact that United States nationality, as we would now call it, was then conceived to be derived exclusively from State citizenship, and that the prerequisites of admission to statehood included a transitional stage of territorial government.[1]

But territorial government was federal government established by federal law and governed by the basic principles of the United States Constitution. This meant, rather sooner than later, the introduction of the jury system at least in criminal cases and with it, of necessity, common-law criminal procedure and evidence, and more or less automatically, the establishment of a system of judicial organization modeled on those prevailing elsewhere in the United States.

Put somewhat more directly, the United States always extended its public law to newly acquired territories even where, starting with the Louisiana Purchase, it had undertaken by treaty to respect pre-existing private property rights. It follows that when present-day Louisiana is denominated a civil law jurisdiction, the focus is on private law. Its legal system as a whole is more properly described as a mixed one, mainly (but not exclusively) because the public law prevailing here, even where it is not United States federal law, is still shaped by notions derived from the common-law tradition peculiar to the United States. It has become customary, therefore, to describe the legal system of Louisiana as a "mixed" one—a term also employed, for similar but not identical reasons, especially for Quebec, Scotland, and South Africa.

How is it, then, that at least in the private-law sphere, the civil law survived in that part of the Louisiana Purchase formerly known as Orleans Territory and now constituting, together with the so-called Florida Parishes, the State of Louisiana? And why is it that private law regimes are different in Arkansas and Missouri—to say nothing of Purchase territories further to the North?

Two further observations may put this question into sharper focus. First, as eager claimants have to be reminded even in these days, treaty guarantees of property rights existing at the time of the transfer of sovereignty do not, as such, ossify or preserve the legal system then in place. Like everything else, these rights are subject to subsequent changes in the legal system, not only as to acquisitive and extinctive prescription but also to more fundamental changes, such as the radical replacement of the civil law by the common law through legislative *fiat* which occurred everywhere in the Continental United States except in Louisiana.

Secondly but perhaps not secondarily, the system for the verification of vested property rights put in place by the United States in the very enactment "erecting Louisiana into two territories, and providing for the temporary government thereof" exhibited special concern for "any bona fide act or proceeding" by actual settlers agreeable not necessarily to the laws, but also if need be to the "usages and customs of the Spanish government"—as understood and practiced *in loco*. As President Lincoln wrote, some four decades thereafter, "liberal measures adopted in reference to actual settlers" had been a prevailing policy in the disposal of the public domain, with a view to "early settlement and substantial cultivation." The confirmation of property rights deriving from foreign sovereigns was not, therefore, primarily an exercise focusing on the accurate determination of the law of the former sovereign. Local practice beneficial to "actual ['Anglo'] settlers" could, and did, trump the learning of Salamanca and the jurisprudence of the Council of the Indies.

Legal Traditions in Place at the Cession

Aside from migratory tribes, legal traditions exist only in settled communities. There were slightly more than half a dozen of these in the Upper Territory on December 20, 1803, and perhaps twice that number in what is now Louisiana. These settlements were made almost exclusively by Frenchmen (including French Canadians), and, outside of New Orleans, the French language remained the idiom of official as well as social communication even in the period of direct Spanish administration which commenced in August 1769 and ended on November 30, 1803.

Between these two dates, the Purchase territory was the Spanish ultramarine province of *Luisiana*, governed by the law of Castile and of the Indies. This legal system was fully in effect at that time, however, only in the capital, New Orleans. There (and only there) we find the full panoply of political and legal administration in Spanish North America: a repository of current royal legislation, a legal advisor who was a genuine university-educated Spanish lawyer, and properly qualified pleaders as well as notaries. Since New Orleans had original jurisdiction in the more important cases and appellate jurisdiction in matters decided by the commandants at the outlying settlements or posts, it might be thought that at the end of more than three decades of direct Spanish rule, Spanish law prevailed throughout Luisiana. That was not, however, the case in all private law transactions of everyday life.

In this connection, I have singled out for special attention the agreed-upon regime of family property, the form of marriage, sales and mortgages of immovables and slaves, and the manumission, by voluntary or compulsory self-purchase, of slaves by their masters.

In France (and in French Louisiana before direct Spanish rule), marital property was all but invariably an agreed-upon family settlement embodied in a marriage contract, concluded in notarial form before (of course) marriage in Roman Catholic form. This was then, as it is now, the most important contract type in French law. In Castilian Spain, however (and consequently, in the ultramarine Spanish empire) a full-blown marriage contract was virtually unknown, and the standard instrument of family wealth planning was the testament.

It is readily established that during the "French" period (from about 1708 to August 1769), the eighteenth century French legal folkway of regulating the property aspects of the marital relationship by an antenuptial notarial marriage contract drafted pursuant to the prototype developed by the Paris notarial profession, and reflecting the Custom of Paris, was firmly rooted in Louisiana. Indeed, the maintenance of this folkway was one of the main functions of the legal institutions of French Louisiana. The Custom of Paris was in force locally and could not be excluded by choice-of-law clauses, and the Superior Council was expressly directed to register donations in marriage contracts. Its *greffier* was regularly a notary who passed such contracts in his notarial capacity. Notaries were appointed for the outlying posts largely to draft marriage contracts. The records show even illiterate prospective spouses entered into marriage contracts. Contemporary accounts of Quebec and Metropolitan French notarial practice demonstrate that this legal folkway was common to continental and colonial pre-Revolutionary France.

How did this tradition fare in the three-plus decades between 1769 and 1803? A survey of the judicial records of some fifteen posts has shown that the French legal folkway of concluding marriage contracts pursuant to the Paris notarial prototype lived on in Luisiana in the Spanish period. This is most readily apparently at the posts, where French-language marriage contracts following French form precedent were routinely used throughout that period, with only the choice-of-law clause modified. In New Orleans, on the other hand, the style of such instruments executed in the Spanish era was Castilian in language and in content.

Like their French prototype, the marriage contracts in use in the Purchase territory throughout the French and Spanish periods were concluded by the prospective spouses before the marriage ceremony, which as routinely provided in the initial clause of the contract had to be celebrated *in facie ecclesiae* (in the presence of a priest). This was so because both under French and under Spanish law as applicable in this part of North America, the Tridentine form of marriage was mandatory for baptized Christians. This requirement was occasionally circumvented where there was no priest available, or avoided, when possible, by non-Catholic spouses especially in the Spanish Floridas. In the period of direct Spanish rule, however, both the Bishop at New Orleans and priests with judicial faculties exercised ecclesiastical jurisdiction both in the Upper and the Lower territories, and Roman Catholic canon law was part of the law of those lands.

Extrapolating for a moment, we might note that further to the North, and before the "property and civil rights" clause of the Quebec Act 1774 affirmed the continued existence of the Civil Law in Canada, the sedentary priest and the ambulatory notary kept the French legal system alive in rural Quebec. The business of the latter is encapsulated by the formula *femme et terre*, or marriage contracts and conveyances, with the occasional mortgage where there was at least the prospect of real money. Marital status and family property, we saw, were governed by the Church and by marriage contract in French as well as Spanish Louisiana, but this left out contracts and real estate transactions *inter vivos*. Two sets of regulations enacted in the initial period of direct Spanish rule sought to regulate the latter.

These two instruments, dated February 12 and November 9, 1770, laid down stringent form and registration requirements for sales, conveyances, donations, and conveyances of immovables and slaves. All such transactions had to be in notarial or, at the posts, in quasi-notarial form (i.e., passed by the Lieutenant Governor or Commandant with two witnesses *de asistencia*; i.e., authenticated). Additionally, mortgages were valid only if registered by the notary of the New Orleans *cabildo* who was *ex officio* the annotator of mortgages, and conveyances had to incorporate a certificate of that official as to the presence or absence of burdens on the property sold.

These requirements were observed fully in New Orleans and in the major posts of the Lower Territory. In the Upper Territory, conveyances and mortgages of land and slaves were in the prescribed quasi-notarial form, but there was, apparently, no compliance with the requirement of registration of mortgages in far away New Orleans. It remains to add that the requirement of public instruments for land transactions was in harmony with the law of French Louisiana at least under Crown rule.

As shown by these enactments in the first full year of direct Spanish rule, slave sales and (even more hideous thought) slave mortgages were an important element in the legal world of the Purchase territory. This brings us to the law of slavery under French and Spanish rule. From a private-law perspective, my focus is on the legal capacity of slaves and on the legal avenues (and obstacles) to their manumission.

The point of departure is the arrival of five hundred African slaves in French Louisiana in the summer of 1719. Five years later, in August 1724, King Louis XV promulgated a slave code for Louisiana, known colloquially as the *Code Noir.* It follows the 1685 code for the French Caribbean Islands in disqualifying slaves from being either witnesses or parties in civil litigation, and in denying them the right to own property or to contract in their own names. Slaves could only be manumitted by their masters once these had reached the age of twenty-five, and by permission of the *Conseil Superieur* (Superior Council, Louisiana's local governing board) for reasons acceptable to the latter. Free persons of color were expressly rendered incapable of receiving either *inter vivos* or *mortis causae* donations from whites. Subject to that exception, however, they were granted the same rights as French subjects of the white race.

The system of slave law just described precluded the development of any judicially enforceable right to self-purchase. Slaves could not possess property or funds with which to buy their freedom; in any event, they could not validly contract on their own behalves. Furthermore, because the courts were closed to them not only as witnesses, but also as plaintiffs, any de facto understanding with their masters lacked the possibility of legal sanction. This is not to say that self-purchase was not practiced. Quite the contrary, article 50 of the Louisiana *Code Noir* expressly mentioned the possibility of "finding masters sufficiently mercenary to put their slaves at liberty for a price." It was believed that the promise held out to slaves by article 50 was apt to lead to theft and to robbery on the part of slaves (presumably to obtain their purchase price). For this reason, 1724's *Code Noir* prohibited the manumission of slaves without the consent of the Superior Council, and further stipulated that such consent was to be granted only if the master's motives in manumitting his slave were deemed legitimate by the Council. In sum, the Louisiana *Code Noir* expressly condemned the practice of self-purchase, and sought to inhibit it by making manumission contingent upon government approval upon a showing of "legitimate" motive (i.e., a non-"mercenary" one).

Although General O'Reilly initially confirmed the continued applicability of the *Code Noir* under direct Spanish rule, the administrative system which he put in place soon thereafter was quite contrary to the basic features of this codification of French slave law. Restrictions on the voluntary manumission of slaves fell with the replacement of the *Conseil Superieur* by the *cabildo* of New Orleans, but even more importantly, the

Spanish judicial machinery installed in that city put into practice the institution of *coartación* which had been developed some centuries earlier for Cuba. This was the right of slaves to purchase their freedom at their appraised value, if need be by order of the court.[2]

Enforced self-purchase was bitterly resisted by the slaveholding population, and at one time, a committee of notables convened for the purpose of codifying the slave law of Spanish Luisiana produced a draft *Code Noir* which would have returned to the French system. Prudently perhaps, the authors and supporters of that scheme did not present it for Royal approval. Compulsory freedom purchase litigation continued with, apparently, only one interruption due to the absence of a law-trained legal advisor of the then Governor who was connected to the local Francophone slaveholding squirarchy by marriage. One or two such cases per year were sufficient, apparently, to induce most masters to agree to reasonable offers of self-purchase by their slaves, with the result that of the 1,921 slaves manumitted in Spanish Luisiana between 1771 and 1803, 452 achieved freedom through self-purchase, 445, through third-party purchase, and only 154 by judicial decree.[3]

Transition, Extinction, Survival, and Revival

The Spanish administrative and legal system in place at New Orleans between 1769 and 1803 was vastly more sophisticated than those of other capital towns in the northern tier of eighteenth-century Spanish North America. The governor and later, the intendant had a *letrado* legal advisor; there was a functioning system of ecclesiastical tribunals and even a bishop in residence for a few years at the end of the period; general and specific legislation expedited by the Council of the Indies was received regularly; two and later three *escribanos* passed notarial acts in due form; and a like number of *procuradores del número* (licensed pleaders) saw to the regularity of filings in court proceedings. Present-day perspective, however, highlights one glaring deficiency: there were no properly qualified lawyers in private practice.

This, too, was the case in Texas, New Mexico, and California, but in Luisiana, it reflected government policy. Indeed, higher authority revoked the New Orleans *cabildo's* admission of an academically qualified customs inspector to private practice, and an aspiring advocate at Pensacola was driven out of the province and colony. Like the French administration at Quebec and Louisiana (but fortunately for the civil law, not that of Saint-Domingue), the Spanish authorities in charge of Luisiana regarded properly qualified lawyers in private practice as undesirable troublemakers.

As we have seen, this Spanish administrative and legal system was not fully operative in the Lower Territory outside of New Orleans and even less so in the Upper Territory: French was the idiom of the Posts, and French folkways persisted especially in family wealth management and transmission. Furthermore, and decisively, there was nothing but instruction from and appeal to New Orleans to sustain Spanish law at the posts. In the capital city itself, the mainstay of that legal system was Spanish officialdom.

With the two transfers of sovereignty in late 1803, the institutions and the officialdom supporting Spanish law in Luisiana simply faded away. Royal and ecclesiastical officials were transferred to other places and functions in Spanish America, including the Floridas (which bordered on Lake Pontchartrain), as were the political archives at the capital and even at the posts. Crucially in retrospect, this included both the legislation expedited by the Council of the Indies to Luisiana and the legislative output of the Governor of that province, which ultimately came to repose in the Archive of the Indies in Seville by way of Pensacola and Cuba. The clerk of the New Orleans *cabildo* remained behind, but changed his first name from Pedro to Pierre and started to pass notarial acts in French form and language—a practice which he was to continue long into the period of United States rule.

Pierre Pedesclaux, and the other *escribanos* continuing their practice as New Orleans notaries, could do so with some confidence because the Organic Act of 1804 and even that of 1805 confirmed the continued effect of the private law in force in Orleans Territory, subject to the disposition of the territorial legislature. This was in marked contradistinction to Congressional disposal of the rest of the Purchase territory, which was placed initially under the administration (executive, legislative, and even judicial) of Indiana Territory and received its own Organic Act in 1805.

We now have a full account of the common law's or perhaps more directly of common lawyers's takeover of the Upper Territory, culminating in the formal reception of the common law by statute in 1816.[4] There is, however, nothing surprising or distinctive in this narrative for historians of what, for lack of a better term, we might call non-American American legal history. As evidenced later by legal developments in the Floridas, in Texas, and in California, massive immigration of "Anglo" settlers and especially of "Anglo" lawyers into sparsely settled civil-law lands is highly likely to lead to the common law's replacement of the civil law.

A short explanation might be that the common law moved with the English language. It did, however, come to prevail also in nineteenth-century New Mexico when that territory was, in the main, still Spanish-speaking if officially bilingual. In the continental United States, Louisiana alone faults the theory that the spread of the common law throughout the United States was invariably a concomitant of Manifest Destiny. Why was (and is) Louisiana exceptional in this respect, at least in the continental United States?

In the following paragraphs, I will share with you some of my views on this subject, which turns out to be, especially in retrospect but to some considerable extent still today, more multi-faceted and controversial than might first appear.[5]

Historical and doctrinal debate about the reasons for the survival as well as the nature and extent of the civil law in what is now Louisiana have centered on four questions. First, was French or Spanish law in force in the Purchase territory at the time of its cession from France to the United States? Secondly, why did the political representatives of the Orleans Territory decide to preserve the legal system in force before the two cessions, in clear and repeated rejection of the common law favored by Washington and its local officials? Thirdly, did the Code or Digest drafted by Moreau Lislet and Brown in 1808 reflect French or Spanish law? Fourth and finally, is the civil law system of Louisiana, as it consolidated in the nineteenth century and developed in the twentieth, French or Spanish in character?

I have already indicated my answer to the first of these questions: Spanish law prevailed officially in Luisiana under direct rule. The folkways of the overwhelmingly Francophone population, however, were French. In the initial territorial period, the influx of United States and of Anglophone migrants and officialdom was counterbalanced perhaps not numerically but I am tempted to say qualitatively by the first wave of French expellees from Saint-Domingue (present-day Haiti). This included, in the words of an irate "Anglo" pamphleteer, a few French lawyers, who, he charged, attempted to monopolize legal practice by establishing a system of law foreign to American attorneys.

The answer to the second question is that in this endeavor, they largely succeeded. The second Organic Act, of March 2, 1805, had signaled Washington's intent to introduce the common law in what was still Orleans territory, but it had also provided for an elected territorial legislature, which (predictably) came to be dominated by the Francophone squirarchy. Governor Claiborne vetoed a declaratory act declaring the law of the territory to be, implausibly in that order, Roman and Spanish, but faced with a bristling manifesto in defense of the inborn rights of the "ancient" inhabitants, he signed a subsequent enactment charging Louis Moreau Lislet and James Brown with the preparation of a civil code for the territory. Two years later, he signed the act giving effect to the "Digest of the Civil Laws now in Force in the Territory of Orleans," and that was that.

Or was it? This brings me to the third question, which is as yet unresolved by legal historians. Brown and Moreau Lislet were charged to make "the civil law by which this territory is now governed, the ground work" of that code. Since it was by then a matter of judicial record that this referred to Spanish law, the question is how closely the redactors of the Digest followed this legislative mandate. Manifestly, they used French as the working language, and manifestly again, they followed both the organizational scheme and, overwhelmingly, the wording of the French Civil Code and of its *projet*. On occasion, however, they followed Spanish rather than French legal precedent—most prominently by choosing the Castilian ganancial community over the community of movables and acquests of the Custom of Paris and of the French Civil Code.

I do not propose to pursue this question any further, since it was overshadowed by two unexpected developments after the change in sovereignty. First, the explusion of French Saint-Domingue refugees from Spanish Cuba in retaliation to Napoleon's invasion of Spain brought some 10,000 French-speaking persons to Louisiana in 1809 and early 1810, divided about equally among white Creoles, free *gens de couleur*, and slaves. Second, Louisiana continued to attract white French immigrants in the antebellum years in considerable numbers—for instance, 8,000 in each of the two decades between 1820 and 1839, and another 11,563 between 1840 and 1848. Many if not most of these immigrants, especially the Saint-Domingue refugees, settled in New Orleans, the antebellum capital.

Whatever the predominant nature of the Code (or Digest) of 1808, the Louisiana Civil Code of 1825 was drafted in a pervasively French environment. Although the Spanish component of Louisiana law survived even that codification, the Legislature repealed, three years thereafter, "all civil laws which were in force" before the Code's promulgation. All this occurred, to repeat, in what might as well have been metropolitan France. As the French consul in New Orleans assured Alexis de Tocqueville on January 1, 1832, "*Ce pays . . . est encore essentiellement français, d'idées, de moeurs, d'opinions, d'usages, de modes*" ("this country . . . is thus essentially French, in ideas, manners, opinions, useages and fashions").

It seems almost indelicate to add that sixteen years later, his successor sought to inhibit the application of the Emancipation Decree of the Second Republic to French slaveholders residing in Louisiana. This was to spare several thousand of them, in his submission, the cruel necessity of becoming naturalized in the United States in order to hold on to their slaves. Prosperous immigrants who retained their links of nationality to France, we may surmise, were likely to prefer living in a legal environment similar to that of their country of origin.

Why Here?

In recent years, legal historians have noted that the Louisiana Civil Code of 1825 ("the first Civil Code of the New World") has furnished legislative precedent for nineteenth-century codifications in Latin America and even in Spain.[6] Its organizational scheme served as a legislatively mandated model for the Civil Code of Lower Canada, and at least one of its concepts (subrogation) even seeped into the common law *via* the jurisprudence of the Louisiana state supreme court. We are dealing, therefore, with a major phenomenon in the civil-law world. Even more remarkable, surely, is the perseverance of the civil law against the common-law tide which swept the continental United States under the banner of Manifest Destiny.

History is supposedly not written by the vanquished, but their voices can be illuminating. Let us listen to one of them. Jeremiah Brown, a Pennsylvania lawyer born in 1776, is the author of *A Short Letter to a Member of Congress Concerning the Territory of Orleans*, published in Washington in 1806, and written in New Orleans in November of that year.[7] Although a common lawyer, he was not unfamiliar with the rudiments of Roman law and able to cope with French-language documents. He feared, justifiably as it turned out, that Moreau Lislet and Brown would use their legislative mandate to codify the laws then in effect in the Territory in consonance with then contemporary French law, to the detriment of English-speaking common lawyers such as, presumably, himself.

Referring to then-recent influx of refugees from Saint-Domingue, he wrote that among them,

> we have within the last two years imported some professional lawyers, most of them men of talents and information by no means despicable. These gentlemen found an easy admission to our courts, and some of them, I understand, have considerable practice. But with this indulgence it would seem they are by no means satisfied. Not content with the privilege of practising law among us, they now insist on dictating the laws which we must practice; and of course give a decided preference to their own.

Warming up to this scheme, he continued that the real object of the Saint-Domingue lawyers was "the introduction, not of the ancient laws and usages of the country, but of the laws and usages of modern France; and that principally with a view to the private emolument of these strangers who have unfortunately acquired such a dangerous degree of ascendancy over the minds of the people." It was a matter of "public notoriety," he added, "that our St. Domingo Lycurgus [Moreau Lislet] is avowedly copying his new code from that of Bonaparte, to the infinite delight of the whole party by whom he is employed."

That party, we may assume, was the Francophone squirarchy headed by Julian Poydras, which dominated the Territorial legislature. But what was the source of the "dangerous degree of ascendancy" which the Saint-Domingue refugee lawyers had acquired over the minds of the good people of Orleans Territory so soon after their arrival? Jeremiah Brown mentions one factor of some importance: the Spanish officials had taken their law books with them, but the Saint-Domingue lawyers had "opportunely arrived with their libraries to supply the deficiency."

That, however, is hardly the full story. Professional proficiency translates into political power only when it holds sway in the forum. It seems reasonable to assume that in a Francophone environment, the polished rhetoric of Saint-Domingue lawyers quickly came to occupy the high ground of public discourse. In one particular forum, surely, it was dominant. Both Organic Acts had introduced, along with United States-style judicial machinery, the jury system for both criminal and civil cases. Since the venire (jury pool) was overwhelmingly Francophone and monolingual at that, the palladium of the common law became, in Orleans Territory, a favorite forum for Ciceronian rhetoric *à la française*.

C'est la vie, one is tempted to conclude. Or, to vary the street pattern of this fair city, Poydras joined Napoleon and crossed over Claiborne. Jeremiah Brown, finally, went back to Pennsylvania and became a politician.

Chapter 18

"A Hard Field to Cultivate": Protestantism in the Lower Mississippi Valley, 1720-1830

Randy J. Sparks

The history of Protestantism in the lower Mississippi Valley from 1720-1830 can be divided in four periods: the French period from 1720-1769, the British period from 1763-83, the Spanish period from 1769-1803, and the American period beginning in 1803. Before 1803, the lower Mississippi Valley was a part of the struggle for territory among Europe's great colonial powers and religion was one of the instruments of empire the European states employed in their colonization schemes. Religion legitimated their claims to the land they took from Native Americans; its agents, particularly priests and missionaries, could be employed in a variety of ways useful to the empire; and, in theory, religion helped sustain the settlers in their hardships and suffering and helped civilize a wild and dangerous frontier and its settlers. For France and Spain, the Catholic religion was the state religion, though transplanting it to the Lower South proved to be a difficult task. Protestantism, even with the arrival of the British, gained only a tenuous foothold. Only with the transfer of the region to the United States did Protestantism emerge as an important cultural force. Even then, however, Protestants struggled throughout the region, but most especially in Louisiana where Catholicism remained deeply embedded. In the early years, the spread of Protestantism owed much to African Americans and women who together made up a majority of its adherents.

The French Period

The idea of one state, one church was deeply ingrained in the very concept of the European nation state, but across Europe that concept had come under attack in the wake of the Protestant Reformation. Many European states, including France, faced challenges from Protestants within their borders. After a long period of warfare followed by an even longer toleration, Louis XIV expelled the French Protestants, known as Huguenots, in 1685. It was a costly decision because France lost hundreds of thousands of useful and prosperous merchants, artisans, and farmers. Even though Louis refused to tolerate French Huguenots in France or the empire, the chronic shortage of settlers willing to come to Louisiana induced the king to allow German Lutherans to settle there, the first recognized Protestants in the lower Mississippi Valley. John Law, French Minister of Finance during the first two decades of the eighteenth century and founder of the Company of the Indies, aggressively recruited Germans and Alsatians to emigrate to Louisiana. Beginning about 1720, German-speaking Protestants began to arrive; often entire villages relocated there. They established their settlements about thirty miles above New Orleans in an area called the German Coast. Catholic priests in the colony deeply resented the presence of the Lutherans among them. Catholic missionaries complained that the Lutheran commandant at the German Coast hindered their work; "his religion . . . was an obstacle to the conversion of several of the inhabitants who are of the same sect," they protested. Despite royal prohibitions, there were Huguenots in Louisiana. Priests scoured the colony in search of French Protestants and did their best to expose them. For instance, Father Raphael complained that Mr. Perry, a member of the Council, "has not attended the sacraments . . . and I am not quite sure what his religion is. There are some who are inclined to think that he is a Huguenot and his talk sometimes causes him to be suspected of being one." Raphael also criticized the commander at Natchez, De Merveilleux, "who makes public profession of the so-called reformed religion, so that this poor parish . . . is greatly to be pitied." Raphael thought "that disorders of this sort would be less prevalent if some exemplary punishment of them were inflicted." The priest reminded officials that "his Majesty does not permit the least officer of justice who does not profess the faith of the Roman church." Raphael's call to punish and banish Protestants may well have been the best way to create a pure Church, but did not help populate a struggling colony. Predictably, these attacks put the officials and priests on a collision course; as Raphael reported, due to "the manner in which we are treated by several members of the Council our ministry becomes almost useless."[1]

The British Period

French rule ended when Louisiana became a bargaining chip in the negotiations ending the Seven Years War in 1763. The Spanish acquired the territory west of the Mississippi, including the Isle of Orleans, while the British took the territory east of the Mississippi, naming it West Florida.[2] The British were not greatly impressed with their new province. One English official referred to it as "a useless territory" and upon his arrival Lieutenant Governor Montfort Browne described its "melancholy and deplorable situation." At the time of the transfer, the entire pre-division colony had a population of about 7,000 whites and 6,000 African slaves, heavily concentrated around New Orleans. Browne was, however, struck by the potential of the western portion of the province around Natchez which he surveyed in a 1766 expedition and devoted "considerable attention" to its development. His efforts were rewarded, and the Natchez region became the most rapidly growing part of the British territory. The district had few settlers in 1770, but by 1774 about 3,000 people resided there, and in 1777 these settlements were in a "flourishing condition."

Religion was not of paramount concern for the British in West Florida, although Governor Peter Chester proposed to offer free transport to all Protestants who would settle in the province. The Bishop of London, through the Church of England's missionary arm called the Society for the Propagation of the Gospel in Foreign Parts, selected Anglican priests for West Florida who were paid by the state. Given the scattered and sparse population, only two Anglican priests came to the colony, one to Mobile and one to Pensacola. Both places were often without ministers. Other Protestants soon began to arrive in the British territory. In 1773 Richard and Samuel Swayze moved from New Jersey and settled near Natchez in an area that became known as the Jersey Settlement. Samuel Swayze was a Congregational minister, "and most of the adults who came with him were communicants."[3]

With the outbreak of the American Revolution, West Florida became an official asylum for British Loyalists, and a steady stream of prosperous new settlers arrived, "families of wealth and distinction," many of them with slaves. Then in 1779 British officials in Pensacola learned that Spain had joined France in the war against Britain. Although the military commanders at Natchez and other garrisons prepared for an invasion from Spanish Louisiana, those preparations were inadequate to resist the Spaniards who quickly captured the Natchez district, and by 1781, all of West Florida. As a result, as many as a third of the residents fled the colony, particularly those Loyalists emigrants, some of whom had resisted the Spaniards with force of arms.[4]

The Spanish Period

The Spaniards learned from the French example, and knew that their colony could not flourish without a larger population, a population not available in Spain. The Spaniards hoped to recruit Americans, but Catholicism was a serious obstacle to overcome in the eyes of Protestant immigrants. As early as 1785 Spanish officials in Louisiana proposed establishing a parish at Natchez staffed by an Irish priest who could then teach and convert non-Catholics in the region. In 1787 Spanish officials in Louisiana appointed an immigration agent in Kentucky and published broadsides inviting American immigrants to the territory. Petitions flooded in, but over and over again those petitioners demanded religious freedom as a precondition for their settlement. Such demands help account for a proclamation issued on April 20, 1789 that immigrants would "not be molested on religious matters, although no other public worship will be permitted to be publickly exercised than that of [the] Roman catholic Church." A later decree explained that once the English-speaking population grew, a number of Irish priests would be brought in to "teach and attract the colonists, their children and families to our Religion. . . ."[5]

Manuel Gayoso de Lemos, Lieutenant Governor at Natchez, supported the plan, which got off to a promising start. Four young Irishmen answered the call for English-speaking priests and arrived in New Orleans in 1787. They were promptly assigned to their respective posts including Natchez and Nogales (now Vicksburg). William Savage served in Natchez from 1787 until his death in 1793, the first of several Irish priests to hold the post.[6] Gayoso recognized his loss when Savage died. Father Francis Lennan, another of the Irish priests, followed Savage, but his overt hostility to Protestants threatened to drive them away and foil Gayoso's well-laid plans. The Protestants, many of them wealthy and well-educated, composed the bedrock of the district. As Gayoso complained, Catholics were few, "mainly Irish and not the best people of their nation . . . of turbulent and intriguing spirits." Despite Lennan's hostile stance, Gayoso continued his remarkably tolerant policy toward non-Catholics.[7]

Lennan's opposition to Gayoso's lax policy soon caused major problems for the governor. The policy strictly prohibited the public exercise of any religion other than the Catholic faith, but Gayoso did not strictly enforce this measure. Samuel Swayze, for example, continued to hold his services in the Jersey Settlement. Swayze reportedly hid his Bible in a hollow sycamore tree and abandoned public services for secret ones until his death in 1784, although the meetings were certainly an open secret. His son carried on the services for a few years, but when he died the church was not reorganized. Perhaps the fact that these services took place outside town in a self-contained settlement made them easier to ignore. Violations in Natchez were a different matter. Under pressure from Lennan, Gayoso ordered the arrest of John Bolls, a Presbyterian elder who preached in Natchez. Bolls's strong republican sympathies also may have played a part. The governor himself was said to have attended a sermon by Adam Cloud, an Episcopalian who lived at Villa Gayoso on Cole's Creek where the governor maintained a summer residence. Cloud's enemies complained to Gayoso's superiors, who ordered Cloud's expulsion over Gayoso's protests.[8]

Another problem was brewing on Cole's Creek where Richard Curtis, Junior, a gifted Baptist preacher, was gaining converts. Given the Spanish regulations, these Baptists met secretly in their homes for services, but their meetings, probably an open secret like the earlier Jersey Settlement services, "soon attracted the attention of the American portion of the population. . . ."[9] Here Gayoso confronted an entirely new breed of Protestant heretofore unknown in the colony, an evangelical.

The governor only dimly perceived the revolutionary potential of these settlers, who more than any others challenged his view of what shape the community should take. Implicit in the early Baptist movement, and deeply embedded within it, was a form of social revolt. Gayoso envisioned a settlement where various religious beliefs would be tolerated, but only one church, the Catholic Church, would meet. With other religions thus marginalized, settlers would be attracted by English-speaking services to the only Church, their children would be educated there, and within a generation, Catholicism would emerge triumphant. Baptists challenged this vision in a variety of ways. First, at the heart of Baptist theology lay a belief in the spiritual equality of all believers; the only authority they recognized was that exercised by brothers and sisters in Christ meeting in fellowship. Their preachers were not selected by a governor, but were raised up from within the congregation after receiving a "call" to exercise that gift before others. Such a call could fall on any man, black or white, from any station in life without reference to family connections, status, or education. Baptists recognized no parish lines; there was no suggestion that their churches encompassed everyone within certain boundaries. This was a community based on faith, a community that quite consciously separated itself from the larger community, in ways completely antithetical to Gayoso's vision.

Perhaps Gayoso could have ignored even these meetings, but problems developed when new converts, including a Spaniard, wanted to be baptized. As their numbers grew, the Baptists became more bold, "believing their cause was the cause of God, . . . [they]

bid their opponents defiance, and even went so far as to have their places of worship guarded by armed men, while they denounced in no very moderate terms the 'image worship' and other unscriptural dogmas and ceremonies [of] the Catholic Church." Despite Gayoso's leniency, he could not ignore such flagrant challenges. In a letter to Gayoso, Ebenezer Drayton, a Presbyterian, dismissed the Baptists as "weak men, of weak minds, and illiterate, and too ignorant to know how inconsistent they act and talk . . . too weak and undesigning to lay any treasonable plans. . . ." But he warned Gayoso, quite correctly, that "they would call any chastisement from Government for their disobedience, persecution, and suffering for Christ. . . ."[10]

In April 1795 Gayoso wrote Curtis ordering him to curb his activities. When Curtis refused, he was arrested and taken before the exasperated Gayoso, who threatened to expel him. For a time, the Americans accepted the prohibitions, but as their numbers grew they became "more and more clamorous for religious, as well as civil, liberty." One high-ranking Spanish official warned that the Curtis case demonstrated that "if disputes and quarrels over religion are not cut off at their roots . . . they will have the most perverse and evil results." As if to verify his prediction, the Baptists resumed their meetings, and Gayoso ordered the arrest of Curtis and two others, one of them Spanish, who fled to South Carolina where Curtis was regularly ordained.[11]

The Baptist challenge to Spanish authority did not end with their flight. In 1795 Spain and the United States signed the Treaty of San Lorenzo (Pinckney's Treaty) that transferred Natchez to the Americans. The number of Americans in the territory had increased in anticipation of the Spanish evacuation, an event they continually delayed, much to the annoyance of the Americans. Under the watchful eye of American officials on the scene to carry out the transfer, evangelical ministers preached under the Stars and Strips to "immense congregations." Barton Hannon, an itinerant Baptist preacher, preached inflammatory anti-Catholic sermons, and "being a weak man, was extremely puffed up with the attention he received. . . ." A native of Virginia who arrived in the territory in 1795, Hannon was a shoemaker who first emigrated to Alabama where he raised livestock before moving to Natchez. Emboldened by his new-found popularity and "a little heightened by liquor" he "entered into a religious controversy in a disorderly part of town" inhabited by Irish Catholics who "gave him a beating." Hannon demanded that the Irishmen be punished and threatened to do the job himself if Gayoso refused to have it done. The governor ordered Hannon placed in stocks inside the local fort.[12]

Armed guards escorted Hannon through town toward the fort. The preacher tried to escape and called on his fellow Americans to help him. Quickly recaptured and placed in stocks, Hannon became a symbol of American resistance. Three hundred armed settlers, including a group at Cole's Creek, threatened to attack Natchez, capture Gayoso, and exchange him for Hannon. Meanwhile, Gayoso called for troops, and violence appeared imminent. Gayoso's calm but firm response and the efforts of more level-headed Americans prevented conflict, although the angry men at Cole's Creek were the last to lay down their arms. Gayoso's generous treatment of the rebels persuaded the discontents to obey

Spanish law until the transition to American rule was completed the following year.[13]

The American Period

Mississippi's evangelical revolt came at the close of the age of empire. At the end of the period as at the beginning, the relationship between faith and government was a conflicted one. As an instrument of empire, religion had been tried and found wanting. For the empire builders, particularly the initial conquerors, religion did serve to legitimate their claims to the land they occupied and the means they employed to subdue the inhabitants. Paradoxically, religion may have been most unsatisfactory as a tool of empire *within* the European colonial communities. The exclusive nature of state churches hampered settlement and trapped European officials in a maze of inconsistencies. As Gayoso discovered, the contradictions between a state church and religious toleration were practically irreconcilable, and his efforts to reconcile them ended predictably in disaster.

The transfer of portions of West Florida to the United States in 1798 and the transfer of Louisiana in 1803 brought a rapid influx of settlers into the Lower South, although at first religion was not of great concern to the immigrants. When the United States took possession of West Florida there were about 5,000 people in the Mississippi Territory, 40 percent of them enslaved Africans and African Americans. According to an 1810 census, more than 76,000 people, about half black and half white, resided in the Territory of Orleans (the state of Louisiana except for the parishes east of the Mississippi River). Already, the future contours of society in the Lower South had largely taken shape, and the elements that would dominate the region throughout the antebellum period—plantation agriculture, slavery, and cotton—were firmly in place. Cotton became an important crop in Mississippi and Louisiana by about 1793, and sugar production expanded in Louisiana after 1797. Mississippi's first governor, the phlegmatic Massachusetts native Winthrop Sargent, described Natchez as "*a most abominable place*" [underlining in the original] teeming with Catholics, Spanish criminals, Africans and Indians. New Orleans' reputation was perhaps even worse. Architect Benjamin Latrobe visited New Orleans in the early nineteenth century and found that "the state of society at any time is puzzling. There are, in fact, three societies here—first, the French; second, the American, and third, the mixed." He found agreement on one score, "Their business is to make money. . . . Their limbs, their heads, and their hearts move to that sole object." Although still a frontier, the Lower South already produced great riches. A wealthy planter elite dominated the territory's economic and political life, but a population boom following the United States's takeover brought thousands of small farmers into rural areas and thousands of immigrants into New Orleans.[14]

Natchez, with a population of about 1,500, was the only town of any consequence in the Mississippi Territory, the center of trade, and the primary seat of the planter elite. Neither the wealthy planters who resided on the bluffs nor the riverboat men and gamblers who congregated below the hill were much interested in religion. Evangelicals lamented the town's wickedness much as Old Testament prophets invoked Nineveh or

Babylon as icons of worldly evil. In 1803 Methodist evangelist Lorenzo Dow reported that "there were not three Christians in the town, either white or black" and called it the center of "irreligion and every form of vice."[15] Evangelicals struggled to gain a foothold in Natchez. Prospects looked grim indeed. A preacher who visited the town in 1812 found the people "very rich, very proud and very polite," but with "little humility, little religion and little piety."[16]

The Baptists at Cole's Creek built the Territory's first Protestant meeting house. When Curtis and his friends returned from South Carolina after Natchez passed into American hands they found a church already built. Curtis officially organized the church in 1798. Appropriately after years of conflict, the Baptists called their church Salem, meaning "peace."[17] The Methodists organized their first church in 1799 in Washington, the territorial capital, but in 1804, only 132 whites and 72 blacks belonged to Methodist churches in Mississippi.[18]

The Presbyterians, plagued by a shortage of ministers because of their high educational requirements, were even slower to establish themselves in the Territory. In 1801 three missionaries sent by the Synod of Carolina arrived in the Natchez District, where they collected congregations, but did not establish churches. In 1804 the Presbyterians organized their first church near Uniontown, in the Natchez region. One of their most prominent early ministers, the Reverend James Smylie, a North Carolinian of Highland Scots ancestry, arrived in the territory in 1805 as a missionary from the Synod of Carolina. He established several churches in Amite and Adams counties, and became one of the most influential ministers in the Old Southwest.[19]

Adam Cloud, who had been banished from the Territory in 1790 for preaching in violation of Spanish law, returned to the territory and in 1820 established the first Episcopal Church, Christ Church, at Church Hill in Jefferson County. The Episcopalians catered to the planter elite, but they also found that the wealthy planters were more interested in the virtues of hospitality than the virtues of Christianity. The Episcopal Diocese of Mississippi was organized in 1826 with only four churches, five priests, and about 100 members.[20]

Evangelical Protestantism expanded rapidly in Mississippi in the wake of the Great Revival, and religious leaders from Mississippi attempted to spread the movement to Louisiana, but growth there was extremely slow. A traditional Creole saying holds that "good coffee and the Protestant religion can seldom if ever be found together," a reference to the sharp division between the northern and southern parts of the state.[21] Protestants had some success in the northern part of Louisiana, settled primarily by emigrants from the southern United States, but struggled to gain a foothold in New Orleans and other areas in the south where Catholics predominated.

The Methodists were the Protestant pioneers in Louisiana. According to tradition, Lorenzo Dow, a famous and rather eccentric evangelist, was the first Methodist minister to preach in the state. In 1803 or 1804 he traveled to the Opelousas region of southern Louisiana to buy mustang ponies, and he reported that he held religious meetings among the few English-speaking residents there. In 1805 the Methodists organized their work in Louisiana. They created the Wilkinson Circuit that occupied the southwestern corner of Mississippi below Natchez and "as far down into west Florida as the Protestant settlements could guarantee the safety of the preacher." In addition, they appointed Elisha Bowman to a newly organized charge in the Opelousas region. A native of Virginia and son of a local Methodist preacher, Bowman was licensed to preach at the age of sixteen. Bowman traveled first to New Orleans where he reported that he was "disappointed in finding but few American people there, and a majority of that few may truly be called the beasts of men." Only a few respectable American families lived in the city, he said, and those few were Episcopalians. The governor promised him the use of the capitol building to hold services, and Bowman published notices of his Sunday service. When he arrived, however, he found the building locked. He preached in the open air to "a few drunken sailors and Frenchmen," and blamed the Episcopal priest for having the doors locked against him. He complained to the governor, who promised him that the building would be open to him on the following Sunday, but it was locked again. Once again, he preached to a handful of people in the open air. He did the same on the following Sunday, but could get few listeners since Sunday was "the day of general rant in this city." By this time, his money was running low, so he set out for the Opelousas country in December 1805, and happily "shook off the dirt from my feet against this ungodly city of Orleans."

He traveled several hundred miles across swamps and rivers, and he reported that "the mosquitoes like to have eaten up me and my horse." He finally reached the Opelousas, but was almost as shocked by what he found there as he had been in New Orleans. Three-fourths of the settlers were French, and although everyone lived very simply with few material possessions, they were rich in herds of cattle and horses. He wrote: "Here I found a few Americans who were swearing with almost every breath; and when I reproved them for swearing, they told me that the priest swore as hard as they did. They said he would play cards and dance with them every Sunday evening after mass! . . . I told them plainly if they did not quit swearing that they and their priest would go to hell together." He found a settlement of Americans, but "they knew very little more about the nature of salvation than the untaught Indians. Some of them, after I had preached to them, asked me what I meant by the fall of man, and when it was that he fell." He rode for miles to reach the scattered American settlements, swam creeks and swamps, preached in private homes and in the open air, and spent most days drenched to the bone. "What I have suffered in body and mind my pen is not able to communicate to you," he mourned, but he added, "while my body is wet with water and chilled with cold, my soul is filled with heavenly fire. . . . I have not a wish but that the will of God may be done in me, through me, and by me." At the end of a year of such labor, he had converted a total of seventeen people. Launer Blackman, Presiding Elder of the Mississippi Conference, visited Bowman and preached with him in Louisiana in 1806. He was discouraged by what he saw there; in his view "the settlements were so scattering, and the people so vastly ignorant, and more than half of them French, and so abominably wicked, we could not do much, and our success was small." When John Jones arrived to preach on the Washita (i.e., Ouachita) Circuit in 1826 he was the only preacher of any denomination in the region except for "two very illiterate Baptist preachers."[22]

In 1807 the Methodists organized another charge in the Washita district where a group of Methodists from Mississippi has recently relocated, but they struggled to build congregations there and faced the same hardships described above. By 1810 these two Louisiana districts reported only thirty members, and in the same year there were forty-three members reported from the Orleans Territory. There was still no Methodist church in the city and it is unclear where the congregation met or who preached to them. The first preacher appointed to New Orleans was Miles Harper in 1812, but the city disappeared as a charge in 1813, reappeared in 1819, and disappeared again until 1824 when it became permanent. That fluctuation reflects the difficulties the Methodists faced there; by 1826 they had only twenty-three white members and sixty blacks.

William Winans came as a missionary to New Orleans in 1814. He rented the bottom floor of a building on Bienville Street in the French Quarter where he ran a school during the day and held services in the evenings and on Sundays. Given the disruptions of the War of 1812 and the attack on the city, he had little success. Winans left New Orleans for Mississippi, but served for many years as a Missionary Agent raising money to build a church in the city.[23]

In 1826 the Methodists bought a lot on Gravier Street and built a simple wooden church with galleries to seat the blacks. The black congregation grew most rapidly and included a Sunday School for black children with over 75 students, many of whom learned to read fluently. The white congregation, however, actually shrank from sixty-four in 1832 to forty-eight in 1836. A separate Louisiana Conference was created in 1845 with 8,101 white and 3,329 black members. Compare those figures to Mississippi where there were 10,095 white and 5,854 black members.[24]

The story of the Baptists in Louisiana is similar to that of the Methodists, and like the Methodists, there were close connections between Mississippi and Louisiana Baptists. According to tradition, the first Baptist sermon in Louisiana was preached by Bailey E. Chaney who was a member of Curtis's early Mississippi congregation. Chaney preached to American settlers near Baton Rouge in 1799, but was arrested by Spanish authorities and ordered out of the territory. Ezra Courtney preached in Amite County, Mississippi, and he crossed the border and preached in Louisiana as early as 1804. Preachers from southwestern Mississippi helped organize the first Baptist churches in Louisiana, including Half Moon Bluff Church in Washington Parish, the first in the state. By 1818 there were five Baptist churches in the state.

One of the most important figures in the history of Baptists in Louisiana is Joseph Willis, a black preacher born in South Carolina who moved to Mississippi in 1798. In 1804 he preached the first Protestant sermon west of the Mississippi River at Vermilion (now Lafayette). Threats of violence forced him to leave, but he moved permanently to St. Landry Parish in 1805. He was formally ordained in 1812 and organized Calvary Baptist Church, the oldest surviving Baptist church in the state. Greatly respected as a man "of some education and great piety," he served for many years as the moderator of the Louisiana Baptist Association and was revered until his death at the age of 92 (significantly, some Baptist histories have "whitewashed" Father Willis by ignoring his race). By 1825 there were only eight Baptist churches and ten preachers west of the Mississippi with a total membership of 150.[25]

Like the Methodists, the Baptists found it difficult to gain a foothold in New Orleans. The Baptist Triennial Convention sent James Raynoldson as a missionary to the city in 1816. He found a few Baptists in the city, including Cornelius Paulding, a native of New York, who allowed Raynoldson to use the upper floor of a building he owned on Dosier Street, below Canal and near the Customhouse. The first baptism was performed in the Mississippi River in 1820 in front of the Customhouse. Raynoldson's congregation included sixteen whites and thirty-two black members. Raynoldson left after two years, glad to leave behind the city he referred to as "the stronghold of Satan." In 1818 the Triennial Society replaced him with Benjamin Davis, sent specifically to "the colored people in New Orleans." Davis remained only a short time, however, and the church dissolved. Black Baptists organized their own church located at Girod and Cypress streets, the most successful Baptist church in the city during the 1820s and '30s. A white Baptist missionary who visited it in 1840 found that "two very pious black preachers" served that congregation. White Baptists reorganized in 1841 and officially formed the First Baptist Church of New Orleans in 1843.[26]

The first Protestants to organize in New Orleans were the Episcopalians and the Presbyterians. A number of prominent English-speaking residents of the city began to meet in 1805 to discuss organizing a church of some denomination. After several discussions, the group put the matter to a vote; 45 voted for the Episcopalians, seven for the Presbyterians, and one for the Methodists. The church was governed by the bishop of New York, and the Reverend Philander Chase was its first minister. Chase labored for six years with the small congregation that was unable to build a church until 1814. The diocese of Louisiana was organized in 1838, and in 1841 Leonidas Polk became its first bishop. In that year there were only six other Episcopal clergymen in the state with 220 church members altogether.

The Connecticut Missionary Society sent the Reverend Elias Cornelius on a missionary tour to New Orleans in 1817. On his way south, Cornelius stopped at Princeton where he met Sylvester Larned, just finishing his training at Princeton Theological Seminary, and urged him to follow him to the Crescent City. Larned arrived in 1818 and went to work to build a church. The cornerstone was laid in January 1819 on St. Charles Avenue. Even though the congregation met regularly and the church was built, it was not officially organized as a Presbyterian church until 1823 when it became part of the Mississippi Presbytery. It was the only Presbyterian church in the state, although a second church of that denomination was organized in New Orleans in 1840. Both the Episcopal and Presbyterian churches were very small, but their congregations were wealthy and socially prominent and that gave them a greater influence than their small numbers might suggest.[27]

Of the Protestant churches in the region, the evangelical churches grew at the most rapid rate and came to dominate religious worship in Mississippi and in some parts of Louisiana. Evangelicals preached the doctrine of Christian equality, a message with powerful appeals to women and blacks. White male evangelicals, however, had no intention of carrying the doctrine of the equality of all believers so far as to threaten the domination of white men throughout southern society. For white women and for blacks of both genders, then, churches were contested terrain. Despite reluctant or resistant men, white women played a vital and active role in the churches. So important was that role that historian Donald Mathews suggested that "women made southern Evangelicalism possible. . . ."[28]

Women responded to the evangelical message in such numbers that they composed a majority in virtually every church, a crucial factor in the evangelical success. Women opened their homes as places of worship, they fed and clothed preachers, they brought their families into the churches, they encourage their husbands to support religious causes, and sometimes they organized churches themselves. For instance, one of the chief benefactors of the Methodists in early New Orleans by William Ross, who moved there in 1811. Ross was an elder in the Presbyterian Church, but he liberally supported the Methodists because his wife belonged to that denomination. The first Methodist society in Monroe, Louisiana, began in 1826 with the conversion of three young women who "began to hold religious conferences, and mutually agreed to make a public profession of religion. . . ."[29] In 1832 nine women organized the Unity Presbyterian Church in Amite County and signed the church's charter.[30] In 1820 a Methodist women's prayer meeting began in the town of Washington, and Methodist minister William Winans mentioned other similar organizations in the 1820s and 1830s. Women's societies were among the largest donors to the Mississippi Methodist Conference and to the Mississippi Baptist Convention.[31] In 1822 Baptist women organized the Ladies Charitable Mission Society, an auxiliary to the Mississippi Baptist Missionary and Education Society. Local groups sprang up in Mississippi and Louisiana and actively raised funds. Their fund-raising events became a regular part of the activities in towns and hamlets across both states.[32] The scope of women's contributions to southern churches, the role religion played in women's lives, and the emergence of a women's culture closely tied to southern churches and religion are topics that remain either under-studied or contested by scholars of southern religion and southern women.

One of the most controversial topics in the study of southern religion is an assessment of the African religious heritage. Did enslaved Africans lose their traditional systems of worship and their collective religious practices? Or can African-American religious practices be traced directly back to their African roots? Most scholars would agree that Africans could not recreate their traditional religious systems anywhere in the Americas, but "What they were able to do, and often very successfully, was to piece together new systems from the remnants of the old." That blending of cultures was nowhere more apparent than in New Orleans where a rich and vibrant Afro-Catholic culture emerged. Indeed, the very existence of that tradition in New Orleans probably hampered the growth of Protestantism there, for Afro-Creoles in the city worked to convert enslaved blacks from the Upper South, many of whom would have been Protestants. Historians "Ginger" Gould and Emily Clark have found that after 1808 "'American' or 'English' bondspeople sold away from the Protestant Upper South began to replace Africans as the primary object of Catholic evangelizers in New Orleans."[33]

Blacks made up roughly half of the population of the Lower South, much higher in the plantation districts that had substantial black majorities. Evangelicals sought to reach out to that large, unchurched population, but their ambivalent position on slavery made masters wary. Among Methodist minister Daniel de Vinne's many complaints against the planter elite was that he could not "get them to feel rich enough to let their poor servants come to preaching."[34] Despite the opposition or indifference of masters, more and more blacks converted, often under the ministry of black preachers.

A remarkable group of African religious leaders emerged throughout the South during the Great Awakening; their congregations served as the "citadels of African evangelism" and produced the first generation of black missionaries after the Revolution. Clearly, these independent black churches also had black preachers, a remarkable group of religious leaders that historian W. E. B. DuBois characterized as "the most unique personality developed by the Negro on American soil." Throughout the antebellum period, both blacks and whites worshiped under the ministry of black preachers.[35] These black preachers, men like Father Willis who helped establish Baptist churches in early Louisiana and Mississippi, had a considerable impact on evangelicalism. Another important black preacher in the region was Henry Adams, a free-born native of South Carolina who lived in Bienville Parish. He was one of the founders of Mount Lebanon Baptist Church, a biracial church, and served as its pastor for two years before becoming pastor of the First African Church in Louisville, Kentucky. Regarded as "a man of education and ability[,] . . . he was much respected by all who knew him."[36]

In early Mississippi blacks organized their own independent "African" churches. Some of the largest churches in the region were these independent African congregations. While it is impossible to know how many independent black churches existed, the scattered references suggest that they were not uncommon. In 1820 the Pearl River Baptist Association had twenty-three member churches, including an African Church that sent black delegates to the association's meetings. In 1825 the largest church in the Union Baptist Association was an African church with 115 members, about one-fifth of the membership of the entire association. At least one African church belonged to the Mississippi Baptist Association from 1810 to 1820. Historian Jon Butler interprets the emergence of these African churches as evidence of a maturing African-American Christianity. The formation of such churches suggests that Christianity was spreading rapidly among the enslaved population, and it was spreading under black control.[37]

The growth of Protestantism in Mississippi and Louisiana stand as studies in contrast. Despite their geographical proximity and close economic ties, vast cultural differences divided the neighboring states and contributed to a radically different history of religious life. The French colonizers attempted to maintain the European tradition of one nation, one church, no matter how detrimental that policy might have been to settlement. Surprisingly it was the Spaniards, long regarded as the most Catholic of all the colonial powers, who were actually willing to experiment with policies that encouraged Protestants to settle in the Lower South. The British, though a Protestant state, made no special effort to promote religion within West Florida.

It was not until the United States acquired the Lower South that Protestantism could expand there. The transfer of Louisiana to the United States coincided with the emergence of the Great Revival that began with a series of remarkable camp meetings in Kentucky in 1802. Suddenly, like wildfire, evangelical Protestantism began to spread outward from the Bluegrass state. The growth of Protestantism in early Mississippi was directly connected to the Great Revival, and many religious leaders in the territory were veterans of the camp meetings. Many of the thousands of emigrants who poured into Mississippi were already converted to evangelical Protestantism or open to it. Those evangelicals attempted to carry their message into Louisiana, but that proved difficult. Louisiana, despite its close proximity, remained culturally distinct. The mixing of Africans, Indians, and Europeans had created a society with many gradations of color and different racial mores. While weak in some parts of Louisiana, Catholicism had taken firm root in New Orleans and proved to be a bulwark against the expansion of Protestantism there, especially among blacks who were often at the forefront of evangelization in other southern cities. The influx of Protestants into the city after the transfer did provide opportunities for some growth, but interest in religion was not high among men on the make in the bustling port city. Protestantism grew most rapidly in rural areas where English-speaking settlers dominated and where community and social life often came to revolve around religious institutions. During the early nineteenth century, the evangelical churches grew at phenomenal rates, and women and blacks played major roles in that growth.

Part III
Learning About the Purchase Territory and Its People
and
Concluding Remarks

Learning about the Purchase Territory and Its People and Concluding Remarks

The third set of essays, "Learning About the Purchase," have the common theme of how persons *not* in the Purchase Territory learned about it. Jessie J. Poesch exams the work of three major artists who ventured into the Purchase Territory before 1860 and returned with watercolors and oil paintings that they produced for patrons and displayed—with collections of Native American handicrafts—in the East and Europe. John R. Hébert looks at The Historic New Orleans Collections' Louisiana Purchase Bicentennial atlas, *Charting Louisiana, Five Hundred Years of Maps,* and then describes selected French manuscript and published maps of the seventeenth and eighteenth centuries that show the slow accumulation of French knowledge of the western drainage of the Mississippi River. John L. Allen takes up that story with a consideration of the Jeffersonian explorations, including Lewis and Clark. He shows how concepts like the "Great American Desert" originated and how misconceptions of the hydrography of the rivers of the Purchase persisted on maps. Of necessity, these essays are published without the numerous, often in-color illustrations displayed when they were presented at the conference.

Finally, John B. Boles's essay reviews what he saw as the themes of the conference and adds some additional perspectives that arise from his own deep knowledge of U. S. history. He summed up the Conference, and these essays, with the observation that they "complexified" the story of the Louisiana Purchase. That is, instead of the shallow, simplistic stories still taught in textbooks, the persons who attended the Conference, and you who will have read these essays, gained a multi-layered, many-voiced picture of an important chapter in our national history, a chapter that contains more than just the great bargain of "four cents an acre" and the Lewis and Clark expedition. Rather, it was the lived experience of a great diversity of peoples of both sexes and many religious and other traditions, an experience that more than in any prior period gave meaning to our national motto: "*E Pluribus Unum.*"

Chapter 19

Points of Departure, Points of Return: Artists in the Louisiana Purchase Territory Before 1860

Jessie J. Poesch

George Catlin, Karl Bodmer and Alfred Jacob Miller each made a major series of works—drawings, watercolors and paintings—based upon their experiences in the new Louisiana Territory in the years 1819 to 1838. Upon their return, this extraordinarily rich body of images was gradually made available to their contemporaries, both in the United States and abroad, through exhibitions and publications. For the first time, many of their contemporaries learned something about the Native American peoples who lived in the Louisiana Territory.

By the beginning of the twentieth century, much of their work had been lost sight of. As these creations have again become known, exhibited and published, we appreciate anew the quality of the work and how much they tell us of Native American peoples and their land as they were before both were radically changed by the impact of American settlers, railroads, changing attitudes and legal restrictions.

A word about being an artist in the 19th century. If one had a sense of having some talent and a desire to be an artist, one had first of all to obtain some training and learn the use of materials. One somehow had to support oneself, to earn money, if possible by finding a marketable subject such as portraits or landscapes. There were few galleries or opportunities for exhibitions. One could advertise and exhibit from one's studio, gain a reputation by word of mouth, or, if lucky, find a patron.

The backgrounds of these three artists and the evolution of their careers were different, but for each the fur trade was important. Its trading expeditions and posts were the means through which they gained access to the Louisiana Purchase Territory.

Before discussing Catlin, Bodmer and Miller, I want to begin with the work of the three other artists, Boqueta de Woiseri, Samuel Seymour, and Titian Peale, and to sketch in some background.

In 1803-04, the little-known artist, John L. Boqueta de Woiseri (fl. c. 1797-1815) created a large painting and two prints celebrating the city of New Orleans and its importance to trade and commerce in the new Territory. Both prints were dedicated to Jefferson and published in Philadelphia. The first, a "View," shows the city and its harbor filled with boats; some of them were very probably loading animal pelts, especially beaver and buffalo, to be shipped to ports on the eastern seaboard and to Europe. The other print is a plan of New Orleans. In the upper left the artist inserted a small map showing the entire length of the Mississippi, thus suggesting the future role of river commerce to the nation. On the western side of the Mississippi several Indian tribes are identified, and a "Route of French to Western Indians" is indicated, both measures of how little was known of this territory before the Lewis and Clark expedition. The route, of course, was used primarily by French and Spanish fur traders.[1]

The fur trade of the upper Missouri was a highly competitive international business, dominated, in the period from 1826 to 1840, by the American Fur Company. Furs were delivered to St. Louis, then carried either by ship or overland to New York, Boston and Montreal. Buffalo hides were made into coats, wraps and blankets. The more precious beaver and finer furs were also sent out, reaching foreign markets, including China and the great annual Leipzig Trade Fair. The fibrous underhair of the beaver was made into the fashionable tall hats.[2]

The intellectual and social climate of the late eighteenth century and early nineteenth century age of Enlightenment is also a part of the story. Philadelphia was the center of scientific scholarship and thought in America. There individuals motivated by curiosity and an almost romantic love and awe of nature began natural history—botany, zoology and geology—as well as ethnography and anthropology. The imperative need was to discover and identify the many different species of the natural world; finding and describing new species is still a fundamental aspect of biology.

The American Philosophical Society, founded in 1743, and the Academy of Natural History, founded in 1812, were in Philadelphia, where Peale's Museum, created by the artist Charles Wilson Peale, was the popular venue for both art and science. Meriwether Lewis spent time in Philadelphia with the scientists preparing himself before departing on the Lewis and Clark expedition. When Lewis and Clark returned, the Museum acquired animal skins that were mounted and displayed. Lewis gave a peace pipe and an ermine skin mantel of a Shoshone Indian chief. An 1822 view of the Museum by Peale's son, Titian (1799-1885) shows the various collections, including some Indian artifacts.[3]

Following Lewis and Clark, several exploring expeditions were sent into the Louisiana Purchase territory. Major Stephen H. Long's Expedition of 1818-1820 brought back scientific knowledge.[4] Originally part of a larger Yellowstone Expedition that fell through, it was broadly commissioned to "explore the country between the Mississippi and Rocky Mountains," and "to acquire as thorough and accurate knowledge as may be practicable" of "this portion of our country." These instructions were based on those Jefferson had given to Lewis and Clark. The military unit was to make geographic measurements and maps while a small group of scientists gathered other information. The latter included Thomas Say, a zoologist from Philadelphia, and Edwin James, a botanist and geologist. There were two artists. Samuel Seymour (1775-1823), a little-known painter and engraver, was assigned to sketch landscapes and make portraits of Indians, and Titian Peale, age 21, as assistant naturalist was to help collect and draw floral and faunal specimens.

The Long expedition departed by steamboat from Pittsburgh and arrived in St. Louis on June 9, 1819. On September 1, it arrived at the military encampment "Engineer Cantonment" in Nebraska. The scientific party stayed there for eight months. The Indian agent, John Dougherty, and two Frenchmen acted as guides and interpretators while the scientists collected specimens and visited several Indian tribes. Because the larger Yellowstone expedition had failed, and an economic depression pervaded the country, the expedition's orders and budget were curtailed by the time Long rejoined it in 1820. Instead of going to Yellowstone, the expedition embarked to trace the sources of the Platte, Arkansas, and Red rivers. On June 30, 1820, the men had their first view of the Rocky Mountains. The expedition then separated into two groups to cover more territory; both parties endured grueling traveling conditions before they reunited at Fort Smith. Some men then returned to their homes overland while others went by way of New Orleans. Historians have tended to give the Long Expedition short shrift for failing to achieve its larger goals and because its members identified, as had others, the western plains as the "great American desert" unsuitable for habitation or cultivation, but it was very important for natural history and ethnology.

Seymour returned with 150 renderings of landscapes and Indians, 60 of which were fully completed.[5] Most of his work has been lost, but among those surviving is a watercolor of the first known view of the Rocky Mountains. Peale brought back 122 sketches.[6] In 1822, Peale's Museum had on display 44 drawings of paintings of birds and 173 sketches of plants, insects, fishes, shells, etc. That same year, he exhibited four small watercolors of animals at the annual exhibition of the Pennsylvania Academy of Fine Arts. (In 1828, Peale's Museum was augmented by a gift of 35 items of the Indian collection that had been in Thomas Jefferson's Poplar Forest estate, including a painted buffalo battle robe that the Lewis and Clark expedition had brought back.)[7]

Among Peale's small-scale watercolors is the first known visual image of a Sioux conical lodge, or "tipi," characteristic of Plains Indians life, and destined to become a symbol of all Native American cultures. Titian Peale also made an image of the American buffalo and several sketches of Indians shooting buffalo with bow and arrow. Two lithographs based on his sketches were published in popular sporting and natural history journals in 1832 and 1836. This became an image of popular culture, painted by any number of artists in subsequent years.

In 1822-1823, Edwin James, using his notes and those of Long and Thomas Say, published *An Account of an Expedition from Pittsburgh to the Rocky Mountains* in Philadelphia. It came out in London the same year, with eleven black and white illustrations. Scholars at the time recognized the significance of the scientific data gathered by the expedition.[8] Contrary to the conclusions of traditional historians, historians of science now also applaud its accomplishments. One has called James's book "a landmark in the literature of American exploration."[9] Two botanists have recently followed the expedition's route, and have concluded that James, the botanist, collected over 700 specimens; among these there were well over 100 plants that were previously unknown.[10]

George Catlin (1796-1872) was living in Philadelphia between 1821 and 1825.[11] Self-taught, he probably learned the rudiments of painting from other artists there. He then painted portraits and miniatures in Philadelphia and Washington for several years. In 1829, no doubt inspired by the growing interest in the unsettled—by Euro-Americans—

land of the West, and having seen some Indians, he had the bold and ambitious idea of painting Native Americans who still had little contact with "civilization." They would be paintings of the "noble savages" whom he feared were doomed to become extinct, would be of historical importance, and might ultimately bring him recognition and income.

By spring 1830, at age 34 and with only financial backing from his family, he was in St. Louis, where he met General William Clark, Superintendent of Indian Affairs, visited Fort Crawford near Prairie du Chien, and made his first group of paintings of Indians. In the fall, he returned to his home in Albany.

In March 1832, Catlin was again in St. Louis and departed on the American Fur Company's steamboat *Yellowstone.* He went as far as Fort Union, 2000 miles northwest of St. Louis, where he stayed at least a month. He returned to St. Louis on October 20, 1832. He had been away seven months, stopping at several fur-trading posts. This proved to be his longest sojourn in the West. During these months, he painted some 170 paintings, some fully finished, some partially finished.

Four portraits of Native Americans illustrate Catlin's work at this time. Catlin captures the individual qualities of each person. One of his favorite sitters, who became a friend, was Four Bears, the second chief of the Mandans, whom he painted in full ceremonial dress.[12] Catlin called him one of "Nature's noblemen . . . no tragedian ever rode the stage with more grace or manly dignity." Catlin later purchased his garments and exhibited these in his Indian Gallery. Another portrait is of the aged Hidatsa chief, Black Mocassin, seated, wearing a Crow robe and holding a long peace pipe (figure 15).[13] He remembered Lewis and Clark from their visit 30 years before. Catlin sat with him in his wigwam, listening to him recount feats from his life. A third strong portrait is of Horse Chief, the Grand Pawnee head chief, probably done on the return trip.[14] An aged man, Horse Chief is shown gazing directly at the viewer, his face and hair reddened with vermilion. He wears various beads and what I believe is a Jefferson peace medal. Buffalo Bull was another Grand Pawnee warrior and the subject of the fourth portrait.[15] Catlin shows him with his *medicine* or *totem* of the head of a buffalo painted on his breast and face. He too wears a peace medal. This painting was never finished, suggesting how Catlin sometimes sketched in a part of a portrait, then completed it later.

In the winter of 1832-1833, Catlin was apparently back East, finishing his paintings and preparing his notes. Ever restless, he showed part of his collection in April in Pittsburgh; many of the paintings were still unfinished. In May he was in Cincinnati where he exhibited around 140 works which were finished and framed. Next, in Louisville, a reviewer wrote that they were portraits "of the manly Indian, as he exists in his own wide plains, joint-tenant with the buffalo, the elk, and the grisly bear; and they exhibit in a striking manner the distinctive features of the tribes to which they belong." In the winter of 1833-1834, Catlin is known to have been in Pensacola and possibly in New Orleans.

Figure 15. George Catlin, *Black Moccasin, Aged Hidatsa Chief, 1841*. From George Catlin, *Letters and Notes on the Manners, Customs and Condition of the North American Indians*, Vol. 1 (London, 1841), figure 72. Courtesy of the Denver Public Library, Western History Collection.

Eager to have his material published, Catlin financed his own publication and prepared most of the engravings himself. This is a much simplified rendering of the painting he made of the aged chief while in the West in 1832.

On July 4, 1832, a fifty-year-old German scientist, Prince Maximilian von Wied,[16] arrived in Boston from Germany. Maximilian had fought with the Prussian Army against Napoleon, then in 1815-1817 had made a two-year trip to Brazil, collecting natural history specimens and recording the customs and the languages of the Indians. In 1820-1821, he published a two-volume account of his travels, illustrating it with his own sketches.[17] In 1832, he decided to make a study of the North American tribes in the Rocky Mountain area. This time he hired a twenty-three-year-old Swiss artist, Karl Bodmer (1809-1893), and David Dreidoppel, a taxidermist and skilled hunter who had been with him in Brazil.[18]

Maximilian was a product of the intellectual ferment taking place in Germany in science, philosophy and history. His mentor was the distinguished naturalist and philosopher, Johan Friedrich Blumenbach, who has been called the founder of the study of anthropology, and who believed that all human beings were probably descended from a single set of parents. One of the many scholars and explorers of that generation, he sought to learn about the variety of human societies and races, especially the primitive.

Maximilian and his party first visited in several places in the East. Of the scientific establishments, he praised only "the museum of Mr. Titian Peale, which contains the best collection of natural history in the United States," and wrote that it "deserves precedence over all public museums in the United States for its arrangements." He noted the excellent stuffed examples of the bison, the big horn or wild sheep of the Rocky Mountains and the prairie antelope.[19]

The party traveled down the Ohio River and reached New Harmony, Indiana, on October 19, 1832. This was the small utopian community founded by Robert Owen and was where Thomas Say and other scientists were then living. Here Maximilian found congenial friends, and a good library. He stayed four months. The diaries he kept throughout his sojourn in the West indicate that he carried James's *Account* of the Long expedition with him as a reference. Bodmer made a visit to New Orleans in the winter, perhaps to purchase supplies.

In the spring Maximilian's party journeyed to St. Louis, arriving on March 24, 1833. Here they called on William Clark and may have seen some of Catlin's paintings in storage there. Among the people they met was William Drummond Stewart, who had arrived sometime that winter with letters of introduction to William Clark and others. Forty-three years old, he was the second son of a Scottish nobleman and a former captain in the British Army who had also fought against Napoleon; he was living on a captain's half-pay. A sportsman and adventurer, he had apparently spent the years since 1815 travelling in Europe and the Middle East.

Maximilian and Stewart momentarily thought of travelling together. However, Maximilian decided to take advantage of the recent return of the *Yellowstone* from New Orleans to go up the Missouri with the American Fur Company. Stewart, on the other hand, decided to take the overland route with the caravan bound for a rendezvous with free trappers (those not in the pay of a company) in the summer. He then spent the next two and one-half years in the West apparently with fur traders, trappers and Indians, possibly going as far as Taos, New Mexico, and did not return to St. Louis until November 1835. More of him later.

Maximilian's party left St. Louis on April 10, 1833. Another passenger on the *Yellowstone* was Major Dougherty, the same man who had been with the Long Expedition for a time. While en route to Fort Union, Bodmer produced a portrait of a young Native American man who was on the boat.[20] He wears what is probably a Navajo blanket and a metal cross. Both are evidence of the trade between the Southwest and Northern Plains tribes—an indication of trade among the tribes that was separate from that between the Indians and the traders.

In May, Maximilian and Bodmer reached Dougherty's Bellevue Agency. By midsummer they were at Fort Union in North Dakota. Near Fort Union Bodmer painted an Assiniboin burial scaffold or "tree grave."[21] (figure 16) This picture demonstrates what a superb watercolorist Bodmer was, catching the texture of the foliage and the light on the branches supporting the scaffold.

On July 16, 1833, Maximilian's party took a smaller keelboat, traveling over 650 miles in 34 days to reach Fort McKenzie (near present-day Bismark, North Dakota) on August 9, the furthest outpost of the American Fur Company and further than Catlin had gone. Here they stayed five weeks. While there, they witnessed a conflict between the rival Blackfeet and Assiniboins. A penetrating portrait by Bodmer, done in September 1833, shows an elderly Blackfoot man in mourning for a young relative who had recently been murdered.[22] His hair is cut; he wears a simple unadorned robe, and has smeared his head and body with gray-white clay. Again, one gets a strong sense of an individual. The portrait of "Child of the Wolf" shows a young man wearing a striped blanket, a wealth of ornament, and a bear-claw necklace. He holds a large feather fan.[23] The pair of bows in his headdress appears to be made of dentalian shells of a type that was traded among the Pacific coast tribes. The long tubular ornaments, on the other hand, have been identified as a type that came from the West Indies via New Jersey and the fur traders. They are made from a particular type of conch shell and were a popular trade item.

In November, Maximilian's party went to Fort Clark to spend the winter, staying until April 1834. Here Bodmer painted a Mandan shrine of buffalo and human skulls, one of several shrines and totems he depicted.[24] Such skull shrines were related to beliefs regarding the human body after death and were used as fasting grounds for those seeking supernatural powers. Bodmer made more than three hundred watercolors and sketches in the West: Sioux and Assiniboin camps, Indian transport such as bull boats, artifacts such as snowshoes, buffalo herds, landscapes such as snags and rock formations on the Missouri, forts, steamboats, and watercolors of natural history specimens.

In April 1834, Maximilian's group left Fort Clark, arriving in St. Louis in late May. In July, they departed for Europe, arriving at LeHavre in August. Unfortunately, Maximilian's scientific collections were lost when the steamboat carrying them burned

Figure 16. Karl Bodmer, *Tombs of Assiniboin Indians on Trees*, 1846. From Maximilian, Prinz von Wied, *Bildatlas: Reise in das innere Nord-America in den Jahren 1832 bis 1834* (Paris, 1843), Tableau 30. Courtesy of the Denver Public Library, Western History Collection, F-28257.

The notations in fine print under the engraving suggest the complex process of creating high quality copper engravings in the nineteenth century: *Karl Bodmer pinx ad natura*—the original painting was done by Karl Bodmer directly from nature; *Aubert père sc.*—the "cutter" was a Parisian engraver, Pierre Eugène Aubert (1789-1847) who signed himself Aubert père after 1840; *Imp. De Bougard*—the copper plate was printed by the shop or firm of Bougard.

and sank. Fortunately his voluminous diary survived, as did Bodmer's watercolors and sketches. Catlin, meanwhile, had decided to return to the West.

Catlin made a second long trip from Fort Gibson, near Tulsa, in the summer of 1834. His advocacy of the Indians and his criticisms of the trade practices of the American Fur Company caused him to travel with the Army. He went with a regiment of dragoons sent on a mission of peace and friendship to the southern Plains tribes, although the size of the force clearly suggested the strength of the United States. This was the territory of Comanches, Kiowa and Wichita. Although it started with 800 men, the hot temperatures and a fever reduced the regiment almost by half. Catlin was among those afflicted and was carried on a stretcher part of the time. His notes and several paintings described how they had a peaceful meeting with the Comanches when they approached with a white flag of truce.[25] He created a series of paintings of that episode. He probably sketched paintings while there and painted them later.

On his return he rode alone on his mustang to St. Louis. There he met his wife. They wintered in Pensacola, then moved to New Orleans. He rented rooms in March and April of 1835 at 78 Chartres Street, accompanying the display of his paintings with a lecture, commenting on them one at a time. The New Orleans *Bee* had two notices of his exhibition on March 14, 1835, and the *Courier* had a long review on April, indicating that he had 200 portraits from 37 different tribes. "We were not only pleased but delighted, and the lucid manner in which Mr. Catlin explained the various groups of Indians, greatly heightened the interest felt by all; and almost forced one to believe that they actually were among them." Catlin had become his own patron, and was beginning to earn some money.

In the summer of 1835 Catlin took a steamboat from New Orleans to Fort Snelling, then went back to Prairie du Chien. In the fall, he gathered together his collection and shipped it to Pittsburgh. In 1836 he made another short trip to the Missouri-Minnesota border region, then returned to Utica, New York, where he worked on finishing his paintings and developing his notes.

We now pick up on the career of the third artist. Alfred Jacob Miller (1810-1874), a native of Baltimore, had studied painting in Europe, come back, put up a shingle in his home town, found business slow, and then moved to New Orleans and advertised himself as an artist at 132 Chartres Street.[26] Sometime in the early spring of 1836 he received a visit from a "very military man" who looked carefully at his work. A few days later the man, Captain William Drummond Stewart, returned, told Miller that he had made several trips to the West, planned to make another, and invited Miller to join his party. Miller checked with the British Consul to be sure the offer was bona fide.

Stewart and his party went first to St. Louis, then in May 1837 left from Westport with the supply caravan of the American Fur Company. Stewart apparently wanted an artist to portray the West he had come to know so well, so that he could have paintings to hang in his home in Scotland. The caravan traveled along the North Platte River, on the route that would become the Oregon Trail. There were several missionaries who also traveled with the caravan, a portent of the settlers who would soon be coming. Because the caravan took the more southerly route it seems to have escaped a deadly smallpox epidemic that almost wiped out the Mandan tribe that summer. Throughout the trip, Miller made many ink and wash sketches as well as watercolors. Some were later developed into larger scale oil paintings. Still later, he made at least two sets of finished watercolors based on his original work. It is very difficult to date precisely much of his work.

More than either Catlin or Bodmer, Miller shows the daily life of the trappers and the Indians as they interacted with each other. The trappers often adopted practices of Indian life such as "taking the Hump Rib of a Buffalo," (figure 17), which was considered the most delicious meat of the buffalo.[27] While en route, near Bellevue, Stewart and his hunter lassoed three buffalo calves, tamed them, and then had them sent back to St. Louis and on to New Orleans, to be shipped to his friend Lord Breadalbane at Taymouth Castle in Scotland.

In another sketch Miller shows a trapper setting traps for a beaver, perhaps unaware that the European market for beaver was diminishing because a new process for making silk hats had been developed.[28] Still another Miller finished watercolor depicts the large supply caravan with which he traveled.[29] He painted Stewart on a white horse. They were on the way to the annual trappers' rendezvous, held each year at a different but prearranged place. The caravan brought supplies for the trappers and materials for trade with the Indians. The caravan carried little food; its members subsisted on meat for the whole journey.

Two of Miller's more important larger oil paintings are of the exterior and interior of Fort Laramie as it appeared only three years after it was built by Stewart's friends and colleagues, William Sublette and Robert Campbell.[30] This was a year-round fort where some of the American Fur Company staff lived and worked. They maintained a large supply of food and trade goods. Indians came there three or four times a year to trade. There was a cannon in the tower over the main entrance. At stated times and in limited numbers, Indians and non-company traders were allowed to come into the open court of the interior.

A fully developed Miller watercolor suggests the lively range of activity at the rendezvous, held that year on Green River.[31] The Indians and the traders have set up camp. In the foreground the artist shows an elaborate procession that the Shoshone Indians staged for their old friend, Captain Stewart. The chief, Ma-wo-ma, is dressed in his finest clothing. He and his companions rode their best horses. About 2,000 people attended these rendezvous. There was horse racing, rifle matches, feasting, much carousing and story-telling as well as shrewd fanatical trading.

At this rendezvous, Stewart and his men rounded up seven mature buffalo, male and female, which in turn were duly shipped to Scotland. Stewart and his party then made a hunting trip to the Wind River Mountains in Wyoming, a favorite hunting ground of his. He was ill for a time, but recovered.

Figure 17. Alfred Jacob Miller, *Taking the 'Hump Rib,'* ink and ink wash over graphite underdrawing on grey card, ca. 1837; Accession 1966.28. By permission of the Amon Carter Museum, Fort Worth, Texas.

Both Miller, in his notes made after his return from the West, and Stewart, in his novel, *Earl Warren* (1854), indicated that the hump rib was the most delicious piece of buffalo meat, prized by Native Americans and traders alike.

The Stewart party arrived back in St. Louis in mid-October 1837. Miller left immediately for New Orleans, where he began to develop his sketches into oil paintings. He made at least 200 watercolors or sketches while on their journey. From New Orleans he went to Baltimore.

Stewart stayed in St. Louis until November, when he learned that he had received an inheritance from his aunt. He then went to New Orleans, staying at the St. Charles Hotel during the winter of 1837-1838.

Stewart, without Miller, again went west from St. Louis in the 1838 season. Miller meanwhile exhibited several of his paintings in Baltimore. When Stewart returned in the fall to St. Louis, he learned that his brother had died in May. In October and November, he was again in New Orleans, living at 46 Bourbon Street; there he learned via the British Consul that his brother's widow was "not with child" and therefore he had inherited the estate—three properties including Murthly Castle. He was now Sir William Stewart. Miller came back to New Orleans to meet Stewart. Stewart, anticipating a return to Scotland, requested his friends in St. Louis to send him a collection of Indian artifacts and some tame deer. He returned to Scotland in May 1839, having been seven years in America. Just before Stewart departed, Miller exhibited eighteen oil paintings at the Apollo Gallery in New York. A favorable review identified and described each one.[32]

Meanwhile, in April 1838, Catlin had further organized his collection and exhibited it in Washington, Baltimore, Philadelphia and Boston. His broadside advertised 330 portraits of Indians from 38 different tribes and 100 landscape paintings (figure 18).

There was some criticism of Catlin's facts, especially his insistence that the Mandans had been totally devastated. At any rate, at this time, using one of his sketches, he added another painting of the Mandans to further document their life.[33] It is a painting of one of their ceremonial bull dances, a three-day ritual he had been allowed to observe and which he described at some length in his notes. As in others of his paintings of the Mandans, he shows their round earth-covered lodges. Each was forty to sixty feet in diameter, with a chimney that also served as a skylight in the center of the roof.

In November 1839, Catlin packed up his collection and sent it to Liverpool; it arrived in January 1840. Because it included a large collection of artifacts as well as paintings, it amounted to eight tons of freight. His exhibit opened in London's Egyptian Gallery and included a total of 485 paintings, a Crow Indian tipi, Indian costumes, weapons and other artifacts. Among the many who came to see it were Queen Victoria and Prince Albert.

As early as 1836, Maximilian had contemplated publishing a deluxe multi-volume account of his travels, addressed to a European audience. Bodmer was engaged to make arrangements with publishers in England and France and to select and supervise the engravers. Progress was slow, especially in the production of large prints. In 1839-1840, the two-volume report, *Reise in das Innere Nord-America in dem Jahren 1832 bis 1834,* was published in Coblenz, Germany, by J. Hölscher. The London edition, published by Ackermann, and the Paris edition, by A. Bertrand, followed. The text was illustrated with 31 vignettes and a map. Most of the vignettes had three imprints—small, crisp images based on selections from Bodmer's drawings and watercolors. The accompanying *Atlas*, with 81 large format copper engravings, was completed in 1843. Because of differences in production and printing, there is variation among these engravings—some copies are simply black and white, some three-color, and some full-color acquatints. Also some individual engravings circulated separately in Europe in the 1840s.[34] The engraving of the Assiniboin "tree grave" (figure 16) catches something of the complexity of Bodmer's original watercolor. The addition of three wolves prowling at the base of the tree conveys a more ominous atmosphere. A shorter version of the *Atlas* was published in 1846 and a second edition in 1851. It is difficult to judge how widely these publications circulated. Clearly, however, the extensive information Maximilian's work contained was a major addition to what Europeans, ever curious, learned about the New World.

In October 1840, Miller arrived at Murthly Castle as the guest of Stewart. Whereas in the field Stewart had often been a strict disciplinarian, now Miller was treated very generously. He painted more paintings for the castle, and also apparently prepared a portfolio of fine watercolors that were still there in 1844. Miller returned to Baltimore in 1841. The hunter, Antoine Clement, and two Indians, who were also guests, returned in 1843.

In October 1841, Catlin published his two-volume *Letters and Notes on the Manners, and Conditions of the North American Indians*.[35] Appearing simultaneously in Britain and America, it has been described as a curious blend of storytelling and perceptive reporting. Although some of its accuracy is questionable, William Truettner, the Catlin scholar, has said that it "remains one of the seminal texts of the period. Much of Plains Indians ethnology is still based on what Catlin observed and recorded."[36] Confident of the importance of his work, Catlin financed the publication himself. British reviews were very favorable, American ones slightly less so. But good reviews don't necessarily mean more income.

While the best of Catlin's paintings are compelling, the steel and wood engravings in these volumes are much simplified, essentially line drawings, such as that of Black Mocassin, the aged chief of the Hidatsa, figure 15. *Letters and Notes* was republished at least eight times by 1860: in New York in 1842 and 1844, in London in 1848 and 1850, in Philadelphia in 1857, 1859, and 1860 and in Sweden in 1848.

Catlin exhibited in England throughout 1843-1845. Though his exhibit was initially well attended, attendance dropped off as the novelty wore off. To enliven his shows, he introduced staged recreations of Plains Indian dances and rituals, first with white men painted to resemble Indians, then, when several groups of Native Americans that had been brought to Europe by other entrepreneurs were stranded, he took them over as performers.[37] He was becoming more showman than spokesman. He often barely made ends meet.

In April 1845, he went to Paris and exhibited for six weeks. King Louis-Philippe ordered copies of fifteen paintings, but in fact these were never paid for, and therefore not delivered. In 1846, Catlin exhibited two paintings in the annual Paris Salon. The first, a vibrant portrait of Buffalo Bull's Back Fat, the head chief, Blood tribe, Blackfoot, painted in 1832, shows him wearing a deerskin tunic ornamented with porcupine quills.[38] The other, done in 1844, is a very poignant painting of Little Wolf, a member of the Iowas who toured with Catlin for a time.[39] Little Wolf's wife and child had died. Catlin catches something of a stoic sense of acceptance of the sorrows of life—a sense of alienation—feelings that Catlin probably shared because of his increasing financial difficulties. The poet, Charles Pierre Baudelaire, was impressed with the quality of these two paintings and wrote: "Mr. Catlin has captured the proud, free character and noble expression of these splendid fellows in a masterly way. . . . I find [in the red color] an element of mystery which delights me more than I can say."[40]

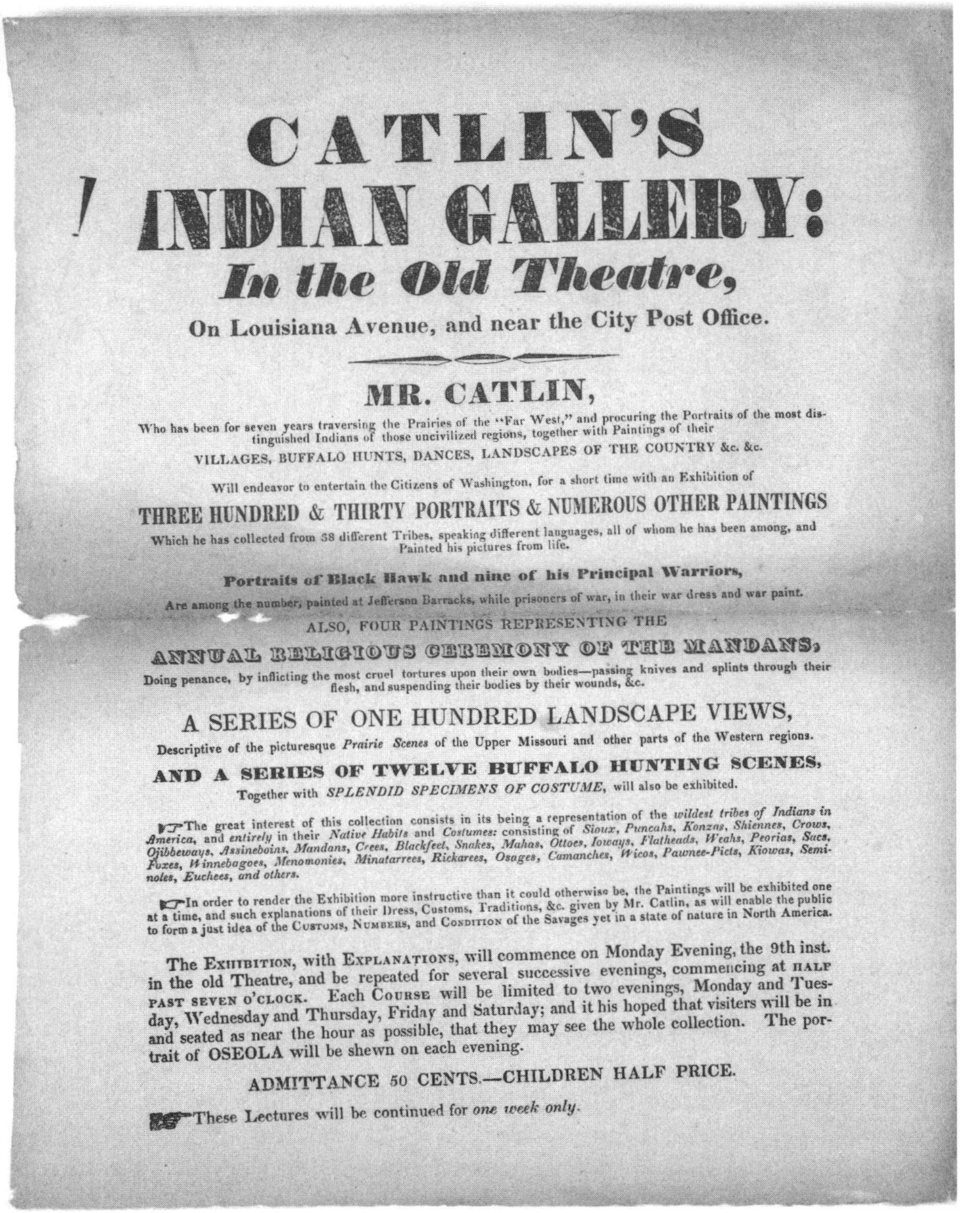

CATLIN'S INDIAN GALLERY:

In the Old Theatre,

On Louisiana Avenue, and near the City Post Office.

MR. CATLIN,

Who has been for seven years traversing the Prairies of the "Far West," and procuring the Portraits of the most distinguished Indians of those uncivilized regions, together with Paintings of their

VILLAGES, BUFFALO HUNTS, DANCES, LANDSCAPES OF THE COUNTRY &c. &c.

Will endeavor to entertain the Citizens of Washington, for a short time with an Exhibition of

THREE HUNDRED & THIRTY PORTRAITS & NUMEROUS OTHER PAINTINGS

Which he has collected from 38 different Tribes, speaking different languages, all of whom he has been among, and Painted his pictures from life.

Portraits of Black Hawk and nine of his Principal Warriors,

Are among the number, painted at Jefferson Barracks, while prisoners of war, in their war dress and war paint.

ALSO, FOUR PAINTINGS REPRESENTING THE

ANNUAL RELIGIOUS CEREMONY OF THE MANDANS;

Doing penance, by inflicting the most cruel tortures upon their own bodies—passing knives and splints through their flesh, and suspending their bodies by their wounds, &c.

A SERIES OF ONE HUNDRED LANDSCAPE VIEWS,

Descriptive of the picturesque *Prairie Scenes* of the Upper Missouri and other parts of the Western regions.

AND A SERIES OF TWELVE BUFFALO HUNTING SCENES,

Together with *SPLENDID SPECIMENS OF COSTUME*, will also be exhibited.

☞The great interest of this collection consists in its being a representation of the *wildest tribes of Indians in America*, and *entirely* in their *Native Habits* and *Costumes:* consisting of *Sioux, Puncahs, Konzas, Shiennes, Crows, Ojibbeways, Assineboins, Mandans, Crees, Blackfeet, Snakes, Mahas, Ottoes, Ioways, Flatheads, Weahs, Peorias, Sacs, Foxes, Winnebagoes, Menomonies, Minatarrees, Rickarees, Osages, Camanches, Wicos, Pawnee-Picts, Kiowas, Seminoles, Euchees, and others.*

☞In order to render the Exhibition more instructive than it could otherwise be, the Paintings will be exhibited one at a time, and such explanations of their Dress, Customs, Traditions, &c. given by Mr. Catlin, as will enable the public to form a just idea of the Customs, Numbers, and Condition of the Savages yet in a state of nature in North America.

The Exhibition, with Explanations, will commence on Monday Evening, the 9th inst. in the old Theatre, and be repeated for several successive evenings, commencing at HALF PAST SEVEN O'CLOCK. Each Course will be limited to two evenings, Monday and Tuesday, Wednesday and Thursday, Friday and Saturday; and it his hoped that visiters will be in and seated as near the hour as possible, that they may see the whole collection. The portrait of OSEOLA will be shewn on each evening.

ADMITTANCE 50 CENTS.—CHILDREN HALF PRICE.

☞These Lectures will be continued for *one week only*.

Figure 18. *Flier for George Catlin's Exhibition of his Indian Gallery in Washington, D. C., April 1846.* Printed Ephemera Collection, Portfolio 198, folder 10a, Library of Congress. (Page 1 only).

Catlin's financial problems increased. In 1845, his wife and son died. In 1848, he self-published a second two-volume work, *Catlin's Notes of Eight Years' Travels and Residence in Europe with His North American Indian Collection*.[41] Carelessly written and anecdotal, it is a less valuable resource than his earlier book. Among the prints is one showing the installation of the Indian Gallery—pictures from floor to ceiling and an Indian tipi set up in the middle of the room—as at the Salle de Séance in Paris. In addition, Catlin published a number of separate catalogs of his Indian Gallery at various times.

Confident that his collection was an invaluable artistic and ethnographic record, he tried to sell his collection to the United States government, but failed. In 1852, the American locomotive manufacturer, Joseph Harrison, came to his rescue and purchased the collection. It remained in storage until Harrison's death. Catlin traveled to South America. In 1864 he was near starvation and finally returned to the United States in 1870, having been away 32 years. He died in poverty at New York in December 1872. In 1879, Harrison's widow bequeathed the collection to the Smithsonian Institution. In 1886, Thomas Donaldson published a lengthy and valuable report on it.[42] Parts of the collection have been on public exhibition since then.

Miller returned to a painting career in Baltimore. His account book of 1846 to 1874 reveals that at irregular intervals individual patrons commissioned finished paintings or watercolors based on his original work done in the field. The most significant was a beautifully finished group of 200 watercolors created between June 1858 and August 1860 for the collector, William T. Walters. These paintings are now in the Walters Gallery in Baltimore.[43]

Stewart continued a life of adventure, including a sentimental return trip to the West in 1842-43, on which he employed a New Orleans journalist to chronicle the trip. Reports were published in the New Orleans newspapers. Stewart published two novels based on his adventures in 1846 and 1854. Largely fictionalized autobiography, they are nonetheless valuable as records of that era in the West.[44] A cartoon in the London journal, *Punch*, of September 15, 1860, showed that Stewart's buffaloes were still startling the natives as they roamed the hills of Scotland.

The aim of these artists and their patrons was to bring back a visual record of life among the Native Americans in the new Louisiana Territory. Theirs is an enduring record; it is because each was first and foremost an artist with a selective eye. There is a continuing history of other depictions of the American West, both myth and reality, into the twentieth century. But no other artists were as prolific as Catlin, Bodmer or Miller and none was to see the Louisiana Purchase territory and its Native American peoples relatively so untouched by contact with Euro-Americans.

Postscript

In the twentieth century there has been an increasing interest in the work of these and other artists who ventured into the American West. New discoveries have been made. Various exhibitions have been organized. For example, when in 1947 Bernard DeVoto published *Across the Wide Missouri*, most of his illustrations were based on examples of Miller's work that were still in private family holdings. Many of these have now entered public collections.

Maximilian's *Reise* and the splendid engravings of the *Atlas*, based on Bodmer's original watercolors and sketches, were known to scholars of the early twentieth century. The original watercolors remained in the Wied estate until after World War II, when they were rediscovered. Sometime in the 1960s they were acquired by the InterNorth Art Foundation and have since been on permanent loan to the Joslyn Art Museum in Omaha. In addition to various publications in which examples of Bodmer's work have been reproduced in the United States, in Germany there have been several illustrated publications and at least one exhibit of the prints since 1970.[45] In 2003, the Amon Carter Museum in Fort Worth featured an exhibition, *A Faithful & Vivid Picture: Karl Bodmer's North American Prints*.[46]

Catlin's work was valued first for its ethnographic value, then for its artistic worth as well. More recently, Catlin's work, and that of other painters of the American West, have been studied as part of the larger context of American expansionism.[47] And in a remarkable exhibition, *George Catlin and His Indian Gallery*, at the Smithsonian in 2002, visitors could experience for themselves the manner in which Catlin, as artist and enterprising showman, presented his collection. For the first time since the middle years of the nineteenth century, the entire collection of paintings was shown, installed much as it had been seen in London and Paris.[48]

Chapter 20

Maps of La Louisiane, 1680-1763

John R. Hébert

Two centuries ago, a chapter ended for European imperial designs on the North American continent, while a new chapter opened for a youthful United States. The occasion was the historic purchase, in 1803, of the vast province called by the French La Louisiane and by the Spaniards, La Luisiana. This moment marked the beginning of the westward thrust of the country's formation and a corresponding shift in national attention from the Atlantic seaboard to the mostly uncharted interior of the continent. The Purchase also represented a cultural shift, as America's Anglo Protestant society found itself associated with Louisiana's Latin and Roman Catholic culture.

In order to observe this significant milestone, the Historic New Orleans collection has pursued for several years the ambitious goal of publishing an atlas that depicts Louisiana's history through maps. Portions of that history are well documented in textual records, books, newspapers, and countless journal articles. Equally valuable but less well-known, understood, and used are thousands of maps found in archives and collections in the United States and abroad. These documents trace the discovery, colonization, and development of the region from its first charting in the early sixteenth century. The cartographic record makes clear the geographical, historical, economic, and cultural importance of Louisiana, from the pre-colonial explorations of Hernando De Soto and Robert Cavelier, Sieur de La Salle, to the very latest twenty-first century offshore oil surveys. These maps denote also the diffusion of information across Europe, as rival cartographers strove to present the very latest news about the American continent to an eager public. In the decades that followed 1803, generations of mapmakers sketched the story of Louisiana as settlers flocked into the Mississippi Valley, founded towns and cities, connected them with roads, rails, and telegraph lines, and cultivated the surrounding fertile lands. Yet despite their value as historical documents and the widespread general interest in and appreciation of maps, there was no existing atlas that reproduced the important maps of Louisiana and its many distinctive parts.

The Atlas: Charting Louisiana

Charting Louisiana: Five Hundred Years of Maps provides in a single volume a rich selection of historic and contemporary maps from various sources that collectively illustrate the broad and diverse reach of the region's history from its multinational colonial experiences to the modern American state. The objective of the atlas is to provide high quality reproductions of significant maps in a convenient format to the broadest possible audience.

Charting Louisiana: Five Hundred Years of Maps presents one hundred and four maps from The Historic New Orleans Collection representing the full range of the institution's cartographic treasures. Many of these maps were originally collected by the institution's founder, General L. Kemper Williams. Also featured in the volume are many important works from the Geography and Map Division of the Library of Congress. Thousands of maps at the Library of Congress pertain to Louisiana, and, as the atlas's cartographic advisor, I have chosen sixty-seven examples to illustrate particular historical and cartographic developments. Other U. S. repositories contributed to this volume, including the Louisiana State Museum in New Orleans, and the Newberry Library in Chicago. Archives in France, Spain, Great Britain, and Mexico generously provided the balance of maps, as befits Louisiana's international history. *Charting Louisiana: Five Hundred Years of Maps* features an unprecedented compilation of 193 significant manuscript and printed maps.

Although the maps are intended to be the primary focus of the atlas, they are supplemented by six essays. These essays provide a broader context for looking at and understanding the maps by concentrating on particular periods and themes relating to the historical development of Louisiana. The essayists are Paul E. Hoffman (Louisiana State University, Baton Rouge), Alfred E. Lemmon (The Historic New Orleans Collection), Ralph E. Ehrenberg (former chief of the Geography and Map Division, Library of Congress), Mark F. Fernandez (Loyola University, New Orleans), Jason R. Wiese (The Historic New Orleans Collection) and John T. Magill (The Historic New Orleans Collection).

Louisiana's history, as depicted in this atlas, begins in the early years of the sixteenth century, when Spanish explorers first encountered and charted the northern Gulf Coast. Indeed, Europe's first pictures of America took the form of maps and charts. Paul E. Hoffman's opening essay examines the early competing ideas concerning the shape of the coast and courses of inland waterways such as the Mississippi River. Initially vague and sometimes contradictory, cartographic knowledge of the region gradually expanded through the two-hundred-year period from ca. 1519 to 1703, informed by early encounters between Europeans and Native Americans and catalyzed by the late seventeenth century French encroachment on the American dominions of Spain.

At the heart of the essay is the notion that in spite of repeated Spanish expeditions along the Gulf Coast and into the interior of the Mississippi Valley, no mapping effectively speaks to the area of North America drained by the Mississippi River until the French explorations down the river in the 1670s and until the Spaniards attempted to find and to dislodge La Salle from the Texas coast in the late 1680s.

The eighteenth century in Louisiana was a politically complex period during which at various times the colony was ruled fully or in part by three Europeans powers: France, Spain, and England. Alfred E. Lemmon's essay describes the continuing evolution of the idea of Louisiana, as expressed not only in maps of the colony but also in the policies of French and Spanish officials. Lemmon also writes of the fundamental tensions between the ideal, wealth-generating colony proposed by Pierre Lemoyne, Sieur d'Iberville in 1699 and the actual impoverished, underpopulated colony incompetently managed by crown officials and administrators of the ill fated Company of the West.

Maps from the eighteenth century dramatize the competing plans for controlling and developing the Mississippi Valley and Gulf Coast regions. In some instances cartographers assumed the role of propagandists for their respective sovereigns. Of particular concern to map makers were the boundaries that defined the various North American colonies. These boundaries constantly changed as European colonial powers won and lost territory through war and diplomacy. Some of these colonial boundaries foreshadow modern state boundaries.

Aside from the continent-wide political maps produced during the eighteenth century, much of the mapping of Louisiana was devoted to the accurate surveying of individual land holdings and the platting of new towns, endeavors thought to be essential in any well ordered society. As Louisiana became settled, towns such as Mobile, Biloxi, Natchitoches, New Orleans, Baton Rouge, and St. Louis were laid out to permit colonial administrators more effective control over the extensive province. Detailed town plans and plats showing early land grants along the colony's waterways provide historians with a wealth of data, including the locations of early plantations, buildings, and fortifications, as well as the names of individual property holders. This section of the book culminates in the historic joint U. S.-Spanish boundary survey undertaken in the final years of the eighteenth century, just before Spain retroceded Louisiana to France and France sold it to the United States.

Ralph E. Ehrenberg's essay concerns itself with the period from the 1803 Louisiana Purchase to the establishment of the modern state boundaries of Louisiana before 1820. By necessity, Louisiana in this chapter has two definitions. One is that vast region that France and later Spain had claimed as La Louisiane and La Luisiana. The other confines itself, more or less, to the physical boundaries of the current state of Louisiana. The essay explores the geographical uncertainty that attended the historic Purchase due to the treaty's vague language concerning Louisiana's boundaries and French maps that made expansive claims that included Texas and the Gulf Coast at least as far east as the Perdido River.

Ehrenberg describes the earliest American attempts to chart the vast province, with attention to the famed expeditions of Meriwether Lewis and William Clark and Zebulon Pike, as well as to their Native American informants. Maps of the Louisiana Purchase territory, and the gradual determination of the present state of Louisiana, are critical for understanding this period, as the immense former colony was subdivided into smaller states and territories.

Of special significance during these two key decades in Louisiana's life was the 1815 battle of New Orleans, which affirmed Louisiana's ties to the United States. If the British had succeeded in their quest to conquer New Orleans and to gain control of the Mississippi River, American history might have taken a radically different direction.

Maps played a vital role in preparing for the battle and in ensuring victory for a jubilant United States, thus creating a closer bond between the peoples of the new state of Louisiana and the nation. Ehrenberg concludes his essay with a discussion of some of the milestones of early state mapping, particularly the efforts of William Darby, John Melish, and Maxfield Ludlow, as well as Barthelemy Lafon's outstanding map of 1806.

Mark F. Fernandez's essay weaves specific maps into a broad historical narrative that traces the often tumultuous political and economic ebbs and flows that characterized the period from 1820 to the beginning of the twentieth century. Developments in agricultural production, transportation, and communications had a huge impact on the fortunes of Louisiana. Mapmakers documented these dynamic changes by showing navigational improvements to rivers, newly constructed railroads, and other timely information. As new settlers rushed in, mapmakers filled in the previously blank western and northern areas of the state. The onset of the Civil War in 1861 forced Louisiana to endure drastic economic and social changes that affected its development well into the final years of the nineteenth century.

Throughout the twentieth century and into the twenty-first, traditional map forms continue to be created and published on Louisiana, particularly those showing infrastructure features such as roads, rail lines, waterways, and new administrative divisions. In the twentieth century mapping was used as well to create change and to document problems requiring solutions. Oil and gas companies, for example, produced geological maps to document their interests and intentions in Louisiana. Also during this period, maps assumed new political, social and economic functions. Demographic data from census records, overlaid on map forms, provided government agencies and city planners with more accurate pictures of the locations and habits of specific populations. Maps were also used to track environmental changes and environmental threats, such as severe weather.

A constant interest in Louisiana mapping revolves around the impact of the major waterways, especially the Mississippi River and the Gulf Intracoastal Waterway system. These routes are vital commercial assets that unfortunately are prone to disaster, whether in the form of springtime floods, coastal erosion, or hurricanes. To place these twentieth century developments into context, Jason R. Wiese explores the ways that modern Louisiana has been affected geographically and politically by the Mississippi River and by a shrinking coastline, as well as the positive and negative effects of globalization on the state.

The dominance of the city of New Orleans in the history of Louisiana as a colony, territory, and state has made it necessary to devote an entire essay to its 300 year existence. John T. Magill discusses the city's development from the earliest plans of LeBlonde de La Tour and Adrien de Pauger to its modern status as the major Mississippi River port and an international tourist mecca. The essay contrasts some of the idealized depictions of the Crescent City, as it appeared in maps, with records of its actual development.

Maps with Magill's essay show the city's humble origins as a wilderness outpost, the slow growth of the French and Spanish colonial capital—twice rebuilt after devastating fires—and later explosive growth that occurred during the first fifty years of American dominion, which culminated in New Orleans's status as Queen of the South. The essay brings the history of New Orleans up to the present by showing the twentieth century urban and suburban development as engineering advances drained the swamps and improved the quality of life in this unique southern metropolis.

Exemplary French Maps, 1680-1763

In the next few pages I will discuss a group of French maps of Louisiana from the 1680s to the end of the French and Indian War, to demonstrate some of the powerful impacts of these objects. In *Charting Louisiana*, these maps are found with the essays on the sixteenth, seventeenth, and eighteenth century Spanish, Dutch, and French attempts to describe the Gulf coast region and the Mississippi Valley. What these French cartographers from the 1680s to 1763 endeavored to do was to establish *La Louisiane* (the greater Louisiana) and to more effectively describe Lower Louisiana, and the Gulf Coast and the Spanish and French areas therein. These maps also show some of the urban plans prepared by the French at the start of their colonial presence along the Gulf Coast.

In the 16th century Spain was the dominant European power in North America and by right of the Papal Bulls of 1493 and the Treaty of Tordesillas of 1494 Spain considered North America its property, a condition that was not challenged, except for minor incidents along the Atlantic coast involving France (1562-65) and England (1584-86), until the beginning of the seventeenth century. From the late seventeenth century through the middle of the eighteenth century, based on the amount of territory claimed, France was the dominant power in North America, especially in the strategic Mississippi Valley. But France did not recognize fully the importance of its strategic holdings. Its failure to provide support to ensure that region's development and retention under French control is the basic reason for France's defeat in the French and Indian War (1756-63). That war ended France's empire in North America.

The dream of finding a Northwest Passage, the river to the west, a quick water route to the Pacific Ocean and legendary riches of Asia, was one of the main purposes for seventeenth century French explorations in the interior of North America. Louis Jolliet, a Canadian-born fur trader, and Jacques Marquette, a Jesuit missionary, were sent in 1673 to discover the mouth of the Mississippi River. Departing Green Bay (Wisconsin) and ascending the Fox River, a quick portage took them to the Wisconsin River. Descending it they reached the Mississippi, which they followed to the mouth of the Arkansas River. At that point they realized that the Mississippi, which ran into the Gulf of Mexico rather than the Pacific, was not the Northwest Passage. Fearful of being captured by the Spaniards, they turned back to bring the news of their discovery to the governor of New France (Canada). In 1682 after a thousand mile journey of exploration, Robert Cavelier, Sieur de la Salle, and his companion Henri Tonti reached the mouths of the Mississippi.

On April 9, 1682, La Salle took possession of all the lands watered by the Mississippi River and its tributaries and christened the new colony La Louisiane in honor of King Louis XIV. Returning to France, he organized an expedition to establish the first settlement in the new colony. La Salle boldly sought colonization along the coast of La Louisiane as a way for France to move closer to the Spanish silver mines in the northern part of Mexico (New Spain) and to drive a wedge that would halt English migration into the Mississippi Valley. In March 1685, after a long and difficult voyage, he landed at Matagorda Bay in Texas, which he thought was one of the Mississippi's branches. After two years of hardship in this unforgiving land, a rebellion by his men resulted in his assassination, putting an end to his ambitious dreams.

La Salle's unsuccessful venture was followed up in 1699 by Iberville's establishment of a French colony near present-day Biloxi, Mississippi. This settlement arose from fears that English traders from Carolina would reach the Mississippi River and trade with various Indian peoples—Creeks, Chickasaws, and Choctaws—north of present-day Mobile. This new venture solidified France's hold in North America, a hold that stretched from Canada (Quebec) to the Great Lakes, down the Ohio and Mississippi Rivers to the Gulf of Mexico.

At its greatest extent La Louisiane extended in French eyes (and maps) from the western slopes of the Appalachian mountains to an ill-defined place far west of the Mississippi River along the eastern edge of the Rocky Mountains or even farther west, and north of Spanish Texas. Some mid-eighteenth century French maps even show Texas and the Florida Peninsula as a part of French La Louisiane. A corps of cartographers soon was involved in the study of the region and noted cartographers and hydrographers in France contributed mightily to the mapping and the circulation of maps regarding this newly described region. We will now consider some of their work.

Father Louis Hennepin's 1683 *Carte de la Nouvelle France et de la Louisiane Nouvellemente decouverte dediée au Roy* begins our story.[1] This continental map is the first published source to name the Mississippi Valley La Louisiane, only a year after La Salle claimed the territory in the name of King Louis XIV. It shows the Mississippi River (Fluve Colbert) from its headwaters south to the Mission des Recollects (on the Arkansas River), but not to the Gulf of Mexico. A dotted line incorrectly projects the remainder of the route from there to the Gulf of Mexico. A few Native American nations are noted. Hennepin, a Belgian Recollect missionary, has been generally recognized as the first European explorer of the upper Mississippi. On the map he names the Falls of St. Anthony in present-day Minnesota. He also identifies California as a peninsula bordering on the Strait of Anian, rather than as an island as was then common. These facts suggest that some of the controversy over the veracity of his travel accounts is misplaced.

Jean Baptiste Louis Franquelin's map of 1684, *Louisiane*, is a classic depiction of the extent of France's Louisiana even before La Salle planted his colony in Texas. It was followed by Franquelin's manuscript map of 1688 *Carte d l'Amerique Septentrionale*, a

Figure 19. Guillaume de L'Isle, *Carte de la Louisiane et du Cours du Mississippi*, Paris, ca. 1718. The LOUISiana Digital Library; also available from the collection of the Geography and Map Division, Library of Congress.

magnificent and beautiful map held in the French national archives and, in a hand drawn facsimile, in the Geography and Map Division of the Library of Congress.[2]

The full map shows the vastness of French claims in North America, and claims French ownership of Mexico before the Spaniards! Particular attention should be paid to the noticeable westward drift of the Mississippi River in this map. Too, the distinction between French Florida and Spanish Florida is clearly shown.

I. Rouillaud's 1691 *Carte generale de la Nouvelle France ou est compris La Louisiane, Gaspesie et le nouveau mexique* is a curious map filled with data reflecting new and old understandings of the Southeastern parts of the United States. For example, the Bay de Spiritu Santo is shown to be Mobile Bay, while the Riviere de Spiritu Santo (River of the Holy Spirit; Río del Espiritu Santo in Spanish) enters the Gulf slightly east of Tallahassee, Florida. Many scholars consider the Riviere de Spiritu Santo to be the early name for the Mississippi River. Hoffman argues in his essay that in De Soto's time it was in fact the Sabine River.

On this map, the Mississippi River falls into the Gulf near the Rio Grande, and for some reason, the Ohio River flows into the Wabash River, which then flows into the Mississippi. The map was printed in two separate 1691 Paris imprints by Chrestien Le Clerc, *Premier etablissment e la foy dans la Nouvelle France* and in *Nouvelle relatio de la Gaspesie.* The intent of the map, in addition to providing a view of the North American continent, is to record the locations of Recollect and Jesuit missions in the new country.

The primary and dominant name in French mapping of Louisiana was that of Guillaume de L'Isle whose 1718 map *Carte de la Louisiane et du cours du Mississippi* provided coverage from the Hudson River in the east to the Rio Grande in the west.[3] This map has been described as one of the most magnificent maps ever made of America (figure 19). The map provides a relatively accurate depiction of the watershed of the Mississippi. The 1718 edition was the first to show New Orleans, and the first to use the name Texas. This map also records the location of La Salle's ill fated colony.

De L'Isle served as map maker to the king, and his map was considered practically an official document that reflected the opinion and policies of the French crown. He expanded French territorial claims at the expense of the British and Spanish empires, extending Louisiana westward to the Pecos River (Rio Salade de Apaches), claiming Texas as part of the French colony, and restricting the British to the eastern slope of the Appalachian mountains. Because his map was printed and well circulated, it must have caused alarm in London and Madrid.

French expansionists at home and English colonists in America were certainly aware of the advantages of gaining control of the American Old Southwest. The French realized that to establish footholds from the mouth of the Mississippi River northward to New France would enable them to dominate the interior corridor of North America, securing a strong grasp on the lucrative fur trade and restricting English colonists to the Atlantic seaboard. Established on the Mississippi River and Gulf Coast, the French would be in an excellent position to threaten the gold and silver mines in Mexico that had financed the Spanish empire since the days of Cortés.

De L'Isle understood the strategic importance of the Mississippi Valley and also recognized Europeans' previous ignorance of the geography north of the Gulf of Mexico. When compiling information on the region, he had studied the routes taken by earlier explorers such as Hernando De Soto, La Salle, and Iberville. He had also received current data from Louis Juchereau de Saint-Denis, who from the new outpost at Natchitoches had made contact in 1714 with the northern Spanish settlements at Chihuahua and Santa Fe, and from reports from the missionary François Lemaire.

In spite of de L'Isle's controversial territorial claims on behalf of France, British cartographers recognized the importance of the geographical information that he provided and were quick to emulate his findings in their own works. In sum, this map, *Carte de la Louisiane de du cours du Mississipi*, became a primary resource for the American Old Southwest for the entire century.

Practically as impressive as De L'Isle's work is that by Nicolas de Fer whose 1718 *La France occidentale* continues the French efforts to claim territory through cartography and to provide relatively detailed information on the Mississippi Valley. De Fer depicts the Mississippi River correctly in his 1718 map.[4]

The prolific Jacques Bellin, in his *Carte de l'amerique septentrional* of 1755 provides a view of French Louisiana at the end of the empire. His map echoes much of the previous work produced by de L'Isle and de Fer. Bellin (1703-1772) was hydrographer to the king of France and the first chief hydrographic engineer of the French *Dépot des cartes, plans et journaux du Ministere de la Marine*. He was one of the most prolific map and atlas producers in the mid-eighteenth century, providing detailed coastal and route maps for French shipping.

Le Page du Pratz, author of a map which originally appeared with his *Histoire de la Louisiane* (1758) and which appears in the 1763 English edition of that work with the title *A Map of Louisiana, with the course of the Missisipi, and the adjaceent Rivers, the Nations of the Natives, The French Establishments and the Mines,*[5] believed that whomever possessed the Mississippi River would command the entire continent. In common with other French expansionists of his time, his 1758 definition of the boundaries of Louisiane is continental. It reads: "Louisiana is that part of North America which is bounded on the South by the Gulf of Mexico, on the east by Carolina, and the English Colony, and by a part of Canada; on the West, by New Mexico, and on the North in part by Canada; in part it extends without any assignable bounds, to the Terra Incognita adjoining Hudson's Bay."

While not an important explorer, Le Page was a keen observer, and carefully synthesized various reports concerning Louisiana colonists and the Natchez Indians. His map locates many Native American tribes and the lead mines of the upper Mississippi. It is further enhanced by intelligence from a captured Spanish manuscript map that gave more accurate geographical information about the Red and Arkansas Rivers as well as a more westerly placement of the Mississippi River. The ready translation of the work and the map demonstrates the rapid movement of North American information throughout Europe during the eighteenth century.

French efforts to more fully understand and to describe the Gulf Coast of the United States is no more evident than in an anonymous French manuscript map, *Carte de la cote de la Louisiane* of 1732.[6] It is notable for its beautiful rendering of various coastal features. While not as comprehensive as the work by d'Anville, it is a very sensitive rendering of that coastal plain which runs from Florida to the Texas border.

The anonymous map should be compared with the *Carte de La Louisiane* of Jean Baptiste d'Anville, also of 1732, but published in 1755.[7] D'Anville was named Royal Cartographer in 1717, and is credited with the rebirth of geography and cartography in eighteenth century France. In this classic map, d'Anville produced one of the earliest detailed depictions of the French settlements in the Gulf Coast region and upper Louisiana. The map's popularity led to frequent re-printings.

A detailed depiction of the Mississippi River segment of Louisiana extending from Bayou Manchac (Iberville River) to the coast below New Orleans is found in Saucier's 1749 *Carte Particuliere du cour du fleuve St. Louis depuis le village sauvage jusqu'au dessous du detour aux anglois*.[8] The River St. Louis was the French name for the Mississippi by this date. The region shown abuts Lakes Pontchartrain and Maurepas on the south. Saucier's map includes not only waterways, and features such as English Turn (see below), but also the locations of European and Native American settlements (notably the Colapissa village), cultivated land, roads, fortifications, and the grid plan for New Orleans. There is also reference to the *Quartier des Allemands*, the famous German Coast.

The region depicted on Saucier's map constitutes the area of Louisiana referred to as the Isle of Orleans, which was first so named by the British upon their receipt of Florida following the French and Indian War. Natural boundaries of the land, especially that portion east of the Mississippi River, are shown. The combined Lakes Maurepas and Pontchartrain form a water boundary with the sandy pine country of what is now referred to as the Florida Parishes in Louisiana, on the north shore of the Lakes.

Alexander de Batz's *Carte General de toute le cote de La Louisiane jusqu'a La Baye St. Bernard* prepared in 1747 is one of my favorite manuscript maps of the Louisiana gulf coast (figure 20).[9] De Batz served as an architect with the French colonial authorities in Louisiana from the 1730s to 1760, and was responsible for a number of maps. This elegant and well executed map recognizes both French and Spanish territories along the Gulf Coast. A careful reading allows one to speculate over the mapmaker's interpretation of political jurisdictions and boundaries, such as the French province of La Florida and a separate Spanish province of Florida. As an engineer and architect, de Batz was also known for his renderings of individual structures in New Orleans, including the Ursuline Convent (the first school for women in what is now the United States) and an observatory.

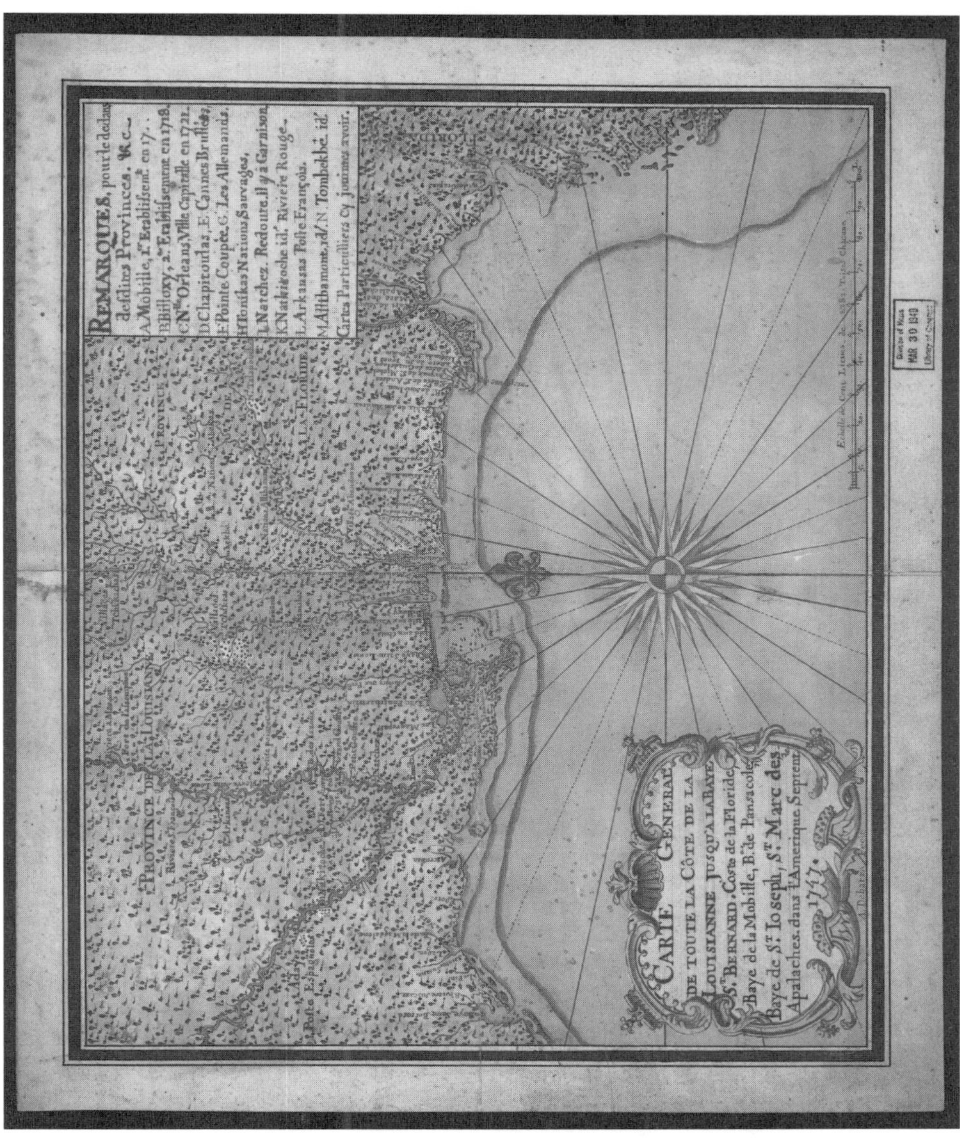

Figure 20. Alexander de Batz, *Carte general de toute la Côte de la Louisianne jusqu'à la Baye St. Bernard . . .*, [New Orleans], 1747. From the collection of the Geography and Map Division, Library of Congress.

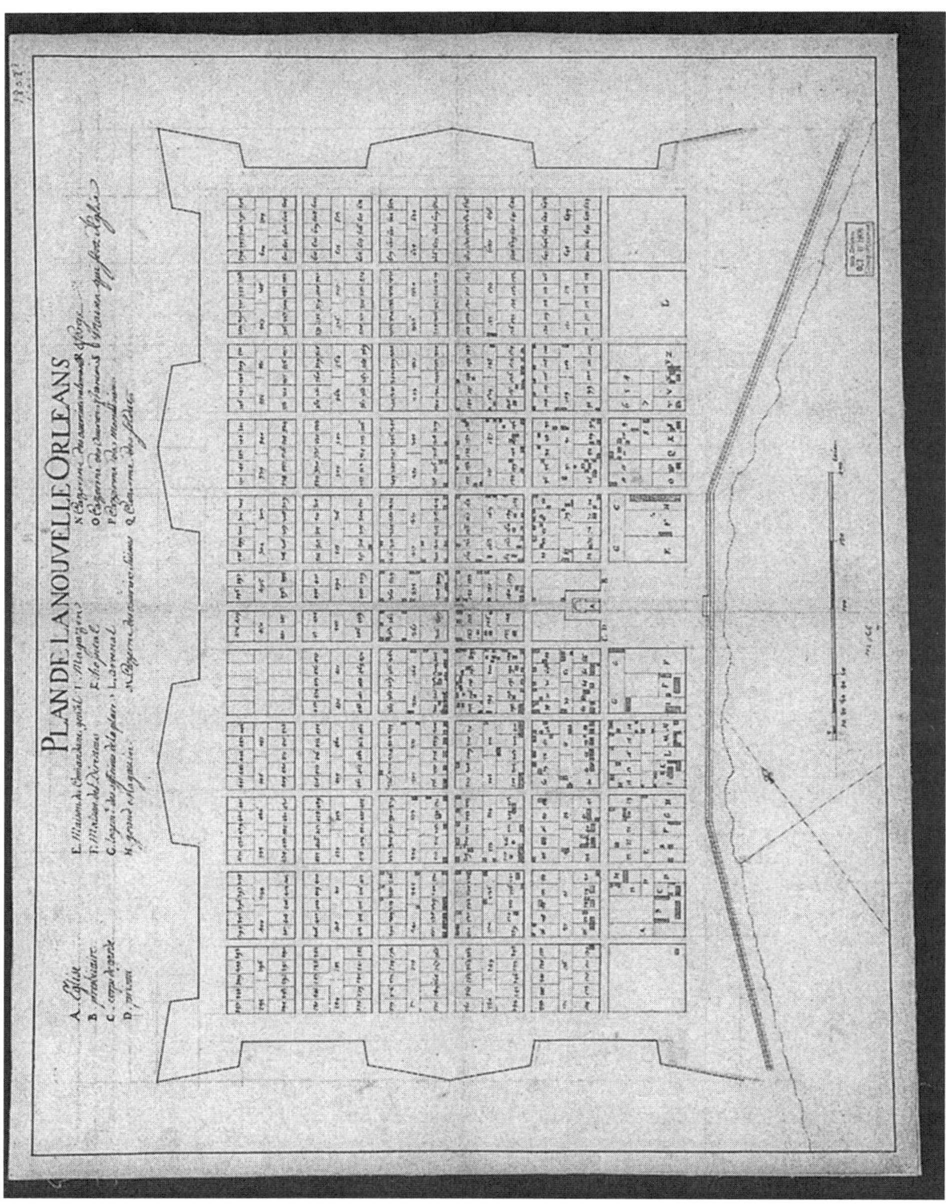

Figure 21. *Plan de la Nouvelle-Orléans* [New Orleans], ca. 1722. From the collection of the Geography and Map Division, Library of Congress.

Urban Plans

Consideration of de Batz leads naturally to the study of representative French military and urban maps from the eighteenth century. A 1743 *Plan of Fort Conde de la Mobile* shows intentions to strengthen that fortification, to protect the city of Mobile from English—and possibly Spanish—incursions. Obviously by the date of the plan the English were more of a threat than the Spaniards.

At the moment that Biloxi lost its important status as La Louisiane's capital, plans were afoot in 1721 to build a fort at New Biloxi, which had been placed on higher ground than the previous settlement. New Biloxi was closer to Ocean Springs, Mississippi, than present-day Biloxi. The fort project is shown in *Plan du forte Projete en Nouveau Biloxy.*

Ultimately the linchpin to French control of the Mississippi Valley was the city of New Orleans, which had been established in 1718 and whose founding was prompted in 1699 by an aborted British attempt to use French Huguenot settlers to establish an English presence on the river. By chance Iberville's brother, Bienville, had been exploring the Mississippi River near the site of New Orleans in search of a location for a fort when he encountered an English ship. The English were forced to turn and proceed to the Gulf, thus giving the name, English Turn, to that portion of the river.

The manuscript *Plan de la Nouvelle-Orléans* prepared about 1722 shows the location of existing buildings and assigned lots (figure 21).[10] It was most likely prepared after the devastating hurricane of 1722, since before that time the town's buildings were arranged without any alignment. It features a gridiron street plan surrounding a central *Place d'Armes*, a layout that has survived to the present day. Lots are marked with alphabetical letters. There was no fortification surrounding the town at this time, and such a project would not be started until 1729. A separate record accompanying this map lists the names of the original grantees, with later annotations regarding changes of ownership to 1734. The plan was apparently prepared by, or after one by Adrien de Pauger, who, along with fellow engineer Le Blonde de La Tour, was responsible for the first street layout of New Orleans.

Summation

Beginning with Iberville's landing on today's Mississippi Gulf Coast in 1699, France attempted colonization of the vast Mississippi Valley to satisfy a variety of political and economic goals. The region known as La Louisiane extended from the Gulf to Canada in the shape of an inverted pyramid and covered roughly one third of what is now the United States. La Louisiane was a vast colony, whose limits were never precisely fixed, and the French mapmakers of the period did not assist us with precise delineation of those boundaries. Although defeat by the English in the French and Indian War eclipsed its French colonial designation after four decades, many of the French settlements endured and the legacy of French maps of the region and of French culture represented in those maps is yet alive in the Mississippi Valley. It can be said that in the late seventeenth and during the first half of the eighteenth centuries, the French pointed out the strategic importance of the Mississippi Valley. Their mapmakers provided the first detailed descriptions of that huge region in what is now the United States, and their cartographic contributions stimulated other national groups, including the U. S. that followed at the end of the eighteenth century, to seek more information about the region, especially that segment located west of the Mississippi River. As we observe the bicentennials of both the Louisiana Purchase and the Lewis and Clark expedition we must recognize that the mapping of those regions covered by both the land purchase and the historical exploration had its origin in the French mapping begun a century and more before those dates.

SUGGESTED READINGS

Cohen, Paul. *Mapping the West: America's Westward Movement, 1527-1890.* New York: Rizzoli, 2002.

Colton, Craig E., ed. *Transforming New Orleans and Its Environs: Centuries of Change.* Pittsburgh: University of Pittsburgh Press, 2000.

Cumming, William P. *The Southeast in Early Maps.* Revised and enlarged by Louis De Vorsey, Jr. 3rd. ed. The Fred W. Morrison Series in Southern Studies. Chapel Hill, N.C.: University of North Carolina Press, 1998.

Delanglez, Jean. *A Jean Delanglez, S. J., Anthology: Selections Useful for Mississippi Valley and Trans-Mississippi American Indian Studies.* Edited with an introduction by Mildred Mott Wedel. The North American Indian. New York, 1985.

________. "The Cartography of the Mississippi. II. La Salle and the Mississippi," *Mid-America*, 31 (1949): 29-52.

________. "The Cartography of the Mississippi. The Maps of Coronelli," *Mid-America*, 30 (1948): 257-284.

________. "Franquelin's Maps And Plans," *Mid-America*, 25 (1943): 29-74.

Eckberg, Carl J. and William E. Foley, eds. *An Account of Upper Louisiana by Nicolas de Finiels.* Columbia, Mo.: University of Missouri Press, 1989.

Galloway, Patricia K., ed. *La Salle and His Legacy: Frenchmen and Indians in the Lower Mississippi Valley.* Jackson, Miss.: University of Mississippi Press, 1982.

González, Julio. *Catalogo de Mapas y Planos de la Florida y la Luisana.* Madrid: Dirección General del Patrimonio Artístico, Archivos y Museos, 1979.

Hébert, John R. and Anthony P. Mullan. *The Luso-Hispanic World in Maps: A Selective Guide to Manuscript Maps to 1900 in the Collections of the Library of Congress.* Washington, D. C.: Library of Congress, 1999.

Jackson, Jack. *Flags Along the Coast: Charting the Gulf of Mexico, 1519-1759: A Reappraisal*. Austin: Book Club of Texas, 1995.

Kennedy, J. Gerald. *The Astonished Traveler: William Darby, Frontier Geographer and Man of Letters*. Baton Rouge, La.: Louisiana State University Press, 1981.

Lewis, G. Malcolm, ed. *Cartographic Encounters: Perspectives on Native American Mapmaking and Map Use*. The Kenneth Nebenzahl, Jr. Lectures in the History of Cartography. Chicago: University of Chicago Press, 1998.

Lockett, Samuel Henry. *Louisiana As It Is: A Geographical and Topographical Description of the State*. Edited by Lauren C. Post. Baton Rouge, La.: Louisiana State University Press, 1970.

Lowery, Woodbury. *The Lowery Collection: A Descriptive List of Maps of the Spanish Possessions Within the Present Limits of the United States, 1502-1820.* Edited with notes by Philip Lee Phillips. Washington, D. C.: Government Printing Office, 1912.

Luebke, Frederick C., Frances W. Kaye and Gary E. Moulton, eds. *Mapping the North American Plains: Essays in the History of Cartography*. Norman: University of Oklahoma Press, 1987.

Nasatir, Abraham P., ed. *Before Lewis and Clark; Documents Illustrating the History of the Missouri, 1785-1804*. Joseph Desloge Fund 3. St. Louis: St. Louis Historical Documents Foundation, 1952.

Schwartz, Seymour and Ralph E. Ehrenberg. *The Mapping of America*. New York: H. N. Abrams, 1980.

Weddle, Robert S. *Changing Tides: Twilight and Dawn in the Spanish Sea 1763-1803*. Centennial Series of the Association of Former Students 58. College Station: Texas A & M University Press, 1995.

Wheat, Carl I. *Mapping the Transmississippi West, 1540-1861*, Vol. 1, *The Spanish entrada to the Louisiana Purchase, 1540-1804*. San Francisco: Institute of Historical Cartography, 1957-63.

Wood, W. Raymond. "Nicholas de Finiels: Mapping the Mississippi & Missouri Rivers, 1797-1798," *Missouri Historical Review*, 81 (July 1987): 387-402.

Chapter 21

"So Fine a Country": The Early Exploration of Louisiana Territory, 1714-1820

John L. Allen

There is a tendency for most Americans—particularly many of those who participated in firing the opening salvo in the Lewis and Clark Bicentennial at Monticello—to view the early exploration of the Louisiana Territory as a single set of lines made by those great captains on a blank map of the American West. But rather than a blank map, Lewis and Clark etched lines across a palimpsest on which the traces of nearly a century of earlier exploration were still visible. Nor were the tracks made by the Corps of Discovery the only ones at the time of the Purchase or during those years thereafter that are known as the period of "Jeffersonian exploration." Lewis and Clark were the first American explorers during this period and they were, without question, the most important. But they did not explore Louisiana alone. It is my responsibility here, as we observe the historical turn of events that made this soil upon which we stand American, to talk about Lewis and Clark, yes, but also to talk about the explorers who preceded and followed them and who are often given short shrift in the history of the exploration of the American West.

If we define the Louisiana Purchase Territory as Thomas Jefferson did in the spring of 1803—the entire western drainage basin of the Mississippi River—then the first Europeans to enter that territory were the Spaniards. Francisco Vásquez de Coronado's *entrada* of 1540-41 reached as far as the grass huts of the Wichita Indians in central Kansas. But the Spaniards were, to put it mildly, not as open with their geographical information obtained through exploration as were the other European colonial powers in North America, with the result that little was known about that first brief etching on the palimpsest until closer to our own time than to that of Jefferson. It remains one of the tragedies of exploratory history that even today the evocative journals of Coronado's chronicler—a foot soldier named Pedro Castañeda—are little known and seldom read. He was the first to describe the "hunch-back Kine" (bison) that frequented the Plains, the Indians who subsisted upon them, and the Plains themselves, "so fine a country," that Castañeda was the first among many to characterize as "a sea of grass . . . [and] the land is in the shape of a bowl."[1] Because the Spanish material was unavailable, the French and British provided the bulk of the information upon which Jefferson based the first official American expedition into the Louisiana Purchase Territory in 1804-06.

Exploration of Louisiana Before Lewis and Clark

French exploration of the land they first named "Louisiana" was, given the time and technology, a remarkable feat. During the century and a half after the nearly simultaneous founding of Jamestown and Quebec, French fur traders and missionary explorers from the St. Lawrence Valley and from the lower Ohio and Mississippi Valleys had penetrated far to the west of the Mississippi, up the Missouri beyond the Platte, and along the Saskatchewan to the outliers of the Rocky Mountains. During the same period the English from Jamestown had only reached the Shenandoah Valley.

The high water mark of French penetration of the interior of North America—or of the PurchaseTerritory—came during the first four decades of the eighteenth century. Three incentives drove this French penetration of Louisiana: a search for a route to the Pacific Ocean by way of the mythical *Mer de l'Ouest* ("The Western Sea") and its river connections; the attraction of commercial profit from the fur trade with Indian nations in the area west of the Great Lakes; and, to the southwest, the establishment of trade between New Orleans and the Spanish settlements in northern New Spain, specifically with Santa Fe.[2] And unlike the Spaniards whose exploratory lore became the secret property of church and state, the journals of French seekers after the Passage to the Pacific became the stuff of French histories and romances and, perhaps most important, of the brilliant maps of such eminent cartographers as Guillaume de L'Isle and Jean d'Anville, maps that Thomas Jefferson relied upon in shaping his own view of the western interior of North America once it became American.

The true extent of French geographical lore about Louisiana as the eighteenth century began is difficult to determine. We know that the heads of Quebec and Montreal fur trading establishments, the Jesuits, and some government officials possessed data on the country from the western shores of Lake Superior to Lake Winnipeg, largely resulting from the penetrations of both French fur traders and missionaries beyond the Great Lakes. French knowledge also included sketchy reports on the prairie country to the south of the Great Lakes, where the *couriers du bois* left behind them the heavily-timbered and rocky Laurentian shield with its tumbling rivers and dense network of linked glacial ponds and entered the tall grass prairie lands of the Ohio country where herds of bison and elk and deer grazed and where the French saw what the Spaniards had two centuries or more before: a sky that met the horizon everywhere one looked. But of the area to the west of the Mississippi Valley that represented France's furthermost penetration into the western interior by 1700, almost nothing was known.

French ignorance of the area west of the Mississippi Valley began to change in 1700 when Louis XIV decreed that the English must be penned up against the Atlantic coast, their colonists not allowed to expand beyond the crest of the Appalachians. The French established one northern rudimentary colonial outpost to block English expansion to the west: Detroit. Detroit stood at a strategically important point along the water route from Montreal to the farther west and thus could control most of the Great Lakes-St. Lawrence waterway and prevent English incursion from the New England/New York region. To halt the possible influx of the English from the Carolina Low Country and Virginia, the French established La Louisiane—with posts at Mobile, New Orleans, Natchez, and Fort Toulouse (near modern Montogmery, Alabama)—as well as a number of posts along the Ohio River. The Louisiana and Ohio settlements, in particular, were intended not just to deny the English access to the continental interior south of the Great Lakes, but to increase French colonial wealth through the burgeoning Indian trade in furs and hides and, hopefully, to open a clandestine trade free of Spanish taxes and duties between French trading posts in the Mississippi Valley and the silver mines of northern New Spain via the Rio Grande Valley. With these twin incentives of blocking the British and increasing their own wealth, the French penetrated far into the trans-Mississippi region of Louisiana, all the while making information available to the cartographers in France who interpreted the information and put it on maps that were, if not geographically precise, among the most beautiful creations of the mapmakers' art (figure 22).

The French officials in Europe and Lower Canada who developed these geopolitical and economic strategies thought that solving two primary puzzles of the interior geography of North America was particularly crucial to the survival of France's establishments there. What was the best route (preferably by water) to link the extensive and French-controlled St. Lawrence and Great Lakes waterway with the Pacific and, hence, the China trade? What was the best overland route to the Spanish silver mines in the Rio Grande Valley? On the first point, the answer for most French geographical theoreticians was the strange concept of a vast inland sea stretching from the Pacific inland into present day Saskatchewan and South Dakota. And on the second point, the solution lay in those Louisiana rivers entering the Mississippi from the west whose source waters were "known" to intermingle with those of the Rio Grande.

Perhaps because the ideas of an inland sea, continental symmetry, and water routes as the primary methods of travel were so dominant in French geographical thought, the reports from both the voyageurs and the missionaries reinforced these French misconceptions of North American geography. Such misconceptions, enhanced by the twin imperial imperatives of the western fur trade and a route to the Rio Grande, conditioned what lay ahead for French explorers in western America. The numbers of these explorers were not great—but the explorations they engaged in before France lost her vast holdings in North America were important. Their names—Claude-Charles Dutisné, Louis Juchereau de Saint-Denis, Bénard de la Harpe, Etienne de Bourgmont, Antoine and Paul Mallet, Father Pierre de Charlevoix, Pierre la Vérendrye, Jean-Baptiste Truteau, and Jacques D'Eglise—were not unknown to Thomas Jefferson as he gathered geographical data on Louisiana prior to dispatching his own explorations.

If the names and in some cases the reports of French explorers were part of Jefferson's geographical lore, so too were those of British explorers who had penetrated the Purchase Territory and returned with information that entered the mainstream of geographical thought on North America. The bulk of British exploration was centered on identifying the key features of Rupert's Land (the drainage basin of Hudson's Bay) and

Figure 22. Jacques Nicolas Bellin, *Map of Louisiana*, ca. 1755. From the collection of the Geography and Map Division, Library of Congress.

Bellin's great map shows the state of geographical awareness of the western interior of Louisiana Territory near the end of the French occupation. Bellin, a naval surveyor, used maps by d'Anville and Guilluame de L'Isle as his primary sources.

locating a route to the Pacific along the Hudson's Bay drainage rivers like the Saskatchewan and rivers that flowed west to the sea beyond what British geographical theorists as early as the late 1600s had postulated was a continental divide. Still, a few British explorers had encroached upon the French territory of Louisiana prior to 1800. Some of these men, like John Evans and James Mackay, were in the employ of the St. Louis fur trade during the Spanish period. Others, like David Thompson, were traders operating out of Montreal, an English colonial city after 1763 and the French surrender of Lower Canada to Great Britain. All three of these travelers reached the Mandan villages near the mouth of the Knife River in what is now central North Dakota. Evans and Mackay approached the Mandans from St. Louis by traveling up the Missouri. Thompson, a North West Company employee and a talented geographer and cartographer, reached this nerve center of the Missouri River fur trade overland from the British fur trading post at Rainy Lake.

The significance of these three late eighteenth-century explorers is that, between them, they explored considerable reaches of the northern portions of the Louisiana Purchase Territory. Not only did they reach the Mandan villages but they provided significant quantities of geographical and cartographic information that became part of the general store of information available to Jefferson immediately prior to the Lewis and Clark expedition. For example, a map of the vicinity of the Mandan villages (figure 23) drawn by Thompson was used in producing a large map of the West that Meriwether Lewis took with him when he left Washington for the West in July, 1803. Mackay's and Evans's maps and other geographical information were obtained by Lewis during the winter of 1803-04 in St. Louis as he and Clark were making the final preparations for what they hoped would be a successful effort to achieve the two-hundred year old goal of finding a water route to the Pacific.

Early American Exploration of Louisiana Territory: Jeffersonian Explorers of the Enlightenment

Just as Lewis and Clark are often erroneously viewed as the first explorers to penetrate the trans-Mississippi area, they are often equally mistakenly portrayed as the only American explorers of the Purchase Territory until the fur trade and John C. Fremont. The expedition of Lewis and Clark is America's epic exploration, but it was not an isolated event. During the period that we generally think of as "Jeffersonian" in an exploratory context, there were a number of important western explorers who added significant geographical information to the American view of the new territory.

That said, we necessarily begin with the Corps of Discovery because the trek of Lewis and Clark across the continent remains one of America's greatest adventure stories. Between May 1804 and September 1806, the Corps of Discovery engaged in the most massive interior exploration of the North American continent to date: up the Missouri to the Continental Divide at Lemhi Pass on the Montana-Idaho border, overland through the Bitterroot Mountains to the Clearwater River of Idaho (where water travel resumed), down the Clearwater to the Snake, the Columbia, and the Pacific. They failed to find the fabled passage although one day after their safe return to St. Louis, Meriwether Lewis rather disingenuously wrote the president that the party led by himself and Clark had "penitrated the Continent of North America to the Pacific Ocean, and sufficiently explored the interior of the country to affirm with confidence that we have discovered the most practicable route which does exist across the continent." But that "most practicable route" was a far cry from the easy water route Jefferson had hoped for. Rather, it involved a lengthy overland crossing suitable only for goods "not bulky brittle nor of a very perishable nature."[3] This was not, as James Ronda has pointed out, Jefferson's "highway to the Pacific."[4]

Thinking of exploration as a series of connected enterprises rather than isolated events, Thomas Jefferson had plans for the investigation of the Louisiana Territory that went beyond Lewis and Clark. As that territory came into official United States

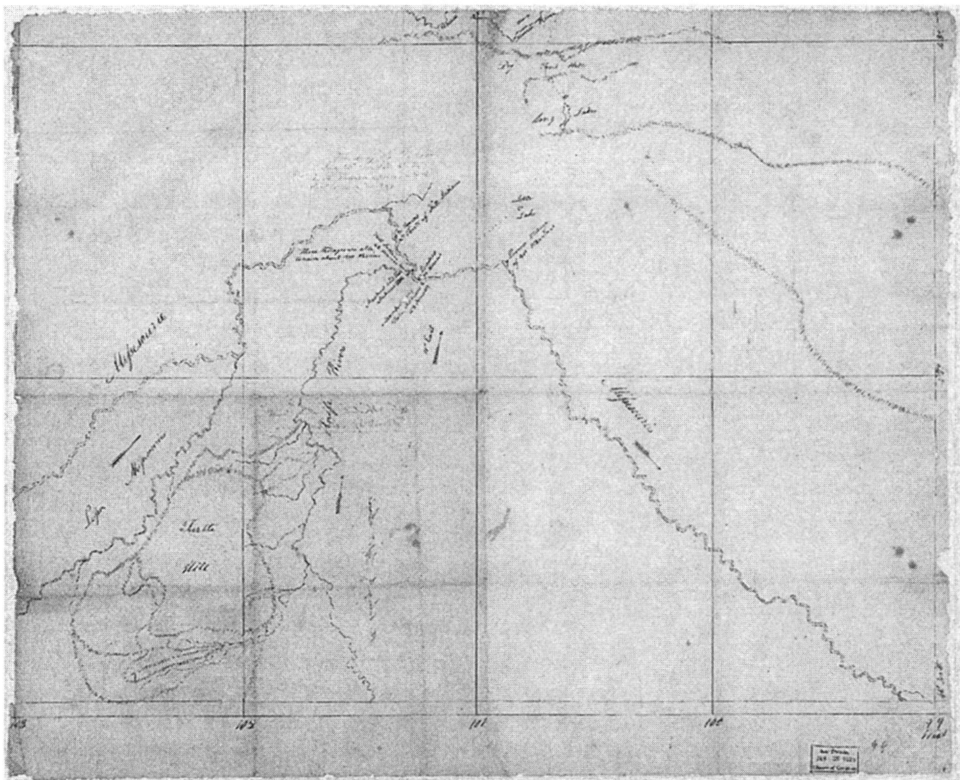

Figure 23. David Thompson, *The Mandan-Hidatsa Villages*, ca. 1798. From the collection of the Geography and Map Division, Library of Congress.

Thompson was a trader/explorer/surveyor for the North West Company out of Montreal in the late eighteenth and early nineteenth centuries. His maps of the American and Canadian West are among the most accurate for the time. This map illustrates the major trading center for the Northern Plains, the Mandan and Hidatsa villages near the confluence of the Knife River and the Missouri River. It was one of the maps available to Lewis and Clark in 1803.

possession, more detailed exploration was necessary to survey the boundaries on the south as well as the north, to establish commercial relations with Indian tribes other than those along the Missouri River, and to increase scientific knowledge beyond that contributed by Lewis and Clark.

As early as March 1804, prior to Lewis's and Clark's departure for the Northwest, Jefferson began to plan an exploration of the Mississippi's great southern tributaries, the Red and Arkansas Rivers. He selected a Natchez planter named William Dunbar, one of Jefferson's frequent correspondents on matters having to do with Louisiana, to lead an expedition into the Red and Arkansas basins. This survey would, Jefferson hoped, "enable us to prepare a map of Louisiana which in its contours and main waters will be perfectly accurate."[5] Dunbar, joined by George Hunter, a Philadelphia naturalist-chemist, and a small contingent of U. S. Army enlisted men, left Natchez in October 1804 and traveled as far as the head of navigation on the Ouachita before returning to Natchez. Although a considerably abbreviated version of what Jefferson had originally intended, Dunbar and Hunter contributed scientific observations and cartographic knowledge that was quickly assimilated into the growing store of information on the trans-Mississippi region. But these were not their only discoveries. Their expedition also pointed up the differences between navigating southwestern waters and the Ohio, Mississippi, or Missouri. More appropriate water craft were needed. The absence of a military commander capable of quick field decisions was also noted as a problem, as was the need for a field strategy that made more sense than the original intent to portage overland over considerable distances between the Red and Arkansas Rivers.

The non-geographic discoveries of the Dunbar-Hunter expedition should have eased planning for subsequent exploration. Unfortunately, they did not and it was not until April 1806 that the larger expedition bound for the Red and Arkansas Rivers was ready to depart the new Army post of Fort Adams, near Natchez, and travel up the Mississippi to the mouth of the Red River. This expedition was led by surveyor Thomas Freeman and a young Philadelphia medical student named Peter Custis. It made little more progress than had that of Dunbar and Hunter. The explorers found the Red River difficult if not impossible to navigate and their plans to travel as far as the head of navigation and then travel by horseback to the river's source before swinging north to the Arkansas were already being re-evaluated when the expedition was intercepted in eastern Texas by a party of Spanish soldiers determined to let no Americans penetrate into what they still considered Spanish territory. Thus was the Freeman-Custis expedition brought to a halt, almost before it began. But the Freeman-Custis expedition should not be branded a failure because even during their abbreviated travels the explorers did much important scientific work and their geographic labors found a place in maps, including William Clark's great master map of 1810 (figure 24).

These explorations organized by Jefferson have been relegated to the dustbin of American memory because of a simultaneous southwestern journey with a history both romantic and slightly twisted. A foremost Western historian has characterized Zebulon Montgomery Pike as "a young army officer cursed by galloping ambition, an inadequate education, and a misplaced loyalty to his commanding officer," General James Wilkinson, commander of the American Army in the West and clandestine Spanish agent.[6]

The orders for Pike's first expedition in 1805 called for him to map the course of the Mississippi River, identify the natural resources of its valley—including appropriate locations for Army forts or commercial trading posts—and make provisions for the visits of Indian delegations to Wilkinson's headquarters in St. Louis. Departing St. Louis on

August 9, 1805, Pike ascended the Mississippi to just above the Falls of St. Anthony (present-day Minneapolis-St. Paul) but failed to locate the river's source. By the end of April, 1806, he had returned to St. Louis, with maps and observations of natural history and "establishment" locations in his journals.

Upon his arrival in St. Louis, Pike learned that he was to have a new assignment that he described as a "long and Ardious" expedition with three sequential missions: he was to return to their homes over 50 Osage Indians who had been held captive by a rival tribe and ransomed by the United States as a way to gain favor with tribes west of the Mississippi. Once at the Osage nation, he was to negotiate a peace between the Kansas and Osage; following that diplomatic task, he was to negotiate an alliance with the Comanches against the Spaniards on the western borderlands of the Louisiana Territory. Seeking the Comanches would take Pike "approximate to the settlements of New Mexico" and he was consequently warned by Wilkinson to "move with great circumspection."[7]

The essence of Pike's real mission, all of this Indian diplomacy notwithstanding, rested in a chronic misunderstanding of western geography since the years of the first French explorers in Louisiana: the belief that the headwaters of the Red and Arkansas Rivers were in close proximity. The more reliable French maps showed the Red River heading a few miles east of Taos, with the Arkansas source springing from an area only slightly to the north and near the sources of the Rio Grande as well. Pike spent a good part of his expedition lost and disoriented—it is little wonder, given the disjunction between his conceptual geography and the geography of reality.

The story of Pike's travels in 1806-07 is well known. In the summer and fall of 1806 his expedition traveled up the Arkansas to what Pike thought was its source, crossed a divide northward to the South Platte, then turned west to intercept the main stem of the Arkansas, believing it to be the Red River—and promptly got into deep trouble. His men were equipped and clothed for summer on the Plains, not winter in the Rockies. And it was not just the weather that posed a problem; so too was the growing realization on Pike's part that his images of the country did not match the reality of the landscape. A journal entry illustrates the scope of his dilemma: "The geography of the country had turned out to be so different from our expectation; we were some what at a loss which course to pursue."[8] Given that he was on the Arkansas River in the Colorado Rockies and believed that he was on the upper waters of the Red River, this statement appears somewhat understated. Finally, in January of 1807, following a struggle to get through the Royal Gorge of the Arkansas, Pike realized which river he was really on. He now had to face a decision to either stay where he was or head southwest for what he assumed would be the valley of the Red River. This was a decision made both more difficult and more important by the scantiness of his supplies, equipment, and clothing, his lack of horses (this was, after all, supposed to be a river expedition like that of Lewis and Clark), and his confusion about the geography of the southern Rocky Mountains. He chose to turn southwest and for nearly three weeks his command struggled through the snows of the Sangre de Cristo Range to the San Luis Valley and the Rio Grande or, in Pike's geography of the imagination, the Red River. Here the party erected a crude log fort to wait out the winter within what Pike always claimed he believed were the territorial limits of the United States. The daily routine and tedium of a frontier army post in mid-winter were dramatically interrupted in late February when a large Spanish detachment reached Pike's stockade and confronted him with the fact that he was on the Rio Grande and in Spanish territory. Continually guarded by Spanish soldiers, the Pike expedition spent the next four months as "guests" of the Spanish colonial government, traveling to Santa Fe, Chihuahua, and San Antonio, Texas before finally arriving back on U. S. soil in June 1807.

Little of Pike's exploration—with the exception of the Colorado peak that bears his name—remains alive in the American consciousness. But in his time, his journals provided one of the first glimpses of what later became, in the minds of some Americans, "the Great American Desert." And his final map added more fuel to the notion that the source waters of western streams were close together because, in addition to portraying the proximity of the sources of the Arkansas and Rio Grande (about which Pike had learned the hard way), Pike showed the sources of the Platte only a short distance away and near the headwaters of that river was "the headwaters of the Yellowstone, branch of the Missouri."[9]

The Early American Fur Trade of the Jeffersonian Era

Although Jeffersonian exploration was characterized by official government expeditions penetrating the Purchase Territory, it would be erroneous to suggest that western exploration during this era was exclusively the province of the United States Army. Moreover, with the exception of Lewis and Clark, the most important exploratory contributions during the first two decades of American possession of Louisiana Territory were made not by the Army but by representatives of competing St. Louis and New York-based fur trading companies. These fur-trade explorers were active on the Missouri even before Lewis and Clark. When the captains traveled north to the Mandan villages in the summer and fall of 1804, they encountered pirogues and dugouts and other rivercraft laden with furs, coming downstream and bound for the warehouses of the Choteaus and other fur-trade magnates of St. Louis. During the long winter at their winter encampment at Fort Mandan in 1804-05 Lewis and Clark were met and hosted by men like Hugh Heney, René Jusseaume, and François-Antoine Larocque. These merchant traders were not insignificant as explorers themselves. Larocque, for example, was the first Euro-American to explore the Yellowstone River, a year before William Clark's reconnaissance on the return journey in 1806. The Missouri River fur trade was an important component of the economic geography of the trans-Mississippi West well before Thomas Jefferson sent his captains west and the nexus of the Mandan villages was an important trading center, not just in the context of continental but also of global trade.[10]

The return of Lewis and Clark and their command to St. Louis in late September 1806 was more than just a celebrated return of the United States' first major western venture. It also provided the American people with their first informative look at the West beyond the horizon. The reports contained in their notebooks that were of most interest to St. Louis entrepreneurs dealt with the abundance of beaver and other fur-bearing animals in the Missouri Basin and with the presence of Indian nations ready to partner with American companies in the fur trade.

First to act on this information was Manuel Lisa, a Spanish trader who had come to St. Louis in the late 1790s. He was soon challenging older and more established concerns for a place in the fur business by organizing a putative journey to open up the long-desired St. Louis-Santa Fe trading connection. Because such an adventure was in conflict with General Wilkinson's ambitions, Lisa wisely gave up his Santa Fe plan in favor of one suggested by the reports of Lewis and Clark. He would travel to the confluence of the Big Horn and Yellowstone, build a fort, and send men into the surrounding country of south-central Montana and northwest Wyoming to induce Indians to come into the fort to trade beaver and buffalo robes for trade goods brought from St. Louis. And that is what he did, employing Lewis and Clark veterans John Colter, George Drouillard, and Daniel Potts as his primary scouts.

Little is known about Colter's, Drouillard's, and Potts's journeys, but Colter's travels have received attention. Traveling alone in the winter of 1807-08, Colter traced a route through Wyoming's Big Horn Basin and Wind River valley that is still subject to dispute because the only documentary evidence that remains is William Clark's copy of a map possibly originally drawn by Colter and/or Drouillard and the subsequent tracing of Colter's route on Clark's 1810 manuscript map. Colter's route, based on Clark's map, took him south from Lisa's fort to the present-day site of Cody, Wyoming where he saw the thermal features that became known as "Colter's Hell" (later erroneously ascribed to Yellowstone). From here he traveled south to the Wind River and followed it to its source in what is called "Lake Biddle" on Clark's map, and then turned north into Yellowstone, traveling along the western edge of the Yellowstone Lake to the Yellowstone River below the Grand Canyon. Here he found the well-traveled Bannock Indian trail east to the Great Plains and the way back to Lisa's fort.

This remarkable solitary journey at such an early date places Colter high on the list of important fur-trade explorers. But there may well have been other American explorers in the mountains during 1807 who still remain shadowy figures. As Lewis and Clark were heading down the Missouri for St. Louis in September 1806 they met a recently-resigned army captain named John McClellan. McClellan told the captains that he intended to reach the "confines of New Spain, with a view to introduce a trade with those people," a mission similar to Pike's.[11] But after hearing Lewis and Clark enthusiastically describe the potential wealth in the beaver streams of the Rocky Mountains, McClellan apparently abandoned thoughts of New Mexico in favor of the northern Rockies, continuing up the Missouri and thence into northwestern Montana in the summer of 1807.

Here he and associates may have trapped and traded until killed by Piegans in the fall of 1810 when those warriors assaulted American traders throughout the upper Missouri country. Contemporary correspondence and cartography from David Thompson of the North West Company suggest the presence of a large party of Americans in an area that the British considered their own territory beyond the Continental Divide and, hence, no longer in Louisiana Territory. Thompson worried that "this establishment of the Americans will give a new Turn to our so long delayed settling of this Country, in which we have entered it seems too late."[12] Were the Americans that Thompson wrote about the party led by McClellan? If so, then to him and his party we would reserve the honor of being the first Americans after Lewis and Clark to winter beyond the Divide.

Meanwhile, Manuel Lisa kept his traders in the field. They gradually developed a finer knowledge of the northern Plains and Rockies and also discovered ways to cross the Rockies south of the Lewis and Clark routes. At least one party of Lisa's men, headed up by Lisa's able field lieutenant Andrew Henry, did in fact cross the Continental Divide in northwestern Wyoming to a tributary of the Snake River. On the tributary of the Snake now known as Henry's Fork, the traders built a fort, the first permanent American post west of the divide. Henry returned to St. Louis in the fall of 1811 where the reports of his travels prompted the *Louisiana Gazette* to offer up an optimistic assessment of western geography: "Mr. Henry, a member of the Missouri Fur Company, and his hunters, have discovered several passes, not only very practicable, but even in their present state, less difficult than those of the Allegany Mountains. These are considerably south of the source of the Jefferson River. It is the opinion of the gentleman last mentioned, that loaded horses, or even wagons, might in its present state, go in the course of 6 or 8 days from a navigable point on the Columbia, to one on the waters of the Missouri—Thus, rendering an intercourse with settlements which may be formed on the Columbia, more easy than between those on the heads of the Ohio, and the Atlantic states."[13] The Northwest Passage that Lewis and Clark had not found was still alive and well in a slightly different form.

The business of collecting trader lore and reducing it to cartographic scale fell to William Clark. His map (figure 24) drawn to illustrate the first "official" narrative account of his and Lewis's travels illustrates the nature of Jeffersonian explorations more than any other. Clark's master map was sent to Nicholas Biddle in December 1810 to become the basis for the engraved "Map of Lewis and Clark's Track Across the Western Portion of North America" published in Biddle's 1814 *History of the Expedition under the Command of Captains Lewis and Clark.*

Clark's great cartographic production demonstrates both the persistence of older and more imaginary geographic features and the coming of changes in American views of the West. A comparison of Clark's 1805 map of the West drawn during the winter at Fort Mandan on the basis of pre-existing geographical knowledge and information obtained from the Indians and his map of 1810 utilizing his own surveys and those of fur-trader explorers like Lisa's men and the Astorians (employees of John Jacob Astor's American

Fur Company) reveals a great "leap forward in both geographic knowledge and cartographic imagination."[14]

Change is most evident in two places. First, like many eighteenth century maps of the interior of North America, Clark's Fort Mandan map portrayed the Rockies as narrow, parallel ridges similar to the ridge-and-valley country of the Blue Ridge. That pre-exploratory image was transformed by field experience in the summer of 1805 during which the long, tortured trek through nearly 600 miles of mountainous terrain taught Clark that the Rockies were not like the Blue Ridge. The convoluted mountain terrain of the Rockies dominates Clark's 1810 map. In the details of Clark's cartography was the end of an old myth: that the Pacific was visible from the crest of the Rockies. Rather, the Rockies were separated from the mountains near the coast (the Cascade Range) by the open Columbian Plateau, a completely unanticipated geographical feature.

The dramatic change in the conceptualization of western mountains was mirrored by Clark's representation of western rivers, his second contribution to geographic knowledge. Where earlier maps had portrayed the headwaters of the Missouri and Columbia as being "interlocked," navigable to sources that were in very close proximity, this newest map of the western mountains (and the first based on direct field observation) portrayed the upper reaches of the Missouri and Columbia drainage systems as rushing, narrow mountain streams, rather than western analogs of the James and Potomac.

As accurate as it was for the areas that Lewis and Clark had actually seen, Clark's map maintained a grand illusory feature in the areas they had not: a core drainage area for major western streams, existing south of the routes that he and Lewis had fashioned across the Montana Rockies. In an area of about 100 miles square Clark placed the source waters of (from 12 o'clock clockwise back to 12 o'clock) the Missouri, the Yellowstone, the Big Horn, the Platte, the Arkansas, the Red, the Rio Grande, the Colorado, the Multnomah (a purely mythical stream created out of the Willamette and necessary, in Clark's hypothetical geography, to drain the country south of the Snake), the Snake or "Lewis's River", and the Clark's Fork of the Columbia. While rejecting the Jeffersonian notion of a short portage between upper Missouri and Columbia, Clark adopted the myth of an easy journey from the upper Bighorn to the "Spanish river"—either the Rio Grande or the Colorado—or to the mythical Multnomah. Jefferson's passage to India by way of the Missouri and Columbia had died; but the illusion persisted in a southern reincarnation that would persist for another four decades on many maps of the West (even if the members of the Rocky Mountain fur trade knew better). Pike's findings and misconceptions helped to reinforce this misunderstanding.

One remaining fur-trade foray into the West during the Jeffersonian period must be mentioned, partly because some information from it was worked into Clark's map and partly because of the significance of this experience for later developments in Louisiana

Figure 24. William Clark, *Map of the American Northwest*, 1814. From Nicholas Biddle, ed., *The History of the Expedition . . . Under the Command of Captains Lewis and Clark . . .* (Philadelphia, 1814). From the collection of the Geography and Map Division, Library of Congress.

Clark's great "master map" of the West dominated western cartography for three decades after its publication in Nicholas Biddle's edition of the Lewis and Clark expedition. Clark's map represents the real contribution to geographical knowledge made by the expedition he and Lewis conducted to the Pacific and back in 1804-1806. It also contains information from the St. Louis fur trade in the 1806-1810 period and from the Astorian venture of 1810.

Territory. In 1811, William Price Hunt was in St. Louis preparing to lead a party of fur traders up the Missouri, intending to cross the Rockies and descend the Columbia to build a fort at the river's mouth for John Jacob Astor's American Fur Company. Conversations with William Clark, John Colter (who was then living in La Charette, Missouri, a short distance upriver from St. Louis), and several veterans of Andrew Henry's 1809 western expedition who already had seen much of the mountain West caused Hunt to revise his plans. Henry's men argued that either the original Lewis and Clark route or a route up the Yellowstone would expose the Astorians to unnecessary Indian dangers. They suggested to Hunt what seemed to be a more direct and less hazardous highway across the mountains: up the Missouri to the Niobrara and then overland on horseback through present-day South Dakota and Wyoming to meet the Wind River near today's Shoshoni, Wyoming. From that point the trail lay up the Wind River to passes (either Union Pass or Togwotee Pass) across "a single mountain ridge . . . [to] the headwaters of the Columbia," by which they meant the Snake River in Jackson's Hole.[15] This was a persuasive argument and the route suggested was that adopted by Hunt, commander of the westbound Astorian party. The decision to descend the Snake nearly proved disastrous, however, and finally Hunt split his expedition into several small parties who left the river to travel overland across Oregon's Blue Mountains to the Columbia, most of them surviving to reach the mouth of the Columbia in February 1812. Here they founded a fur-trade post that was quickly lost to the British North West Company in 1813 as an outgrowth of the War of 1812.

Some of the dispossessed Astorians departed the Northwest via British and American ships and others, led by Robert Stuart, returned overland to discover what would become the key to the riddle of the geography of the American interior. Retracing Hunt's route across the Blue Mountains to the Snake River Plain and up the Snake to the low pass between the Snake and the upper waters of the Green River in 1812, Stuart made a fateful decision. Instead of crossing the Continental Divide by the now well-known Union Pass, Stuart—on the strength of Indian advice—followed the Green River south to the southern end of the Wind River Range where he turned east and crossed a broad tableland that could not be properly called a mountain pass to the headwaters of the Sweetwater River, a branch of the Platte. Stuart had crossed South Pass, which eventually became an essential part of the Oregon and California and Mormon Trails.

New Englander Stephen H. Long led the penultimate Jeffersonian exploration. Long was an officer in the U. S. Army whose reach to do great deeds exceeded his grasp of what it took to lead an exploratory expedition. Originally intended to explore the Yellowstone Valley, Long's 1819 command was turned back by Indian troubles in the Missouri Valley and his mission redefined to include a survey in 1820 of the central and southern Great Plains as far as the Rockies. The expedition, the first government survey to include trained scientists and artists, departed St. Louis in June 1820 and struck the Platte two weeks later. A fortnight after it reached the junction of the North and South Platte at present-day North Platte, Nebraska. Following the South Platte to the Colorado

Rockies, Long and his scientists and artists took note of topography, climate, and many of the Great Plains plants and animals recorded earlier by Lewis and Clark. But where Lewis and Clark had seen the Great Plains as a Garden, the New Englander Long and his eastern scientists filled their accounts with words like "arid," "barren," and "sterile." The chronicler of the expedition, Dr. Edwin James, found the landscape not only exotic but unsettling: "the monotony of a vast unbroken plain, like that in which we had now travelled, nearly one hundred and fifty miles, is little less tiresome to the eye, and fatiguing to the spirit, than the dreary solitude of the ocean."[16] Long's party reached the site of present-day Denver in early July, attempted an ascent of Pike's Peak, and viewed the Platte headwaters running from the mountains. This settled a long-standing question about the proximity of the Platte's sources to those of the Missouri and Snake and what remained was to clarify the relationship between the Platte and the Arkansas. Long's instructions had included a western probe along the Arkansas but Long failed to pursue that goal, instead turning his expedition downriver on a homeward journey that did little but to confuse the Red with the Canadian River and fail to clarify the relationship of these streams with each other or with the Arkansas. The three primary streams of the southern plains were still poorly understood more than a century after their discovery by the French explorers seeking a route to Santa Fe.

Long's ambition had been to lead a grand scientific reconnaissance of the West. In that he must have been bitterly disappointed. But his expedition was something of a transition for western exploration because it involved citizen scientists and artists and because it focused not on a route to the Pacific but on a better understanding of what would soon become the American middle border. The scientists and artists accompanying Long gave the American public the accurate first visual images of the West beyond the horizon. Long certainly gave the notion of the Louisiana Purchase Territory as a desert a powerful boost, and on his major map of the Great Plains, Long gave the American public a geographical oddity that confused American images of the West for the remainder of the century, stretching the words "Great American Desert" across the Great Plains.

After Long's exploration there still remained the one important geographical question to be answered by the final Jeffersonian era exploration: where was the actual source of the Mississippi River? Michigan territorial governor Lewis Cass, with scientist Henry Rowe Schoolcraft accompanying, mounted an expedition in 1820 to locate "the sources of the Mississippi river, which have continued to be the subject of dispute,"[17] but failed to do so. It was not until 1832 that the final major riddle in the geography of Louisiana Territory was solved when another expedition led by Schoolcraft determined the ultimate source of the Mississippi to be in a lake Schoolcraft named "Itasca, a name compounded from the last two syllables of *veritas* and the first syllable of *caput*."[18] Perhaps of equal importance with the discovery of the Mississippi's source was that the map accompanying Schoolcraft's report, drawn by Lieutenant James Allen, clearly showed the dividing ridge between the Mississippi drainage and that of the Red River of

Nicollet and John Charles Fremont in 1838 and would mark the transition in western exploration from Jeffersonian explorers to the U. S. Army Corps of Engineers, the successor and heir to the principles of Jeffersonian exploratory science.

The early exploration of Louisiana Territory laid the foundations of empire. But, as James Ronda has pointed out, "that handiwork did not promise all North Americans an equally bright future."[19] Joseph Conrad reminds us in his novel of exploration, *Heart of Darkness*, that "the conquest of the earth, which mostly means the taking of it away from those who have a different complexion or slightly flatter noses than ourselves, is not a pretty thing when you look at it too much."[20] Close scrutiny of exploration's outcomes in the Louisiana Purchase Territory during the century separating Bernard la Harpe from Stephen Long reveals no sure and steady progress of "civilization" or geographical knowledge but, rather, scenes of imperial and commercial ambition, heightened international rivalry, geographic confusion, and ultimately conquest and invasion. Shortly after the Purchase of Louisiana Territory was announced, Jefferson wrote a letter to a prominent member of the Senate in which the president spelled out his vision for national expansion: "we may lay off a range of States on the Western bank [of the Mississippi], from the head to the mouth, and so, range after range, advancing compactly as we multiply."[21] This was nothing more than geopolitical ambition writ large and it would create the same kind of attitudes about the conquest of lands adjacent to the Louisiana Purchase Territory that Jefferson claimed to find abhorrent in the behavior of imperial Britain.

Finally, there was something else happening at the end of the early exploration of Louisiana Territory and that was a fundamental change in the character of exploration itself. Up to the end of the Jeffersonian period explorers has seen themselves as faithful "servants" of the state or corporate entity, or sometimes both. Whatever they found, whatever glory they attained belonged to the cause of nation or company. There was nothing self-effacing about Etienne de Bourgmont or Meriwether Lewis but in the final analysis they saw themselves as "men doing dangerous work as ordered, . . . as ordinary men who faced sometimes extraordinary challenges."[22] But after the last of the Jeffersonian explorations, new explorers—whether military commanders or civilian scientists—would actively court the favor of the public and demand attention not as public servants but as national heroes. Where William Clark lived out his life as a soldier who continued to do his duty in service to his nation, John Charles Fremont styled himself as "Pathfinder" and rode that label nearly to the White House.

SUGGESTED READING

Allen, John Logan. *Passage through the Garden: Lewis and Clark and the Image of the American Northwest.* Urbana, Ill.: University of Illinois Press, 1975. Reprint edition published as *Lewis and Clark and the Image of the American Northwest,* New York: Dover Publications, 1991.

published as *Lewis and Clark and the Image of the American Northwest,* New York: Dover Publications, 1991.

________, ed. *North American Exploration*, 3 vols. Lincoln: University of Nebraska Press, 1997.

Cox, Issac Joslin. *The Early Exploration of Louisiana*. University Studies 2:2:1. Cincinnati: University of Cincinnati Press, 1906.

DeVoto, Bernard. *Course of Empire*. Boston: Houghton-Mifflin, 1952.

Goetzemann, William. *Exploration and Empire: The Explorer and The Scientist in the Winning of the American West.* New York: Knopf, 1967. Reprint, New York: Norton, 1978, and Austin: Texas State Historical Association, 1994.

Jackson, Donald. *Letters of the Lewis and Clark Expedition, with Related Documents 1783-1854*. 2nd edition. 2 vols. Urbana, Ill.: University of Illinois Press, 1978.

________, ed. *The Journals of Zebulon Montgomery Pike with Letters and Related Documents.* 2 vols. Norman: University of Oklahoma Press, 1966.

James, Edwin. *Account of an Expedition from Pittsburgh to the Rocky Mountains: Performed in the Years 1819 and '20, by the order of the Hon. J. C. Calhoun, Secretary of War; Under the Command of Major Stephen H. Long*. 2 vols. Philadelphia: H. C. Carey and I. Lea, 1823.

Moulton, Gary. *The Lewis and Clark Journals: An American Epic of Discovery; An abridgement of the definitive Nebraska Edition*. Lincoln: University of Nebraska Press, 2003.

Nasatir, Abraham P. *Before Lewis and Clark: Documents Illustrating the History of the Missouri, 1785-1804.* 2 vols. St. Louis: St. Louis Historical Documents Foundation, 1952. Reprint Lincoln: University of Nebraska Press, 2003.

Ronda, James P. *Astoria and Empire.* Lincoln: University of Nebraska Press, 1990.

Winsor, Justin. *The Mississippi Basin; the Struggle in America between England and France, 1697-1763, with full Cartographical Illustrations from Contemporary Sources*. Boston and New York: Houghton Mifflin and Company. Reprint, Freeport, N. Y.: Books for Libraries Press, 1972.

Chapter 22

The Louisiana Purchase Bicentennial Conference Closing Remarks

John B. Boles

We forget how controversial the Louisiana Purchase was in 1803, particularly in New England, where those conservative Federalists—at that time themselves "men of little faith"—feared the consequences of the territorial enlargement on the future of the nation. "A great waste, a wilderness unpeopled with any beings except wolves and wandering Indians," complained the Boston *Columbian Centinel* on July 13, 1803. "We are to give money of which we have too little, for land of which we already have too much."[1] The *New Hampshire Sentinel* published a long diatribe in graphic display:

On the 12 inst., was celebrated in a few sections
Of our country, by a few individuals,
A NATIONAL JUBILEE,
To celebrate
The purchase of an immense Tract of Wild
Land
Filled with buffaloes, deer, mammoths,
Prairies and salt mountains,
Which was purchased by incurring a
Debt to Bonaparte
Of
Fifteen millions of Dollars.
An event, of dire portent to
The Liberty,
The Happiness,
The Peace,
The Security,
The Prosperity,
The Glory, of
The Northern States, and particularly of New-England,
And perhaps eventually to the subversion of
Representative Government,
And to the dissolution of
These United States.
An event, resulting from the embarrassed state
Of

European Nations,
And not from the exclusive wisdom of
Thomas Jefferson,
Whose acts of administration, in the Removal
From place, of
Old Revolutionary Officers, and
Real Patriots, &c, &c,
Will never entitle him to the character of
The Man of the People,
Or the
Plaudits of Posterity.
The
Acquisition of Louisiana
Opens to the foreigners, convicts, and deserters of every clime,
A vast prairie for the enjoyment of
Self Government:
For transplanting all the vices and miseries of
European nations,
And a prospect of one day swallowing up
The American Character,
By an unnatural mixture with
Foreigners,
An event, which has already made necessary, a
Government
Strong as monarchy;
And in which almost the whole power is administered,
Under the direction
Of the Republican T. Jefferson,
By one individual, the
Governor General,
An event, which holds out to the world, by actual
Example,
The singular instance of a
Representative Government,
Fostering in its bosom,
One which bears more resemblance to
A Monarchy,
Than
A Republic.[2]

This New England rant, of course, did not represent Jefferson's attitude. He was a man of great optimism who imagined the spread of basic American institutions across the Mississippi and eventually to the far Pacific. Jefferson, sharing James Madison's idea that Republican government would be safeguarded by a larger nation, specifically referred to the Northeastern fears in his Second Inaugural Address on March 5, 1804: "I know that the acquisition of Louisiana has been disapproved by some, from a candid apprehension that the enlargement of our territory would endanger its union. But who can limit the extent to which the federative principle may operate effectively? The larger our association, the less will it be shaken by local passions. . . ."[3] And in addition to that philosophical position that the health of a republican system of government was enhanced by geographical size and diversity, Jefferson had long had what can only be called a love affair with the West.

It has often been noted that Jefferson sited Monticello, a classically designed home, facing westward on a small mountaintop, symbolically borrowing from the best of Old Europe but optimistically looking to the West and the future. For twenty years or more Jefferson had read voraciously all the travel and geography books he could buy, and he had attempted or promoted explorations of the West in 1783 with George Rogers Clark; in 1785 with an adventurer named John Ledyard; with a scheme for army exploration in 1789; and again with a traveling French botanist, André Michaux, in 1793. He had planned what became the Lewis and Clark expedition long before the purchase of Louisiana was a remote possibility, and he had remarked that control of New Orleans and the right to navigate the Mississippi River were essential to the prosperity and security of the new nation before Napoleon dangled the bargain before the American ministers.[4] I should add parenthetically that about the only thing Jefferson did as president that John Adams approved of was the purchase of Louisiana, which "seemed most expedient to [Adams] because he was convinced that 'if the union of the Northern, Southern, and Western states was to continue, the free navigation of the Mississippi was essential to its preservation.'"[5] For Jefferson, the most important goal, the most important cause, of his life and age was protecting and promoting the success of the new nation. Hence compromising the principle of strict construction of the Constitution—the extra-legal acquisition of the Louisiana Purchase—for the safeguarding of the nation's future was not a lapse of principle but a prioritizing of principles.

Jefferson had sent a secret message to Congress on January 18, 1803, proposing a scientific trip to explore the upper reaches of the Mississippi-Missouri watershed, when the territory still—so far as he knew—belonged to the Spaniards. That proposal necessarily emphasized the scientific aspect of the trip. Later, to facilitate Congressional approval, he emphasized the commercial aspects of this "Voyage of Discovery," but an examination of Jefferson's letter of instruction to Meriwether Lewis on June 20, 1803, reveals the dominance of Jefferson's scientific motives.[6] His passionate interest in the West had been piqued by recent evidence that a British traveler had reached the Pacific across the northern mountains and had urged his British readers to settle the region. Jefferson also had read several of the reports of Captain Cook's exploratory voyages and knew how important for such long-distance expeditions planning was, and how important it was to draw maps, keep detailed records, sketch the flora, fauna, and scenes one encountered, and thereby contribute to the world's storehouse of knowledge. Accordingly he directed Lewis to observe the terrain, the geology, the wildlife, the climate, and especially the people—the Indians—they met. Jefferson understood the potential commerce with Indians and wished to promote it (and he hoped to find a mostly water route to the Pacific for obviously commercial reasons), but he was personally more interested in the scientific aspects of the exploration. The Lewis and Clark expedition was to be primarily what we would later think of as an ethnographic, an anthropological foray, to reveal what existed in this strange but wonderful and potentially valuable new land that would turn out to become, by reason of the Louisiana Purchase that occurred in the midst of the planning of the trek by the Corps of Discovery, a part of the nation. But with all the current attention to Lewis and Clark, it is salutary for Professor John W. Allen to call our attention to earlier French and English explorers and to other exploratory expeditions authorized or inspired by Jefferson: those of William Dunbar and George Hunter, Thomas Freeman and Peter Custis, Zebulon Montgomery Pike of Pike's Peak fame, and Stephen Long.

I like to think that the participants in this 2003 Bicentennial Conference are likewise a modern-day academic Corps of Discovery, sent, as it were, into that different and sometimes exotic and unfamiliar world that we call the past, assigned to report on what was there in that great expanse of land we call the Louisiana Purchase, both before 1803 and afterwards. The resulting essays have given a history to the people—Native Americans, the French and Spaniards, women and slaves—whose presence in this region has been shortchanged if not denied by much of the popular history of our day. The essays have demonstrated to us how the Louisiana Purchase was perceived by British, Spanish, and French contemporaries; they have quite wonderfully illustrated how the vast territory was described and depicted by explorers, artists, and cartographers and shown us a portion of the visual record; they have described for us the religious traditions of the various peoples who have populated the region and have contextualized the Purchase in the legal traditions and conventions of the time. They have helped us to understand Jefferson's motives and ambitions and have shown us the way in which American national identity was reshaped by the presence of an empire of millions of acres of land and the prospects for commerce and population that bounty opened up. We have heard music akin to what the early Spanish and French inhabitants heard. And we all have experienced this city, established in 1718, whose Old World architecture and hybrid culture and foodways suggest the complex variety of peoples whose history has been caught up in the development of this region since the eighteenth century.

My simple assignment was to summarize all this, craft a conclusion, and send us all on our ways more appreciative of the combined heritage and history we have heard discussed. But I obviously don't have time here to comment on every paper, as interesting or valuable as they might have been.

First, a general conclusion that surprised me: how little the actual Louisiana Purchase was mentioned and how little influence was often attached to it. It seems to have had such negligible immediate influence on the quotidian lives of Indians, slaves, women, pioneers, and French settlers as to have been hardly more than a diplomatic blip on the inevitable westward demographic tide of Anglo-Americans. Maybe that view simply reflects the kind of history now most often practiced. But now to some highlights from the papers.

Spain—Sylvia Hilton incisively told us—had seen Louisiana primarily as a buffer against the increasingly powerful and populous Anglo-American colonists and then the United States, both of whom might potentially threaten Spain's more valuable holdings to the West and Southwest, especially its silver mines in Mexico. Spain felt that U. S. movement westward was inevitable (France too, it turns out, had believed at least since the 1780s that U. S. expansion was inevitable), but Spain wanted to resist the extension of U. S. population and control as long as possible. Complicated European events forced Spain to cede Louisiana to France in 1800. In 1802 France had assured Spain that it (France) would never give Louisiana to another power. Consequently Spain felt double-crossed in 1803 by France's sale of Louisiana to the United States, which, remember, Spain saw as a threat to its interests in Texas and Mexico. Item 62 in the "Fusion of Nations, Fusion of Cultures" exhibit at The Historic New Orleans Collection was the irate letter from the Spanish ambassador in Paris to the French minister of foreign affairs, Charles Maurice de Tallyrand-Périgord, complaining that the Spaniards had neither been informed nor consulted about the transaction. (Parenthetically, Professor David Geggus outlined for us the three basic reasons for France's about-face: fear of U. S. opposition to the original transfer of Louisiana from Spain to France, fear of an eminent war with the British, and frustration over trying to maintain her colony on Saint-Domingue.)

By the end of the eighteenth century, as Gene Smith pointed out, the major European players all recognized that control of the Mississippi was key to the eventual control of the Continent. And Jefferson too (along with John Adams) was fully aware of this geopolitical truism.

Light T. Cummins and Glenn R. Conrad have reminded us again of the multinational makeup of the Louisiana population in the eighteenth century and beyond. Cummins emphasized the Spanish officials' desire to attract setters of various nationalities, even from the English colonies, as part of their efforts at "social control." He concluded that the Anglo-Americanization of Louisiana began decades before 1803. Conrad emphasized the various streams of French-speaking settlers. In addition to the original French settlers, there were French-speaking newcomers from Acadia. Later, as a result of the general European disruption associated with the French Revolution and the Age of Napoleon, refugees from the Haitian revolt arrived, including hundreds of planters of mixed race, the so-called *gens de couleur libres*. In 1809-1810 there was another surge of about 10,000 French-speaking whites, blacks, and mixed-race refugees who were expelled from Spanish Cuba in retaliation for Napoleon's having invaded Spain. And throughout much of the first half of the nineteenth century there were immigrants from France itself. The various waves of "French" settlers were distinct in their political and social attitudes and in economic resources, and they complicate any easy portrayal of the French influence on Louisiana. The disunity among French-speaking Louisianians also weakened their political influence and hence their cultural influence on such matters as language. Louisiana could have stayed more "French" had its French citizens been less fractious. Yet while Spain had controlled Louisiana during the latter decades of the eighteenth century, the Spanish legal procedures were mediated by French folkways, and most of the people of southern Louisiana were culturally French even after they had accepted the political control and political institutions of the United States. In the mid-nineteenth century, New Orleans had the largest French population of any city in North America, including Montreal. The heritage of French and Spanish civil law, Professor Hans W. Baade demonstrates, continued to shape legal procedures in subtle and persisting ways in the Orleans Territory, which later of course became the state of Louisiana.

The history of the people of the Louisiana Purchase includes many groups, and we tend to think primarily perhaps of the French and then the Anglo population as both demographically and culturally dominant. But two papers, one by Peter Wood and the other by Celia Naylor-Ojurongbe, have reminded us of the complex and changing face of the black population: slaves, free blacks, the free people of color (*gens de couleur libres*) in the southern portion of Louisiana especially, and of the slaves owned by Native Americans. These two speakers have emphasized both the chronological and geographical extent of the black presence in the region, from Esteban in the 1530s to the present, and from the mouth of the Mississippi all the way to the territories of Iowa and even Minnesota. At different times in different places these various blacks created their own cultural institutions, worked out a variety of accommodations with the majority white population, and by borrowing cultural attributes from the French and Anglo settlers, the Indians, and blacks from many African and Afro-Caribbean traditions, synthesized new folkways with regard to religion, music, food, and dance. Black society and culture were never static and never defined by simple or simplistic conceptions of slavery. Those who were enslaved discovered diverse ways to hold on to their humanity, revolted in a variety of ways, resisting their bondage both psychologically and physically. And the continuing controversy over whether slavery should be legal in the states eventually carved out of the original Louisiana Purchase territory proved to be one of the key festering issues that led to the Civil War, a conflict ultimately and profoundly over the institution of slavery.

Patricia Galloway and Susan A. Miller have shown us anew the complex Indian cultures that existed throughout the region and indicated their rich history in the millennia before European invasion. In our popular culture the Indian past looks flat, and Indians are often assumed to have lived in timeless fashion without change for centuries before the White Man appeared. Our presenters have complicated that antihistorical prejudice by outlining the evolution of Indian societies and cultures, from the earliest hunter-gatherer societies, to the introduction of better species of maize and the spread of corn cultivation, and eventually to the rise of large, town-based population centers along some of the river valleys. These societies would later be disrupted by the explorations and maraudings of Francisco Vásquez de Coronado, Hernando De Soto, the French fur trappers, and—slightly later—the Spanish and Anglo traders and settlers with their more sophisticated technologies.

A wide variety of Indian peoples and lifestyles obtained in the vast region stretching from the Gulf of Mexico to the Rocky Mountains and what we now call the Canadian border, and there were huge differences between the Caddo and the Choctaw, for example, and the Mandan and Blackfeet in the Dakotas and Montana. The Indian polities had far-flung trading relationships, first among themselves and then with various European trading companies.

Three biological invasions impacted the Indian population: deadly microorganisms (pathogens) from the Old World; the horse, also from the Old World, primarily by way of the Spaniards in Mexico; and Europeans and Africans, both transient and permanent. The effect on Indian populations and societies was substantial and ultimately devastating. Climatic and ecological changes over the millennia likewise affected the human populations. And of course in the nineteenth century the five so-called Civilized Tribes in the Southeast, along with many others from east of the Mississippi, were forcibly moved to the region west of the Arkansas Territory, a tragic "trail of tears" that still brings sorrow and shame to our history. Overlaying the entire history of European invasion is the arrogance with which Europeans justified their take-over of indigenous peoples' lands. I believe this is almost universally recognized today, but here, as in roughly similar situations all over the world, there really is no satisfactory—or politically feasible—method of going back and rescripting history to make things right.

Several decades ago much history was written as though only political, economic, and military issues mattered, and these were primarily male domains. One of the great advances in historical scholarship—in addition to black history and, increasingly, at last, for the South, the history of Native Americans—has been the discovery of women's history, an advance that now includes gender more broadly as an analytical category. Certainly our picture of the past was incomplete and flawed when it did not include women as reluctant pioneers, as farm wives, as plantation mistresses, as enslaved workers, as promoters of folkways and religion, and so on and on. Women often experienced the migration west, and subsequent life there, very differently than did men. The presentations by Johanna Miller Lewis and Lucy E. Murphy exemplify this fruitful new field of inquiry.

Adding gender to the repertoire of interpretative tools has significantly affected how we understand political and labor history, legal history, the history of race relations, and the most basic social unit of all, of course, the family. Nothing it seems has been untouched by the new recognition of and attention to gender. We now see, for example, that the very gender of Sacajawea may have been her most important contribution to the Lewis and Clark expedition. Certainly her geographical knowledge in several specific parts of the trip was valuable; her language skills proved to be essential; and her kinship to the Shoshone village chief Cameahwait—who turned out to be her brother—allowed the Corps of Discovery to obtain horses necessary for the arduous and dangerous trek over the Rockies as winter approached. But the sight of a young woman, carrying her infant, signaled to Indian scouts across the West that the Lewis and Clark troop was not a military force. That image no doubt saved the explorers from ambush and annihilation again and again and allowed them to complete their journey to the Pacific and back and into the history books.

Time does not allow even the briefest summary of the rich information we have feasted on these last several days. But I must at the very least applaud what has been achieved here, in part at least because it corrects so many common misperceptions. The way U. S. history is often taught, it so privileges the eastern seaboard that students and the general public forget the rest of the story. As a result, Louisiana seems to come into existence in 1803 when the U. S. buys it, the same way that Texas seems to spring into existence in the 1820s when Moses Austin begins to lead Anglo setters from the older southern states into that Mexican territory. Popular history sometimes suggests nothing much happened before European intervention—a misperception disproved by many of these essays—and that everything changed after European involvement, an idea specifically disproved in the economic sphere by Daniel Usner's essay. Few of our citizens realize that both New Orleans and San Antonio—two of our nation's most unique cities today—were both founded in 1718 by French and Spanish authorities respectively. It is therefore important on such occasions as this to develop a carefully nuanced history of the era of French and Spanish rule in Louisiana. If nothing else, this attention to the pre-1803 history of New Orleans helps tourists to understand why the iconic architecture of the French Quarter is mostly Spanish. In similar fashion it is beneficial to understand more of the complicated history of international rivalries of the late-eighteenth and early-nineteenth centuries. That helps us to know more about the convoluted imperial jousting and competition for territory not just in 1803 with regard to Louisiana but also shortly later with the acquisition of Florida and then Texas; and in fact these earlier imperial rivalries help explain the timing of the initial stages of European exploration and settlement in the South and Southwest. With respect to this broader geographical perspective, Selwyn H. H. Carrington illustrates the complicated trade relationships between Europe, the Caribbean islands, and the mainland colonies. The essays on the French, the slaves, and the free people of color bring needed complexity to popular conceptions of life, labor, and license in the region as well as make more sophisticated and precise our understanding of exactly what Creole meant.

Facing squarely and honestly what injustices have been done to Indians and blacks is in part what taking history seriously means, but that fair and overdue critisism does not exhaust the lessons of history. All these topics have been simplified and oversimplified in classroom and textbooks for reasons of pedagogical convenience, and students have usually walked away with an even more simplified version. What we are doing here is very salutary because we are complexifying that past instead of simplifying it, and by such careful complexifying comes true knowledge.

One obvious example of making the story more complex is Randy Sparks's brief history of the rise of Protestant religions in the southern portion of the Louisiana Purchase. Many Americans rather reflexively associate the region exclusively with the Catholic Church, and understandably so. But Protestants began establishing their churches here as early as 1720, and the rise of the evangelical denominations quickened the pace of popular religion, with a particular influence on both women and enslaved blacks. Sparks noted in the longer, preliminary version of his paper that one early Methodist minister in 1812 described the people of Natchez as having "little humility, little religion, and little piety." One cannot help but wonder today what he might have thought of the people of New Orleans.

Considerations of complexification bring us back to Mr. Jefferson. Jefferson had an expansive vision of empire both geographical and human. Unlike the New England naysayers who could imagine only "wolves and wandering Indians" peopling the region, along with convicts and foreigners "transplanting the vices and miseries of European nations," Jefferson was willing to welcome immigrants to the nation and guarantee basic rights to the European natives of the new territory. He expected the region to eventually become a number of states after going through the territorial process in a way analogous to the process by which Kentucky, Tennessee, and the eventual states of the Northwest Territory—beginning with Ohio in 1803—evolved into states. He could only imagine Indians surviving as a people if they somehow were pressured into giving up Indian ways and became in effect whites, a failure of imagination on his part, perhaps, more than a failure of heart. He did not know how black slavery might evolve; it troubled him for years and he never resolved the issue, never made the transition from eighteenth-century slaveholder to modern American. In the 1780s he had fully accepted the Northwest Ordinances that prohibited slavery in the territory north of the Ohio River. Why did he not extend that limitation against slavery into the Louisiana Territory? Had Eli Whitney's improvements in the cotton gin in 1793 and the growing power and prosperity of the slave-based economy made such a bold move politically impossible in 1803, in effect, closed that 1780s window of opportunity? Did he place his hope afterwards in what Professor Ellis calls diffusion because he already envisioned stopping forever the importation of slaves from abroad and expected as a result a proportionate fall in their numbers to such an extent in the near future that, as in the northern states beginning with Massachusetts in 1780, slavery would eventually be abolished? We don't know his motivation. We do know that he recognized that the Constitution allowed, but did not require, the ending of the African slave trade in 1808. Not wanting to miss *this* window of opportunity, Jefferson in his annual message to Congress on December 2, 1806, called on the legislature to pass the ban quickly in 1807 so that it could go into effect immediately on January 1, 1808. Jefferson could hardly wait to "withdraw the citizens of the United States from all further participation in those violations of human rights which have so long continued on the unoffending inhabitants of Africa, and which the morality, the reputation, and the best interests of our country, have long been eager to proscribe."[7] Congress took up the issue and approved the ban in March 1807. Alas, whatever Jefferson might have intended or hoped, slavery did not diffuse and weaken, and it required a bloody war to end the institution.

Would this whole tragic history have been different had the Louisiana territory been acquired in 1783 rather than 1803? It surely disappoints us today that Jefferson, this great "apostle of liberty," could not break free from his racism and work to extend liberty to slaves. But to note that Jefferson, ultimately, was a racist should be a rather obvious if accurate observation about him and not be confused with a thoughtful conclusion or total summation of his life and career. To casually dismiss Jefferson because he was a so-called dead white male—or because he was not John Adams—is a disservice to scholarship.

The New England Federalists and anti-Jeffersonians might have terribly feared the settlement of "foreigners" in the region, but the millions of acres did beckon to the poor and oppressed of Europe and elsewhere, with the result that immigrants by the thousands from Ireland, from Germany and Scandinavia, from England and Scotland and France and Italy and other places flocked to the region. (Some might say, Italy? But simply think of the Monteleone Hotel down Royal Street from where we sit today. Thousands of Italians and Sicilians came to southern Louisiana in the late nineteenth century.) These immigrants to the Mississippi-Missouri basin helped create the breadbasket of the nation, they contributed in myriad ways to the economy and politics and literature of the nation. Classics as varied as Willa Cather's *My Antonia* and Laura Ingalls Wilder's *Little House on the Prairie* have enriched our collective lives. The mighty Mississippi with its connection to the Missouri and Ohio Rivers has been an avenue of commerce and culture. European brass bands in the immigrant towns of Cincinnati and St. Louis migrated down river to the cosmopolitan city of New Orleans, where peoples of all colors, cultures, and nationalities, with various religious and musical traditions, mixed and borrowed from one another. One of the creations was jazz, which then migrated back up the river to places like Chicago from whence it eventually spread across the nation and the world. New Orleans for one-and- a-half centuries was the largest city in the South, and its blending of cultures and the excitement and anonymity it offered allowed it to become a nurturing incubator for the talent of writers, artists, and composers of all sorts. The Mississippi River itself was the primary setting for Mark Twain's *Huckleberry Finn*, arguably our greatest novel and the first to really capture American "talk." Rather than threatening the nation or "swallowing up the American character," as the New Hampshire editorial writer feared in 1803, the admixture of people and cultures in the land of the Louisiana Purchase helped create and define the American character. Jefferson, more than most of his more fearful contemporaries, expected and would have welcomed that development.

Perhaps the only thing that the typical high school student tends to remember about the Louisiana Purchase, other than the "bargain" aspect of the purchase itself, is Andrew

Jackson's victory over the British at the Battle of New Orleans in 1815. Their teachers often tell them that this battle occurred after the peace treaty had already been signed, so the so-called great victory—ha, ha—meant nothing. But it did mean something. The treaty had been signed on Christmas Eve, 1814, at Ghent, but it had not yet been ratified by the British Parliament (or by the U. S. Senate), and it meant nothing until it had been formally accepted by both governments. England still harbored hopes for the invasion force bearing down on New Orleans. On board the ships commanded by Admiral Alexander Cochrane (with army troops under the leadership of General Edward Michael Packenham) were the staff for a complete civil government, including an attorney general, a judge, a colonial secretary, and a superintendent for Indian affairs; a proclamation disclaiming the Louisiana Purchase as fraudulent; and a plan to name General Packenham the governor of a new British province. If Packenham had been victorious, the Americans would have been ousted from the region, the British installed, and the tide of history perhaps changed in ways we cannot imagine. So Andy Jackson's victory did mean something.

But does it serve any useful purpose to even try to imagine alternative pasts? Had England acquired the great middle section of the continent in 1815, would that have only led eventually to a third war with England? And can Jefferson be charged, as some present-minded historians have lately done, with causing the Civil War by virtue of his Louisiana Purchase allowing the spread of slavery westward?[8] But of course slavery was already there in French and Spanish days, and cotton and slavery (and the cotton gin) had spread to the region before 1800. Had England acquired such a large territory so adaptable to slave labor and cotton culture, would she have ended slavery in her empire in 1833? Blaming Jefferson for the Civil War simply ascribes far too much influence to one individual and vastly oversimplifies the subsequent history of the nation.

On a related issue, some Francophiles in Louisiana still decry the supposed illegality of France's selling of the region to the United States, although perhaps their anger should be directed at the earlier Spanish transfer of Louisiana to France. But do those Francophiles who lament the purchase really believe they would be more free or more prosperous today had the purchase never occurred?

It is also well known, and I think even college students remember this, that a surge of nationalism swept over the nation after the victory at New Orleans, and songs like "The Hunters of Kentucky" made Andy Jackson, the Hero of New Orleans, a military celebrity and eventually propelled him to the White House. This issue of nationalism that swelled in the breasts of many Americans is related to that concept of "identity" that Drew Cayton discusses and what Peter J. Kastor calls "attachment." Certainly there were imperfections—especially with regard to Indians and African Americans for generations—but it is significant the degree to which a very diverse population came to identify themselves as Americans and found intellectual and emotion attraction to the rhetorical ideals of Americanism. Jefferson had always believed, unlike, for example, Alexander Hamilton, that the power of ideals should be the flux that welds a people together into nationhood, not simply economic self-interest.

I realize that it is not the fashion for historians to be positive about aspects of the past—after all, it is always so easy to find past individuals not living up to our ideals—but the blending of indigenous populations and peoples from around the world into a nation, *E Pluribus Unum*, even though imperfectly and with hypocrisy and prejudice aplenty has worked amazingly well compared to many other places in the world. Just think of modern Europe, for instance, where even today nations like Germany and Switzerland make it almost impossible for "foreigners" to ever become citizens. And then there are nations such as Denmark and the Netherlands, where the presence of two to five percent of "non-native" people is considered a national menace and laws are passed, for example, in Denmark within the last two years, severely limiting the numbers and rights of such non-Danish people. Compare this to the original language of the Treaty between the United States of America and the French Republic, finalized on April 30 and signed May 2, 1803. I quote from Article III: "The inhabitants of the ceded territory [remember they were of French, Spanish, and German extraction] shall be incorporated in the Union of the United States and admitted as soon as possible according to the principles of the federal Constitution to the enjoyment of all the rights, advantages and immunities of citizens of the United States, and in the mean time they shall be maintained and protected in the free enjoyment of their liberty, property and the Religion which they profess."[9] Yes, the blacks and Indians were treated differently to our everlasting disgrace, but even so, such relative openness to absorbing new peoples is even today, two centuries later, seldom to be found in the world.

Despite the failures and inconsistencies that tragically intervened, the basic openness to the future, the optimistic assumption that many peoples could eventually become one people, Americans, seen here imperfectly in 1803, remains an ideal worth upholding and strengthening. Held in this old, richly multicultural city whose blending of traditions has so enriched its food, its music, and our nation, this conference, by examining the many peoples who have made this region and nation, suggests that this essential American tradition of pluralism is alive and well. And openness to other peoples and other cultures and other religions is a particularly valuable part of our heritage that we should strive to defend, enhance, and extend in these perilous times when suspicion of "others" has almost become national policy.

Contributors

JOSEPH ELLIS, Professor of History, Mount Holyoke College. In 2001 he won the Pulitzer Prize for *Founding Brothers: The Revolutionary Generation* (New York, 2000). His biography of Thomas Jefferson, *American Sphinx: The Character of Thomas Jefferson* (New York, 1997) won the National Book Award.

SYLVIA L. HILTON, Professor of American History, Universidad Complutense, Madrid. Among her books are *Las Indias en la diplomacía española, 1739-1759* (Madrid, 1980); (edited with Steve J. S. Ickringill) *European Perceptions of the Spanish-American War of 1898* (New York, 1999); and (edited with Cornelis van Minnen) *Federalism, Citizenship and Collective Identities in U. S. History* (Amsterdam, 2000), and *Nation on the Move: Mobility in U. S. History* (Amsterdam, 2002).

DAVID P. GEGGUS, Professor of History, University of Florida. He has brought much new light to the history of Saint-Domingue (Haiti) and other parts of the Caribbean during the era of the French Revolution. Among his books are *Slavery, War and Revolution: The British Occupation of Saint-Domingue, 1793-1798* (New York, 1982); (as co-editor), *A Turbulent Time: The French Revolution and the Greater Caribbean* (Bloomington, 1997); (as editor), *The Impact of the Haitian Revolution in the Atlantic World* (Columbia, S. C., 2001); and (as author) *Haitian Revolutionary Studies* (Bloomington, 2002).

GENE A. SMITH, Professor of History, Texas Christian University. He is known for his studies of the era of the War of 1812 found in *"For the Purposes of Defense": The Politics of the Jeffersonian Gunboat Program* (Newark, 1995); (with Frank L. Owsley, Jr.) *Filibusters and Expansionists: Jeffersonian Manifest Destiny, 1800-1821* (Tuscaloosa, 1997); (as editor) *Arsene Lacarriere Latour, Historical Memoir of the War in West Florida and Louisiana, 1814-1815: With an Atlas* (New Orleans and Gainesville, Fla., 1999); and *Thomas Catesby Jones: Commodore of Manifest Destiny* (Annapolis, 2000).

SELWYN H. H. CARRINGTON, Associate Professor of History, Howard University. Publication of his dissertation, *The British West Indies during the American Revolution* (London, 1988) established him as an authority on the British Caribbean in the era of the American Revolution. More recently he has become known for his work on the late historian Eric Williams' controversial thesis (about how shifting uses for British capital led to the abolition of slavery) with publications such as *Capitalism and Slavery Fifty Years Later: Eric Eustace Williams-A Reassessment of the Man and His Work* (with Heather Cateau) (Peter Lang, 2000). The University of Florida Press has recently published his major work, *The Sugar Industry and the Abolition of the Slave Trade, 1775-1810*

(Gainesville, 2003) on the state of the West Indian economy at the end of the eighteenth century and at the beginning of the nineteenth century.

DANIEL H. USNER, JR., Professor of History, Vanderbilt University. His award-winning study of the early economic history of Louisiana, *Indians, Settlers, and Slaves in a Frontier Exchange Economy: The Lower Mississippi Valley before 1783* (Raleigh, 1992) has become a classic among studies of Louisiana's colonial history. He contributed to Native American history with works such as *American Indians in the Lower Mississippi Valley: Social and Economic Histories* (Lincoln, 1998) and "Iroquois Livelihood and Jeffersonian Agrarianism: Reaching behind the Metaphors and Models," in *Native Americans and the Early Republic*, ed. Frederick E. Hoxie, et al (Charlottesville, 1999), 200-225.

PATRICIA GALLOWAY, Assistant Professor of Library and Information Science, University of Texas, Austin. Among her award-winning scholarly works is *Choctaw Genesis 1500-1800* (Lincoln, 1995). She has edited and contributed to many volumes of essays on all aspects of the early history of the Mississippi Valley, notably *The Hernando de Soto Expediton: History, Historiography, and "Discovery" in the Southeast* (Lincoln, 1997) and *Southeastern Ceremonial Complex: Artifacts and Analysis* (Lincoln, 1989).

SUSAN A. MILLER, Tiger Clan and Tom Palmer Band of the Seminole Nation, Assistant Professor of History, Arizona State University. Her first book is *Coacoochee's Bones: A Seminole Saga* (Lawrence, 2003).

PETER H. WOOD, Professor of History, Duke University. He established his scholarly reputation with *Black Majority: Negroes in Colonial South Carolina from 1670 through the Stono Rebellion* (New York, 1974). His work in early Southern history includes an important article about the French explorer La Salle (*American Historical Review*, 1984) and pioneering estimates of colonial-era population figures in *Powhatan's Mantle* (1989). He is also the author of *Strange New Land* (New York, 1996), a short survey of early African American history, and *Winslow Homer's Images of Blacks: The Civil War and Reconstruction Years* (with Karen C. C. Dalton) (Austin, 1998). He has just completed a collaboration on a new U. S. history survey text titled *Created Equal* (Longman, 2003).

CELIA E. NAYLOR-OJURONGBE, Assistant Professor of History, Dartmouth College. She received her Ph.D. in History (2001) from Duke University. She was one of the coordinators of the historic conference "'Eating Out of the Same Pot': Relating Black and Native (Hi)stories," held at Dartmouth College in April 2000. Her dissertation, "'More at home with the Indians': African-American Slaves and Freedpeople in the Cherokee Nation, Indian Territory, 1838-1907," has already yielded a number of articles and conference papers. Her most recent published work is a chapter entitled "'Born and raised among these people, I don't want to know any other': Slaves' Acculturation in Nineteenth-Century Indian Territory" in the anthology *Confounding the Color Line: The Indian-Black Experience in North America*, edited by James F. Brooks (Lincoln, 2002).

GLENN R. CONRAD, University Distinguished Professor of History and Director, Center for Louisiana Studies, University of Louisiana at Lafayette and 2001 Louisiana Endowment for the Humanities Humanist of the Year. Known for his numerous books and articles on various aspects of the history of Acadiana, including published compilations of primary sources, he was also an editor of great skill, having served as editor of *Louisiana History* for twenty years and more recently as the general editor of the center's Louisiana Purchase Bicentennial Series in Louisiana History (19 volumes).

LIGHT T. CUMMINS, Guy B. Bryan Professor of History, Austin College. Known for his work on Anglo-Americans and Spanish Louisiana he has published the award-winning *Spanish Observers and the American Revolution, 1775-1783* (Baton Rouge, 1991) and is at work on a biography of Oliver Pollock, a project that has produced "Oliver Pollock's Plantations: An Early Anglo Landowner on the Lower Mississippi, 1769-1824," *Louisiana History*, 29 (1988): 35-48, among other essays.

LUCY ELDERSVELD MURPHY, Assistant Professor of History, Ohio State University, Newark. Through her book, *A Gathering of Rivers; Indians, Métis, and Mining in the Western Great Lakes, 1737-1832* (Lincoln, 2000) and (with Wendy Hamand Venet, editors) *Midwestern Women: Work, Community, and Leadership at the Crossroads* (Bloomington, 1997) and a number of articles she has established herself as an historian of women in the upper Mississippi Valley.

JOHANNA MILLER LEWIS, Professor of History and Chair of the History Department, University of Arkansas at Little Rock. A public historian and student of women's history, with publications such as *Artisans in the North Carolina Backcountry* (Lexington, 1995) and "Equality Deferred, Opportunity Pursued: The Sisters of Wachovia," in *Women of the American South: A Multicultural Reader*, ed. Christine Farnham (New York, 1997) she has also been active in the creation of the Central High Museum in Little Rock and served as curator for a number of exhibits connected with it.

ANDREW R. L. CAYTON, Distinguished Professor of History, Miami University (Ohio). Among his publications are *Frontier Indiana* (Bloomington, 1996) and *Ohio: The History of a People* (Columbus, 2002) as well as the anthology, co-edited with Fredrika J. Teute, *Contact Points: American Frontiers from the Mohawk Valley to the Mississippi* (Chapel Hill, 1998). He is currently completing a book with Fred Anderson entitled *The Dominion of War: Liberty and Empire in North America, 1500-2000.*

PETER J. KASTOR, Assistant Professor of History and American Culture Studies and Assistant Director of American Culture Studies, Washington University, St. Louis. He is the editor of *The Louisiana Purchase: Emergence of an American Nation* (Washington, D. C., 2002), and is currently working on a book entitled *"An Apprenticeship to Liberty": The Incorporation of Louisiana and the Struggle for Nationhood in the Early American Republic, 1803-1820.* He is the author of close to a dozen articles and essays, including "'Motives of Peculiar Urgency': Local Diplomacy in Louisiana, 1803-1821," the *William and Mary Quarterly* 3d. ser., 58 (2001):819-48 and "'Equitable Rights and Privileges': The Divided Loyalties of Washington County, Virginia, During the Franklin Separatist Crisis," the *Virginia Magazine of History and Biography*, 105 (1997):193-226.

HANS W. BAADE, Hugh Lamar Stone Chair in Civil Law, University of Texas, Austin. His work on the interactions of the Spanish and French civil law traditions with each other and with American Common Law has clarified important issues. Among his publications are "Marriage Contracts in French and Spanish Louisiana: A Study in Notarial Jurisprudence," *Tulane Law Review*, 53 (1978): 1-92; "The Law of Slavery in Spanish Luisiana, 1769-1803," *Louisiana's Legal Heritage*, ed. Edward F. Haas (Pensacola, 1983): 43-86; and "The *Gens de Couleur* of Louisiana: Comparative Slave Law in Microcosm," *Cardozo Law Review*, 18 (1996): 535-86.

RANDY J. SPARKS, Associate Professor of History, Tulane Univeristy. His books are *On Jordan's Stormy Banks: Evangelical Religion in Mississippi, 1773-1876* (Athens, 1994) and *Mississippi's Religious Heritage* (Jackson, 2001). While at the College of Charleston he co-edited three of the proceedings volumes from their Carolina Low Country and the Atlantic World conferences.

JESSIE J. POESCH, Professor Emeritus of Art History, Tulane University and 1993 Louisiana Endowment for the Humanities Humanist of the Year. Dr. Poesch has published on a variety of Southern arts and artists in works such as her *The Art of the Old South: Paintings, Architecture and the Products of Craftsmen, 1560-1860* (New York 1983) and *Titian Ramsay Peale, 1799-1885, and His Journals of the Wilkes Expedition* (Memoirs of the American Philosophical Society, Vol. 52, 1961). She has guest curated and/or authored essays in catalogs for exhibits on *Painting in the South* (Virginia Museum of Fine Arts, 1983-84); *Newcomb Pottery: An Enterprise for Southern Women, 1895-1940* (Smithsonian Institution Traveling Exhibition Services, 1984-87); *Will Henry Stephens (1881-1949)* (South Carolina, 1987-88); *David Hunter Strother* (1997-98); and *Arthur Wesley Dow and American Arts and Crafts* (1999-2000).

JOHN R. HÉBERT, Chief, Geography and Map Division, Library of Congress. He is a well-known student of cartography, with publications such as *Luso-Hispanic World in Maps; A Selective Guide to Manuscript Maps to 1900 in the Collections of the Library of*

Congress (with Anthony P. Mullan) (Washington, D. C., 1999); (as editor) *1492: An Ongoing Voyage* (Washington, D. C., 1992); and *Vincente Sebastián Pintado, Surveyor General of Spanish West Florida, 1805-1817: The Man and His Maps* (Washington, D. C., 1985). He is also the consulting editor of the historical atlas *Charting Louisiana* (New Orleans, 2003).

JOHN L. ALLEN, Professor and Chair of Geography, University of Wyoming. His *Passage Through the Garden: Lewis and Clark and the Image of the American Northwest* (Urbana, 1975; reprinted as *Lewis and Clark and the Image of the American West* (1991), and (as editor) *North American Exploration* (3 vols., Lincoln, 1997) and several dozen book chapters and articles have established him as one of the leading students of the exploration and settlement of the American West.

JOHN B. BOLES, William Pettus Hobby Professor of History, Rice University, and the editor of the *Journal of Southern History.* He is known for his work on antebellum religion published as *The Great Revival, 1787-1805: The Origins of the Southern Evangelical Mind* (Lexington, 1972) and *Religion in Antebellum Kentucky* (Lexington, 1976). His *Black Southerners, 1619-1869* (Lexington, 1983) is a classic, and his textbook, *The South Through Time: A History of an American Region* (Prentice Hall, 1999), is widely used in college classes.

PAUL E. HOFFMAN, Paul W. and Nancy W. Murrill Distinguished Professor, Department of History, Louisiana State University. An authority on the early Spanish presence in the American Southeast, his publications include the Parkman Prize-winning *A New Andalucia and a Way to the Orient: The American Southeast During the Sixteenth Century* (Baton Rouge, 1990, 2004) and *Florida's Frontiers* (Bloomington, 2002). He was program chair for the Conference as well as editor of this volume.

Endnotes

Notes, Chapter 1

[1]Merrill Peterson, *The Jefferson Image in the American Mind* (New York, 1960), 271-74; Joseph J. Ellis, *American Sphinx: The Character of Thomas Jefferson* (New York, 1996), 290-302. My earlier effort to tell the story of Jefferson's role in the Louisiana Purchase is in ibid., 202-313, and the current effort derives its shape and some of its language from that account.

[2]The standard account is Alexander DeConde, *This Affair of Louisiana* (New York, 1976); Dumas Malone, *Jefferson and His Time*, 6 vols. (Boston, 1948-81), 4:285-360, for the treatment in the authoritative biography. Two more recent exceptions are Robert W. Tucker and David C. Hendrickson, *Empire of Liberty: The Statecraft of Thomas Jefferson* (New York, 1990); and Peter S. Onuf, *Jefferson's Empire: The Language of American Nationhood* (Charlottesville, 2000). Most recently, see Jon Kukla, *A Wilderness So Immense: The Louisiana Purchase and the Destiny of America* (New York, 2003).

[3]Henry Adams, ed., *Documents Relating to New England Federalism, 1800-1815* (1877; Boston, 1905), 46-63, 338-65.

[4]Ibid., 230-32, 321-22; Linda Kerber, *Federalists in Dissent: Imagery and Ideology in Jeffersonian America* (Ithaca, 1970), 69-70; Leonard Levy, *Jefferson and Civil Liberties: The Darker Side* (Cambridge, 1963), 158-76; Jan Ellen Lewis and Peter S. Onuf, eds., *Sally Hemings and Thomas Jefferson: History, Memory, and Civic Culture* (Charlottesville, 1999). My conclusions about the Sally and Tom question are in "Jefferson: Post-DNA," *William and Mary Quarterly*, 3rd ser., 57 (2000): 125-38.

[5]Jefferson to James Monroe, November 24, 1801, in Paul Leicester Ford, ed., *The Writings of Thomas Jefferson*, 20 vols. (New York, 1892-99), 8:103-6; Jefferson to William Henry Harrison, February 27, 1803, in Andrew A. Lipscomb and Albert Ellery Bergh, eds., *The Writings of Thomas Jefferson*, 20 vols. (Washington, D. C., 1905), 10:368-73. For the most recent scholarly treatment of Jefferson's posture towards the Native American question, see Anthony F. C. Wallace, *Jefferson and the Indians: The Tragic Fate of the First Americans* (Cambridge, 1999).

[6]Turner was noted for his "frontier" thesis. See Frederick Jackson Turner, "The Significance of the Frontier in American History," *Proceedings of the Forty-First Annual Meeting of the State Historical Society of Wisconsin* (Madison, 1894), 79-112. Also in Turner, *The Frontier in American History* (New York, 1920), 1-38. This essay has been reprinted many times.

[7]Drew R. McCoy, *The Elusive Republic: Political Economy in Jeffersonian America* (New York, 1980). See also Jefferson to Nathaniel Niles, March 22, 1801, in Ford, ed., *Writings*, 8:24.

[8]Jefferson to Robert R. Livingston, April 18, 1802, ibid., 143-47; Jefferson to James Monroe, 13 January 1803, ibid., 190-92.

[9]For a nice summary of the historiography on the agency question, see John M. Belohlavek, "Politics, Principle, and Pragmatism in the Early Republic: Thomas Jefferson and

the Quest for American Empire," *Diplomatic History*, 15 (1991): 599-606. An excellent narrative of the collaboration among Jefferson, Madison and Monroe is in James Morton Smith, ed., *The Republic of Letters: The Correspondence Between Thomas Jefferson and James Madison 1776-1826*, 3 vols. (New York, 1995), 2:1254-57. For Channing's remark, see George Dangerfield, *Chancellor Robert R. Livingston of New York* (New York, 1960), 369.

[10]Douglas R. Egerton, *Gabriel's Rebellion: The Virginia Slave Conspiracies of 1800 and 1802* (Chapel Hill, 1993), 45-48, 160-61, 168-72, for Jefferson's posture towards Toussaint L'Ouverture.

[11]Smith, ed., *Republic of Letters*, 2:1291, for the Talleyrand quotation; Jefferson to James Monroe, January 8, 1804, in Ford, ed., *Writings*, 8:289. See also Jefferson to John Breckinridge, August 12, 1803, ibid., 243; Jefferson to William Dunbar, September 21, 1803, ibid., 256.

[12]Draft of a Proposed Constitutional Amendment on Louisiana, [July 1803], in Smith, ed., *Republic of Letters*, 2:1269; Jefferson to James Madison, August 18, 1803, ibid., 1278; Jefferson to John Colvin, September 20, 1810, in Ford, ed., *Writings*, 11:146.

[13]Jefferson to Meriwether Lewis, April 27, 1803, ibid., 8:193-94; Confidential Message on Expedition to the Pacific, January 18, 1803, ibid., 202.

[14]Smith, ed., *Republic of Letters*, 2:1272-73, 1290-91.

[15]Jefferson to John Breckinridge, November 24, 1803, in Ford, ed., *Writings*, 8:279-81; James Madison to Robert Livingston, January 31, 1804, quoted in Malone, *Jefferson and His Time*, 4:353.

[16]Ibid., 359-60; the first use of the phrase "empire of liberty" that I could find is in Jefferson to James Madison, April 27, 1809, in Smith, ed., *Republic of Letters*, 3:1585-86. See also Jefferson to DeWitt Clinton, December 2, 1803, in Ford, ed., *Writings*, 8:282-83.

[17]Ellis, *American Sphinx*, 144-52; Onuf, *Jefferson's Empire*, passim.

[18]Jefferson to John Holmes, April 22, 1820, in Ford, ed., *Writings*, 10:157-58; John Adams to Louisa Catherine Adams, January 29, 1820, *The Microfilm Edition of the Adams Papers*, 608 reels (Boston, 1954-59), Reel 124. See also John Chester Miller, *The Wolf by the Ears: Thomas Jefferson and Slavery* (New York, 1977), 221-52.

[19]Jefferson to Henry Dearborn, August 17, 1821, in Ford, ed., *Writings*, 10:191-92. For the Adams view of Jefferson's diffusion doctrine, see Joseph J. Ellis, *Passionate Sage: The Character and Legacy of John Adams* (New York, 1993), 140-41.

[20]Ibid., 217-19; Peterson, *Jefferson Image in the American Mind*, 221-26. See also, Joyce Appleby, "Jefferson and His Complex Legacy," in Peter S. Onuf, ed., *Jeffersonian Legacies* (Charlottesville, 1993), 1-18.

Notes, Chapter 2

[1]Marques Gonzalez de Castejón, Dictamen, February 3, 1777, Archivo Historico Nacional (AHN), Madrid, Estado, legajo 3884, in Juan F. Yela Utrilla, *España ante la independencia de los Estados Unidos* (Lérida, 1925), 2:55.

[2]"Plan, presupuestos y proyecto para dar nueva instrucción a Don Diego de Gardoqui, sobre la negociación de limites y navegación exclusiva del Misisipi," September 1, 1786, AHN, Estado, legajo 3886, in Manuel Serrano y Sanz, ed., *Documentos historicos de la Florida y la Luisiana, siglos XVI al XVIII* (Madrid, 1912), 382.

[3]Manuel Gayoso de Lemos to the viceroy of New Spain, Miguel Joseph de Azanza, New Orleans, August 2, 1798, Archivo General de la Nación, Mexico, Sección Historia, tomo 334, folios. 30-38, in Jack D. L. Holmes, "La ultima barrera: La Luisiana y la Nueva España," *Historia Mexicana*, 10 (1961): 641.

[4]Carlos Martinez de Irujo to Pedro Cevallos, Mont Plaisant, July 24, 1802, no. 288, AHN, Estado, legajo 5630.

[5]Carlos Martinez de Irujo to Secretary of State, James Madison, Washington, November 5, 1803, cited in Jerónimo Becker, *Historia de las relaciones exteriores de España durante el siglo XIX. (Apuntes para una Historia diplomática). Tomo I (1800-1839)* (Madrid, 1924), 97.

[6]Marques de Casa Irujo to Pedro Cevallos, Philadelphia, December 24, 1804, AHN, Estado, legajo 5631.

Notes, Chapter 3

[1]The meeting occurred April 10, 1803. François Barbé-Marbois, *Histoire de la Louisiane et de la cession de cette colonie par la France aux États-Unis de l'Amérique septentrionale* (Paris, 1829), 293-97, does not identify the minister in question but mention of his military service in North America leaves little doubt it was Berthier.

[2]Ibid., 287-89, 299.

[3]E. Wilson Lyon, *Louisiana in French Diplomacy, 1759-1804* (Norman, 1934), 19-35; Alexander DeConde, *This Affair of Louisiana* (New York, 1976), 85.

[4]Pierre Pluchon, *Histoire de la colonisation française* (Paris, 1991), 367-68.

[5]Lyon, *Louisiana*, 44-54, 57-60.

[6]Edward S. Corwin, *French Policy and the American Alliance of 1778* (Princeton, 1916) proved that the *Mémoire historique et politique sur la Louisiane* (Paris, 1802) falsely claims that the French royal government wanted Louisiana before 1789. But the *Mémoire* still misleads scholars, most recently Ramiro Guerra, *La Expansión territorial de los Estados Unidos a expensas de España y de los países hispanoamericanos* (Havana, 1964), 64.

[7]E. Wilson Lyon, "Moustier's Memoir on Louisiana," *Mississippi Valley Historical Review*, 22 (1935): 251-66.

[8]Jean Tarrade, *Le Commerce colonial de la France à la fin de l'Ancien régime*, 2 vols. (Paris, 1972).

[9]Jean Tarrade, "La France et la Louisiane espagnole à la fin de l'Ancien régime (1763-1789)," in *L'Europe, l'Alsace et la France: problèmes intérieurs et relations internationales. Études en l'honneur du doyen Georges Livet* (Colmar, 1986), 337-44; Arthur P. Whitaker, *The Mississippi Question, 1795-1803: A Study in Trade, Politics, and Diplomacy* (New York, 1934), 82-83; John G. Clark, *New Orleans, 1718-1812: An Economic History* (Baton Rouge, 1970), 226-28.

[10]DeConde, *This Affair of Louisiana*, 42; Lyon, *Louisiana*, 160.

[11]DeConde, *This Affair of Louisiana*, 78.

[12]Frederick J. Turner, "The Origin of Genet's Projected Attack on Louisiana and the Floridas," *American Historical Review*, 3 (1898): 650-71; Harry Ammon, *The Genet Mission* (New York, 1973). The spelling "Genêt," common in modern U. S. works, is incorrect.

[13]Alexander DeConde, *The Quasi-War:Tthe Politics and Diplomacy of the Undeclared War with France, 1797-1801* (New York, 1966).

[14]Henry Adams, *History of the United States of America*, 9 vols. (New York, 1889-1891), 1:354-58; DeConde, *This Affair of Louisiana*, 82-89.

[15]Differing sets of trade figures can be found in Jesús Lorente Miguel, "Commercial relations between New Orleans and the United States," in *The North American Role in the Spanish Imperial Economy, 1760-1819*, eds. Jacques Barbier, Allan J. Kuethe (Manchester, 1984), 177-91; Clark, *New Orleans*, 228; Whitaker, *The Mississippi Question*, 130-37; John Coatsworth, "American Trade with European Colonies in the Caribbean and South America, 1790-1812," *William and Mary Quarterly*, 3rd ser., 24 (1967): 243-66.

[16]Arthur P. Whitaker, "Louisiana in the Treaty of Basel," *Journal of Modern History*, 8 (1939): 1-26; Lyon, *Louisiana*, 81-86. Whitaker disproved the French negotiator's later claim that he deliberately subverted the aims of the revolutionary government. Whitaker also hypothesized that the Spanish chief minister Godoy wanted to keep Louisiana at least until he had negotiated Pinckney's Treaty with the United States (October 1795). This helps explain Godoy's otherwise perplexing offer in December 1795 to exchange Louisiana for Saint-Domingue, which the French then refused.

[17]Henri Blet, *Histoire de la colonisation française* (Paris, 1946), 29-30; Charles-Maurice de Talleyrand, *Mémoires complets et authentiques de Charles-Maurice de Talleyrand*, 6 vols. (Paris, 1967), 1:70-79. See Carl Ludwig Lokke, "French Dreams of Colonial Empire under Directory and Consulate," *Journal of Modern History*, 2 (1930): 239.

[18]J. Christopher Herold, *Bonaparte in Egypt* (New York, 1962).

[19]Yves Bénot, *La Démence coloniale sous Napoléon* (Paris, 1991), 9, 100; Bénot, "Bonaparte et la démence coloniale," in *Mourir pour les Antilles: indépendance nègre ou esclavage, 1802-1804*, eds. Michel Martin and Alain Yacou (Paris, 1991), 13-35.

[20]Paul Gaffarel, *La Politique coloniale en France de 1789 à 1830* (Paris, 1908), 133-38, 154. among others; see also, Jules-François Saintoyant, *La Colonisation française pendant la période napoléonienne (1799-1815)* (Paris, 1931), 70-76; Charles Victor Emmanuel Leclerc, *Les Lettres du général Leclerc, commandant en chef de l'armée de Saint-Domingue*, ed. Paul Roussier (Paris, 1937), 33.

[21]Gustav Roloff, *Die Kolonialpolitik Napoleons* (Munich, 1899), 254.

[22]See DeConde, *This Affair of Louisiana*, 108-9; Ronald D. Smith, "Napoleon and Louisiana: Failure of the Proposed Expedition to Occupy and Defend Louisiana, 1801-1803," in Dolores Labbé, ed., *The Louisiana Purchase and its Aftermath, 1800-1830*, vol. 3 of *The Louisiana Purchase Bicentennial Series in Louisiana History* (Lafayette, La., 1998), 61. Some Jeffersonians thought Bonaparte might adopt General Collot's 1796 plan, and journalist William Cobbett imagined him extending it to Mexico.

[23]Decrès's instructions to the would-be Captain-General of Louisiana, written in November 1802, recommmend merely the defense of Louisiana and maintaining the colony's existing trade links with Spanish possessions. See James A. Robertson, trans. And ed., *Louisiana under the Rule of Spain, France, and the United States, 1785-1807*, 2 vols. (Cleveland, 1911), 359-76; See also Turner, "Genet," 662-63.

[24]Additions were to be made to the Duchy of Parma, ruled by a relative of the Spanish monarchs.

[25]Talleyrand appears to have played along with Dupont so as to defuse American hostility. Inconclusive evidence, suggestive of an early willingness to sell, is summarized in Lyon, *Louisiana*, 141n; DeConde, *This Affair of Louisiana*, 96, 119, 130.

[26]The argument was made in Lyon, *Louisiana*, 191-92, and given primacy in Richard Stenberg, "Napoleon's Cession of Louisiana: A Suggestion," *Louisiana Historical Quarterly*, 21 (1938): 354-61.

[27]Lyon, *Louisiana*, 147 (quotation), 202-4, 214. Although DeConde's is a general study of the Purchase and not focused on the French, it contains details on French policy not found in Lyon's book. DeConde stresses Jefferson's bellicosity and provides the best detail on French knowledge of U. S. opinion, but also observes that the American and European factors were interdependent.

[28]Albert H. Bowman, "Pichon, the United States, and Louisiana," *Diplomatic History*, 1 (1977): 257-70, corrects Lyon, *Louisiana*, in showing that Pichon's most important dispatches arrived too late to affect the decision to sell.

[29]Lyon, *Louisiana*, 203; DeConde, *This Affair of Louisiana*, 157; David A. Carson, "The Role of Congress in the Acquisition of the Louisiana Territory," *Louisiana History*, 26 (1985): 369-83.

[30]Bénot, *La Démence coloniale*, 102; Barbé-Marbois, *Histoire de la Louisiane*, 285-87, 335.

[31]Roloff, *Die Kolonialpolitik Napoleons*, 149; Francis Paul Renaut, *La Question de la Louisiane, 1796-1806* (Paris, 1918), 117. Jefferson himself later mentioned he had not expected the French to sell Louisiana until after war broke out with Britain. See Merrill D. Peterson, *Thomas Jefferson and the New Nation: A Biography* (New York, 1970), 761.

[32]It is not mentioned at all in Marc de Villiers du Terrage, *Les Dernières années de la Louisiane française* (Paris, 1920), 384-94; Maurice Besson, *La Tradition coloniale française* (Paris, 1931), 123; Jacques Stern, *Les Colonies françaises: passé et avenir* (Paris, 1943), 94; Bernard Faÿ, *L'Aventure coloniale* (Paris, 1962), 559-62; Émile Lauvrière's chapter on late-colonial Louisiana, in *Histoire des colonies françaises*, eds. Gabriel Hanotaux, Alfred A. Martineau, 3 vols. (Paris, 1929-1931), 1:368-71; and only in passing in Barbé-Marbois, *Histoire de la Louisiane*, 285; Renaut, *La Question de la Louisiane*, 116-19, and Saintoyant, *La Colonisation française pendant la période napoléonienne*, 273-80. Georges Hardy, *Histoire de la colonisation française* (Paris, 1928), 138, does no more than raise the question.

[33]Adams, *History of the United States*, 1:378, 2:23.

[34]See Bénot, *Démence*, 331n2, which cites Barbé-Marbois; and Dolores Hernández Guerrero, *La Revolución haitiana y el fin de un sueño colonial* (Mexico, 1991), 115, which relied on the lightweight and unreliable Donald B. Chidsey, *Louisiana Purchase* (New York, 1972), 133-34, which presents Saint-Domingue as just a "pause" en route to Louisiana and on Ludwell Lee Montague, *Haiti and the United States, 1714-1938* (Durham, 1940), 43.

[35]The instructions are printed in Roloff, *Die Kolonialpolitik Napoleons*, 244-54; the correspondence is in Leclerc, *Les Lettres du général Leclerc*.

[36]Smith, "Napoleon and Louisiana," 57-59; Lyon, *Louisiana*, 132-39.

[37]Lyon, *Louisiana*, 193-194; DeConde, *This Affair of Louisiana*, 151.

[38]Bénot, "Bonaparte et la démence coloniale," 19n11.

[39]Roloff, *Die Kolonialpolitik Napoleons*, 142-44; Ott, *The Haitian Revolution*, 179-80, 186.

[40]Lyon, *Louisiana*, 141-42; Barbé-Marbois, *Histoire de la Louisiane*, 271.

[41]A closely documented accounting has yet to be made. Historians often mix up deaths, desertions, and repatriations, and soldiers, sailors, and civilians. One on-the-spot assessment reckoned that the army and navy had lost 30,000 of 43,000 men by May 1803. See Francisco de Arango y Parreño, *Obras*, 2 vols. (Havana, 1952), 1:354-55.

[42]These included General Thouvenot and the former prefect Wante in Saint-Domingue, the Cuban intellectual Arango y Parreño, and war minister Berthier. See Arango y Parreño, *Obras*, 1:369-70; Barbé-Marbois, *Histoire*, 296.

[43]Lyon, *Louisiana*, 196, 199-201; Bowman, "Pichon," 269; Smith, "Napoleon and Louisiana," 59-62. The documents Lyon cites (pp. 202-7) to show Bonaparte's "prime motive was to placate the United States" suggest just as much the centrality of the British threat.

[44]See below, note 47. See also, E. Wilson Lyon, *The Man Who Sold Louisiana: The Career of François Barbé-Marbois* (Norman, 1942).

[45]Roloff, *Kolonialpolitik Napoleons*, 141-42.

[46]Lyon, *Louisiana*, 141-42; Smith, "Napoleon and Louisiana," 59.

[47]Barbé-Marbois, *Histoire de la Louisiane*, 2, 269-87, 298-99, 307; DeConde, *This Affair of Louisiana*, 156-57 (on Monroe).

[48]Adams, *History of the United States*, 2:13-17; Lyon, *Louisiana*, 195-96, 199-200; Robert Paquette, "Revolutionary Saint-Domingue in the Making of Territorial Louisiana," in *A Turbulent Time: The French Revolution and the Greater Caribbean*, eds. David B. Gaspar and David P. Geggus (Bloomington, 1997), 205-11.

[49]Signaling renewed plans of conquest in the Middle East, the report increased British reluctance to withdraw from Malta, which was a major cause for the renewal of hostilities. Harold C. Deutsch, *The Genesis of Napoleonic Imperialism* (Cambridge, 1938), 116-20, tentatively suggests that the report should not be seen as a turning-point but a petulant outburst that the French rapidly sought to excuse. A similar media-related puzzle was created the previous spring, when, although the retrocession of Louisiana was officially denied, the government-controlled *Gazette de France* argued that France should curb U. S. westward expansion by occupying Louisiana and detaching Kentucky and Tennessee. See Bowman, "Pichon," 266; Lyon, *Louisiana*, 151.

[50]The phrase comes from a 1799 letter to Aaron Burr. See Tim Matthewson, "Jefferson and Haiti," *Journal of Southern History*, 61 (1995): 217.

[51]See Adams, *History of the United States*, 1:362-63, 2:46-48; Barbé-Marbois, *Histoire de la Louisiane*, 327-36; Lyon, *Louisiana*, 143, 223.

[52]François-René de Chateaubriand, *Atala, ou, les amours de deux sauvages dans le désert* (Paris, 1801); Baudry des Lozières, *Voyage à la Louisiane*, and *Second voyage à la Louisiane*, 2 vols. (Paris, 1803); Louis Dubroca, *L'Itinéraire des Français dans la Louisiane* (Paris, 1802); Nicolas Jacquemin, *Mémoire sur la Louisiane contenant la description du sol et des productions de cette île, et les moyens de la rendre florissante en peu de temps* (Paris, 1803); Berquin-Duvallon, *Vue de la colonie espagnole du Mississipi ou des provinces de Louisiane et Floride Occidentale, en l'année 1802* (Paris, 1803).

Notes, Chapter 4

[1]Charles Elliott, "Bienville's English Turn Incident: Anecdotes Influencing History," *Gulf South Historical Review*, 14 (1999): 7-15.

[2]Pierre Le Moyne d'Iberville, *Iberville's Gulf Journals* (Tuscaloosa, 1991), 109; Elliott, "Bienville's English Turn Incident," 16; Werner W. Crane, *The Southern Frontier: 1670-1732* (Ann Arbor, 1956), 58-59.

[3]For a discussion of the struggle for the Great Lakes regions and the Ohio Valley see Richard White, *The Middle Ground: Indians, Empire, and Republics in the Great Lakes*

Region, 1650-1815 (New York, 1991); Eric Hinderaker, *Elusive Empires: Constructing Colonialism in the Ohio Valley, 1673-1800* (New York, 1997); Michael N. McConnell, *A Country Between: The Upper Ohio Valley and Its Peoples, 1724-1774* (Lincoln, 1992); Jeremy Adelman and Stephen Aron, "From Borderlands to Borders: Empires, Nation-States, and the Peoples in between in North American History," *American Historical Review*, 104 (1999): 818-21.

[4]Daniel H. Usner, Jr., *Indians, Settlers, and Slaves in a Frontier Exchange Economy: The Lower Mississippi Valley Before 1783* (Chapel Hill, 1992), 276-77; Marquis de la Galissonière, "Memoir on the French Colonies in North America, December 1750," cited in Alexander DeConde, *This Affair of Louisiana* (New York, 1976), 22.

[5]Carl A. Brasseaux, *The Founding of New Acadia: The Beginnings of Acadian Life in Louisiana* (Baton Rouge, 1987), 73-115; J. Barton Starr, *Tories, Dons, and Rebels: The American Revolution in British West Florida* (Gainesville, 1976), 230-40; Gilbert C. Din, "The Canary Islander Settlements of Spanish Louisiana: An Overview," *Louisiana History*, 27 (1986): 353-73; Robin A. Fabel, *The Economy of West Florida, 1763-1783* (Tuscaloosa, 1988), 6-21.

[6]J. Leitch Wright, Jr., *Britain and the American Frontier, 1783-1815* (Athens, 1975), 4, 8-9.

[7]Ibid., 45-48; Frank T. Reuter, *Trials and Triumphs: George Washington's Foreign Policy* (Fort Worth, 1983), 116-18; Samuel Flagg Bemis, *Pinckney's Treaty: America's Advantage from Europe's Distress, 1783-1800* (1926; rev. ed., New Haven, 1960), 120-22; 138-39.

[8]A. L. Burt, *The United States, Great Britain, and British North America From the Revolution to the Establishment of Peace after the War of 1812* (New York, 1961), 112-13; Wright, *Britain and the American Frontier*, 50-56.

[9]J. Leitch Wright, *William Augustus Bowles: Director General of the Creek Nation* (Athens, 1967), 40-50.

[10]Ibid., 51-54; J. Leitch Wright, "British Designs on the Old Southwest: Foreign Intrigue on the Florida Frontier, 1783-1803," *Florida Historical Quarterly*, 44 (1966): 275-76.

[11]Kathryn E. Holland Braund, *Deerskins and Duffels: The Creek Indian Trade with Anglo-America, 1685-1815* (Lincoln, 1993), 174; Wright, "British Designs on the Old Southwest," 275-76, 276n.

[12]Wright, *William Augustus Bowles*, 65-86; Wright, "British Designs on the Old Southwest," 275-77; Wright, *Britain and the American Frontier*, 64-65.

[13]Braund, *Deerskins and Duffels*, 174; Wright, "British Designs on the Old Southwest," 278-79.

[14]Alexander DeConde, *This Affair of Louisiana* (New York, 1976), 59-62.

[15]Thomas Perkins Abernethy, *The South in the New Nation, 1789-1819* (Baton Rouge, 1961), 172-81; Wright, "British Designs on the Old Southwest," 280-81.

[16]Wright, *William Augustus Bowles*, 160-71; Wright, "British Designs on the Old Southwest," 283-84.

[17]Wright, *Britain and the American Frontier*, 137-44.

[18]John Jerry Pritchett, "Selkirk's Views of British Policy toward the Spanish-American Colonies, 1806," *Canadian Historical Review*, 24 (1943): 381-82; Keith S. Dent, "The British Navy and the Anglo-American War of 1812 to 1815" (M.A. thesis, University of Leeds, 1949), 352; Wright, *Britain and the American Frontier*, 122-25, 135-36.

[19]John Borlase Warren to Lord Melville, November 18, 1812, November 16, 1813, Warren Papers, National Maritime Museum, Greenwich, England.

[20]James Stirling to Viscount Melville, March 17, 1813, James Stirling Memorandum, Historic New Orleans Collection, New Orleans, Louisiana; Henry Hotham Book of Remarks, 1813, Hotham Collection, DDHO 7/99, Brynmor Jones Library, University of Hull, Hull, England.

[21]Alexander F. I. Cochrane's Observations to Lord Melville Relative to America, 1814, War of 1812 MSS, Lilly Library, Indiana University, Bloomington, Indiana; Lord Melville to William Domett, July 23, 1814, and Domett to Melville, 26 July 1814, both in Melville Castle Muniments, GD 51/2/523/1-2, National Archives of Scotland, Edinburgh; John Wilson Croker to Alexander Cochrane, August 10, 1814, Great Britain, Public Record Office, War Office 1/141, 15-24; Earl Bathurst to Robert Ross, August 10, 1814, loc. cit. 6/2, 6-8.

[22]Wright, *Britain and the American Frontier*, 179-81.

[23]Ibid., 184-85.

Notes, Chapter 5

[1]William M. Stone, "World Aspects of the Louisiana Purchase," *American Historical Review*, 9 (1904): 507-21.

[2]American State Papers. In the same period, U.S. exports and re-exports to the British West Indies averaged $1,942,598 and $5,435,976, respectively, per annum.

[3]Stone, "World Aspects," 517-18.

[4]Ibid.

[5]John G. Clark, *New Orleans, an Economic History* (Baton Rouge, 1970), for the trade decree of 1782 that fully restored the trade, subject to a 6% tariff on non-Spanish goods.

[6]E. Wilson Lyon, "Moustier's Memoir on Louisiana," *Mississippi Valley Historical Review*, 22 (1935): 251-66; Jacques-Pierre Brissot, *Nouveau voyage aux États-Unis* (Paris, 1791).

[7]Jon Kukla, *A Wilderness So Immense: The Louisiana Purchase and the Destiny of America* (New York, 2003), 239-41.

[8]"Remarks on the trade of the different Governments on the continent of North America," no date, British Library (hereafter BL), Additional MS. 38,342, folios 211-212d; Richard Pares, *Yankees and Creoles* (London, 1956), 27.

[9]Lieutenant-Governor Stuart to the Earl of Dartmouth, September 24, 1773, Great Britain, Public Records Office (hereafter PRO), Colonial Office (hereafter CO) 71/4, folio 71.

[10]Dartmouth to Stuart, April 6, 1774, loc. cit., folio 118.

[11]"Account of the total quantities of imports from North America to the British West Indies . . . ," no date, BL, Additional MS. 12,431, folio 170.

[12]Edward Long, "History of Jamaica," BL, Additional MS. 12,404, folio 463d.

[13]Ibid, folio 433.

[14]John Baker Holroyd, 1st Earl of Sheffield, *Observations on the Commerce of the American States* (London, 1783; reprint New York, 1970), Appendix, No. 5.

[15]Long, "History of Jamaica," folio 422. Minutes of the Committee of the Privy Council for Trade and Plantations, April 16, 1784, BL, Board of Trade (hereafter BT) 5/1, folios 158-59.

[16]Long, "History of Jamaica," folio 390. Jamaica provided a larger part of her own food than the other islands, but the provisions taken lasted only a few weeks.

[17]Ibid., folio 402.

[18]Jean Tarrade, *Le commerce colonial de la France à la fin de l'Ancien Régime: L'évolution du régime de "l'Exclusif" de 1763 à 1789*, 2 vols. (Paris, 1972), 1:362-63, 388n68.

[19]Kukla, *A Wilderness So Immense*, 114.

[20]Sheffield, *Observations*, Appendix IV.

[21]"Account of all the sugar, rum, coffee and molasses exported from Jamaica to America from 1768-1774," no date, PRO, BT 6/84, folio, 259.

[22]"Minutes of the Committee of the Privy Council for Trade," March 16, 1784, loc. cit., 5.1, folio 25.

[23]Long, "History of Jamaica," folios 420-421d.

[24]Answers to Queries, 1774, PRO, CO 137/70, folio 90.

Notes, Chapter 6

[1]Amos Stoddard, *Sketches, Historical and Descriptive, of Louisiana* (Philadelphia, 1812), 310.

[2]Daniel H. Usner, Jr., "Between Creoles and Yankees: Writing Colonial Louisiana into American History," *Colonial Louisiana*, ed. Bradley Bond (Baton Rouge, forthcoming).

[3]Francis Parkman, *The Conspiracy of Pontiac* (1851; reprint New York, 1962), 435; Frederick Jackson Turner, "The Rise and Fall of New France," *The Chautauquan*, 24 (1896), reprinted in *Minnesota History*, 18 (1937).

[4]Jay Gitlin, "On the Boundaries of Empire: Connecting the West to Its Imperial Past," *Under an Open Sky: Rethinking America's Western Past*, eds. William Cronon, George Miles, and Jay Gitlin (New York, 1992), 71-89; Jeremy Adelman and Stephen Aron, "From Borderlands to Borders: Empires, Nation-States, and the Peoples in Between in North American History," *American Historical Review*, 104 (1999): 814-41; Alan Taylor, *American Colonies* (New York, 2001).

[5]Fernand Braudel, *Capitalism and Material Life, 1400-1800* (New York, 1967), xi-xv; Karl Polanyi, *The Great Transformation: The Political and Economic Origins of Our Time* (Boston, 1957).

[6]John W. Verano and Douglas H. Ubelaker, eds., *Disease and Demography in the Americas* (Washington, D. C., 1992), 173; David J. Weber, *The Spanish Frontier in North America* (New Haven, 1992), 274.

[7]John Fahey, *The Flathead Indians* (Norman, 1974), chapters 1 and 2; W. Raymond Wood and Thomas D. Thiesssen, eds., *Early Fur Trade on the Northern Plains: Canadian Traders among the Mandan and Hidatsa Indians, 1738-1818* (Norman, 1985); James P. Ronda, *Lewis and Clark among the Indians* (Lincoln, 1984), 155-56.

[8]Morris Arnold, *Colonial Arkansas, 1686-1804: A Social and Cultural History* (Fayetteville, 1991); Carl J. Ekberg, *French Roots in the Illinois Country: The Mississippi Frontier in Colonial Times* (Urbana, 1998).

[9]Tanis C. Thorne, *The Many Hands of My Relations: French and Indians on the Lower Missouri* (Columbia, 1996); Jay Larry Gitlin, "Negotiating the Course of Empire: The French Bourgeois Frontier and the Emergence of Mid-America, 1763-1863" (Ph.D. diss., Yale University, 2002).

[10]Daniel H. Usner, Jr., *Indians, Settlers, and Slaves in a Frontier Exchange Economy: The Lower Mississippi Valley before 1783* (Chapel Hill, 1992).

[11]Carl A. Brasseaux, *The Founding of New Acadia: The Beginnings of Acadian Life in Louisiana, 1765-1803* (Baton Rouge, 1987); Philip D. Uzee, ed., *The Lafourche Country: The People and the Land* (Lafayette, La., 1985), 1-42.

[12]W. W. Pugh, "Bayou Lafourche from 1820 to 1825—Its Inhabitants, Customs and Pursuits," *Louisiana Planter and Manufacturer*, 1 (1888): 143; Sara Russell, "Ethnicity, Commerce and Community on Lower Louisiana's Plantation Frontier, 1803-1828," *Louisiana History*, 40 (1999): 389-405; Peter Kastor, *An Apprenticeship to Liberty: The Incorporation of Louisiana and the Struggle for Nationhood in the Early American Republic, 1803-1820* (New Haven, forthcoming).

Notes, Chapter 7

[1]Eric Wolf, *Europe and the People without History* (Berkeley, 1982).

[2]Johannes Fabian, *Time and the Other: How Anthropology Makes Its Object* (New York, 1983).

[3]See Shepard Krech, *The Ecological Indian: Myth and History* (New York, 1999).

[4]For a summary of the emergence of gathering and agriculture as subsistence in the American South, see Gayle Fritz, "The Development of Native Agricultural Economies in the Lower Mississippi Valley," in *The Natchez District in the Old, Old South*, ed. Vincas P. Steponaitis, Southern Research Report #11 (Chapel Hill, 1998), 23-47.

[5]For Cahokia and the trajectory of Mississippian polities in general see Timothy Pauketat and Thomas Emerson, eds., *Cahokia: Domination and Ideology in the Mississippian World* (Lincoln, 1997).

[6]Henry Dobyns, *Their Number Become Thinned: Native American Population Dynamics in Eastern North America* (Knoxville, 1983). Sharp critiques have been rendered to Dobyns's claims; see David Henige, *Numbers from Nowhere: The American Indian Contact Population Debate* (Norman, 1998). This discussion has a political edge as well as a scholarly one.

[7]See Ann Ramenofsky, *Vectors of Death: The Archaeology of European Contact* (Albuquerque, 1987).

[8]See, for the Creeks, Gregory Waselkov and Marvin Smith, "Upper Creek Archaeology," 242-64; and John Worth, "The Lower Creeks: Origins and Early History," 265-298, both in Bonnie McEwan, ed., *Indians of the Greater Southeast: Historical Archaeology and Ethnohistory* (Gainesville, 2000); for the Choctaw, see Patricia Galloway, *Choctaw Genesis, 1500-1700* (Lincoln, 1995); for the Caddo, Timothy Perttula, *The Caddo Nation: Archaeological and Ethnohistoric Perspectives* (Austin, 1992).

[9]See the extended work of Jeffrey Brain, *Tunica Treasure*, Papers of the Peabody Museum of Archaeology and Ethnology, 71 (Cambridge, 1979), *Tunica Archaeology*, Papers of the Peabody Museum of Archaeology and Ethnology 78 (Cambridge, 1988); more recently on Tunicas and Quapaw, see Marvin Jeter, "From Prehistory through Protohistory to Ethnohistory in and near the Northern Lower Mississippi Valley," in *The Transformation of the Southeastern Indians, 1540-1760*, eds. Robbie Ethridge and Charles Hudson (Jackson, 2002), 177-223.

[10]Remarkably, the relatively small Taensa group not only retained its coherence living in the Mobile delta region, but in 1764 moved back west of the Mississippi to settle around the Red River. See John Swanton, *Indians of the Lower Mississippi Valley and Adjacent Coast of the Gulf of Mexico*, Bureau of American Ethnology Bulletin 43 (Washington, 1911).

[11]For these activities of the French and Spaniards, see Marcel Giraud, *A History of French Louisiana, Volume 2: Years of Transition, 1715-1717*, trans. Brian Pearce (Baton

Rouge, 1993).

Notes, Chapter 8

[1]Archaeologists categorize the way of life of the Spiro Mounds people as Mississippian of the Southern Cult type; west of the Mississippi, archaeologists refer to that Mississippian type as Caddoan.

[2]After Spaniards set up their colonial administration in New Orleans, the Caddoan trade supplied them with horses, which they supplied in turn to the Spanish colonial headquarters in Havana, Cuba.

[3]Scholars classify the languages of the former group as Chiwere languages and of the latter group as Deghiha languages and group them all with the languages of the Dakota peoples in what linguists call the Siouan language family.

[4]Pekka Hamalainen, "The Rise and Fall of Plains Indian Horse Cultures," *Journal of American History*, 90 (2003).

[5]The source for the Mandan, Hidatsa, and Sahnish dates is the Three Affiliated Tribes webpage, http://www.mhanation.com/history/The_three_tribes.shtml.

[6]Hamalainen, "The Rise and Fall of Plains Indian Horse Cultures."

[7]Ibid.

[8]Mildred Mayhall, citing a Kiowa traditional narrative, *Handbook of Texas Online*, http://www.tsha.utexas.edu/handbook/online/articles/view/KK/bmk10.html.

[9]Hamalainen, "The Rise and Fall of Plains Indian Horse Cultures," says that the Kiowas first obtained the horse in the Black Hills.

[10] Mayhall, *Handbook of Texas Online*.

[11]Hamalainen, "The Rise and Fall of Plains Indian Horse Cultures."

[12]Ibid.; Richard White, "The Winning of the West: The Expansion of the Western Sioux in the Eighteenth and Nineteenth Centuries," *Journal of American History*, 65 (1978): 322-23; Gary Clayton Anderson, "Early Dakota Migration and Intertribal War: A Revision," *Western Historical Quarterly*, 11 (1980): 17-36.

[13]Hamalainen, "The Rise and Fall of Plains Indian Horse Cultures."

[14]Charles C. Royce, *Indian Land Cessions in the United States*, in Smithsonian Institution Bureau of American Ethnology, *Eighteenth Annual Report* (Washington, D. C., 1899).

[15]John R. Wunder, *"Retained by the People": A History of American Indians and the Bill of Rights* (New York, 1994), 8.

[16]"Doctrine of Discovery and *Terra Nullius*," presentation to the General Synod of 2001, The Anglican Church of Canada, n.d., available online, copy in file of the author.

[17]Vince Deloria, Jr., "The Evolution of Federal Indian Policy Making," in *American*

Indian Policy in the Twentieth Century, ed. Vince Deloria, Jr. (Norman, 1985), 240.

[18]Richard White, *It's Your Misfortune and None of My Own: A History of the American West* (Norman, 1991), 214.

[19]Henry F. Dobyns, "Diseases," in Frederick E. Hoxie, ed., *Encyclopedia of North American Indians* (Boston, 1996), 164.

[20]Ibid.; David J. Wishart, *An Unspeakable Sadness: The Dispossession of the Nebraska Indians* (Lincoln, 1994), 7.

[21]Dobyns, "Diseases," 164; Wishart, *Unspeakable Sadness*, 63, 80.

[22]Wishart, *Unspeakable Sadness*, 77, 81, 99.

[23]Dobyns, "Diseases," 164-65.

[24]Arrel M. Gibson, *The American Indian: Prehistory to the Present* (Lexington, Mass., 1980), 358.

[25]Wishart, *Unspeakable Sadness*, 87, 89, 93.

[26]Dobyns, "Diseases," 165.

[27]Gibson, *The American Indian*, 289-331.

[28]Ibid., 309.

[29]Ibid., 310-12.

[30]Ibid., 312.

[31]Ibid., 315.

[32]Grant Foreman, *The Last Trek of the Indians* (Chicago, 1946), 110-18.

[33]Ibid.

[34]R. David Edmunds, *The Potawatomis: Keepers of the Fire* (Norman, 1978), 266-68.

[35]William E. Unrau, *The Emigrant Indians of Kansas* (Bloomington, 1979), 3, 24.

[36]Gibson, *The American Indian*, 359.

[37]H. Craig Miner and William E. Unrau in *The End of Indian Kansas: A Study of Cultural Revolution, 1854-1871* (Lawrence, 1978), ix-x.

Notes, Chapter 9

[1]Peter H. Wood, "The Changing Population of the Colonial South: An Overview by Race and Region, 1685-1790," Table I, in Peter H. Wood, Gregory A. Waselkov and M. Thomas Hatleym, eds., *Powhatan's Mantle: Indians in the Colonial Southeast* (Lincoln, 1989), 38-39. (Second edition forthcoming.) The preceding numbers are based on this research.

[2]Colin G. Calloway, *First Peoples: A Documentary Survey of American Indian History*

(Boston, 1999), 4.

[3]In 1508, fourteen years after Columbus reached the Americas, García Ordoñez de Montalvo translated from Portuguese into Spanish a four-book romance called the *Amadís de Gaula*, concerning Christian-Moslem conflicts during the Crusades. Montalvo added a fifth book of his own which included California. According to Montalvo, "There ruled on that island of California, a queen great of body, very beautiful for her race." Scholars suspect that the popularity of this 1508 fabrication prompted Cortés to select the name. See Dora Beale Polk, *The Island of California: A History of the Myth* (Lincoln, 1991), 121-32 (quotations p. 125).

[4]Cyclone Covey, ed., *Cabeza de Vaca's Adventures in the Unknown Interior of America* (Albuquerque, 1961).

[5]Cleve Hallenbeck, *The Journey of Fray Marcos de Niza* (Dallas, 1987).

[6]"The Narrative of the Expedition of Coronado by Casteñada," in Frederick W. Hodge, ed., *Spanish Explorers in the Southern United States, 1528-1543* (1907; reprint Austin, 1984), 333. Casteñada continues: "If this had struck them while they were upon the plain, the army would have been in great danger of being left without its horses, as there were many which they were not able to cover. The hail broke many tents, and battered many helmets, and wounded many of the horses, and broke all the crockery of the army, and the gourds, which was no small loss, because they do not have any crockery in this region."

[7]See, for example, "a Moor from Barbary, [who was] the slave of Don Carlos Enríquez;" quote from Lawrence A. Clayton, Vernon James Knight, Jr., and Edward C. Moore, eds., *The De Soto Chronicles: The Expedition of Hernando De Soto to North America in 1539-1543*, 2 vols. (Tuscaloosa, 1993), 2:315.

[8]Peter H. Wood, *Strange New Land: Africans in Colonial America* (New York, 2002), 6-8.

[9]Clayton, et al, *The De Soto Chronicles*, 2:326.

[10]Gwendolyn Midlo Hall, *Africans in Colonial Louisiana: The Development of Afro–Creole Culture in the Eighteenth Century* (Baton Rouge, 1992), 10, 35.

[11]Daniel H. Usner, Jr., *Indians, Settlers, and Slaves in a Frontier Exchange Economy: The Lower Mississippi Valley before 1783* (Chapel Hill, 1992), 58.

[12]Ibid., 98-99 (quotation p. 72).

[13]Ibid., 74-75.

[14]Hall, *Africans in Colonial Louisiana*, 106-111.

[15]Ira Berlin, *Many Thousands Gone: The First Two Centuries of Slavery in North America* (Cambridge, 1998), 77. [Editor's note: Equally important, or even more important than African resistance, was the unwillingness of the Company of the Indies to import more slaves until those already imported had been paid for.]

[16]Ibid., 199.

[17]Governor Bienville to the Company, April 25, 1721, quoted in Carl J. Ekberg, *Colonial Ste. Genevieve: An Adventure on the Mississippi Frontier* (Gerald, Mo., 1985), 200.

[18]Chapter on "Black Slavery French Style," in Ekberg, *Colonial Ste. Genevieve*, 196-239; Charles J. Balesi, *The Time of the French in the Heart of North America, 1673-1818* (Chicago, 1991; 2nd ed., 1996), 246, 280-81. Greg Robinson, entry on "St. Louis, Missouri," in *Encyclopedia of African-American Culture and History*, 5 vols. (New York, 1996), 5:2378.

[19]William Loren Katz, *Black Indians: A Hidden Heritage* (New York, 1986), 94-96; Mansur N. Nuruddin and Greg Robinson, "Jean Baptiste Pointe Du Sable," in *Encyclopedia of African-American Culture and History*, 1:819-20.

[20]Robert B. Betts, *In Search of York: The Slave Who Went to the Pacific with Lewis and Clark*, rev. ed. (Boulder, 2000), 83-94.

[21]Betts, *In Search of York*, 11. We also know that York received occasional abuse from the white company because Clark states in one journal entry: "My Servent York nearly loseing an Eye by a man throwing Sand into it." In Reuben Gold Thwaites, ed., *Original Journals of the Lewis and Clark Expedition, 1804-1806*, 8 vols. (New York, 1904-1905), 1:53.

[22]Quoted in Betts, *In Search of York*, 16.

[23]Thwaites, *Original Journals*, 1:186, 243.

[24]William Clark to Jonathan Clark, November 9, 1808, quoted in James J. Holmberg, "Epilogue," in Betts, *In Search of York*, 157.

[25]Quoted in Betts, *In Search of York*, 135. Betts (135-143) gives a full and balanced discussion of this possibility.

Notes, Chapter 10

[1]At the heart of this debate is Frank Tannenbaum's thesis regarding the better treatment (or less inhumane treatment) of Blacks in the Spanish and Portuguese colonies compared to other colonies. Part of Tannenbaum's argument centers around the manumission laws and the significant number of free people of color in areas like New Orleans. See Frank Tannenbaum, *Slave and Citizen: The Negro in the Americas* (New York, 1947) and Stanley Elkins, *Slavery: A Problem in American Institutional and Intellectual Life* (Chicago, 1959). For a few responses related to Tannenbaum's thesis, see Herbert S. Klein, *Slavery in the Americas: A Comparative Study of Virginia and Cuba* (Chicago, 1967); Gwendolyn Midlo Hall, *Social Control in Slave Plantation Societies: A Comparison of St. Domingue and Cuba* (Baltimore, 1971); David C. Rankin, "The Tannenbaum Thesis Reconsidered: Slavery and Race Relations in Antebellum Louisiana," *Southern Studies*, 18 (1979): 5-31; and Thomas N. Ingersoll, "Free Blacks in a Slave Society: New Orleans, 1718-1812," *William and Mary Quarterly*, 3rd ser., 48 (1991): 173-200.

[2]Judith Kelleher Schafer, *Slavery, the Civil Law, and the Supreme Court of Louisiana* (Baton Rouge, 1994). See also, Judith Kelleher Schafer, *Becoming Free, Remaining*

Free: Manumission and Enslavement in New Orleans, 1846-1864 (Baton Rouge, 2003).

[3]The 1724 *Code Noir* was based primarily on the 1685 edict "promulgated to establish an orderly system of slave labor and race relations for French possessions in the Caribbean." *Coartación* allowed "slaves to petition to have themselves appraised and to purchase themselves from even unwilling masters or mistresses at their judicially appraised market value," Schafer, *Slavery*, 1-3.

[4]Ibid., 5.

[5]Ibid., 6, 220-49. Reiterating the rights of slaves in this particular area, the 1825 Civil Code of Louisiana stated that a slave "cannot be party in any civil action, either as plaintiff or defendant, except when he has to claim or prove his freedom," ibid., 220.

[6]See, for example, Paul F. Lachance, "The Formation of a Three-Caste Society: Evidence from Wills in Antebellum New Orleans," *Social Science History*, 18 (1994): 211-42.

[7]Paul F. Lachance has begun a conversation about the integration of the 2,731 whites, 3,102 free people of color and 3,226 slaves from Saint-Domingue who arrived in 1809. See Paul F. Lachance, "The 1809 Immigration of Saint-Domingue Refugees to New Orleans: Reception, Integration and Impact," *Louisiana History*, 29 (1988): 109-41. This influx of refugees resulted in "doubling the population of free persons of color and substantially increasing the population of whites and slaves in New Orleans overnight," Schafer, *Slavery*, 151. Further study is needed of the factors that led to their incorporation or exclusion and the effects they had on the separate communities in New Orleans.

[8]Virginia Meacham Gould's presentation of the letters and journal entries of the free women of color in the families of Ann Battles Johnson (in Natchez) and Adelia Johnson Miller (in New Orleans) highlights the importance of unveiling and examining freedwomen's voices and lives. See Virginia Meacham Gould, ed., *Chained to the Rock of Adversity: To Be Free, Black and Female in the Old South* (Athens, 1998).

[9]Mary M. Williams, "Private Lives, Public Orders: The Heno Family and the Legal Regulation of Sexuality in Early National Louisiana," presented at the 12th Berkshire Conference on the History of Women, University of Connecticut, Storrs, June 7, 2002. Williams is currently a doctoral candidate at Brown University. Her dissertation is entitled "Negotiating Private Lives: Gender, Race and Society in Louisiana, 1770-1830."

[10]Tamara D. McNeill is currently a doctoral candidate at the University of California, Berkeley. The tentative title of her dissertation is "The *Gens de Couleur Libres*, 1800-1850."

[11]Shirley E. Thompson, *The Passing of a People: Creoles of Color in Mid-Nineteenth Century New Orleans* (Cambridge, forthcoming). Thompson completed her dissertation on this topic at Harvard University in 2001.

[12]See Joe Gray Taylor, *Negro Slavery in Louisiana* (Baton Rouge, 1963); Ann Patton Malone, "The Nineteenth Century Slave Family in Rural Louisiana: Its Household and Community Structure" (Ph.D. diss., Tulane University, 1985) and *Sweet Chariot: Slave Family and Household Structure in Nineteenth-Century Louisiana* (Chapel Hill, 1992);

Walter Livezey Johnson, "Masters and Slaves in the Market of Slavery and the New Orleans Trade, 1804-1864" (Ph.D. diss., Princeton University, 1995); and Thomas C. Buchanan, "The Slave Mississippi: African-American Steamboat Workers, Networks of Resistance, and the Commercial World of the Western Rivers, 1811-1880" (Ph.D. diss., Carnegie-Mellon University, 1998).

[13]Taylor, *Negro Slavery in Louisiana*, 133-34. Taylor's chapter entitled "Religion among Louisiana Slaves" focuses on slaves' Christian indoctrination, especially by members of the Catholic Church.

[14]Katherine Olukemi Bankole, "An Afrocentric Analysis of Enslavement and Medicine in the Southeastern Parishes of Antebellum Louisiana" (Ph.D. diss., Temple University, 1996).

[15]Although Joe Gray Taylor's work includes a chapter on "Runaways" and another on "Control of Slaves," he only begins to address the various forms and techniques of Louisiana slaves' resistance to their enslavement.

[16]Junius Peter Rodriguez, Jr., "Ripe for Revolt: Louisiana and the Tradition of Slave Insurrection, 1803-1865" (Ph.D. diss., Auburn University, 1992). Also see James H. Dormon, "The Persistent Specter: Slave Rebellion in Territorial Louisiana," *Louisiana History*, 18 (1977): 389-404.

[17]For example, future studies should also examine slaves who stole, feigned illness, damaged property, or ran away, as well as those who murdered owners and their children.

[18]For a brief analysis of the complexity surrounding the passage of the Kansas-Nebraska Act, see Roy F. Nichols, "The Kansas-Nebraska Act: A Century of Historiography," *Mississippi Valley Historical Review*, 43 (1956): 187-212.

[19]United States, *Population of the United States in 1860; compiled from the original returns of The Eighth Census, under the direction of the Secretary of the Interior* (Washington, D. C., 1864), 166. All Black residents were listed as "native born." One of the 266 mulattoes was identified as "foreign born." There were 189 individuals classified as "Indians" who were included in the "white" category.

[20]As scholar Richard B. Sheridan explains, "Kansas was born in a struggle for liberty and freedom, a struggle that raised the curtain on the Civil War and sounded the death knell of slavery." "From Slavery in Missouri to Freedom in Kansas: The Influx of Black Fugitives and Contrabands into Kansas, 1854-1865," *Kansas History*, 12 (1989): 28.

[21]Even before the passage of the Kansas-Nebraska Act, free and enslaved African Americans made a temporary home in Nebraska on the way to their final destination. During the winter of 1846-47, members of the Mormon Church, en route to Utah from Illinois, camped just north of the city of Omaha. Included in this group were free and enslaved African Americans. One free Black member of this group, Jane Manning James, traveled with her husband Isaac James. While camping in Nebraska, Jane Manning James gave birth to their son Silas James. Bertha W. Calloway and Alonzo N. Smith, *Visions of Freedom on the Great Plains: An Illustrated History of African Americans in Nebraska* (Virginia Beach, 1998), 24. For more on Jane Manning James, see Colleen Whitley, ed., *Worth Their Salt: Notable But Often Unnoted Women of Utah* (Logan, 1996), 14-30.

[22]Dorothy Devereux Dustin, *Omaha and Douglas County: A Panoramic History* (Woodland Hills, Calif., 1980), 19. By 1861, the number of African Americans in Nebraska remained low, a total of 82 out of 28,841 residents, Calloway and Smith, *Visions of Freedom*, 24.

[23]The advertisement for the slave auction of Hercules and Martha appeared in the *Nebraska City News* on November 24, 1860. For a copy of the ad, see Calloway and Smith, *Visions of Freedom*, 24.

[24]Calloway and Smith, *Visions of Freedom*, 24-26. These restrictive laws forbade interracial marriages, supported the disenfranchisement of African Americans and initially enforced segregation in public schools.

[25]Ibid., 24.

[26]The Underground Railroad stations in Nebraska Territory included Falls City, Little Nehmaha, Camp Creek and Nebraska City. Fugitive slaves crossed the Missouri River at Nebraska City and traveled on to Tabor, Iowa. See James D. Bish, "The Black Experience in Selected Nebraska Counties, 1854-1920" (M.A. thesis, University of Nebraska at Omaha, 1989), 8; and Calloway and Smith, *Visions of Freedom*, 24.

[27]United States. Census Office, *Sixth Census. Compendium of the Enumeration of the Inhabitants and Statistics of the United States: As Corrected at the Department of State in 1840* (1841; reprint New York, 1990), 100-2.

[28]The Territory of Iowa's act was a version of the Territory of Michigan's "Act to Regulate Blacks and Mulattoes, and to Punish the Kidnapping of Such Persons." The Michigan act required blacks and mulattoes to file their certificate of freedom before being allowed to reside in the territory, as well as to produce a $500 bond within 20 days of relocating to the territory.

[29]Easton presented himself as "the owner of a certain negro woman named Rachel aged about 45 years and a slave for life to your said Petitioner." Bill Silag, ed., *Outside In: African-American History in Iowa, 1838-2000* (Des Moines, 2001), 61.

[30]Ibid., 62.

[31]Ibid.; *Iowa Territorial Gazette*, May 18, 1839, newspaper's emphasis.

[32]Richard Lord Acton and Patricia Nassif Acton, *To Go Free: A Treasury of Iowa's Legal Heritage* (Ames, 1995), 40-44.

[33]Acton and Acton, *To Go Free*, 46.

[34]For specific cases of Iowa's enforcement of the fugitive slave law of 1793, see Silag, *Outside In*, 65. However, in 1855, the United States Court for the District in Iowa ruled in favor of freeing a fugitive slave named "Dick" (ibid., 68). Although slavery had been outlawed in Iowa by the Missouri Compromise, resident and visiting slave owners freely and openly brought their slaves to this area. Other non-slaveholding Iowa residents supported the efforts of slave catchers from the neighboring state of Missouri.

[35]Ibid., 65-66.

[36]Ibid., 68.

[37]The trail from Iowa to Kansas was utilized often by a number of abolitionists including John Brown in his successful efforts to assist slaves escaping from Kansas. For more information on Iowa stations of the Underground Railroad, see O. A. Garretson, "Travelling on the Underground Railroad in Iowa," *Iowa Journal of History and Politics*, 22 (1924): 418-53; and Curt Harnack, "The Iowa Underground Railroad," *The Iowan*, 4 (1956), 20-23, 44, 47. For a general overview of the anti-slavery and pro-slavery segments of the Iowa Territory, see Morton M. Rosenberg, *Iowa on the Eve of the Civil War: A Decade of Frontier Politics* (Norman, 1972); Joel H. Silbey, "Proslavery Sentiment in Iowa 1838-1861," *Iowa Journal of History*, 55 (1957): 289-318; and James Connor, "The Antislavery Movement in Iowa, Part I," *Annals of Iowa*, 3rd ser., 40 (1970): 343-76 and "Part II," ibid., (1970): 450-79.

[38]William D. Green, "Eliza Winston and the Politics of Freedom in Minnesota, 1854-1860," *Minnesota History*, 57 (2000): 113-15.

[39]Scott and his wife's residency at Fort Snelling for two years represented part of their appeal in their 1857 U. S. Supreme Court case, *Dred Scott v. Sandford.* See Lea Vandervelde and Sandhya Subramanian, "Mrs. Dred Scott," *Yale Law Journal*, 106 (1997): 1033-122.

[40]Green, "Eliza Winston," 108. Southern vacationers appeared comfortable with the idea of bringing their slaves to the "free" state of Minnesota. However, because of St. Paul's proximity to the Mississippi River, there was at least one Underground Railroad station in this area used by fugitive slaves in their journey to freedom. Taylor, *African Americans in Minnesota*, 6.

[41]At the time of her case, Winston was a slave of Col. Richard Christmas of Mississippi. Christmas and his wife were vacationing in Minnesota. During that summer, Winston had voiced her wish for her freedom to free Black seamstress Emily Grey, who had shared her concern with abolitionists in the area. They, in turn, had requested that Judge Charles E. Vanderburgh issue a writ of habeas corpus so that Winston would be brought before him in the district court. When Eliza Winston appeared before Judge Vanderburgh at approximately 5 p.m. on August 21, 1860, Christmas' lawyer focused on the Dred Scott decision as the basis for Eliza Winston's continued enslavement in Minnesota, but her lawyer, Francis R. E. Cornell, countered with the Article 1, Section 2 of Minnesota's constitution prohibiting slavery and involuntary servitude in the state. Judge Vanderburgh quickly ruled in favor of Eliza Winston. He stated that "'she was free to go where, and with whom she chose.'" *Minneapolis State Atlas*, August 22, 1860. A photocopy of this newspaper article on the case is reproduced in Green, "Eliza Winston," 110. Minnesota newspapers printed Eliza Winston's sworn statement, as well as those of others associated with her case, including William Babbitt, Ariel S. Bigelow and Deputy Sheriff Joseph H. Canney (Green, "Eliza Winston," 108-16).

[42]Green, "Eliza Winston," 117-18. Reports concerning Winston's future movements are uncertain and contradictory. Newspapers reported that she spoke at an anti-slavery society meeting in Minnesota on October 19, 1860. Hostile whites harassed the Greys and other abolitionists for several months after the trial. Ibid., 119-20.

[43]For an examination of the struggle over segregation in Minnesota's public schools and Black male suffrage, see William D. Green, "Race and Segregation in St. Paul's Public Schools, 1846-1869," *Minnesota History*, 55 (1997): 139-49.

[44]Clipping, files of Dr. Modupe Labode, Chief Historian, Colorado Historical Society, Denver, Colorado.

[45]As a result of her significant contribution to the area, the Central City Opera (in Central City, Co.) will premiere an opera based on Clara Brown's life in the summer of 2003.

[46]Larry Borowsky, "Aunt Clara Brown," *Colorado History NOW: Newsletter of the Colorado Historical Society* (November 2001), 3.

[47]Brown often donated to various individuals and organizations in Colorado. Unfortunately, due to the extensive damage to her real estate as a result of fires and floods, by the end of the 1870s she had to rely on the charity of others. She died in Colorado in 1885. Both the governor of Colorado (James Grant) and the mayor of Denver (John Routt) attended her funeral. The Colorado Pioneer Association, of which she was a member, held funeral services in Denver (ibid.).

[48]The mining communities of Independent, Hawkeye, and Cooper districts all prohibited the Black franchise. The Larimer County Claim Club Association, created in 1860, excluded African Americans even before any Blacks resided there. See Harmon Mothershead, "Negro Rights in Colorado Territory (1859-1867)," *Colorado Magazine*, 40 (1963): 213-14. Reflecting the views of a large number of Southern-born residents, the Colorado territorial legislature barred interracial marriages (ibid., 214-15). For more on the struggle regarding Colorado's public schools, see William M. King, "Black Children: White Law: Black Efforts to Secure Public Education in Central City, Colorado: 1864-1869," in *Essays and Monographs in Colorado History*, ed. David Wetzel (Denver, 1984), 55-79.

[49]The eleven-year period (1810-1821) that marked Mexico's wars of independence not only signaled Mexico's challenge to Spain's colonial power, it also reflected Mexicans' desire for an egalitarian society. When priest Miguel Hidalgo y Costilla issued the Grito de Delores (cry of Delores) on September 16, 1810, it demanded racial equality and the redistribution of land. Eleven years later, in February 1821, Spanish general Agustín de Iturbide and rebel leader Vicente Guerrero negotiated the Plan de Iguala, which called for social equality, the abolition of slavery, and the right of citizens of all races to hold office.

[50]Due to the colonization laws of independent Mexico, promoters and individuals were granted tracts of land. African Americans from the United States believed that they, too, were entitled to land of their own. One attractive area for fugitive slaves was Matamores, a well-established community of fugitive slaves from the United States. For an analysis of Mexico as a place of refuge for runaway slaves, see Ronnie C. Tyler, "Fugitive Slaves in Mexico," *Journal of Negro History*, 57 (1972): 1-12. Also see, Paul Lack, *The Texas Revolutionary Experience: A Political and Social History, 1835-1836* (College Station 1992).

[51]For his colony, Austin selected the area between the Brazos and Colorado rivers.

[52]Randolph B. Campbell, *An Empire for Slavery: The Peculiar Institution in Texas, 1821-1865* (Baton Rouge, 1989), 19.

[53]H. P. N. Gammel, comp., *The Laws of Texas 1822-1897*, 10 vols. (Austin, 1898), 1:424. In November 1827, the Congress passed a law allowing slaves to be sold between slaveowners. Ibid., 202.

[54]Fred Robbins, "The Origin and Development of the African Slave Trade in Galveston, Texas, and Surrounding Areas from 1816 to 1836," *East Texas Historical Journal*, 9 (1971): 153-61.

[55]Campbell, *An Empire for Slavery*, 45-47.

[56]Ibid., 55.

[57]United States, *The Seventh Census of the United States: 1850* (Washington, D. C., 1853), 504.

[58]United States, *Population of the United States in 1860*, 486. Included in the slave population were 157,579 Blacks and 24,987 mulattoes. There were 355 "free colored" persons listed in this census of Texas. There were also 403 "Indians" included in the "white" population.

[59]Campbell, *An Empire for Slavery*, 115-89.

[60]Because scholars have primarily focused on the controversy regarding Missouri Territory's status as a new "slave state" and the Missouri Compromise, fur trading in Missouri has been generally neglected. Established in 1812, the Territory of Missouri did not become an important site for Euro-American settlement until travel along the Mississippi by steamboat. Because of Missouri's historical position as a vibrant fur-trading center in the eighteenth and the early nineteenth centuries, scholarly work focused on the racially diverse participants in fur trading in this and other areas remains crucial and necessary.

[61]One scholar in particular, William W. Gwaltney, has focused on uncovering the African-American presence in fur trading in the western United States. See William W. Gwaltney, "Beyond the Pale: African-Americans in the Fur Trade West," http://www.coax.net/people/lwf/furtrade.htm. Gwaltney has worked with the National Park Service in Fort Davis, Texas, and Fort Laramie, Wyoming, and is stationed currently in the Denver, Colorado, office. The Museum of the Fur Trade in Chadron, Nebraska, is another resource regarding the fur-trading economy.

[62]For more information regarding the Bonga family, see Kenneth W. Porter, "Negroes and the Fur Trade," *Minnesota History*, 15 (1934): 426-436. In his article Porter highlights a number of free people of African descent who worked in various positions related to the fur trade. Also see David Vassar Taylor, *African Americans in Minnesota* (St. Paul, 2002), 3.

[63]Gwaltney, "Beyond the Pale." Another important site of fur-trading activity was at Fort Union, located near the convergence of the Yellowstone and Missouri rivers, along the current-day Montana and North Dakota border. Established in 1828, Fort Union was a trading post of the American Fur Company.

[64]Gwaltney, "Beyond the Pale," 3. Also see Taylor, *In Search of the Racial Frontier*, 50-51.

[65]Like Pierre and George Bonga, Beckwourth married Native American women. While living in Montana, Beckwourth married two Absaroka (Crow) women. The life of Edward Rose also illustrates the activity of one African-American fur trader and interpreter who eventually became a member of two Native societies: the Absaroka (Crow) Nation along the Wyoming-Montana border and the Arikara Nation of present-day South Dakota (ibid., 49-50). Slave-born fur trapper John Taylor also married two Native American women in his lifetime. The first woman he married in New Mexico. After he moved to the Pine River area in Colorado, he met and married his second Native American wife, Car-ni-ta (Kitty Cloud) from the Ute Nation. Because of his marriage to Car-ni-ta, Taylor became a member of the southern Ute nation. John Taylor and Car-ni-ta had a daughter (Euterpe in 1899) and son (Henry). Euterpe Taylor served on the Southern Ute Tribal Council between 1949 and 1951 and 1961 and 1963.

[66]Other Native nations also owned African-American slaves. For example, the controversy surrounding slavery within the limits of the current state of Kansas did not begin with the Kansas-Nebraska Act. Rather, as Kevin Abing's recent work demonstrates, it was the question of the antebellum enslavement of African-Americans by the Shawnees that proved to be divisive in this area. Kevin Abing, "Before Bleeding Kansas: Christian Missionaries, Slavery and the Shawnee Indians in Pre-Territorial Kansas, 1844-1854," *Kansas History*, 24 (2001): 54-70.

The early work on slavery in the Five Tribes provided an overview of the historical development of the peculiar institution within specific nations. In the 1930s and 1940s, Annie H. Abel, Kenneth W. Porter, James Hugo Johnston and Wyatt F. Jeltz introduced this area of inquiry. See Annie H. Abel, *The American Indian and the End of the Confederacy, 1863-1866* (Lincoln, 1992); *The American Indian as Participant in the Civil War* (Lincoln, 1992); and *The American Indian as Slaveholder and Secessionist* (Lincoln, 1992); Kenneth W. Porter "Relations between Negroes and Indians Within the Present Limits of the United States," *Journal of Negro History*, 17 (1932): 287-367; and "Notes Supplementary to 'Relations between Negroes and Indians,'" *Journal of Negro History*, 18 (1933): 282-321; James Hugo Johnston, "Documentary Evidence of the The Relations of Negroes Indians," *Journal of Negro History*, 14 (1929): 21-43; and Wyatt F. Jeltz, "The Relations of Negroes and Choctaw and Chickasaw Indians," *Journal of Negro History*, 33 (1948): 24-37.

In the 1970s, more than a generation later, the work of Rudi Halliburton, Jr., Daniel F. Littlefield, Jr., and Theda Perdue presented a more thorough understanding of the development and evolution of slavery within specific Native American nations. See Rudi Halliburton, Jr., *Red over Black: Black Slavery among the Cherokee Indians* (Westport, 1977); Theda Perdue, *Slavery and the Evolution of Cherokee Society, 1540-1866* (Knoxville, 1979); Daniel F. Littlefield, Jr., *Africans and Seminoles: From Removal to Emancipation* (Westport, 1977); *The Cherokee Freedmen: From Emancipation to American Citizenship* (Westport, 1978); *Africans and Creeks: From the Colonial Period to the Civil War* (Westport, 1979); and *The Chickasaw Freedmen: A People Without a Country* (Westport, 1980).

In the past couple of years scholars have begun to explore to a greater extent the complex lives of free and enslaved African Americans among the Five Tribes. See, for example, Tiya A. Miles, "'Bone of My Bone': Stories of a Black Cherokee Family, 1790-1850" (Ph.D. diss., University of Minnesota, 2000); and Celia E. Naylor-Ojurongbe, "'More at Home With the Indians': African-American Slaves and Freedpeople in the Cherokee Nation, Indian Territory, 1838-1907" (Ph.D. diss., Duke University, 2001).

[67]For a detailed historical analysis of Indian slavery, see Almon W. Lauber, *Indian Slavery in Colonial Times Within the Present Limits of the United States* (Williamstown, 1970). Also see Perdue, *Slavery and the Evolution of Cherokee Society.*

[68]Michael F. Doran, "Population Statistics of Nineteenth-Century Indian Territory," *Chronicles of Oklahoma*, 53 (1976): 501.

[69]The laws of these nations often differentiated between the limitations placed on slaves and the rights of free Blacks, particularly persons of combined Black and Native descent. Nonetheless, free Blacks living in Indian Territory were cognizant of their precarious position and restrained liberties as residents in slaveholding communities. Just as other free Blacks in the United States were vulnerable to kidnapping and reenslavement, so too were free Blacks in Indian Territory often the victims of abduction. See, for example, *Cherokee Advocate*, October 7, 1847.

[70]Naylor-Ojurongbe, "More at Home with the Indians," passim.

[71]George P. Rawick, ed., *Oklahoma and Mississippi Narratives*, vol. 7 of *The American Slave* (Westport, 1973); and *Oklahoma Narratives*, vol. 12, Supplement, ser. 1 of *The American Slave* (Westport, 1977).

[72]Naylor-Ojurongbe, "More at Home with the Indians."

Notes, Chapter 11

[1]By far, the outstanding work on the establishment of the French colony in the Mississippi valley is Marcel Giraud's *A History of French Louisiana* in 5 vols. Volumes 1-4 were originally published in French under the series title *Historie de la Louisiane française* (Paris, 1953). Volumes 1, 2 and 5 have been translated and published by Louisiana State University Press as, respectively, *The Reign of Louis XIV, 1698-1715*, trans. Joseph C. Lambert (Baton Rouge, 1974); *Years of Transition, 1715-1717*, trans. Brian Pearce (Baton Rouge, 1991); *The Company of the Indies, 1723-1731*, trans. Brian Pearce (Baton Rouge, 1993). See also, Mathé Allain, *"Not Worth a Straw": French Colonial Policy and the Early Years of Louisiana* (Lafayette, La., 1988); and John C. Rule, "Jérôme Phélypeaux, Comte de Pontchartrain and the Establishment of Louisiana," in *Frenchmen and French Ways in the Mississippi Valley*, ed. John Francis McDermott (Urbana, 1969).

[2]The hardships realized by early colonial settlers have been treated in numerous scholarly works in addition to Giraud's comprehensive analysis. See, for example, Jay Higginbotham, *Old Mobile: Fort Louis de la Louisiane, 1702-1711* (Mobile, 1977), which recounts the early years of the French colonial experience on the Gulf Coast. See also Charles Edwards O'Neill, *Church and State in French Colonial Louisiana: Policy and*

Politics to 1732 (New Haven, 1966). Also of some value in this regard are John-Baptiste Bénard de La Harpe, *The Historical Journal of the Establishment of the French in Louisiana*, trans. Joan Cain and Virginia Koenig, ed. and annot. Glenn R. Conrad (Lafayette, La., 1971) and *Immigration and War: Louisiana 1718-1721, from the Memoir of Charles le Gac*, trans., ed. and annot. Glenn R. Conrad (Lafayette, La., 1970).

[3]A detailed account of the founding and early years of New Orleans is found in Marc Villiers du Terrage, *Historie de la fondation de la Nouvelle-Orléans* (Paris, 1917). John Smith Kendall covers approximately two hundred years of New Orleans history in *History of New Orleans*, 3 vols. (Chicago, 1922). A noteworthy study is John G. Clark, *New Orleans, 1718-1812: An Economic History* (Baton Rouge, 1970). For an account of some people "who built the colony with a musket, an axe, and a plow," see the article by Gary D. Mills, "The Chauvin Brothers: Early Colonists of Louisiana," *Louisiana History*, 15 (1974): 117-31. For studies of localized pioneering, see J. Hanno Deiler, *The Settlement of the German Coast of Louisiana and Creoles of German Descent* (1909; reprint Baltimore, 1969); Helmut Blume, *The German Coast during the Colonial Era, 1722-1803*, trans., ed. and annot. Ellen C. Merrill (Destrehan, La., 1990); Lillian C. Bourgeois, *Cabanocey: The History, Customs, and Folklore of St. James Parish* (New Orleans, 1957); for Natchitoches, see Milton Dunn, "History of Natchitoches," *Louisiana Historical Quarterly*, 3 (1920): 26-56; the early history of Natchez can be found in James Register, *Fort Rosalie: The French at Old Natchez (1682-1762)* (Shreveport, La., 1969).

[4]For an account of the initial introduction of African slaves into French Louisiana, see Henry Plauché Dart, "The First Cargo of African Slaves for Louisiana, 1718," *Louisiana Historical Quarterly*, 14 (1931): 163-77; Daniel H. Usner, Jr., "From African Captivity to American Slavery: The Introduction of Black Laborers in Colonial Louisiana," *Louisiana History*, 20 (1979): 25-48; Joe Gray Taylor, *Negro Slavery in Louisiana* (Baton Rouge, 1963); James Thomas McGowan, "Creation of a Slave Society: Louisiana Plantations in the Eighteenth Century" (Ph.D. diss., University of Rochester, 1976).

[5]Unfortunately for Louisiana scholarship, there is at present no truly objective study of the emergence of Creole society. Perhaps one can get a sense of the metamorphosis from Frenchman to Creole in the following work: A. Prioult, *Le Chevalier de Pradel: Vie d'un Colon français en Louisiane aux XVIIIe siècle . . .* (Paris, 1928). One gets an insight into the evolution of Creole society in Fontaine Martin, *A History of the Bouligny Family and Allied Families* (Lafayette, La., 1990), particularly in chapters two through seven. The attitudes of Creole society are clearly revealed in the events surrounding the Rebellion of 1768. For accounts of Creole thinking leading to that event and the event itself, see Carl A. Brasseaux, *Denis-Nicolas Foucault and the New Orleans Rebellion of 1768* (Ruston, La., 1987); John Preston Moore, *Revolt in Louisiana: The Spanish Occupation, 1766-1770* (Baton Rouge, La., 1976); and David Kerr Texada, *Alejandro O'Reilly and the New Orleans Rebels* (Lafayette, La., 1970).

[6]There are many accounts of the founding and cultural evolution of Acadia; however, two recent scholarly studies are Andrew Hill Clark, *Acadia: The Geography of Early Nova Scotia to 1760* (Madison, 1968); and Naomi Griffiths, *The Acadians: Creation of a People* (Toronto, 1973).

[7]Three accounts leading to the events of the Acadian exile, *le grand dérangement*, are

N. E. S. Griffiths, ed., *The Acadian Deportation: Deliberate Perfidy or Cruel Necessity?* (Toronto, 1969); Carl A. Brasseaux, *"Scattered to the Wind": The Dispersal and Wanderings of the Acadian Exiles, 1755-1809* (Lafayette, La., 1991); and Oscar W. Winzerling, *Acadian Odyssey* (Baton Rouge, 1955).

[8]A notable work concerned with the arrival of the Acadians in Louisiana is the compilation, translation, and annotation of original source materials by Carl A. Brasseaux, Emilio Fabian García, and Jacqueline K. Voorhies, eds., trans., annots., *Quest for the Promised Land: Official Correspondence Relating to the First Acadian Migration to Louisiana, 1764-1769* (Lafayette, La., 1989).

[9]The only scholarly monograph on the establishment of the Acadians in Louisiana is Carl A. Brasseaux, *The Founding of New Acadia: The Beginning of Acadian Life in Louisiana, 1764-1769* (Baton Rouge, 1987). For additional details on the Acadian establishment in the Attakapas District, where bayou country and prairie meet, see Glenn R. Conrad, ed., *Land Records of the Attakapas District. Volume I, The Attakapas Domesday Book: Land Grants, Claims and Confirmation in the Attakapas District, 1764-1826* (Lafayette, La., 1990).

[10]Good accounts of the Haitian Revolution are Thomas O. Ott, *The Haitian Revolution, 1789-1804* (Knoxville, 1973), and C. L. R. James, *The Black Jacobins: Toussaint L'Ouverture and the San Domingo Revolution*, 2nd ed. (New York, 1963). For an account of the Saint-Domingue colonists in refuge in Louisiana, see Carl A. Brasseaux and Glenn R. Conrad, eds. and annots., *The Road to Louisiana: The Saint-Domingue Refugees, 1792-1809* (Lafayette, La., 1992). The contributions of Thomas Fiehrer and Paul Lachance to this work are outstanding pieces of scholarship.

[11]The Creole lifestyle of early nineteenth-century New Orleans is excellently detailed in Liliane Crété, *Daily Life in Louisiana, 1815-1830*, trans. Patrick Gregory (Baton Rouge, 1981). There are older standard works on the Creoles of New Orleans, such as Grace King, *Creole Families in New Orleans* (New York, 1921); George Washington Cable, *The Creoles of Louisiana* (London, 1885); and Hélène d'Aquin Allain, *Souvenirs d'Amérique et de France, par une Créole* (Paris, 1883).

[12]The only piece of recent scholarship focusing on nineteenth-century French immigration to Louisiana is Carl A. Brasseaux, *The "Foreign French": Nineteenth-century French Immigration into Louisiana, Volume I, 1820-1839; Volume II, 1840-1848* (Lafayette, La., 1990, 1992).

[13]Warren M. Billings, "From This Seed: The Constitution of 1812," in *In Search of Fundamental Law: Louisiana's Constitutions, 1812-1974*, eds. Warren M. Billings and Edward F. Haas (Lafayette, La., 1993), 7-8.

[14]See Peter Kastor's article in this volume for their strategy.

[15]Joseph G. Tregle, Jr., *Louisiana in the Age of Jackson: A Clash of Cultures and Personalities* (Baton Rouge, 1999), 25, 28. This is, by far, the outstanding work on Louisiana in the antebellum era. It is thoroughly researched, beautifully written, and superbly interpreted by someone with keen insight into the era.

Notes, Chapter 12

[1]J. S. Roucek, ed., *Social Control*, 2nd ed. (New York, 1956), 3.

[2]See, however, Hans Baade's essay in this volume, which argues for the influence of French lawyers, especially from Haiti.

[3]Light T. Cummins, "Spanish Louisiana Land Policy: Antecedents to the Anglo-American Colonization of East Texas," *East Texas Historical Journal*, 33 (1995): 21.

[4]Gilbert C. Din, *Spaniards, Planters, and Slaves: The Spanish Regulation of Slavery in Louisiana, 1763-1803* (College Station, 1999), 43.

[5]Light T. Cummins, "Luis de Unzaga," in Joseph G. Dawson III, ed., *The Louisiana Governors* (Baton Rouge, 1990), 54.

[6]Carl A. Brasseaux, "The Baron de Carondelet," in ibid., 69.

[7]Bennett H. Wall, et al., *Lousiana: A History*, 4th ed. (Chicago, 1997), 78.

[8]Quoted in Jeremy Adelman and Stephen Aron, "From Borderlands to Border: Empires, Nation-States, and the Peoples in Between in North American History," *American Historical Review*, 104 (1999): 828.

[9]"Message of Thomas Jefferson to the Senate and House of January 16, 1804," from *A Compilation of the Messages and Papers for the Presidents*, 57th Congress, 1897, accessed on November 15, 2002 from the Avalon Project, Yale University at www.yale.edu/lawweb/avalon/president/messages/tj006.htm.

Notes, Chapter 13

[1]C. Fred Williams, et al., *A Documentary History of Arkansas* (Fayetteville, 1978), 59.

[2]Malcolm Rohrbough, *The Trans-Appalachian Frontier: People, Societies, and Institutions, 1775-1850* (New York, 1978), 4.

[3]Ibid., 5.

[4]Ibid., 91, 42.

[5]Julie Roy Jeffrey, *Frontier Women: The Trans-Mississippi West, 1840-1880* (New York, 1979), xii.

[6]William G. Boyd, ed., *William Byrd's Histories of the Dividing Line Betwixt Virginia and North Carolina* (New York, 1967), 304.

[7]James William Miller, ed. and trans., *In the Arkansas Backwoods: Tales and Sketches by Frederick Gerstacker* (Columbia, 1991), 49.

[8]Johanna Miller Lewis, "Women and Economic Freedom in the North Carolina Backcountry," in *Women and Freedom in Early America*, ed. Larry D. Eldridge (New York, 1997), 191-208.

[9]Joan E. Cashin, *A Family Venture: Men and Women on the Southern Frontier* (Baltimore, 1991), 3-7.

[10]Ibid., 33-34.

[11]Ibid., 47.

[12]Ibid., 45.

[13]Ibid., 66-67.

[14]Jeffrey, *Frontier Women*, xii; Cashin, *A Family Venture*, 7; Barbara Welter, "The Cult of True Womanhood: 1820-1860," *American Quarterly*, 18 (1966): 151-74.

[15]Cashin, *A Family Venture*, 23-25.

[16]Ibid., 7.

[17]Rohrbaugh, *Trans-Appalachian Frontier*, 91.

[18]Morris S. Arnold, *Colonial Arkansas, 1686-1804: A Social and Cultural History* (Fayetteville, 1991), 5.

[19]Joe Gray Taylor, *Louisiana: A Bicentennial History* (New York, 1976), 3-15, 25; Charles L. Dufour, *Ten Flags in the Wind: The Story of Louisiana* (New York, 1967), 60-61, 90.

[20]Rohrbaugh, *Trans-Appalachian Frontier*, 109, 281-82.

[21]Ibid., 113-14.

[22]John Wilds, et al., *Louisiana,Yesterday and Today: A Historical Guide to the State* (Baton Rouge, 1996), 28.

[23]Rohrbaugh, *Trans-Appalachian Frontier*, 129.

[24]Ibid., 158-59; James A. Henretta, "Families and Farms: *Mentalité* in Pre-Industrial America," *William and Mary Quarterly*, 3rd series, 35 (1978): 3-32.

[25]Carl A. Brasseaux, *Acadian to Cajun: Transformation of a People, 1803-1877* (Jackson, 1992), 21-25, 42; Allan Kulikoff, "The Transition to Capitalism in Rural America," *William and Mary Quarterly*, 3rd ser., 46 (1989): 25.

[26]Rohrbaugh, *Trans-Appalachian Frontier*, 281-282.

[27]Miller, *In the Arkansas Backwoods*, 50.

[28]Diary of Mrs. Maria Toncray Watkins, 1820-1830, Arkansas History Commission; Nancy W. Long, "'This Wilderness of Sorrow': White Women in Frontier Arkansas," paper presented at the Conference on Southern Women's History, Rice University, 1995 (Collection of the author).

[29]Watkins Diary, Arkansas History Commission.

Notes, Chapter 14

[1]Bernard DeVoto, ed., *The Journals of Lewis and Clark* (Boston, 1953), 186. According to LaRay Buckskin, Research Assistant of the Cultural Resource Department, Tribal/Department of Energy, Shoshone-Bannock Tribe, Fort Hall, Idaho, this word does indicate a European or Euro-American, but is not related to the word for the color *white*. Telephone conversation, September 10, 2002.

[2]Meriwether Lewis, in ibid., 189-90.

[3]Ibid., 190-91.

[4]Nicholas Biddle in ibid., 202. The quotations to which notes 4 and 5 refer came originally from Biddle's *History of the Expedition Under the Command of Captains Lewis and Clark* (Philadelphia, 1814) based on William Clark's notes and interviews with George Shannon, a member of the expeditionary party (ibid., viii).

[5]Nicholas Biddle in DeVoto, *Journals*, 203.

[6]Clara Sue Kidwell, "Indian Women as Cultural Mediators," *Ethnohistory*, 39 (1992): 97-107.

[7]Tamara Miller, "'Those with Whom I feel Most Nearly Connected': Kinship and Gender in Early Ohio," in Lucy Eldersveld Murphy and Wendy Hamand Venet, eds., *Midwestern Women: Work, Community, and Leadership at the Crossroads* (Bloomington, 1997), 121-40, makes this point in particular with regard to white Anglo pioneer women.

[8]*Captivities of Mrs. J. E. De Camp Sweet, Nancy McClure and Mary Schwandt* (1894; reprint New York, 1977).

[9]Bruce Paulson, "Komick, 1822-84, a Biography," unpublished manuscript, collection of the author. I thank Mr. Paulson for sharing his research with me. Quotation from John M. Ware, ed., *A Standard History of Waupaca County, Wisconsin* (Chicago, 1917), 1:71.

[10]Paulson, "Komick, 1822-84, a Biography."

[11]"Memoir of Antoine LeClaire, Esquire, of Davenport, Iowa," in *Annals of Iowa*, 12 vols. (Des Moines, 1863-74), 1:144-47; Harry E. Downer, *History of Davenport and Scott County, Iowa* (Chicago, 1910), 394-405.

[12]Downer, *History of Davenport*, 400.

[13]David Bishop and Craig G. Campbell, *History of the Forest Preserves of Winnebago County, Illinois* (Rockford, Ill., 1979), 35; Elihu B. Washburne, "Col. Henry Gratiot—A Pioneer of Wisconsin," *Collections of the State Historical Society of Wisconsin*, 20 vols. (1888-1931), 10:258; Walter O'Meara, *Daughters of the County* (New York, 1968), 297.

[14]*Leonard Bryant and Mary Bryant v. Alexander Neavill and Elias Griggs*, April 12, 1832; *Dunkey v. William Morrison*, October 2, 1829, both in Jo Daviess County, Illinois, Court Records held by the State Historical Society of Wisconsin, Branch, Wisconsin Room, Karrmann Library, University of Wisconsin, Platteville.

[15]Gerald Early, ed., *"Ain't But a Place:" An Anthology of African American Writings About St. Louis* (St. Louis, 1998), 34-35.

[16]Deed Record Book A, Crawford County, Wisconsin, 198-99.

[17]Galena, *Miner's Journal*, September 13, 1828, 2. After being flogged, he was incarcerated in a makeshift jail, from which he escaped.

[18]According to historian Carl Ekberg, both the French and Spanish legal codes of the early Mississippi Valley made it "illegal to break up a conjugal slave family by selling individual members," although these separations sometimes did illegally take place. Intermarriage, however, was illegal under the French Code Noir. See Carl J. Eckberg, *Colonial Ste. Genevieve: An Adventure on the Mississippi Frontier*, 2nd ed. (Tucson, 1996), 205.

[19]William Wells Brown, excerpt from *Narrative of William Wells Brown, A Fugitive Slave, Written by Himself* in Early, ed., *"Ain't But a Place,"* 22.

[20]Ibid., 26.

[21]Eventually he escaped to Canada and later wrote a memoir in 1847. Ibid., 15.

[22]Ibid., 14-15.

[23]Melton A. McLaurin, *Celia, A Slave* (1991, reprint Avon, 1993).

[24]John Mack Faragher, *Sugar Creek: Life on the Illinois Prairie* (New Haven, 1986); Miller, "'Those with Whom I Feel Most Nearly Connected'"; Marilyn Ferris Motz, *True Sisterhood: Michigan Women and Their Kin, 1820-1920* (Albany, 1983). Generalizations made about these Midwestern states may also be applied to white settlers in the trans-Mississippi West.

[25]Emily M. Austin, *Mormonism; or, Life among the Mormons* (1882, fac. ed., New York, 1971); Lucy Eldersveld Murphy, "Journeywoman Milliner: Emily Austin, Migration, and Women's Work in the Nineteenth-Century Midwest," in Murphy and Hamand Venet, eds., *Midwestern Women*, 38-59.

[26]E. Adamson Hoebel, *The Cheyennes: Indians of the Great Plains*, 2nd ed. (Fort Worth, 1978), 67; Glenda Riley, *The Female Frontier: A Comparative View of Women on the Prairie and the Plains* (Lawrence, 1988), 100, 148-93.

[27]Tanis C. Thorne, *The Many Hands of My Relations: French and Indians on the Lower Missouri* (Columbia, 1996), 153-54.

[28]Hallie Q. Brown, *Homespun Heroines and Other Women of Distinction* (New York, 1988), 34-45.

Notes, Chapter 15

[1]Forrest McDonald, *The Presidency of Thomas Jefferson* (Lawrence, 1976), 60-66.

[2]Henry Adams, *History of the United States of America During the Administrations of*

Jefferson and Madison, ed. Ernest Samuels (Chicago, 1967), 183-86.

[3]Andrew R. L. Cayton, "Looking for America with Lewis and Clark," *William and Mary Quarterly*, 3d ser., 59 (2002): 697-709.

[4]James E. Lewis, Jr., *The American Union and the Problem of Neighborhood: The United States and the Collapse of the Spanish Empire, 1783-1829* (Chapel Hill, 1998), 12-40.

[5]David Waldstreicher, *In the Midst of Perpetual Fetes: The Making of American Nationalism, 1776-1820* (Chapel Hill, 1997).

[6]Karen Ordahl Kupperman, ed., *America in European Consciousness, 1493-1750* (Chapel Hill, 1995).

[7]Washington to James Duane, September 7, 1783, in John C. Fitzpatrick, ed., *The Writings of George Washington from the Original Manuscript Sources, 1745-1799*, 39 vols. (Washington, D. C., 1931-44), 27:136; Samuel Holden Parsons to William S. Johnson, November 26, 1785, William S. Johnson Papers, Library of Congress, Washington, D. C.

[8]Andrew R. L. Cayton, "'Separate Interests and the Nation-State': The Washington Administration and the Origins of Regionalism in the Trans-Appalachian West," *Journal of American History*, 78 (1992): 39-67; Cayton, "'When Shall We Cease to Have Judases?': The Blount Conspiracy and the Limits of the 'Extended' Republic," in Ronald Hoffman, ed., *Launching the "Extended" Republic: The Federalist Era* (Charlottesville, 1996), 156-89; and Cayton, "Noble Actors Upon the 'Theatre of Honor': Power and Civility in the Treaty of Greenville," in Andrew R. L. Cayton and Fredrika J. Teute, eds., *Contact Points: North American Frontiers from the Mohawk Valley to the Mississippi* (Chapel Hill, 1998), 235-69.

[9]Peter S. Onuf, *Jefferson's Empire: The Language of American Nationhood* (Charlottesville, 2000), 109-46; Lewis, *The American Union and the Problem of Neighborhood*; Thomas Perkins Abenethy, *The Burr Conspiracy* (New York, 1954); and Arthur Preston Whitaker, *The Mississippi Question, 1795-1803: A Study in Trade, Politics and Diplomacy* (1934; reprint Gloucester, Mass., 1962).

[10]Thomas Jefferson to John C. Breckinridge, August 12, 1803, in Thomas Jefferson, *Writings*, ed. Merrill D. Peterson (New York, 1984), 1138.

[11]Jan Lewis, "'Those Scenes for Which Alone My Heart Was Made': Affection and Politics in the Age of Jefferson and Hamilton," in Peter N. Stearns and Jan Lewis, eds., *An Emotional History of the United States* (New York, 1998), 52-65; Gordon S. Wood, "The Trials and Tribulations of Thomas Jefferson," in Peter S. Onuf, ed., *Jeffersonian Legacies* (Charlottesville, 1993), 395-417.

[12]Jefferson, "First Inaugural Address," March 4, 1801, in Jefferson, *Writings*, 493.

[13]Jefferson, "Instructions to Captain Lewis," June 20, 1803, in ibid., 1128, 1129.

[14]Jefferson to Gov. William Henry Harrison, February 27, 1803, in ibid., 1118.

[15]Ellen K. Rothman, *Hands and Hearts: A History of Courtship in America* (Cam-

bridge, Mass., 1984), 17-84.

[16]John Routledge to Harrison Gray Otis, October 1, 1803, in Samuel Eliot Morrison, *Life and Letters of Harrison Gray Otis, Federalist, 1765-1848*, 2 vols. (Boston, 1913), 1:279.

[17]*Orleans Gazette and Commercial Advertiser*, July 5, 1806, quoted in Waldstreicher, *In the Midst of Perpetual Fetes*, 283.

[18]*Time Piece* (St. Francisville), July 4, 1811, quoted in ibid., 284.

[19]McDonald, *The Presidency of Thomas Jefferson*, 120-30.

[20]Quoted in Milton Lomask, *Aaron Burr: The Years from Princeton to Vice President, 1756-1905* (New York, 1979), 90.

[21]"The United States," March 1-13, 1810, in "Documents Delivered to the Ministry of Foreign Affairs," in Mary-Jo Kline, ed., *Political Correspondence and Public Papers of Aaron Burr*, 2 vols. (Princeton, 1983), 2:1103-4.

[22]"John Quincy Adams's Notes on Burr's Farewell Address to the Senate," [March 2, 1805], in ibid., 2:913.

[23]Quoted in Mari-Jo Kline, "Editorial Note: Burr's Farewell Address to the Senate," in ibid., 2:910-11.

[24]Robert V. Remini, *Andrew Jackson and the Course of American Empire, 1767-1821* (New York, 1977), 162.

[25]"Order to Brigadier Generals of the 2nd Division," in Sam B. Smith, et al., eds., *The Papers of Andrew Jackson*, 6 vols. (Knoxville, 1980-), 2:112.

[26]Jackson to James Winchester, January 1, 1807, in ibid., 2:130.

[27]"To the 2nd Division," [January 10, 1807], in ibid., 2:143.

[28]"To the Officers of the 2nd Division," April 20, 1808, in ibid., 2:191.

[29]"Address to the Citizens of Nashville," January 16, 1809, in ibid., 2:210.

[30]"To the Tennessee Volunteers," July 31, 1812, and "To the 2nd Division," September 8, 1812, in ibid., 2:317, 231, respectively.

[31]Jackson to Pathkiller, October 23, 1813, in ibid., 2:440-41.

Notes, Chapter 16

[1]Philip D. Gleason, "Identifying Identity: A Semantic History," *Journal of American History*, 69 (1983): 910-31.

[2]Joseph G. Tregle, "Creoles and Americans," in *Creole New Orleans: Race and Americanization*, ed. Arnold R. Hirsch, et al. (Baton Rouge, 1992), 131-85, 132-34. Tregle provides a cogent and compelling interpretation of the battle over the title "Creole," which

many Caribbean migrants as well as free people of color applied to themselves. While he applies this analysis to much of the nineteenth century, his evidence begins in the mid-1820s. In the two preceding decades, those same migrants were called and often called themselves "French" in an effort to claim a cosmopolitan sophistication which the Creoles of Louisiana lacked.

[3]Carl A. Brasseaux, *Denis-Nicolas Foucault and the New Orleans Rebellion of 1768* (Ruston, 1987); John Preston Moore, *Revolt in Louisiana: The Spanish Occupation, 1766-1770* (Baton Rouge, 1976), 143-64, 185-215; Daniel H. Usner, Jr., *Indians, Settlers, and Slaves in a Frontier Exchange Economy: The Lower Mississippi Valley Before 1783* (Chapel Hill, 1992), 116-18; Sidney Louis Villeré, *Jacques Philippe Villeré, First Native-Born Governor of Louisiana, 1816-1820* (New Orleans, 1981), 13-18.

[4]C. Richard Arena, "Philadelphia-Spanish New Orleans Trade in the 1790s," *Louisiana History*, 2 (1961): 429-45; Peggy K. Liss, *Atlantic Empires: The Network of Trade and Revolution, 1713-1826* (Baltimore, 1983), 142-44; Jesús Lorente Miguel, "Commercial Relations Between New Orleans and the United States, 1783-1803," in *The North American Role in the Spanish Imperial Economy, 1760-1819*, eds. Jacques A. Barbier and Allan Kuethe (Manchester, 1984), 177-91.

[5]T. H. Breen, "Ideology and Nationalism on the Eve of the American Revolution: Revisions *Once More* in Need of Revising," *Journal of American History*, 84 (1997): 31, 36; Jack P. Greene, *Peripheries and Center: Constitutional Development in the Extended Polities of the British Empire and the United States* (New York, 1986), 79-87; James H. Kettner, *The Development of American Citizenship, 1608-1870* (Chapel Hill, 1978), 173-209; Rogers M. Smith, *Civic Ideals: Conflicting Visions of Citizenship in U. S. History* (New Haven, 1997); David Waldstreicher, *In the Midst of Perpetual Fetes: The Making of American Nationalism, 1776-1820* (Chapel Hill, 1997), 124-25, 129.

[6]Jane Frances Heaney, *A Century of Pioneering: A History of the Ursuline Nuns in New Orleans (1727-1827)* (New Orleans, 1993), 18-20; Robert L. Paquette, "Revolutionary Saint-Domingue in the Making of Territorial Louisiana," in *A Turbulent Time: The French Revolution and the Greater Caribbean*, ed. David B. Gaspar, et al. (Bloomington, 1997), 204-25.

[7]"Remonstrance of the People of Louisiana Against the Political System Adopted by Congress for Them," in *American State Papers: Documents, Legislative and Executive, of the Congress of the United States: Miscellaneous* (Washington, 1832-61) (hereafter cited as *ASP-MI*), 1:396; Louisianais (Pierre Derbigny), *Esquisse de la situation politique et civile de la Louisiane . . .* (New Orleans, 1804); *Instructions from the Inhabitants of the Territory of Orleans to their Representatives in the Legislature* (New Orleans,1810); *Reflections on the Cause of the Louisianians* (Washington, 1803).

[8]Charles I. Bevans, comp., *Treaties and Other International Agreements of the United States of America, 1776-1949*, 13 vols. (Washington, 1968-76), 8:813.

[9]James Madison to Robert R. Livingston and James Monroe, March 2, 1803, in *The Papers of James Madison: Secretary of State Series*, ed. Robert J. Brugger, et al., 6 vols. (Charlottesville, 1986-2002) (hereafter cited as *PJM-SS*), 4:364-78. For the administration's limited territorial goals in 1803, see James E. Lewis, Jr., *The American Union and*

the Problem of Neighborhood: The United States and the Collapse of the Spanish Empire, 1783-1829 (Chapel Hill, 1998), 12-40; Robert W. Tucker, et al., *Empire of Liberty: The Statecraft of Thomas Jefferson* (New York, 1990), 121-35.

[10]*Annals of Congress: Debates and Proceedings of the Congress of the United States, 11th Congress, 3rd Session* (Washington, 1834-56), 496.

[11]In keeping with these principles, the administration intended to postpone the naturalization of whatever people they acquired through a cession from France, only to have the French establish immediate and unquestioned citizenship as a treaty requirement. See Madison to Livingston and Monroe, March 2, 1803, in *PJM-SS*, 4:371.

[12]*Annals of Congress, 8th Congress, 2nd Session*, 1016-1017.

[13]Resolution of the Orleans Territorial Legislature, February 20, 1807, *Territorial Papers of the United States* (Washington, U. S. National Archives, Record Group 59, Microfilm Copy M116 (Florida), T260 (Orleans), 9:707). For similar testimonials, see "Remonstrance of the People of Louisiana Against the Political System Adopted by Congress for Them," *ASP-MI*, 1:396; Territorial House of Representatives to Thomas Jefferson, January 19, 1810, *Thomas Jefferson Papers* (Washington: Library of Congress Microfilm Collection), Reel 74. See also Representatives to Jefferson, March 29, 1808, ibid., Reel 66.

[14]*Louisiana Courier* (New Orleans), July 4, 1810.

[15]John Prevost to Monroe, February 3, 1812, *Miscellaneous Letters of the Department of State* (Washington, U. S. National Archives, Record Group 59, Microfilm Copy M179), Reel 25. See also, Edward Livingston to Monroe, February 2, 1812, ibid.

[16]Dennis C. Rousey, *Policing the Southern City: New Orleans 1805-1889* (Baton Rouge, 1996), 16-18.

[17]For efforts to build public schools, see William C. C. Claiborne to the Territorial Legislature, March 24, 1806, William C. C. Claiborne, *Official Letter Books of W. C. C. Claiborne, 1801-1816*, ed. Dunbar Rowland, 6 vols. (Jackson, Miss., 1917) (hereafter cited as *Claiborne Letterbooks*), 3:274-79; Claiborne to Jefferson, January 16, 1804, *The Territorial Papers of the United States*, ed. Clarence E. Carter, 28 vols. (Washington, 1934) (hereinafter abbreviated as *Carter*), 9:161. See also Claiborne to Madison, January 24, 1804, *Claiborne Letterbooks*, 1:344-49. *Acts Passed at the Legislature of the Territory of Orleans* (New Orleans, 1806-1812), 8-11, 20-22, 50-53, 304-21; Stuart Noble Grayson, "Governor Claiborne and the Public School System of the Territorial Government of Louisiana," *Louisiana Historical Quarterly*, 11 (1928): 638-39. For examples of private academies, see *Louisiana Courier*, October 17, 1810, October 24, 1810, November 29, 1811, March 1, 1813, March 15, 1813, March 17, 1813, March 19, 1813, June 17, 1818, July 8, 1818, October 19, 1818, December 11, 1818.

[18]Petition to Congress by Lawyers of the Territory (no date), enclosed in James Brown to Samuel Smith, November 28, 1805, *Carter*, 9:539. See also Pierre Derbigny to John Watkins, January 24, 1806, *Messages from the Mayor to the Conseil de Ville* (New Orleans: New Orleans Public Library Microfilm Collection), 1:12-14. See also Mark F. Fernandez, "The Appellate Question: A Comparative Analysis of Supreme Courts of Appeal

in Virginia and Louisiana, 1776-1840" (Ph.D. diss., College of William and Mary, 1991), 102. For the major legal texts, see James Brown, et al., *A Digest of the Civil Laws Now in Force in the Territory of Orleans . . . Adapted to its Present System of Government* (New Orleans, 1808); *The Public Statutes at Large of the United States of America*, 8 vols. (Boston, 1845), 2:324-29; *Acts Passed at the Legislature of the Territory of Orleans [1805]*, 151-213.

[19]*The Election of a President* (Pittsburgh, 1812).

[20]*Proceedings of the Conseil de Ville* (New Orleans: New Orleans Public Library Microfilm Collection), 10:92, 101, 163, 166, 168, 170, 172-77.

[21]Louisiana's Congressional delegation was particularly confusing and election returns particularly spotty, but the available information indicates that American Congressional candidates consistently won majorities in Creole districts and American senatorial candidates won in the Louisiana General Assembly. The only Creole to serve in either house, Jean Nöel Destrehan, resigned his election to the Senate for unknown reasons before ever taking his seat. His colleague, a Kentuckian named Allan Bowie Magruder, resigned as well. Fromentin took Magruder's spot but did not seek re-election in 1818, preferring to return to Louisiana, where he eventually became a judge. In the meantime, the legislature selected James Brown, Henry Johnson, Thomas Posey, and William C. C. Claiborne as senators. Thomas Bolling Robertson was Louisiana's lone Congressman from 1812-1818, when he was succeeded by Thomas Butler. See "Louisiana Congressional Election Papers"; James Sterrett to Fulwar Skipwith, September 8, 1812, Louisiana State University, Louisiana and Lower Mississippi Valley Collections, *Fulwar Skipwith Papers*, Folder 3. Butler's election coincided with news of Robertson's resignation, and the new Congressman from Louisiana assumed office immediately. See *Louisiana Gazette* (New Orleans), August 6, 1818. Claiborne appointed Thomas Posey to fill Destrehan's seat, but the General Assembly eventually selected Brown for the position. Brown was unsuccessful in his bid for re-election in 1816, losing to Claiborne. He won the state's other seat in 1818, however, when Fromentin left the Senate. Johnson assumed Claiborne's seat in 1817 when the former governor died. *Biographical Directory of the American Congress, 1774-1961* (Washington, 1961), 934, 1062, 1434, 1679.

[22]*Annals of Congress, 11th Congress, 3rd Session*, 485.

[23]Peter J. Kastor, "'Motives of Peculiar Urgency': Local Diplomacy in Louisiana, 1803-1821," *William and Mary Quarterly*, 3rd. ser., 58 (2001): 833-35.

[24]Claiborne to Marquis de Casa Calvo, October 30, 1804, *Claiborne Letterbooks*, 2:382-83. See also Claiborne to Madison, October 5, 1807, Carter, *Territorial Papers*, 9:765. For this ongoing dispute, see Edward Turner to James Wilkinson, October 15, 1804, *Letters Received by the Secretary of War: Registered Series* (Washington, U. S. National Archives, Record Group 107, Microfilm Copy M22, (hereafter cited as *Letters Received, Registered Series*), 2:466. See also Turner to Claiborne, October 16, 17, 1804, *Claiborne Letterbooks*, 2:385-86 and 361-63; Claiborne to Turner, November 3, 1804, ibid., 2:389-90; Claiborne to Madison, October 17, 1807, ibid., 4:135-36. For the broader contours of conflict on the borderlands, see Kastor, "'Motives of Peculiar Urgency,'" 819-48.

[25]For an indication of the complex efforts to establish federal sovereignty over West Florida, see Claiborne to Robert Smith, January 5, 1811, *Claiborne Letterbooks*, 5:81; Claiborne to William Flood, January 5, 1811, ibid., 5:82-84; Claiborne to Smith, January 5, 1811, ibid, 5:82-84; Claiborne to William Eustis, January 5, 1805, *Letters Received, Registered Series*, 35:C-342. See also Kastor, "'Motives of Peculiar Urgency,'" 839-40.

[26]John Shaw to Paul Hamilton, January 18, 1811, *Letters Received by the Secretary of the Navy from Captains* (Washington, U. S. National Archives, Record Group 45, Microfilm Copy M125), 19:35. For the slave revolt, see James Dormon, "The Persistent Specter: Slave Rebellion in Territorial Louisiana," *Louisiana History*, 18 (1977): 394; Paquette, "Revolutionary Saint-Domingue in the Making of Territorial Louisiana," 204-25.

[27]"James Sterling Memorandum." Edward Nicholls Broadside, August 29, 1814, The Historic New Orleans Collection, *Edward Nicholls and William H. Percy Letters*, Folder 1; William Percy, orders to an anonymous recipient, August 30, 1814, *Edward Nicholls and William H. Percy Letters*, Folder 2; Edward Nicholls to an anonymous recipient, September 1, 1814, ibid.

[28]Jacques Philippe Villeré to the Louisiana General Assembly, January 6, 1819, *Journal of the House of Representatives of the State of Louisiana* (New Orleans, 1812-1820), 5.

Notes, Chapter 17

[1]Sarah H. Cleveland, "Powers Inherent in Sovereignty: Indians, Aliens, Territories, and the Nineteenth Century Origins of Plenary Power over Foreign Affairs," *Texas Law Review*, 81 (2002), 167-81, discusses the constitutionality of the Purchase in historical perspective.

[2]Hans W. Baade, "The Law of Slavery in Spanish Louisiana," *Louisiana's Legal Heritage*, ed. Edward F. Haas (Pensacola, 1983), 43-86, supplies the background for the Spanish period and slave law under Spanish rule.

[3]Kimbery L. Hanger, *Bounded Lives, Bounded Places: Free Black Society in Colonial New Orleans, 1769-1830* (Durham, 1997) is the definitive study of this topic. Hans W. Baade, "The Gens de Couleur of Louisiana: Comparative Slave Law in Microcosm," *Cardoso Law Review*, 18 (1996), 535-86, documents subsequent developments.

[4]Stuart Banner, *Legal Systems in Conflict: Property and Sovereignty in Missouri, 1750-1860* (Norman, 2000).

[5]George Dargo, *Jefferson's Louisiana: Politics and the Clash of Legal Traditions* (Cambridge, 1975), provides background and overview on the topics to be discussed.

[6]For example, Rolf Knütel, "Influences of the Louisiana Civil Code in Latin America," *Tulane Law Review*, 70 (1996), 1445-80.

[7]Available in microfiche in *Early American Reprints*, 2nd ser., No. 10041.

Notes, Chapter 18

[1]Mississippi Department of Archives and History, *Mississippi Provincial Archives: French Dominion*, trans. and eds. Dunbar Roland, A.G. Sanders, 3 vols. (Jackson, 1927-1932), 2:465, 488 (second quotation), 490 (first quotation), 520 (fourth and fifth quotations), 528 (third quotation), 531 (sixth quotation), 532 (seventh quotation). (Hereafter *MPA:FD.*) This essay is based in part on Randy J. Sparks, *On Jordan's Stormy Banks: Evangelicalism in Mississippi, 1773-1876* (Athens, Ga., 1994), Chaps. 1 and 2, and Sparks, *Religion in Mississippi* (Jackson, 2001), Chaps. 1-4.

[2]*MPA:FD*, 3:13.

[3]Robert R. Rea, "British West Florida: Stepchild of Diplomacy," in Samuel Proctor, ed., *Eighteenth-Century Florida and Its Borderlands* (Gainesville, 1975), 69 (first quotation); Byrle A. Kynerd, "British West Florida," in Richard A. McLemore, ed., *A History of Mississippi*, 2 vols. (Hattiesburg, 1973), 1:134-44 (second quotation, p. 144), 145 (third quotation), 154 (fourth quotation); Jack D. L. Holmes, *Gayoso: The Life of a Spanish Governor in the Mississippi Valley, 1789-1799* (Baton Rouge, 1968), 22.

[4]John F. H. Claiborne, *Mississippi, as a Province, Territory, and State, with Biographical Notices of Eminent Citizens* (1880, reprint, Jackson, 1964), 115 (first quotation), 116, 127-34; Daniel Usner, Jr., *Indians, Settlers, and Slaves in a Frontier Exchange Economy: The Lower Mississippi Valley Before 1783* (Chapel Hill and London, 1992), 112-13.

[5]Holmes, *Gayoso*, 23, 68 (first and second quotations), 69-72; Usner, *Indians, Settlers, and Slaves*, 280.

[6]Holmes, *Gayoso*, 71-77.

[7]Ibid, 77.

[8]John G. Jones, *A Concise History of the Introduction of Protestantism into Mississippi and the Southwest* (St. Louis, 1866), 20-21, 23-24, 27-47, 70-71; Daniel S. Farrar, ed., "Alexander K. Farrar's Deed to Kingston Church, 1874," *Journal of Mississippi History*, 17 (1955): 135-41; Jack D. L. Holmes, "Spanish Religious Policy in West Florida: Enlightened or Expedient?" *Journal of Church and State*, 15 (1973): 259-69; Claiborne, *Mississippi*, 106-7, 209, 210, 342, 528 (quotation).

[9]Jones, *Concise History*, 20-21, 23-24, 27-47, 70-71 (quotation, p. 31); Charles H. Otken, "Richard Curtis in the Country of the Natchez," *Publications of the Mississippi Historical Society, Centenary Series*, 14 vols. (Oxford, 1898-1914), 3:147-53; Walter Brownlow Posey, *The Baptist Church in the Lower Mississippi Valley, 1776-1845* (Lexington, 1957), 5-7; Richard Aubrey McLemore, *A History of Mississippi Baptists, 1780-1970* (Jackson, 1971), 6-7.

[10]Jones, *Concise History*, 33 (first quotation); D. Clayton James, *Antebellum Natchez* (Baton Rouge, 1968), 39; Jack D. L. Holmes, "Barton Hannon in the Old Southwest," *Journal of Mississippi History*, 44 (1982): 69-79 (second quotation, p. 79); and Holmes, *Gayoso*.

[11]Jones, *Concise History*, 35-45; Holmes, *Gayoso*, 83 (second quotation).

[12]Holmes, "Barton Hannon," 69-73 (first quotation. p. 69; second quotation, p. 71); Holmes, *Gayoso*, 189-91.

[13]Holmes, "Barton Hannon," 73-79; James, *Antebellum Natchez*, 70-72; Holmes, *Gayoso*, 191-99; Terry Alford, *Prince Among Slaves* (New York and London, 1977), 62. Hannon became an American citizen and landowner, although there is no evidence of further religious activity on his part.

[14]Sparks, *On Jordan's Stormy Banks*, 7, 14; James Hebron Moore, *The Emergence of the Cotton Kingdom in the Old Southwest: Mississippi, 1770-1860* (Baton Rouge, 1988), 8-12, 75-77; James, *Antebellum Natchez*, 45, 48; Charles Sydnor, *A Gentleman of the Old Natchez Region* (Durham, N. C., 1938), 9-13; Claiborne, *Mississippi*, 1:208 (quotation).

[15]Sparks, *On Jordan's Stormy Banks*, 11-12; John G. Jones, *A Complete History of Methodism in the Mississippi Conference* (Nashville, 1908), 164 (first quotation). Young looked aghast at "Americans, French, Spaniards, English, Irish, Dutch, negroes, and mulattoes—all mingling as 'fellows well met.' Many Kentuckians were lying in their flatboats, along the wharf, drinking, fighting, swearing, and acting like demons." Young, *Autobiography of a Pioneer . . .* (Cincinnati, 1857), 222-23. Latrobe, quoted in John T. Christian, *History of the Baptists of Louisiana* (Shreveport, La., 1923), 58.

[16]Sparks, *On Jordan's Stormy Banks*, 11-12; Jones, *History of Methodism*, 164 (first quotation); Young, *Fifty Years in the Itineracy*, 222-23; Henry G. Hawkins, *Methodism in Natchez* (Jackson, 1937), 38 (third quotation); see also Winans' Autobiography (Cain Archives, Mississippi State University Archives), 56-57; Samuel J. Mills and Daniel Smith, *Report on a Missionary Tour. . .* (Andover, 1815), 26; Flint, *Recollections*, 295.

[17]Ibid.

[18](?) to Rev'd Brother, April 1, 1833, Tobias Gibson Subject File (Mississippi Department of Archives and History); Sparks, *On Jordan's Stormy Banks*, 10-11.

[19]Sparks, *On Jordan's Stormy Banks*, 11.

[20]Samuel S. Hill, ed., *Encyclopedia of Religion in the South* (Macon, Ga., 1984), 487.

[21]Louisiana Library Commission, *Louisiana: A Guide to the State* (New York, 1941), 228.

[22]John G. Jones, *A Complete History of Methodism as Connected with the Mississippi Conference of the Methodist Episcopal Church, South*, 2 vols. (Nashville, 1887), 1:35-36, 148-53. Bowman to William Burke, January 26, 1806 reproduced in ibid, 148-52. Blackman Journal reproduced in ibid, 1:174; 2:105 (final quotation).

[23]Ibid, 242-44, 342.

[24]Ibid, 2:81, 259.

[25]Christian, *A History of the Baptists of Louisiana*, 42-43, 47-48, 50-53 (quotation, p. 52). Christian makes no mention of Willis's race.

[26]Ibid, 59-65 (first and second quotations, p. 60; third quotation, p. 64).

[27]*Biographical and Historical Memoirs of Louisiana*, 2 vols. (Chicago, 1892), 2:146-49.

[28]Donald Mathews, *Religion in the Old South* (Chicago, 1977), 101-24 (quotation, p. 102).

[29]Ibid, 44-45.

[30]Jones, *Complete History of Methodism . . . Connected with the Mississippi Conference*, 1:243-44; 2:108.

[31]C. T. Stiles to W. Winans, March 11, 1820, Winans Correspondence; Winans Journal, 1 November 1823, Cain Archives; First Methodist Church, Columbus, Second Conference, 1837, Mississippi State University Archives; Jones, *Complete History of Methodism . . . Connected with the Mississippi Conference*, 2:388 (second quotation); *Tennessee Baptist*, June 12, 1847 (final quotation); Sparks, *On Jordan's Stormy Banks*, 52-53.

[32]Baptist State Convention, *Second Annual Report . . . 1824* (Natchez, 1825), 3; Mississippi Baptist State Convention, *Proceedings of A Meeting . . . December, 1836* (Natchez, 1837), 21 (third quotation); Woman's Missionary Union of Mississippi, *Hearts the Lord Opened: The History of Mississippi Woman's Missionary Union* (Jackson, 1954), 13, 14-18, 21 (first quotation, p. 14; second quotation, p. 15; fourth quotation, p. 17); James Adair Lyon Journal, October-December, 1854 (quotation); Jesse L. Boyd, *A Popular History of the Baptists in Mississippi* (Jackson, 1930), 277-78; *Mississippi Baptist*, April 14, 28, November 3, 1859; Moore, *Emergence of the Cotton Kingdom*, 199-200 (final quotation, p. 200); Sparks, *On Jordan's Stormy Banks*, 53.

[33]Sylvia R. Frey and Betty Wood, *Come Shouting to Zion: African American Protestantism in the American South and British Caribbean to 1830* (Chapel Hill, 1988), 33, 40, 117; Emily Clark and Virginia Meacham Gould, "The Feminine Face of Afro-Catholicism in New Orleans, 1727-1852," *William and Mary Quarterly*, 3rd ser., 59 (2002): 435.

[34]Daniel de Vinne to Benjamin Drake, August 22, 1823, Drake Correspondence (Cain Archives); *Minutes and Resolutions of the Religious Convention of Christian Denominations Held at Washington, (Miss.) on November 19, 1818* (Natchez, 1818), 16; James E. Davis, *Frontier America 1800-1840: A Comparative Demographic Analysis of the Settlement Process* (Glendale, Calif., 1977), 128; Sparks, *On Jordan's Stormy Banks*, 61.

[35]Kenneth M. Stampp, *The Peculiar Institution: Slavery in the Ante-Bellum South* (New York, 1956), 158-61; John W. Blassingame, *The Slave Community: Plantation Life in the Antebellum South* (New York, 1979), 84-87; Eugene D. Genovese, *Roll, Jordan, Roll: The World the Slaves Made* (New York, 1974), 202-09; William B. DuBois, *The Souls of Black Folk* (Greenwich, Conn., 1963), 141.

[36]Mathews, *Religion in the Old South*, 202; Albert E. Casey, *Amite County, Mississippi, 1699-[1865]*, 2 vols. (Birmingham, 1948-50), 2:315, 321, 323, 324, 330; Sparks, *On Jordan's Stormy Banks*, 66; Christian, *History of the Baptists of Louisiana*, 73 (quotation).

[37]Frey and Wood, *Come Shouting to Zion*, 33, 40, 117.

Notes, Chapter 19

[1]"Boqueta de Woiseri, J. L.," in John H. Mahé and Roseanne McCaffrey, eds., *Encyclopedia of New Orleans Artists, 1718-1918* (New Orleans, 1987), 46-47, and Jessie Poesch, "New Orleans, Site of the Transfer, Prize of the Purchase," in *Jefferson's America and Napoleon's France, An Exhibition for the Louisiana Purchase Bicentennial* (New Orleans, 2003), 225-37.

[2]Valuable studies of the fur trade include H. M. Chittenden, *The American Fur Trade of the Far West* (New York, 1902), John E. Sunder, *The Fur Trade on the Upper Missouri, 1840-1865* (Norman, 1965); and David J. Wishart, *The Fur Trade of the American West, 1807-1840* (Lincoln, 1979).

[3]Jessie Poesch, "A Precise View of Peale's Museum," *Antiques* (October 1960), 343-45.

[4]Edwin James, comp., *Account of an Expedition from Pittsburg to the Rocky Mountains; Performed in the Years 1819 and '20, by order of the Hon. J. C. Calhoun, Sec'y of War, Under the Command of Major Stephen H. Long; From the Notes of Major Long, Mr. T. Say and Other Gentlemen of the Exploring Party, compiled by Edwin James, Botanist and Geologist for the Expedition*, 2 vols. with an atlas (Philadelphia, 1822-23).

[5]John F. McDermott, "Samuel Seymour: Pioneer Artist of the Plains and the Rockies," *Annual Report of the Smithsonian Institution* (Washington, D. C., 1950), 497-509. Most of the surviving Seymour work is in the Samuel Seymour Collection in the Beinecke Rare Book and Manuscript Library of Yale University Library.

[6]Jessie Poesch, *Titian Ramsay Peale, 1799-1885, and His Journals of the Wilkes Expedition*, Memoirs of the American Philosophical Society 52 (Philadelphia, 1961), 20-35. The American Philosophical Society, the Historical Society of Pennsylvania, and the American Museum of Natural History in New York each hold substantial collections of Titian Peale papers.

[7]Charles Coleman Sellers, *Mr. Peale's Museum: Charles Wilson Peale and the First Popular Museum of Natural Science and Art* (New York, 1980), 258-60.

[8]Roger L. Nichols and Patrick L. Halley, *Stephen Long and American Frontier Exploration* (Newark, 1980), 174-79, and Appendix, 224-32, in which list there are about 14 articles or books dealing in whole or in part with the specimens collected or identified by the scientists on the Long expedition. They summarize the expedition's accomplishments in biology, botany, geography, ethnography, geology, geography and cartography, astronomic observations, and weather data. Among the fourteen are Thomas Say's three volume *American Entomology, or Descriptions of the Insects of North America* (Philadelphia, 1824-28), the first publication on the insects of North America. It has 21 exquisite illustrations by Titian Peale.

[9]Savoie Lottinville in Paul Wilhelm, *Travels in North America, 1822-1824*, ed. Savoie Lottinville, trans. W. Robert Nitske (Norman, 1973), xiv and 128, 201n, 203, and 296 as cited in Nichols and Halley, *Stephen Long*, 180 and 250n42. Lottinville also notes that Paul Wilhelm, Duke of Wurtemberg, used James's *Account* as his guide and was im-

pressed with the scientific accomplishments of the Long expedition in cartography, archaeology, and comparative linguistics.

[10]George J. Goodman and Cheryl A. Lawson, *Retracing Major Stephen H. Long's 1820 Expedition: The Itinerary and the Botany* (Norman, 1995), xii-xiv, 123-336.

[11]There is an extensive bibliography on Catlin. Three valuable recent publications, each with an extensive bibliography, are William H. Truettner, *The Natural Man Observed: A Study of Catlin's Indian Gallery* (Washington, D. C., 1979); Brian W. Dippie, *Catlin and His Contemporaries: The Politics of Patronage* (Lincoln, 1990); and Smithsonian American Art Museum, *George Catlin and His Indian Gallery* (Washington, D. C., 2002). Catlin's works are held by various museums; the largest collection is in the Smithsonian Institution.

[12]Truettner, *Catlin*, 23, 26, 92, 103-fig. 105, cat. #128. Smithsonian Museum of American Art Collection. (Hereafter, Smithsonian Collection.)

[13]Ibid., 23, 87, 93-fig. 88, cat. #171. Smithsonian Collection.

[14]Ibid., 23, 28-fig. 28, 92, cat. #99. Smithsonian Collection.

[15]Ibid., 105-fig. 109, cat. #100. Smithsonian Collection.

[16]Alexander Philipp Graf zu Wied-Neuwiedk, 1782-1867.

[17]Maximilian, Prinz von Wied, *Beiträge zur Naturgeschichte von Brasilien*, 4 vols. in 6 parts (Weimar, 1825-33).

[18]Joslyn Art Museum, *Bodmer's America* (Lincoln, 1984) is the most valuable reference on Bodmer. It has an introduction by William H. Goetzmann, annotations by David C. Hunt and Marsha V. Gallagher, and the artist's biography by William J. Orr. The largest collection of Bodmer's work and related papers of Maximilian of Wied are on permanent loan to the Joslyn Art Museum, Omaha, Nebraska, from the InterNorth Art Foundation.

[19]Maximilian, Prinz von Wied, *Travels in the Interior of North America, 1832-1834,* trans. Hannibal Evans Lloyd, 2 vols. (London, 1843), as printed in Reuben Gold Thwaites, ed., *Early Western Travels, 1748-1846*, vol. 22 (Cleveland, 1906), 69. This is a translation of *Reise im das Innere Nord-America in den Jahren 1832 bis 1834*, 2 vols. (Coblenz, 1839-41). Volumes 22-25 of Thwaites include both volumes of the English edition of Maximilian's publication, an Appendix with additional extracts and adaptations from sections in the German and English editions, and the *Atlas*.

[20]Joslyn Museum, *Bodmer's America*, 254-fig. 257.

[21]Ibid., 196-fig. 198.

[22]Ibid., 244-fig. 246.

[23]Ibid., 257-fig. 260.

[24]Ibid., 294-fig. 363.

[25]Truettner, *Catlin*, 31, 32-fig. 23, cat. #353. Smithsonian Collection.

[26]Two valuable studies of Miller are: Marvin C. Ross, *The West of Alfred Jacob Miller* (Norman, 1951); and Ron Tyler, ed., *Alfred Jacob Miller: Artist on the Oregon Trail* (Fort Worth, 1982). The largest collection of Miller's work is in the Walters Art Gallery, Baltimore. For a biography of Stewart see Mae Reed Porter and Odessa Davenport, *Scotsman in Buckskin* (New York, 1963). See also, Lisa Strong, "Images of Indigenous Aristocracy in Alfred Jacob Miller," *American Art* (Spring 1999), 63-83; and "American Indians and Scottish Identity in Sir William Drummond Stewart's Collection," *Winterthur Portfolio* (Summer/Autumn, 2000), 127-55.

[27]Tyler, *Miller*, cat. #46. Amon Carter Museum Collection.

[28]William H. Goetzmann and Joseph Porter, with artists' biographies in David C. Hunt, *The West as Romantic Horizon* (Omaha, 1981), 66 and 68-fig. 15. Joslyn Museum Collection.

[29]Tyler, *Miller*, cat. #82. Walters Art Gallery Collection.

[30]Ibid., cat. #s 56 and 57. Walters Art Gallery Collection.

[31]Paul A. Rossi and David C. Hunt, *The Art of the Old West* (New York, 1971), 120, 324. Gilcrease Institute, Tulsa.

[32]Ross, *Miller*, xxi-xxiii.

[33]Truettner, *Catlin*, 63, 64-fig. 63, reference cat. #505. Smithsonian Collection.

[34]Bernard A. DeVoto, *Across the Wide Missouri* (Boston, 1947), 452-53, note 11. Marsha Gallagher, Curator, to author, July 24, 2003, indicated that the Joslyn Museum is in the process of publishing a detailed study of the prints based on Bodmer's originals.

[35]George Catlin, *Letters and Notes on the Manners, Customs, and Condition of the North American Indians; Written During Eight Years' Travel Amongst the Wildest Tribes of Indians in North America in 1832-39; in Two Volumes with Four Hundred Illustrations, Carefully Engraved from his Original Paintings*, 2 vols. (London and New York, 1841).

[36]Truettner, *Catlin*, 43.

[37]Ibid., 41-48.

[38]Ibid., 20, 48, and 124; 22-fig. 15, cat. #149. Smithsonian Collection.

[39]Ibid., 49, 50, 87, 124; 50-fig. 40, cat. #521. Smithsonian Collection.

[40]Quoted in Lois Marie Fink, *American Art at the Nineteenth-Century Paris Salons* (Cambridge and New York, 1990), 54.

[41]Catlin, *Catlin's Notes of Eight Years' Travels and Residence in Europe with His North American Indian Collection; With Anecdotes and Incidents of the Travels and Adventures of Three Different Parties of American Indians Whom He Introduced to the Courts of England, France, and Belgium* (London, 1848). In the same year it was published in New York by Burgess, Stringer, and Company. See also a video, "George Catlin, The Printed Works, Computer File" (Cincinnati, 2000).

[42]"The George Catlin Indian Gallery in the U. S. National Museum (Smithsonian Institution) with Memoir and Statistics," *Annual Report of the Smithsonian Institution for 1885*, part 5 (Washington, D. C., 1886).

[43]Ross, *Miller*, xxxiii-xxxvii.

[44]*Altowan* (New York, 1846); and *Edward Warren* (London, 1854). The latter is considered the superior. It has been reprinted in the *Classics of the Fur Trade Series*, Winfred Blevins, general editor (Missoula, 1986). The newspaper articles written in 1842-43 are gathered together in Matt Field, *Prairie and Mountain Sketches*, ed. Kate L. Gregg and John McDermott (Norman, 1960).

[45]Karl Bodmer, *Bildatlas: Reise zu den Indianern am oberen Missouri, 1832-1834* (Frankfort, 1970); Maximilian Prinz von Wied, *Der Reise des Prinzen Wied zu den Indianern* (Pfaffenhofen-llm, 1977); and Maximilian, Prinz von Wied, *Reise in das innere Nord-America* (Berlin, 1982). The later was an exhibit honoring the two hundredth birthday of Maximilian.

[46]Brandon K. Rund, "Karl Bodmer's North American Prints," *American Art Review* (Aug. 2003), 88-91.

[47]For example, in 1991, a Smithsonian exhibit, *The West as America: Reinterpreting Images of the Frontier, 1820-1920*, aroused much discussion and criticism. Two commentaries reflect the discussion: Alan Trachtenberg, "Contesting the West," *Art in America* (Sept. 1991), 118-52; and William H. Truettner, "The West and the Heroic Ideal: Using Images to Interpret History," *The Chronicle of Higher Education* (Nov. 20, 1991), B1-B2. For another contextual study of paintings of the American west see Yale University Art Gallery, *Discovered Lands, Invented Pasts, Transforming Visions of the American West* (New Haven, 1992), with essays by seven authors.

[48]Smithsonian American Art Museum, *George Catlin and His Indian Gallery*, September 6, 2002 to January 19, 2003.

Notes, Chapter 20

[1]*Charting Louisiana: Five Hundred Years of Maps*, eds. Alfred E. Lemmon, John T. Magill, and Jason R. Wiese; consulting ed. John R. Hébert (New Orleans, 2003), Map 5; also in Seymour L. Schwartz and Ralph E. Ehrenberg, *The Mapping of America* (New York, 1980), Figure 73.

[2]*Charting Louisiana*, Map 8; Schwarz and Ehrenberg, *Mapping*, Figure 74.

[3]*Charting Louisiana*, Map 18; also in Jack Jackson, *Flags Along the Coast; Charting the Gulf of Mexico, 1519-1759: A Reappraisal* (Austin, 1995), Plate 24; and, William P. Cumming, *The Southeast in Early Maps*, ed. Louis De Vorsey, Jr., 3rd ed. (Chapel Hill, 1998), Plate 47.

[4]Jackson, *Flags Along the Coast*, Plate 15.

[5]*Charting Louisiana*, Map 32.

[6]*Charting Louisiana*, Map 23.

[7]*Charting Louisiana*, Map 24.

[8]*Charting Louisiana*, Map 27.

[9]*Charting Louisiana*, Map 26 and Jackson, *Flags Along the Coast*, Plate 48.

[10]*Charting Louisiana*, Map 167.

Notes, Chapter 21

[1]From Samuel Purchas, *Hakluytus Posthumus or, Purchas His Pilgrims, Contayning a History of the World in Sea Voyages and Lande Travells by Englishmen and Others* (London, 1612), cited in John L. Allen, "New World Encounters: Exploring the Great Plains of North America," *Great Plains Quarterly*, 13 (1993): 74.

[2]An excellent recent source for French exploration during the period prior to the American purchase of Louisiana may be found in John L. Allen, ed., *North American Exploration*, 3 vols. (Lincoln, 1997), vol. 2, chapters 10 and 11.

[3]Lewis to Jefferson, September 23, 1806, in Donald Jackson, ed., *Letters of the Lewis and Clark Expedition, with Related Documents, 1783-1854*, 2nd. ed., 2 vols. (Urbana, 1978), 2:319-24.

[4]James P. Ronda, "Exploring the American West in the Age of Jefferson," in Allen, *North American Exploration*, 3:32.

[5]Jefferson to William Dunbar, Washington, March 12, 1804, Jefferson Papers, Library of Congress.

[6]Ronda, "Exploring the American West in the Age of Jefferson," in Allen, *North American Exploration*, 3:40-41.

[7]Donald Jackson, ed., *The Journals of Zebulon Montgomery Pike with Letters and Related Documents*, 2 vols. (Norman, 1966), 1:286.

[8]Ibid., 1:358.

[9]Pike's map is discussed in John L. Allen, "Patterns of Promise: Mapping the Great Plains, 1800-1860," in Frederick Luebke, ed., *Mapping the Plains: Essays in Historical Cartography* (Norman, 1987).

[10]See Susan Miller's essay in this volume for details.

[11]Cited in Reuben Gold Thwaites, ed., *The Original Journals of Lewis and Clark*, 8 vols. (New York, 1904-05), 5:387.

[12]Thompson to the North West Company, Kootenay House, September 23, 1807, in *Oregon Historical Quarterly*, 38 (1937): 394-95.

[13]*Louisiana Gazette*, October 11, 1811.

[14]Ronda, "Exploring the American West in the Age of Jefferson," in Allen, *North American Exploration*, 3:56.

[15]Washington Irving, *Astoria; or, Anecdotes of an Enterprise beyond the Rocky Mountains* (1836, reprint Norman, 1964), 256. Irving's text is a paraphrasing from a letter of Hunt's that was in his possession but is now lost.

[16]Edwin James, *Account of an Expedition from Pittsburgh to the Rocky Mountains*, 2 vols. (Philadelphia, 1823), 1:460.

[17]Henry R. Schoolcraft, *Narrative Journal of Travels . . . from Detroit . . . to the Sources of the Mississippi River* (Albany, 1821), xii.

[18]Martha Coleman Bray, *Joseph Nicollet and His Map* (Philadelphia, 1980), 166.

[19]Ronda, "Exploring the American West in the Age of Jefferson," in Allen, *North American Exploration*, 3:73.

[20]Ibid.

[21]Jefferson to John Breckinridge, Monticello, August 12, 1803, Jefferson Papers, Library of Congress.

[22]Ronda, "Exploring the American West in the Age of Jefferson," in Allen, *North American Exploration*, 3:74.

Notes, Chapter 22

[1]Quoted by Dayton Duncan and Ken Burns, *Lewis and Clark: The Journey of the Corps of Discovery, An Illustrated History* (New York, 1997), 15.

[2]Facsimile of original reproduced as a sidebar in ibid.

[3]James D. Richardson, ed., *A Compilation of the Messages and Papers of the Presidents*, 20 vols. (New York, 1897), 1:366-70 (quotation, p. 367).

[4]Jefferson wrote to Archibald Stuart on January 25, 1786, that "Our confederacy must be viewed as the nest from which all America, North and South, is to be peopled. We should take care to not . . . press too soon on the Spaniards. Those countries cannot be in better hands. My fear is that they are too feeble to hold them till our population can be sufficiently advanced to gain it from them peice by piece [*sic*]. The navigation of the Mississippi we must have." In Julian Boyd, ed., *The Papers of Thomas Jefferson*, 29 vols. (Princeton, N. J., 1950-), 9:217-19 (quotation, p. 218).

[5]Page Smith, *John Adams*, 2 vols. (New York, 1962), 2:1094.

[6]The letter has often been reprinted, usually in histories of the subsequent expedition. See, for example, David Freeman Hawke, *Those Tremendous Mountains: The Story of the Lewis and Clark Exedition* (New York, 1980), 26-32.

[7]Richardson , *Messages and Papers of the Presidents*, 1:408.

[8]See, for example, Roger G. Kennedy, *Mr. Jefferson's Lost Cause: Land, Farmers,*

Slavery, and the Louisiana Purchase (New York, 2003).

[9]The treaty is conveniently reprinted as Appendix B in Jon Kukla, *A Wilderness So Immense: The Louisiana Purchase and the Destiny of America* (New York, 2003), 350-53 (quotation, p. 351). A number of interpretive essays about the purchase, with supporting documents reprinted, are available in Peter J. Kastor, ed., *The Louisiana Purchase: Emergence of an American Nation* (Washington, D. C., 2002).

Index